Arata
THE LEGEND

15

We are Man, born of Heaven and Earth,
Moon and Sun and everything under them.

Eyes, Ears, Nose, Tongue, Body, Mind...

Purity will pierce evil and
open up the world of darkness.

All life will be reborn and invigorated.

Appear now.

STORY & ART BY
Yuu Watase

Arata
THE LEGEND

CHARACTERS

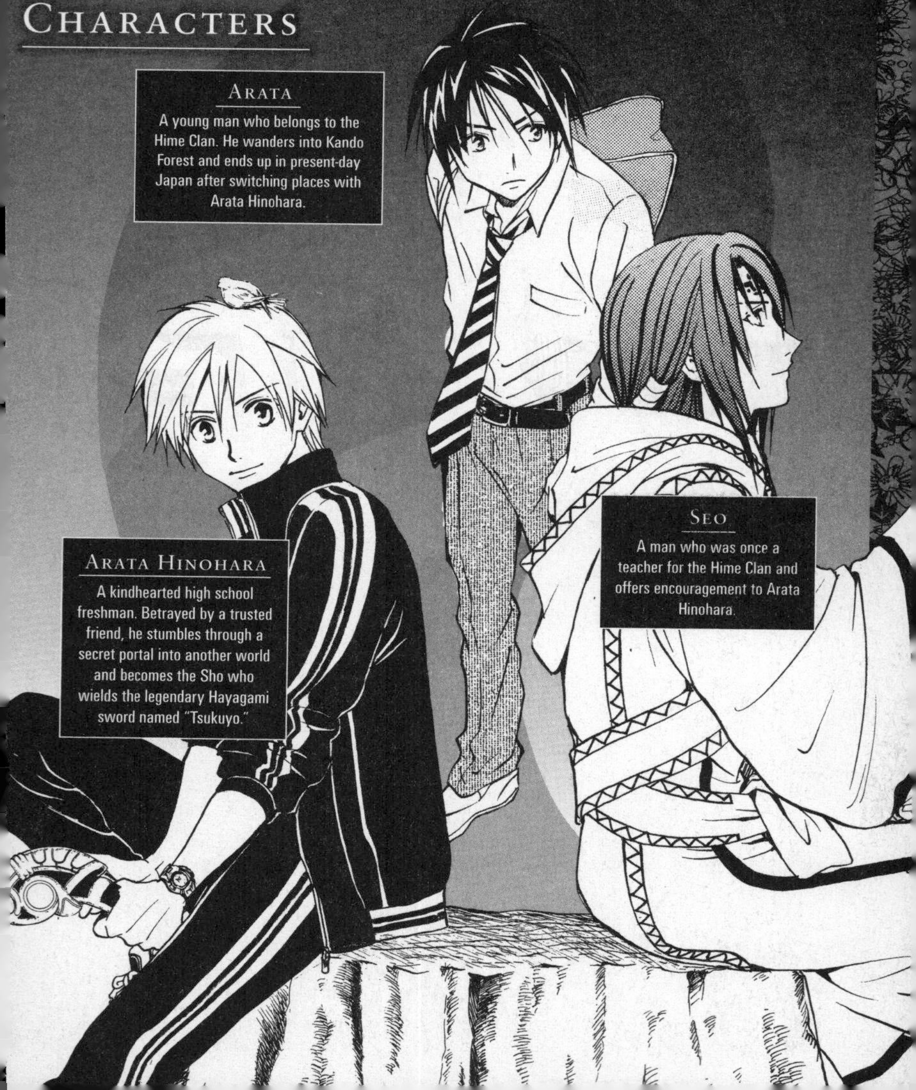

ARATA

A young man who belongs to the Hime Clan. He wanders into Kando Forest and ends up in present-day Japan after switching places with Arata Hinohara.

SEO

A man who was once a teacher for the Hime Clan and offers encouragement to Arata Hinohara.

ARATA HINOHARA

A kindhearted high school freshman. Betrayed by a trusted friend, he stumbles through a secret portal into another world and becomes the Sho who wields the legendary Hayagami sword named "Tsukuyo."

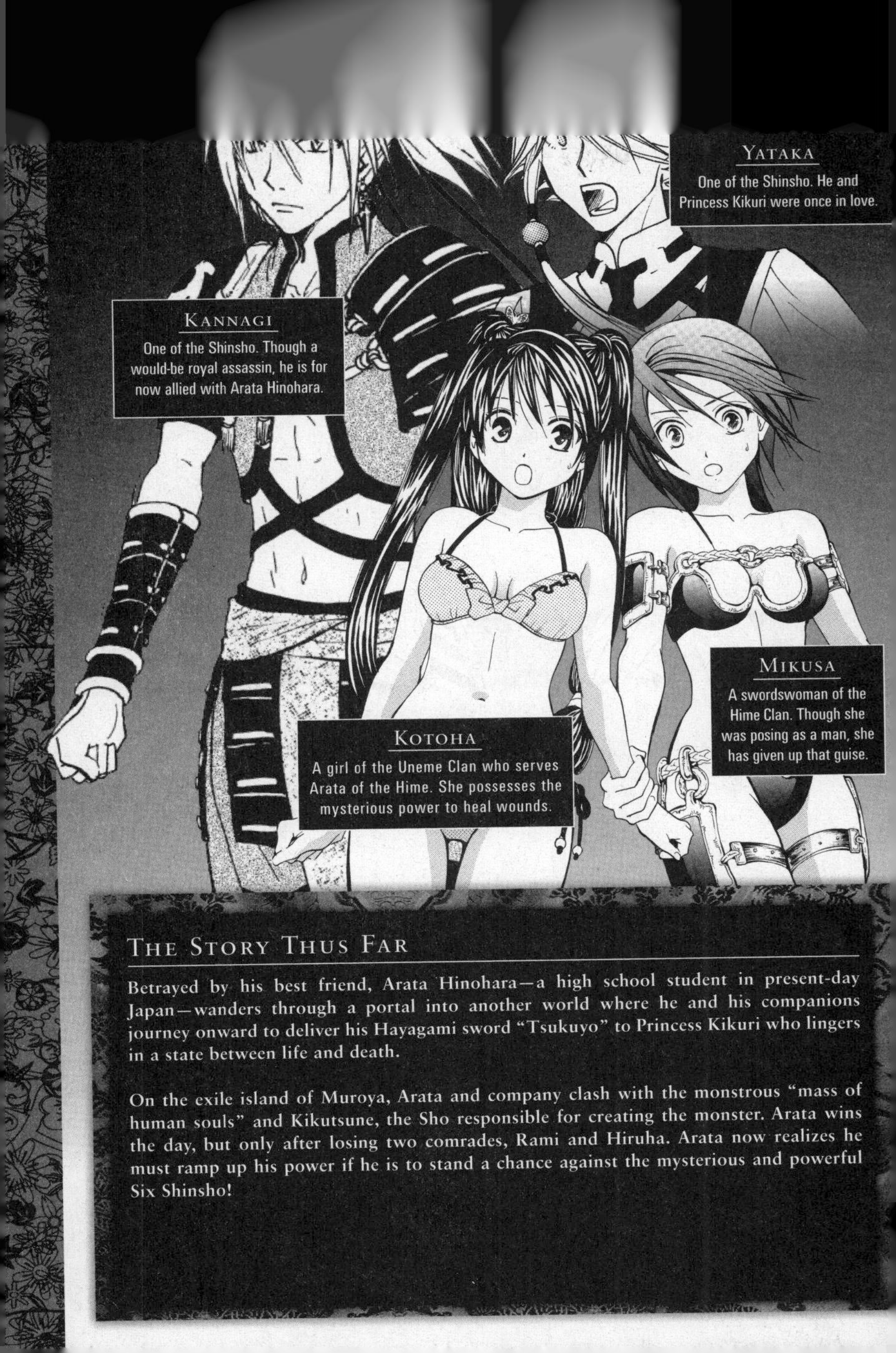
YATAKA
One of the Shinsho. He and Princess Kikuri were once in love.
KANNAGI
One of the Shinsho. Though a would-be royal assassin, he is for now allied with Arata Hinohara.
MIKUSA
A swordswoman of the Hime Clan. Though she was posing as a man, she has given up that guise.
KOTOHA
A girl of the Uneme Clan who serves Arata of the Hime. She possesses the mysterious power to heal wounds.

THE STORY THUS FAR

Betrayed by his best friend, Arata Hinohara—a high school student in present-day Japan—wanders through a portal into another world where he and his companions journey onward to deliver his Hayagami sword "Tsukuyo" to Princess Kikuri who lingers in a state between life and death.

On the exile island of Muroya, Arata and company clash with the monstrous "mass of human souls" and Kikutsune, the Sho responsible for creating the monster. Arata wins the day, but only after losing two comrades, Rami and Hiruha. Arata now realizes he must ramp up his power if he is to stand a chance against the mysterious and powerful Six Shinsho!

15

Arata
THE LEGEND

CONTENTS

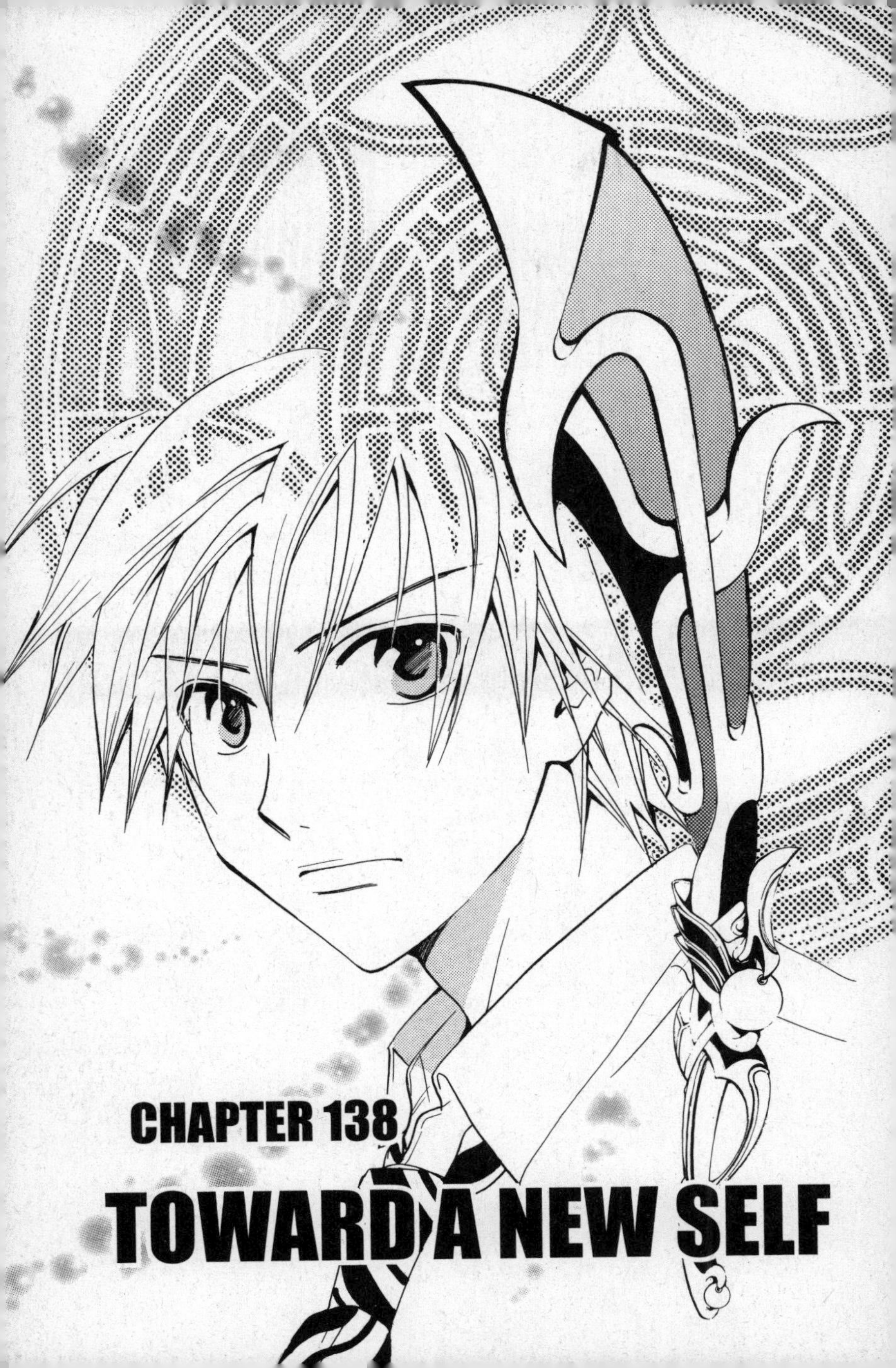

CHAPTER 138

TOWARD A NEW SELF

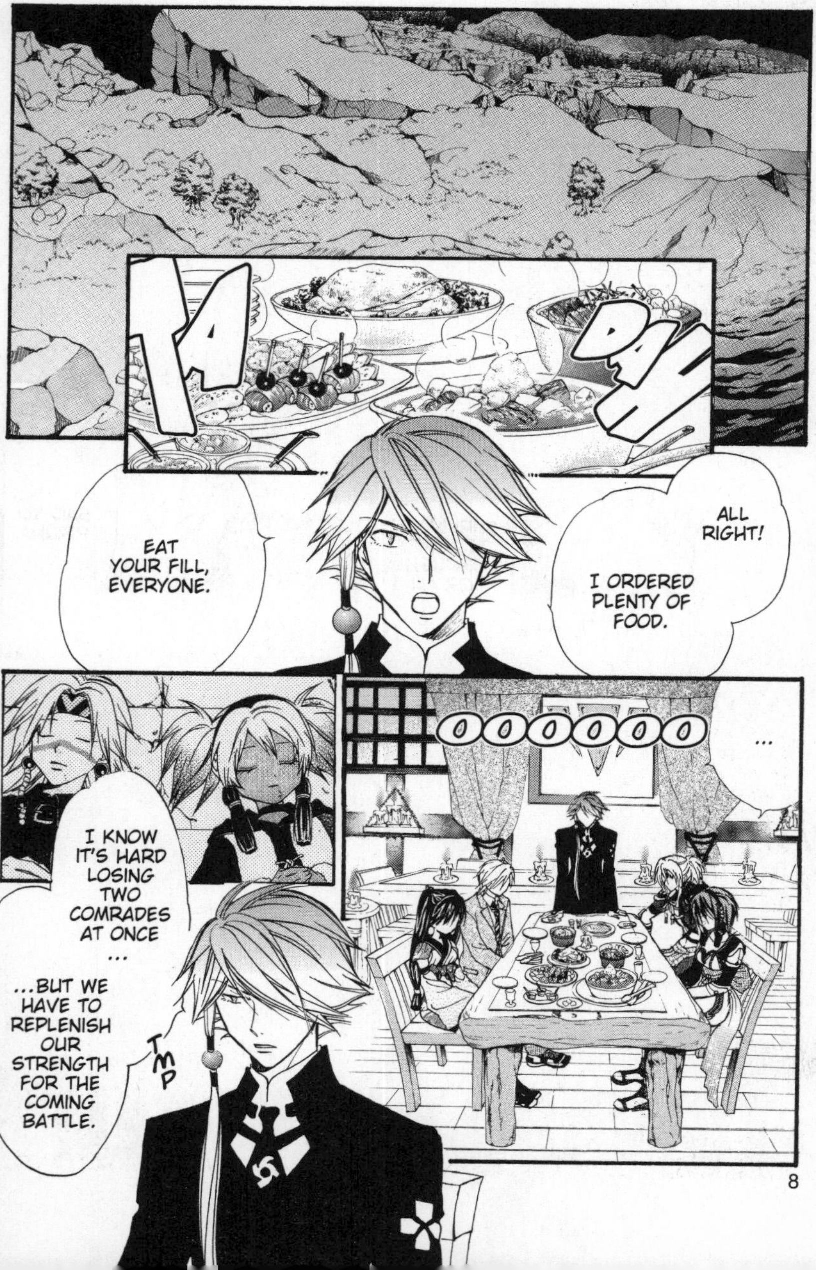
DA
TA
ALL RIGHT!
I ORDERED PLENTY OF FOOD.
EAT YOUR FILL, EVERYONE.
...
I KNOW IT'S HARD LOSING TWO COMRADES AT ONCE...
...BUT WE HAVE TO REPLENISH OUR STRENGTH FOR THE COMING BATTLE.
TMP

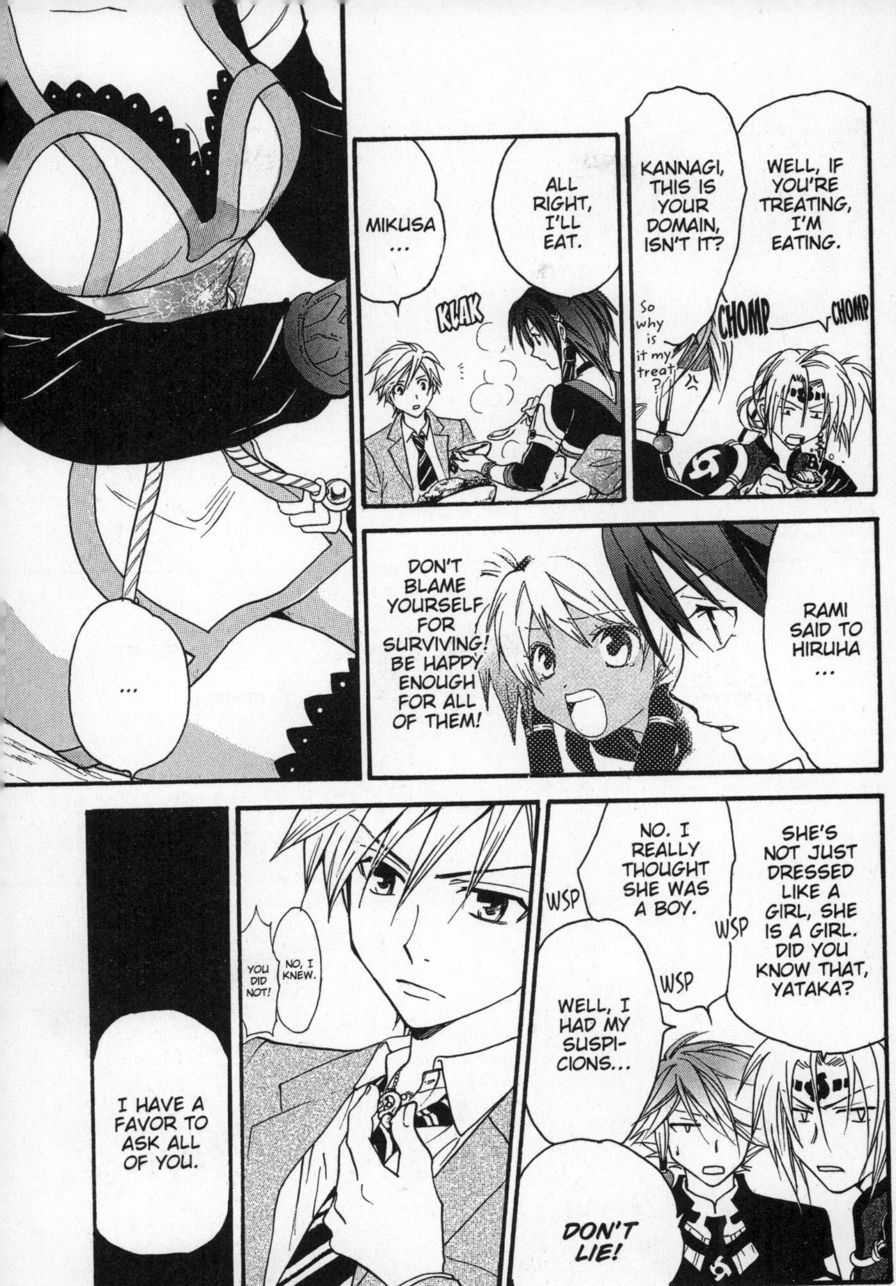
WELL, IF YOU'RE TREATING, I'M EATING.
KANNAGI, THIS IS YOUR DOMAIN, ISN'T IT?
CHOMP
CHOMP
So why is it my treat?
ALL RIGHT, I'LL EAT.
KLAK
MIKUSA ...
RAMI SAID TO HIRUHA ...
DON'T BLAME YOURSELF FOR SURVIVING! BE HAPPY ENOUGH FOR ALL OF THEM!
...
SHE'S NOT JUST DRESSED LIKE A GIRL, SHE IS A GIRL. DID YOU KNOW THAT, YATAKA?
WSP
NO. I REALLY THOUGHT SHE WAS A BOY.
WSP
WSP
WELL, I HAD MY SUSPICIONS...
DON'T LIE!
NO, I KNEW.
YOU DID NOT!
I HAVE A FAVOR TO ASK ALL OF YOU.

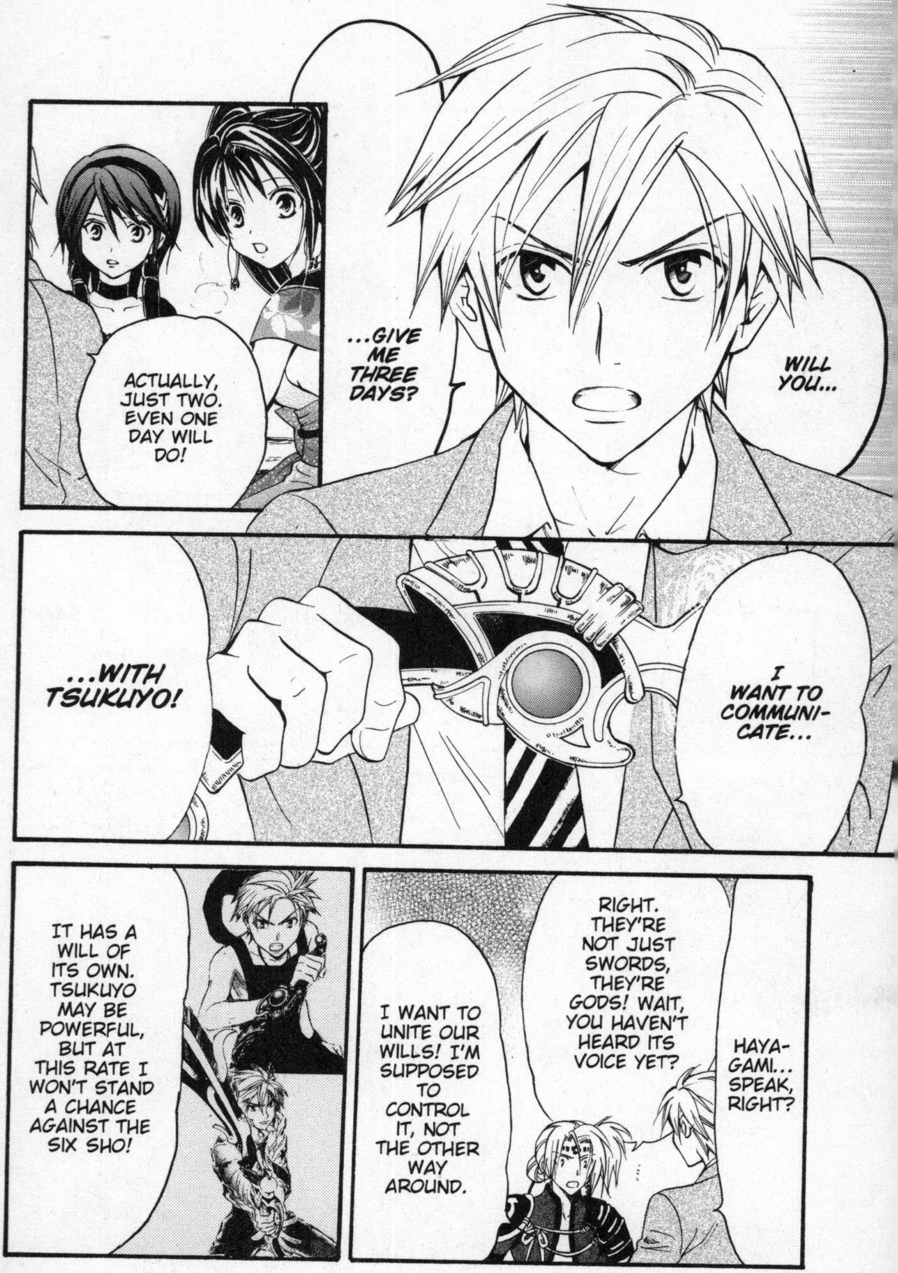
WILL YOU...
...GIVE ME THREE DAYS?
ACTUALLY, JUST TWO. EVEN ONE DAY WILL DO!
I WANT TO COMMUNICATE...
...WITH TSUKUYO!
HAYAGAMI... SPEAK, RIGHT?
RIGHT. THEY'RE NOT JUST SWORDS, THEY'RE GODS! WAIT, YOU HAVEN'T HEARD ITS VOICE YET?
I WANT TO UNITE OUR WILLS! I'M SUPPOSED TO CONTROL IT, NOT THE OTHER WAY AROUND.
IT HAS A WILL OF ITS OWN. TSUKUYO MAY BE POWERFUL, BUT AT THIS RATE I WON'T STAND A CHANCE AGAINST THE SIX SHO!

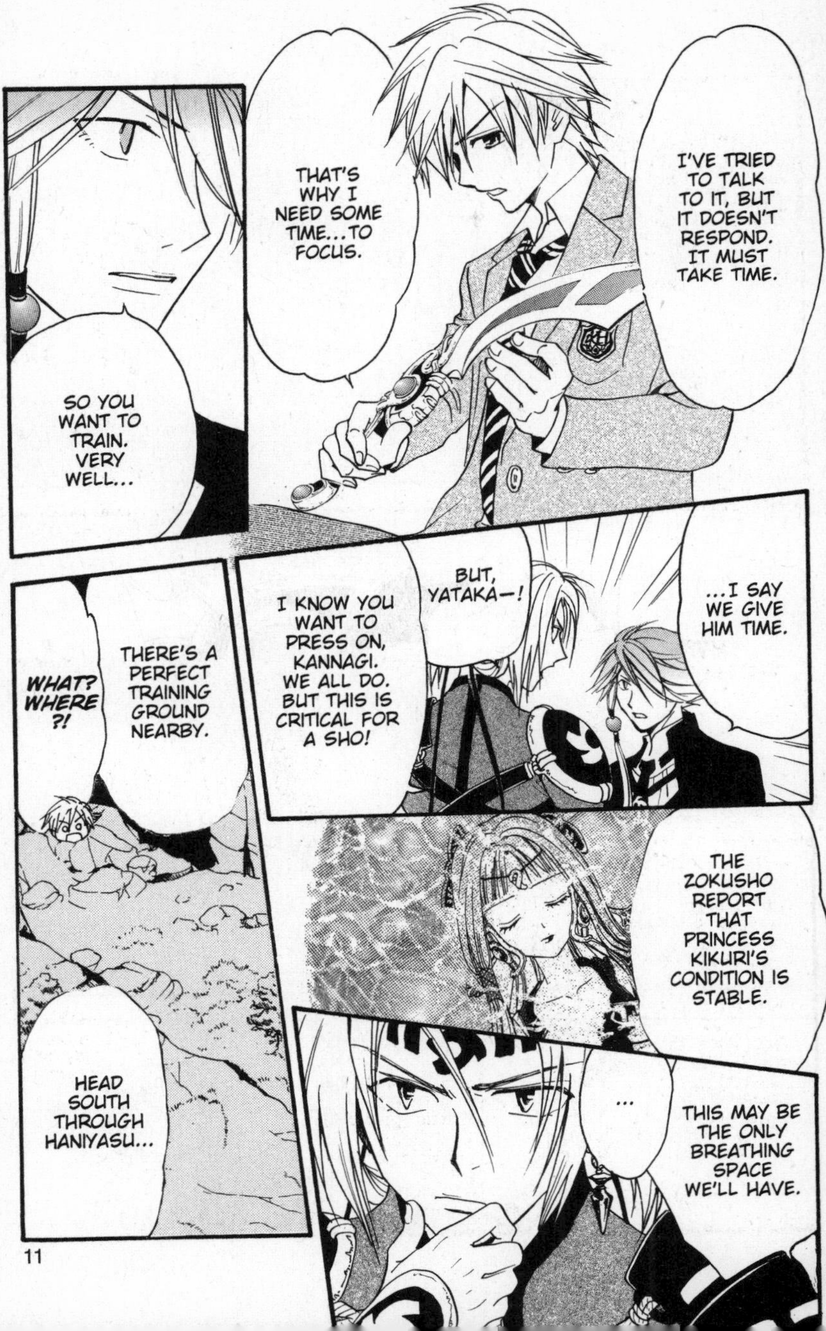
I'VE TRIED TO TALK TO IT, BUT IT DOESN'T RESPOND. IT MUST TAKE TIME.
THAT'S WHY I NEED SOME TIME...TO FOCUS.
SO YOU WANT TO TRAIN. VERY WELL...
...I SAY WE GIVE HIM TIME.
BUT, YATAKA—!
I KNOW YOU WANT TO PRESS ON, KANNAGI. WE ALL DO. BUT THIS IS CRITICAL FOR A SHO!
THE ZOKUSHO REPORT THAT PRINCESS KIKURI'S CONDITION IS STABLE.
THIS MAY BE THE ONLY BREATHING SPACE WE'LL HAVE.
...
THERE'S A PERFECT TRAINING GROUND NEARBY.
WHAT? WHERE?!
HEAD SOUTH THROUGH HANIYASU...

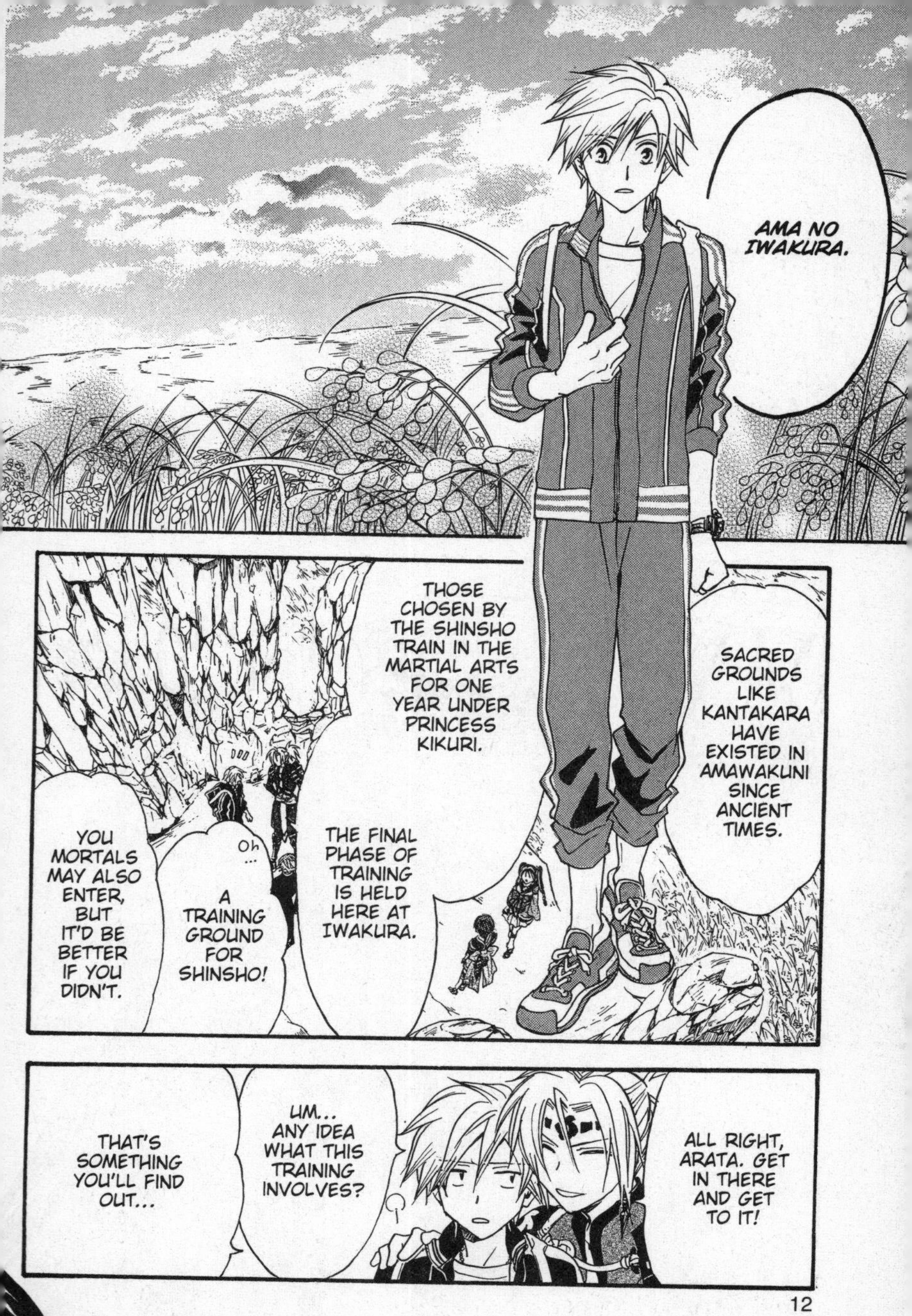
AMA NO IWAKURA.
SACRED GROUNDS LIKE KANTAKARA HAVE EXISTED IN AMAWAKUNI SINCE ANCIENT TIMES.
THOSE CHOSEN BY THE SHINSHO TRAIN IN THE MARTIAL ARTS FOR ONE YEAR UNDER PRINCESS KIKURI.
THE FINAL PHASE OF TRAINING IS HELD HERE AT IWAKURA.
Oh ...
A TRAINING GROUND FOR SHINSHO!
YOU MORTALS MAY ALSO ENTER, BUT IT'D BE BETTER IF YOU DIDN'T.
ALL RIGHT, ARATA. GET IN THERE AND GET TO IT!
UM... ANY IDEA WHAT THIS TRAINING INVOLVES?
THAT'S SOMETHING YOU'LL FIND OUT...

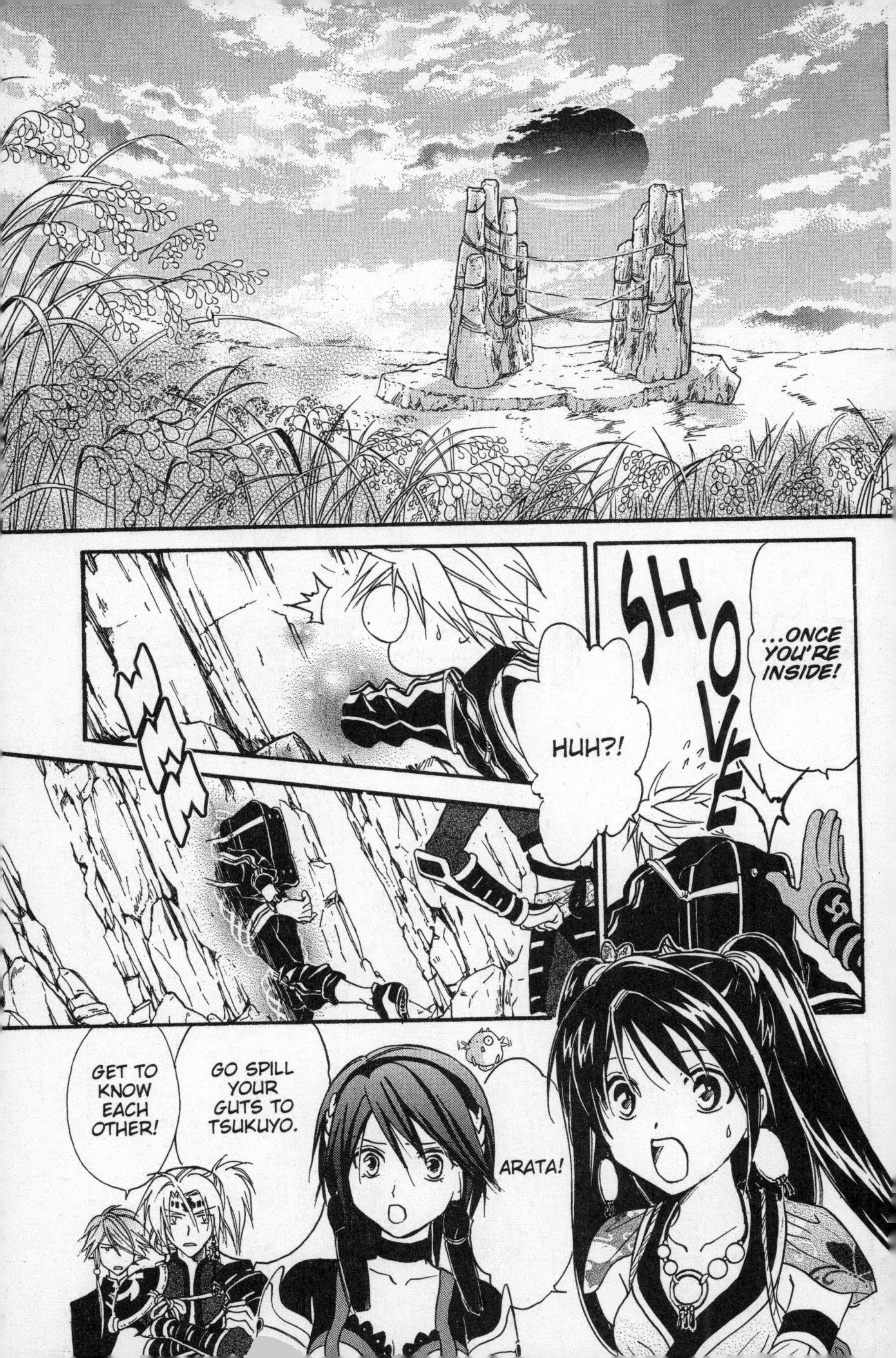
...ONCE YOU'RE INSIDE!
SHOVE
HUH?!
ARATA!
GO SPILL YOUR GUTS TO TSUKUYO.
GET TO KNOW EACH OTHER!

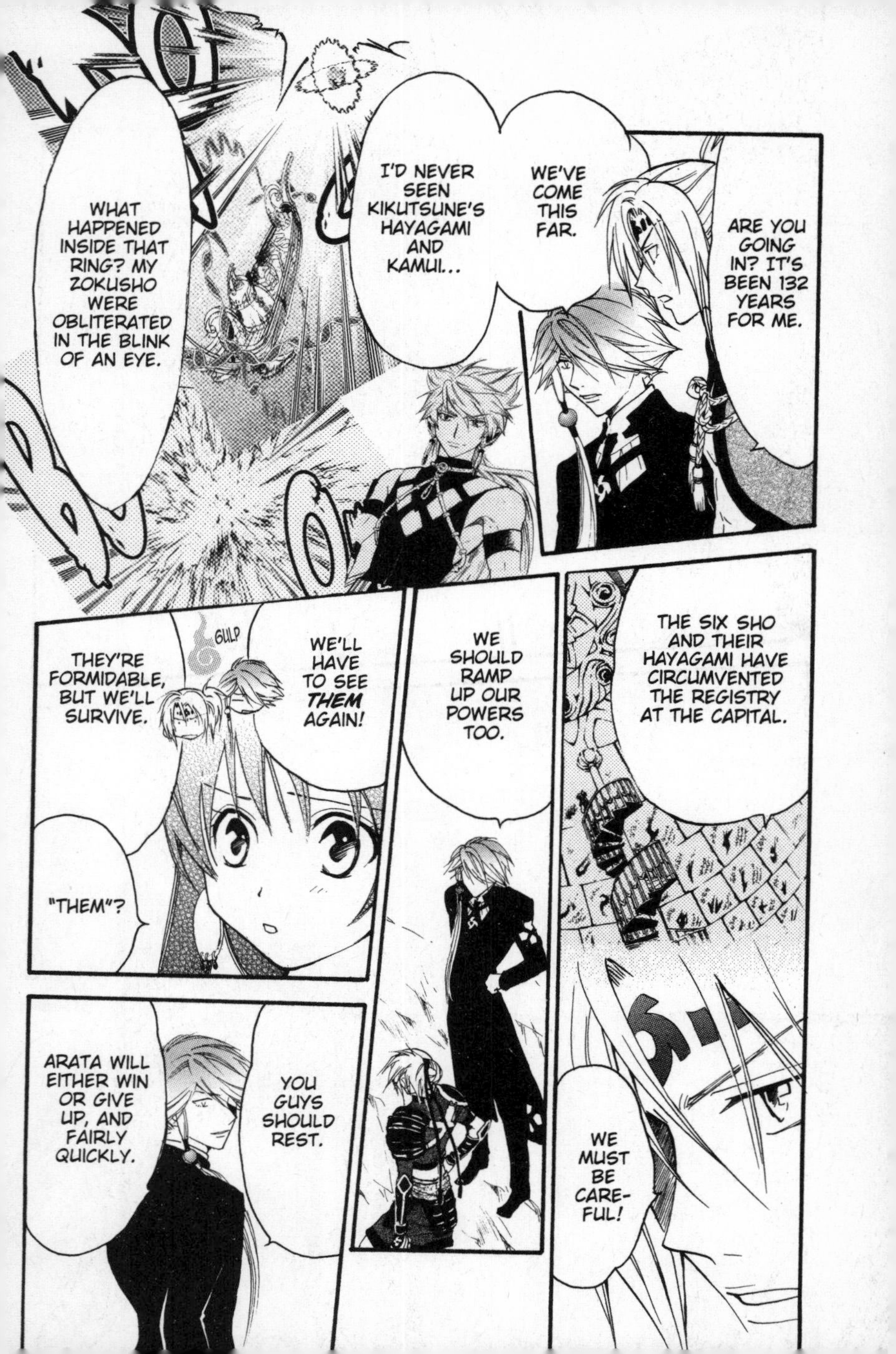
ARE YOU GOING IN? IT'S BEEN 132 YEARS FOR ME.
WE'VE COME THIS FAR.
I'D NEVER SEEN KIKUTSUNE'S HAYAGAMI AND KAMUI...
WHAT HAPPENED INSIDE THAT RING? MY ZOKUSHO WERE OBLITERATED IN THE BLINK OF AN EYE.
THE SIX SHO AND THEIR HAYAGAMI HAVE CIRCUMVENTED THE REGISTRY AT THE CAPITAL.
WE SHOULD RAMP UP OUR POWERS TOO.
WE'LL HAVE TO SEE *THEM* AGAIN!
GULP
THEY'RE FORMIDABLE, BUT WE'LL SURVIVE.
"THEM"?
WE MUST BE CARE-FUL!
YOU GUYS SHOULD REST.
ARATA WILL EITHER WIN OR GIVE UP, AND FAIRLY QUICKLY.

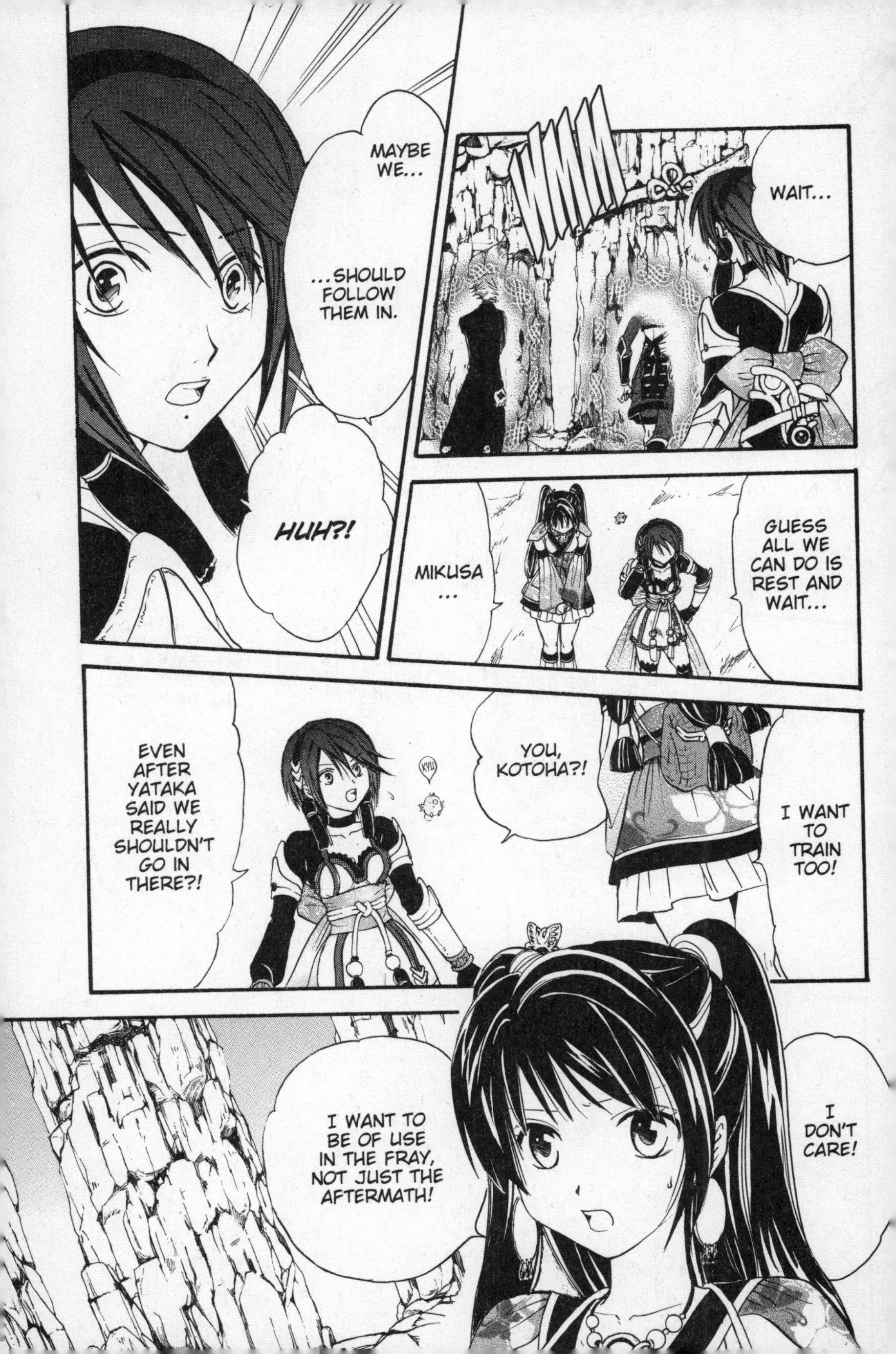
WAIT...
VMMM
GUESS ALL WE CAN DO IS REST AND WAIT...
MIKUSA...
MAYBE WE...
...SHOULD FOLLOW THEM IN.
HUH?!
I WANT TO TRAIN TOO!
YOU, KOTOHA?!
KYU
EVEN AFTER YATAKA SAID WE REALLY SHOULDN'T GO IN THERE?!
I DON'T CARE!
I WANT TO BE OF USE IN THE FRAY, NOT JUST THE AFTERMATH!

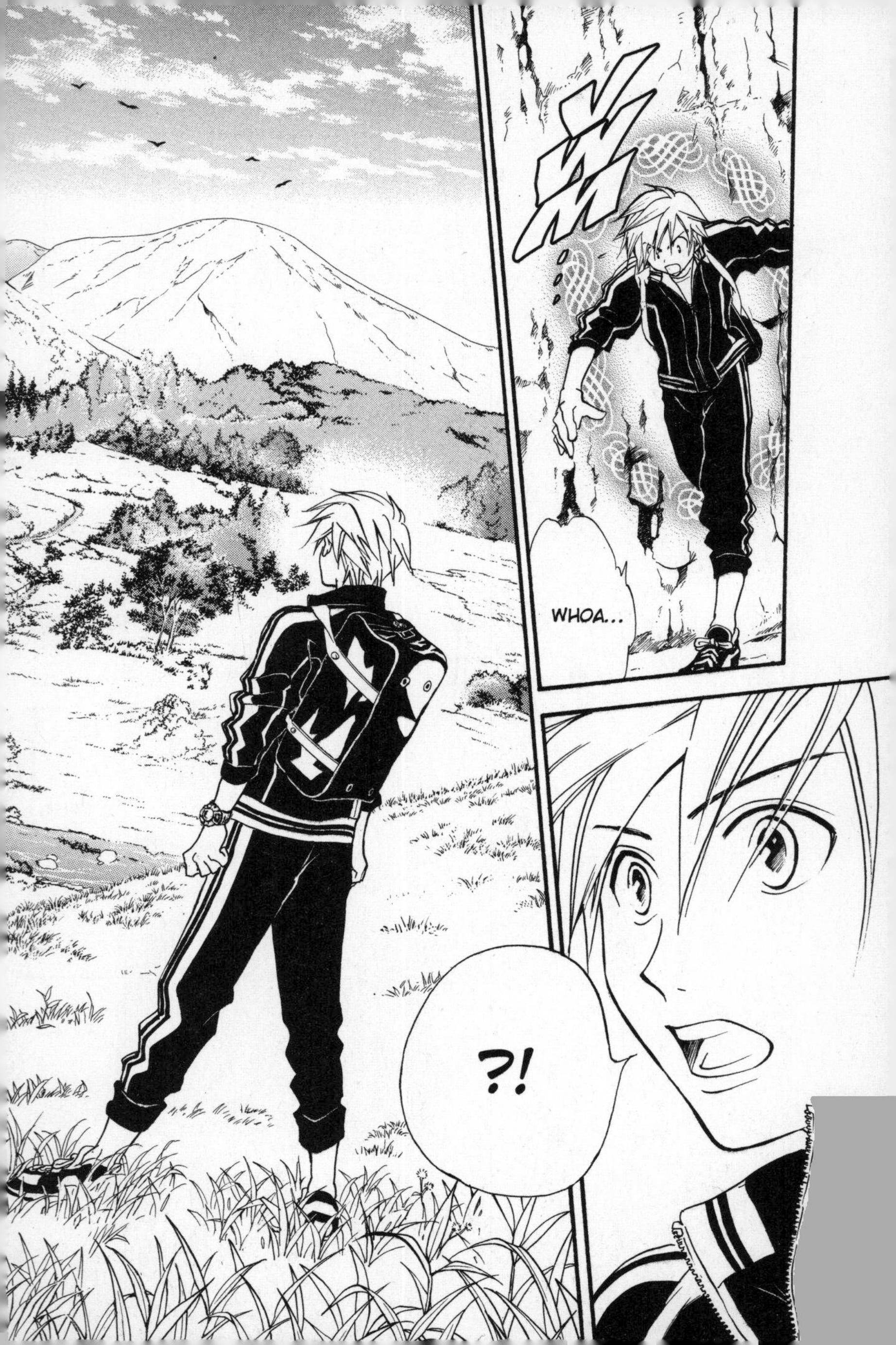
WHOA...
?!

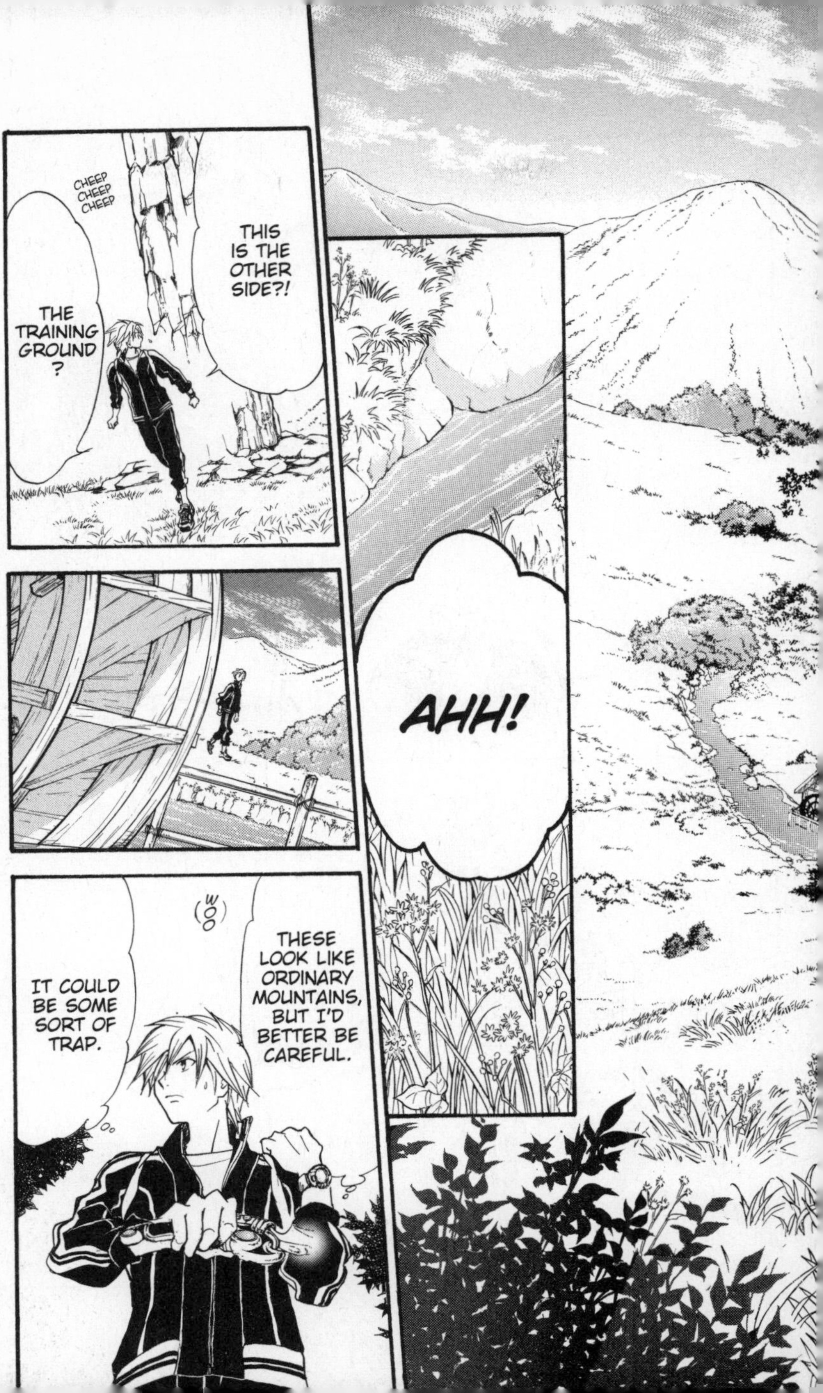
AHH!
THIS IS THE OTHER SIDE?!
CHEEP CHEEP CHEEP
THE TRAINING GROUND?
WOO
THESE LOOK LIKE ORDINARY MOUNTAINS, BUT I'D BETTER BE CAREFUL.
IT COULD BE SOME SORT OF TRAP.

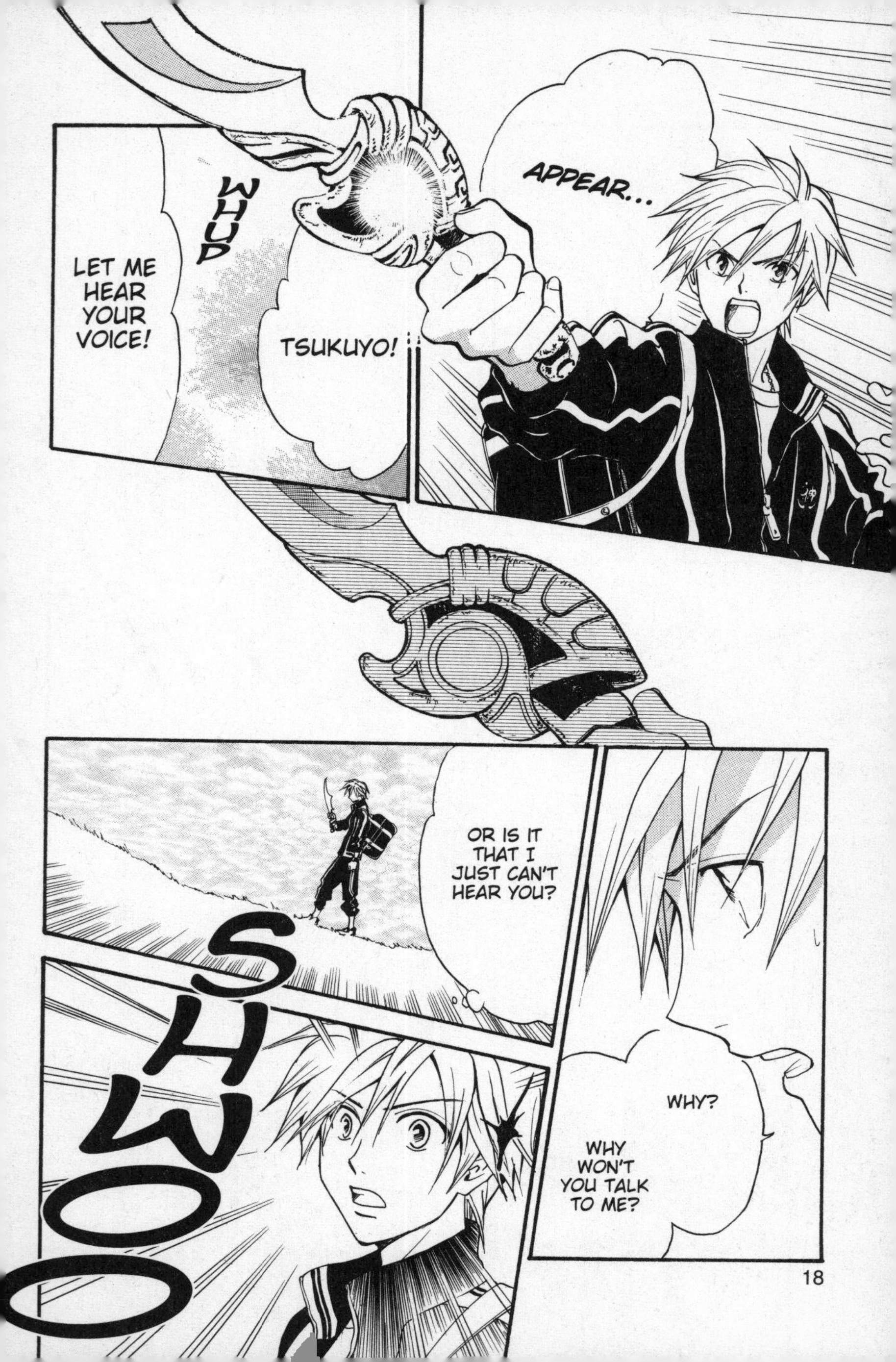

APPEAR...
TSUKUYO!
WHUP
LET ME HEAR YOUR VOICE!
WHY?
WHY WON'T YOU TALK TO ME?
OR IS IT THAT I JUST CAN'T HEAR YOU?
SHWOO

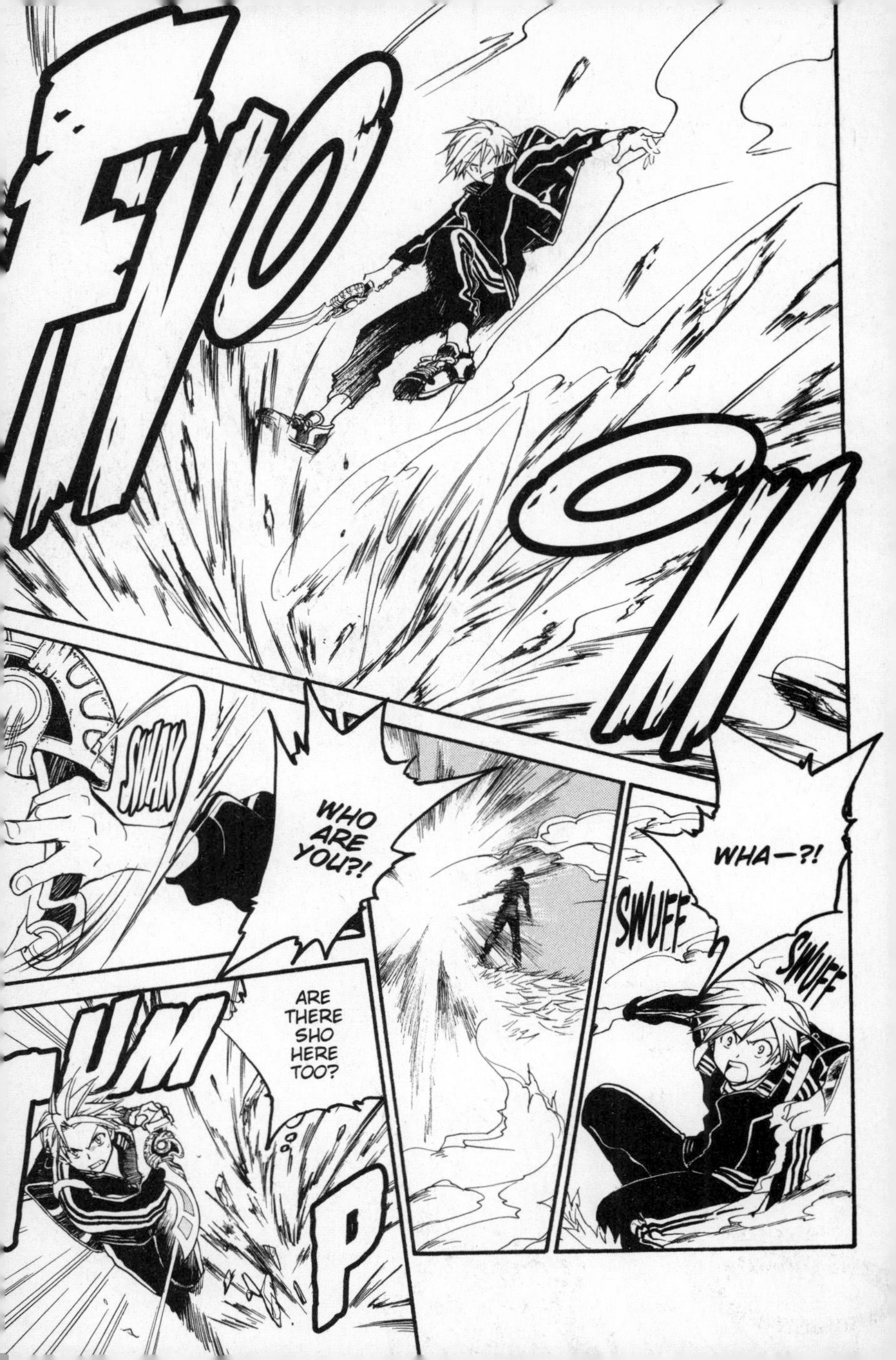
WHA—?!
SWUFF
SWUFF
WHO ARE YOU?!
SWAK
ARE THERE SHO HERE TOO?

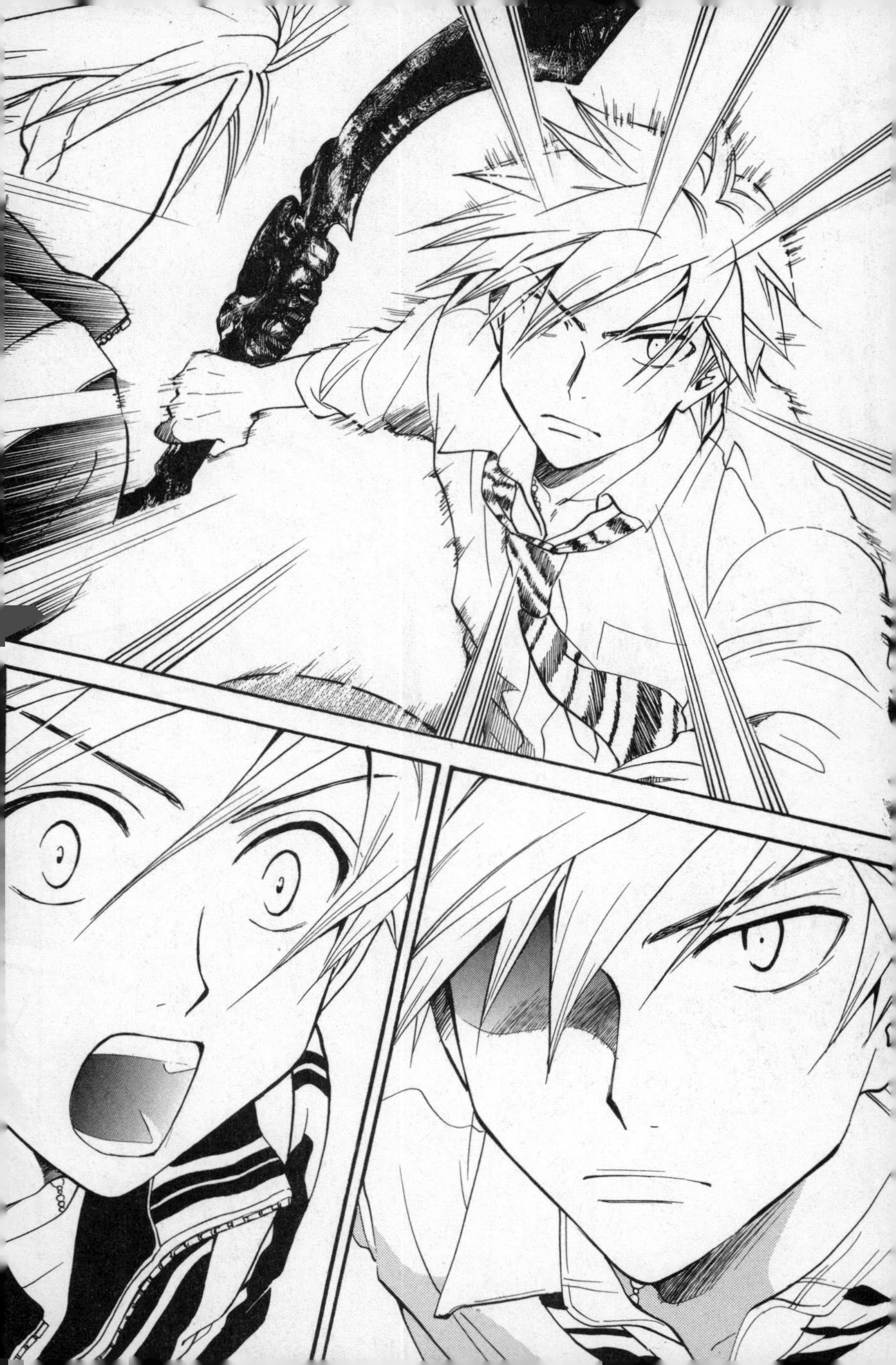

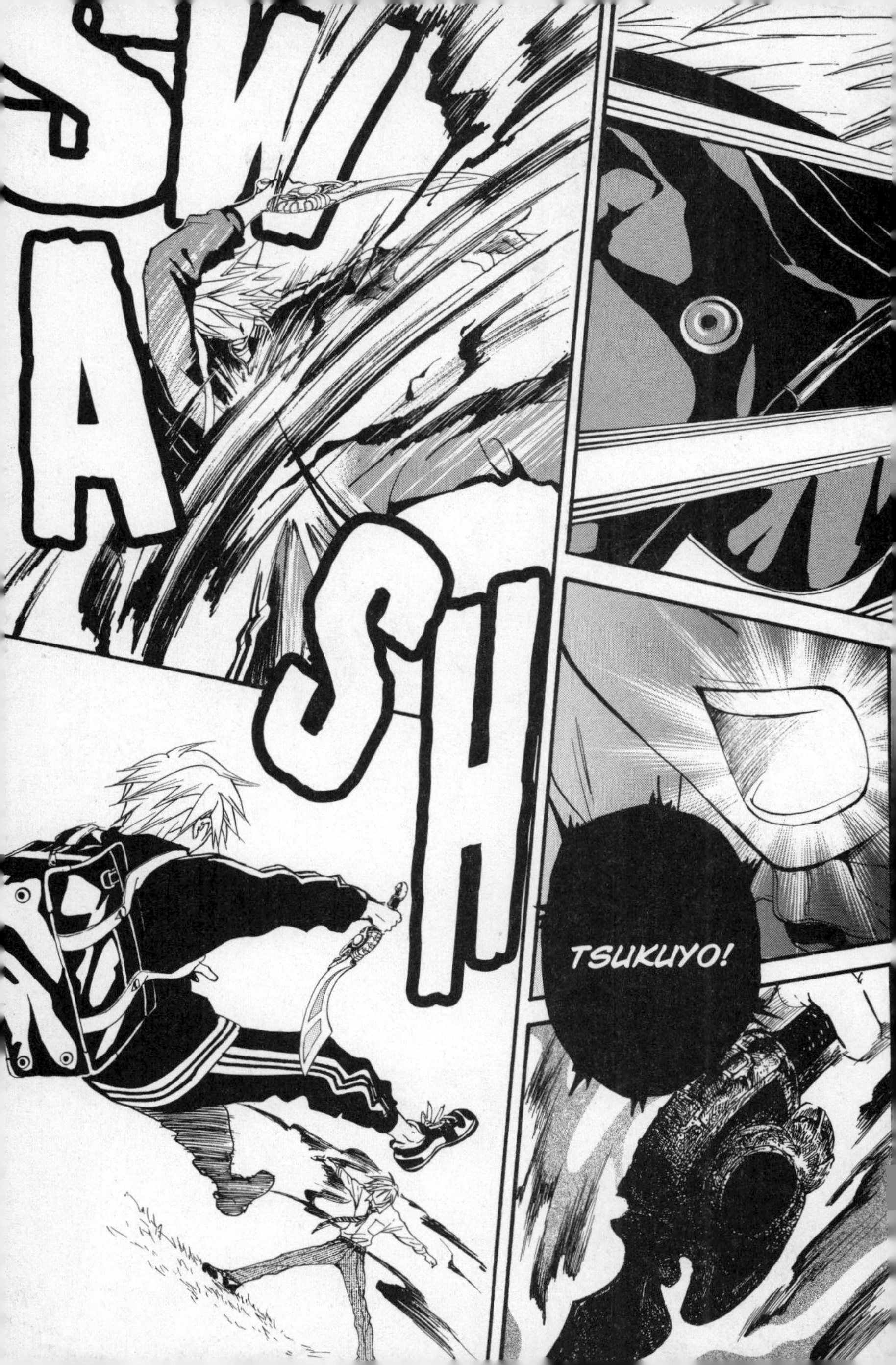
TSUKUYO!
SWASH

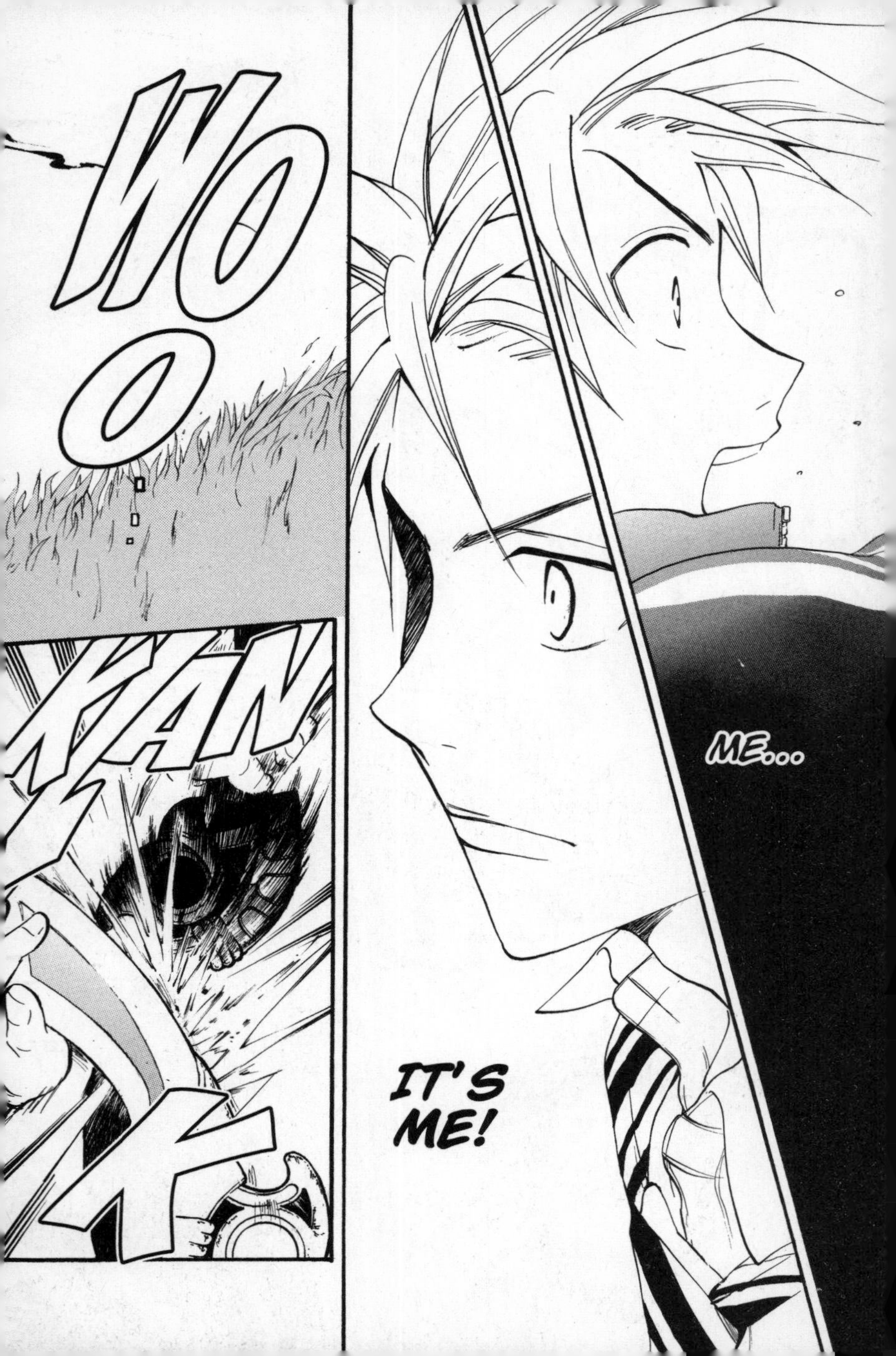
ME...
IT'S ME!
WOO
KANK

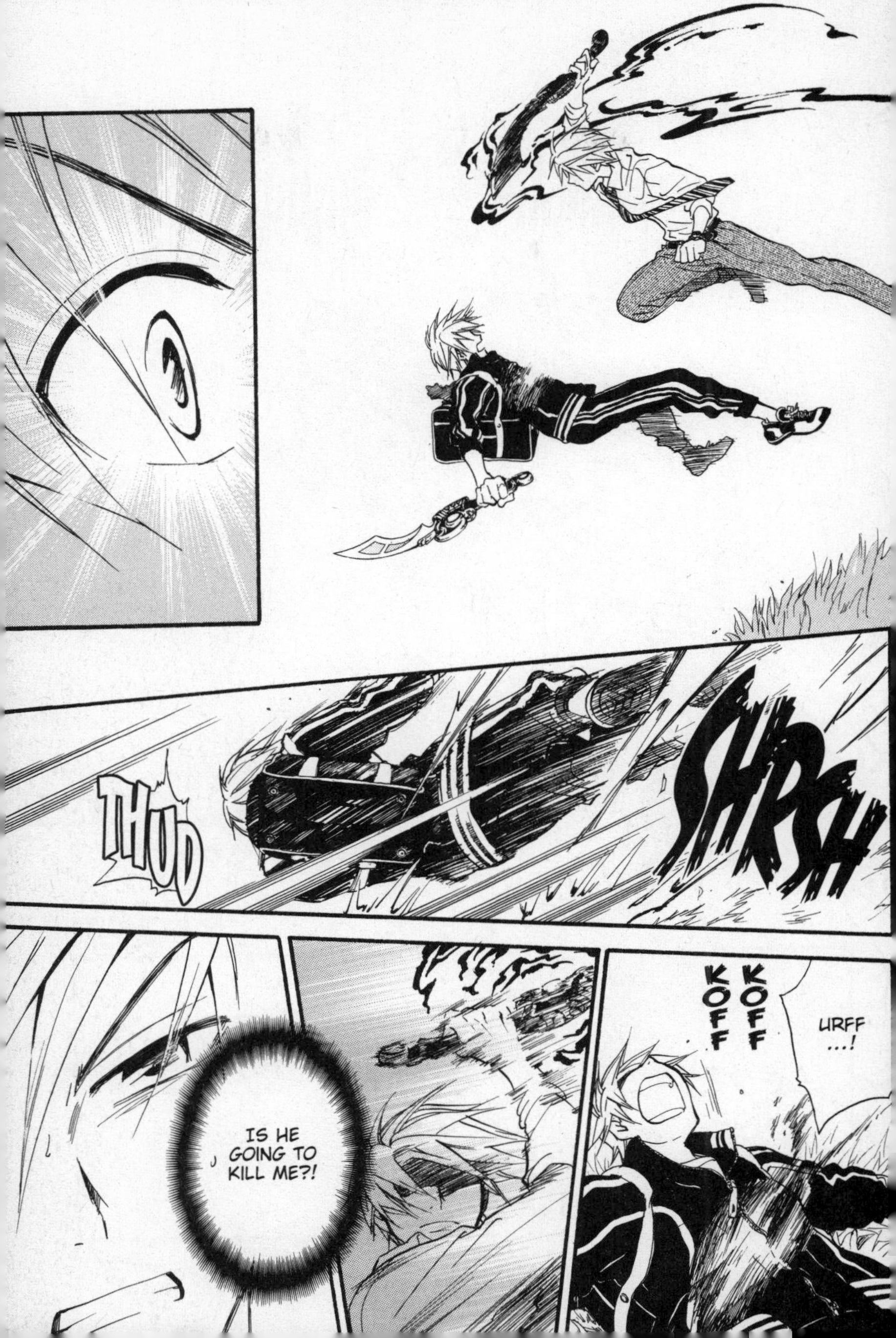
SHRSH
THUD
KOFF KOFF
URFF ...!
IS HE GOING TO KILL ME?!

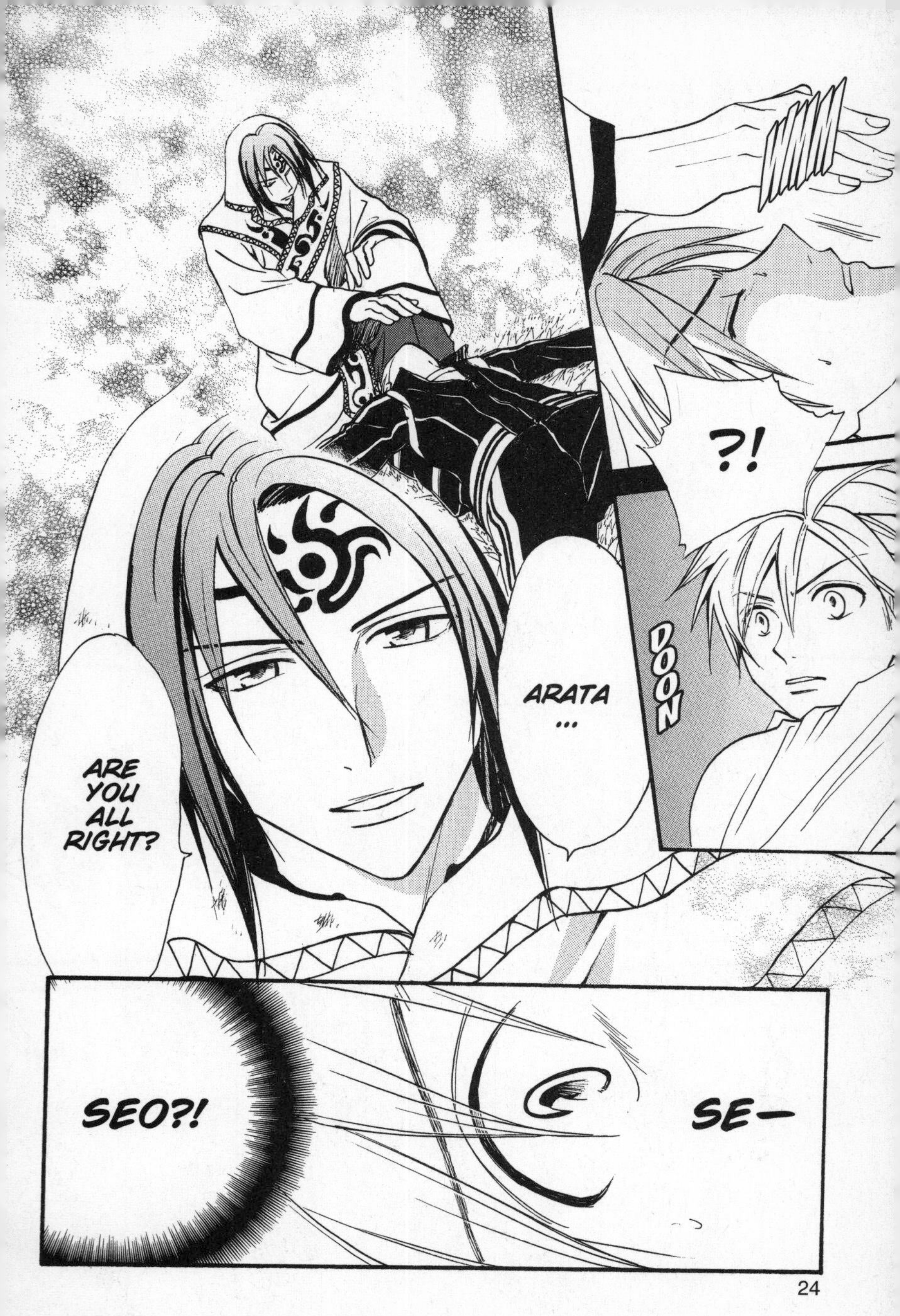
?!
DOON
ARATA ...
ARE YOU ALL RIGHT?
SE—
SEO?!

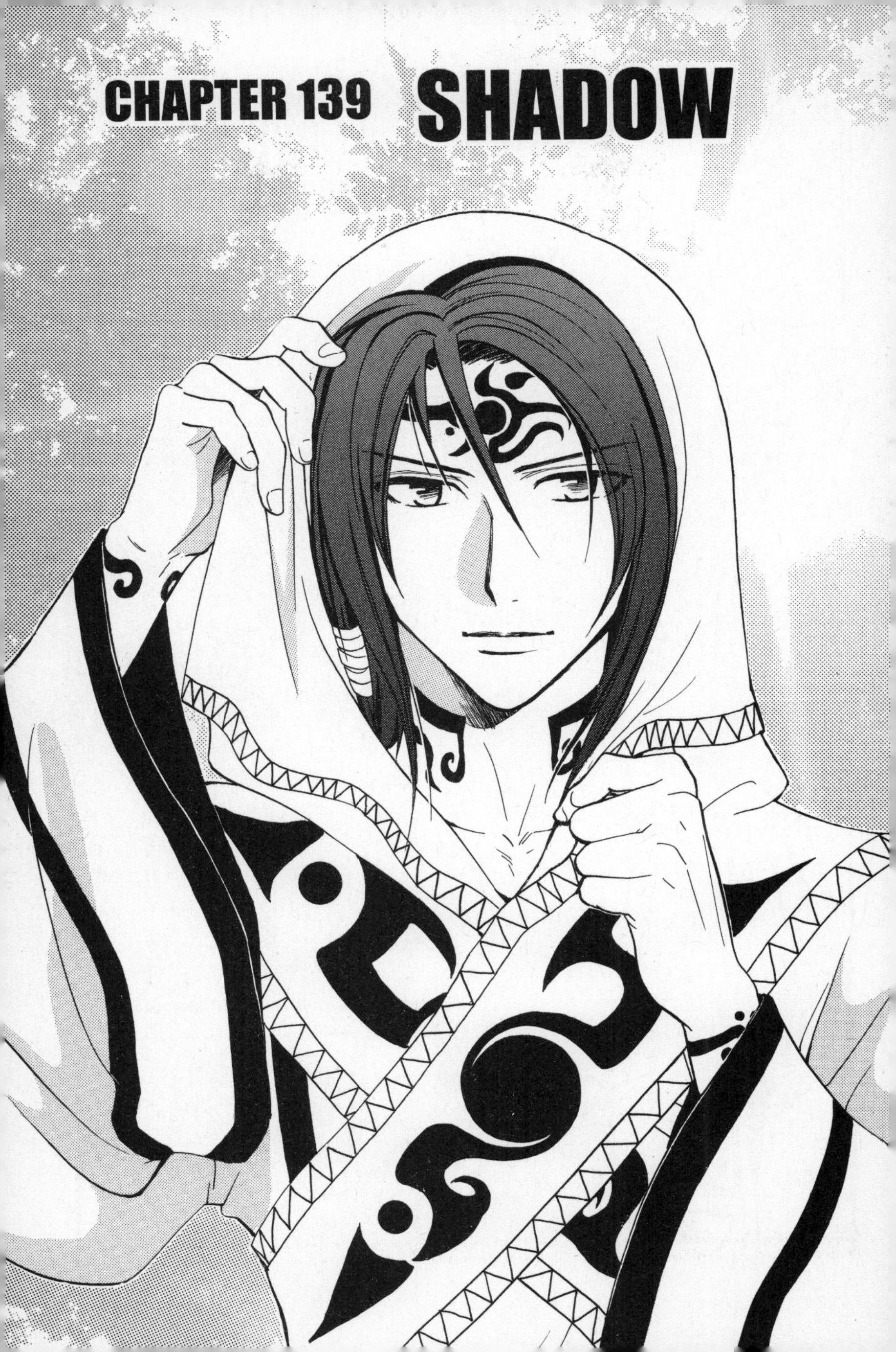
CHAPTER 139 SHADOW

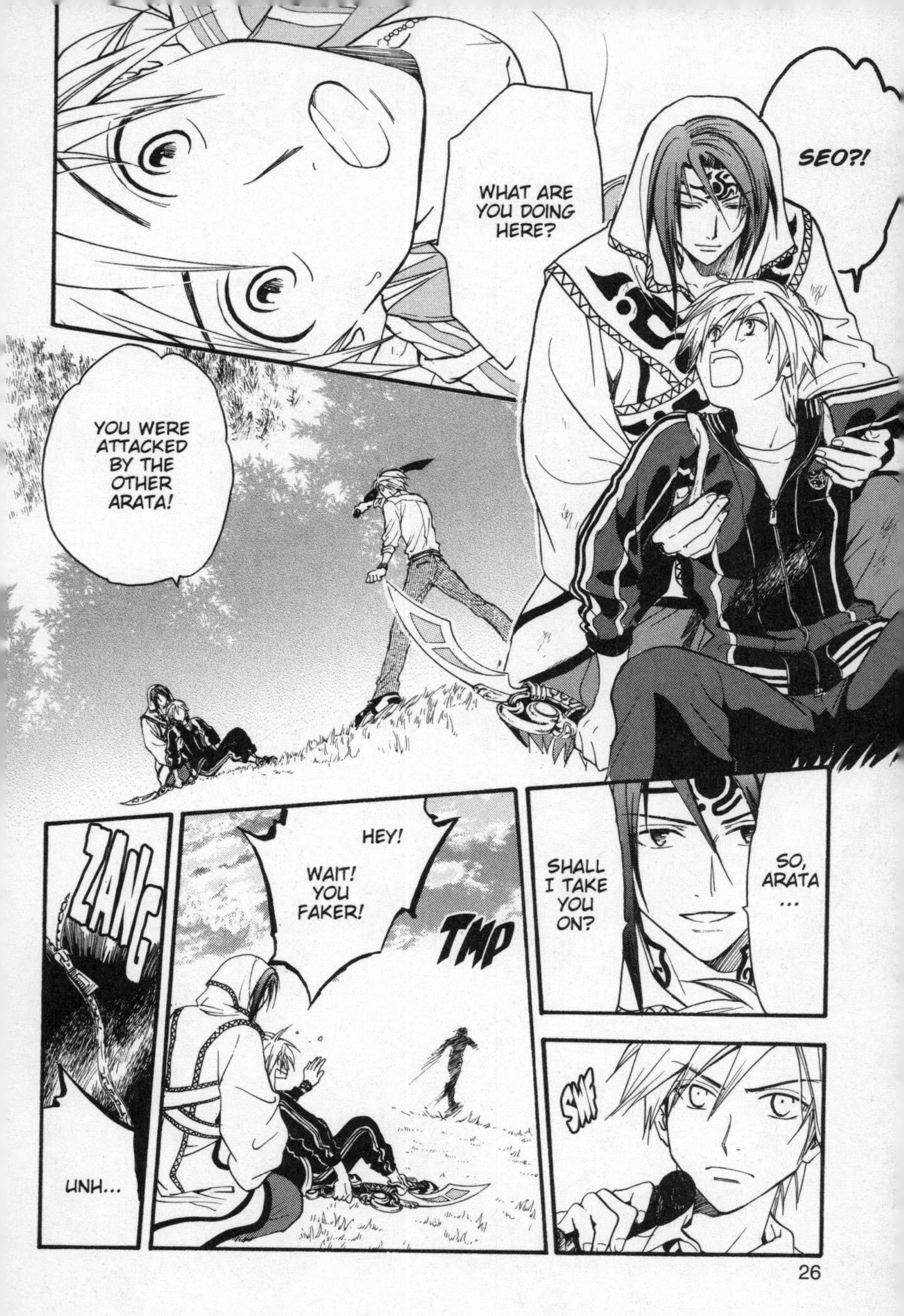
SEO?!
WHAT ARE YOU DOING HERE?
YOU WERE ATTACKED BY THE OTHER ARATA!
SO, ARATA...
SHALL I TAKE YOU ON?
SWF
HEY!
WAIT! YOU FAKER!
TMP
ZANG
UNH...

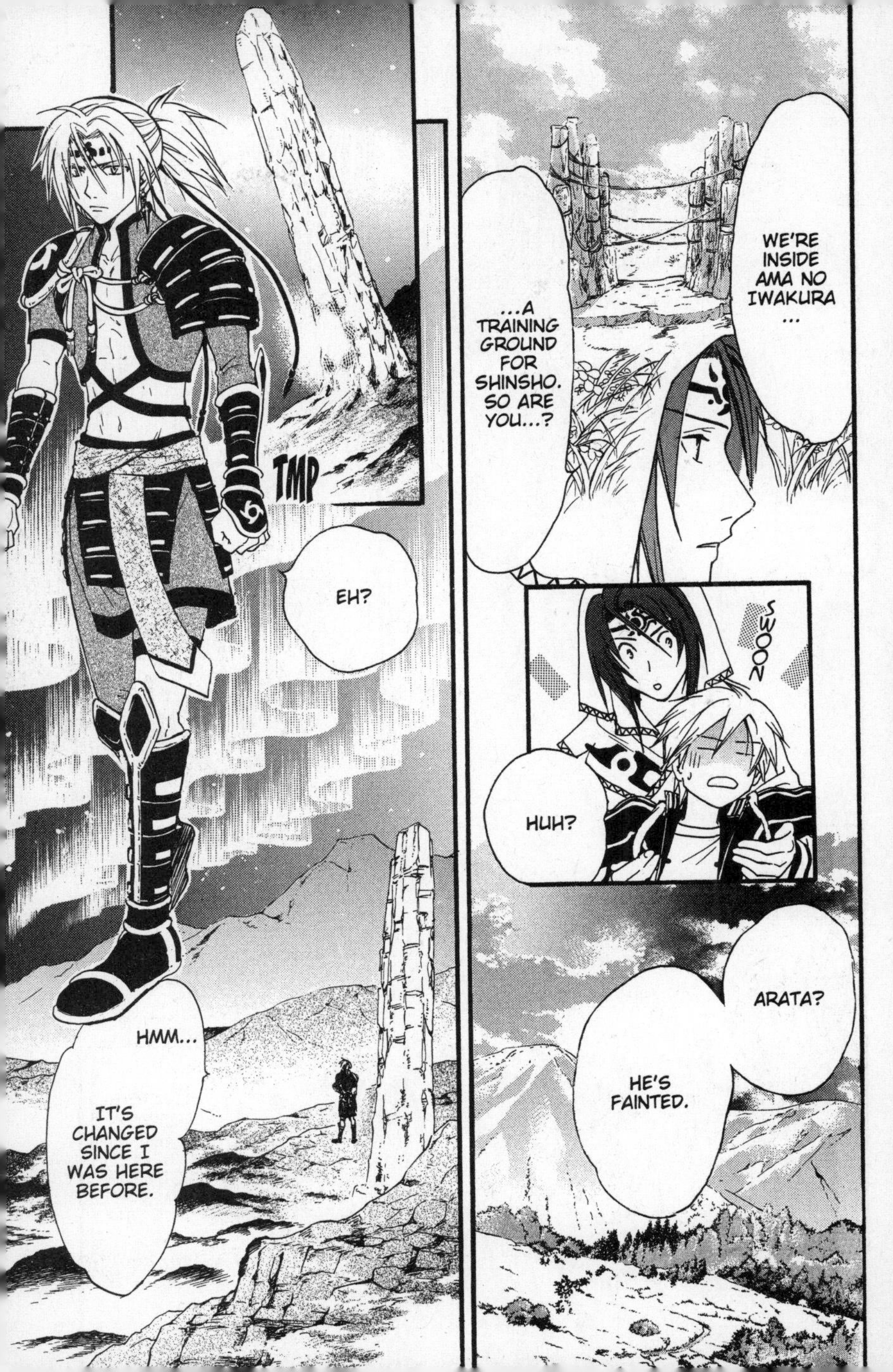
WE'RE INSIDE AMA NO IWAKURA...
...A TRAINING GROUND FOR SHINSHO. SO ARE YOU...?
SWOON
HUH?
ARATA?
HE'S FAINTED.
TMP
EH?
HMM...
IT'S CHANGED SINCE I WAS HERE BEFORE.

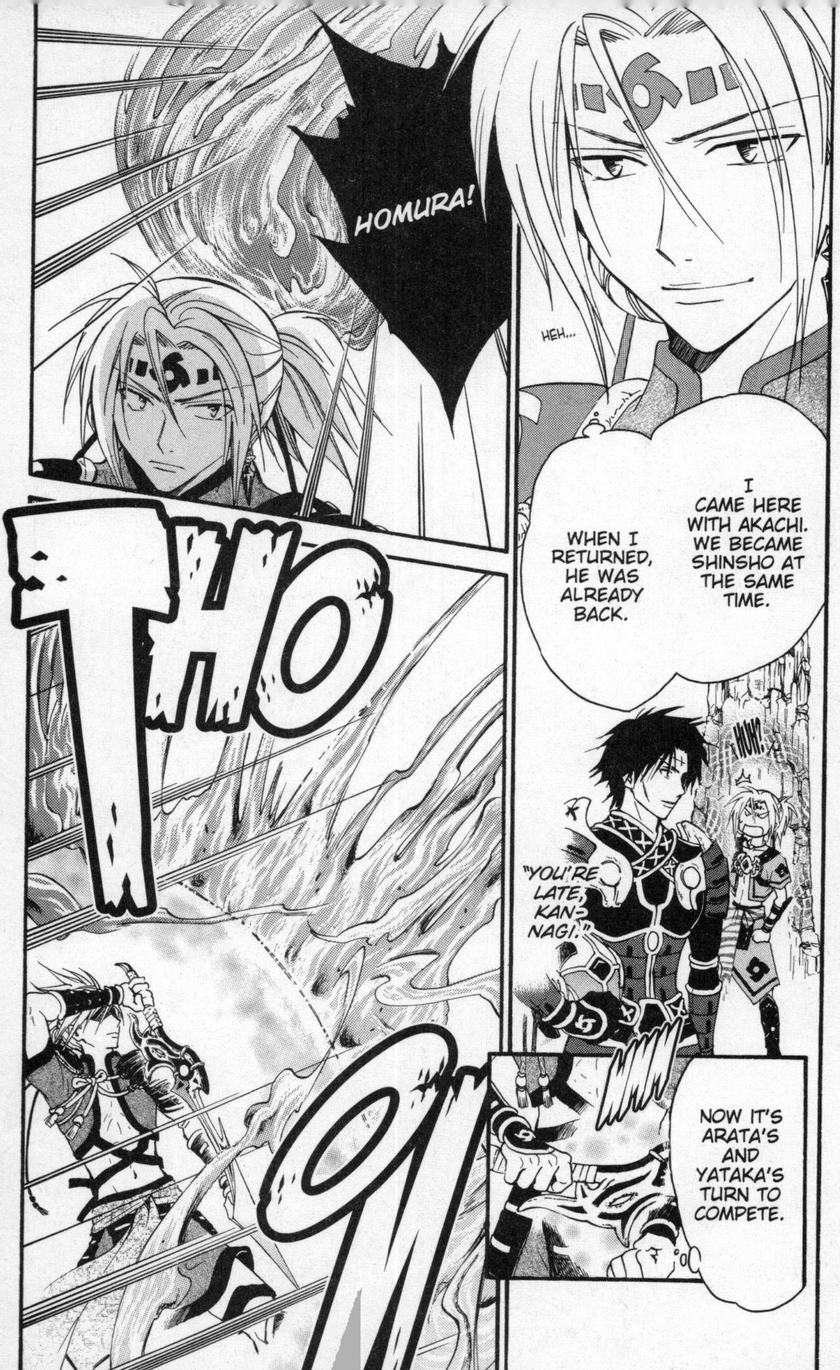
HEH...
I CAME HERE WITH AKACHI. WE BECAME SHINSHO AT THE SAME TIME.
WHEN I RETURNED, HE WAS ALREADY BACK.
HUH?
"YOU'RE LATE, KAN-NAGI."
NOW IT'S ARATA'S AND YATAKA'S TURN TO COMPETE.
HOMURA!
THO

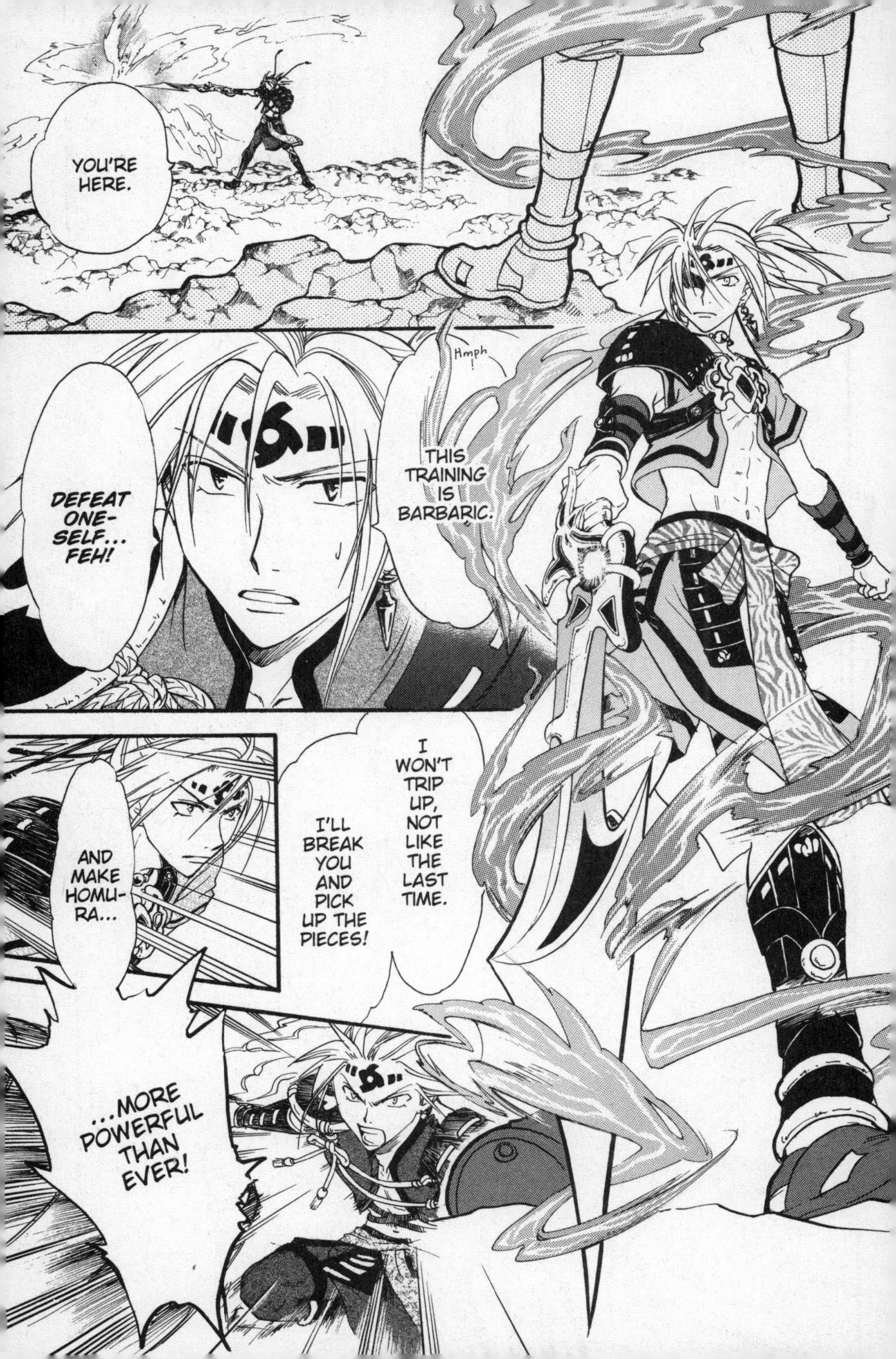
YOU'RE HERE.
Hmph!
THIS TRAINING IS BARBARIC.
DEFEAT ONE-SELF... FEH!
I WON'T TRIP UP, NOT LIKE THE LAST TIME.
I'LL BREAK YOU AND PICK UP THE PIECES!
AND MAKE HOMU-RA...
...MORE POWERFUL THAN EVER!

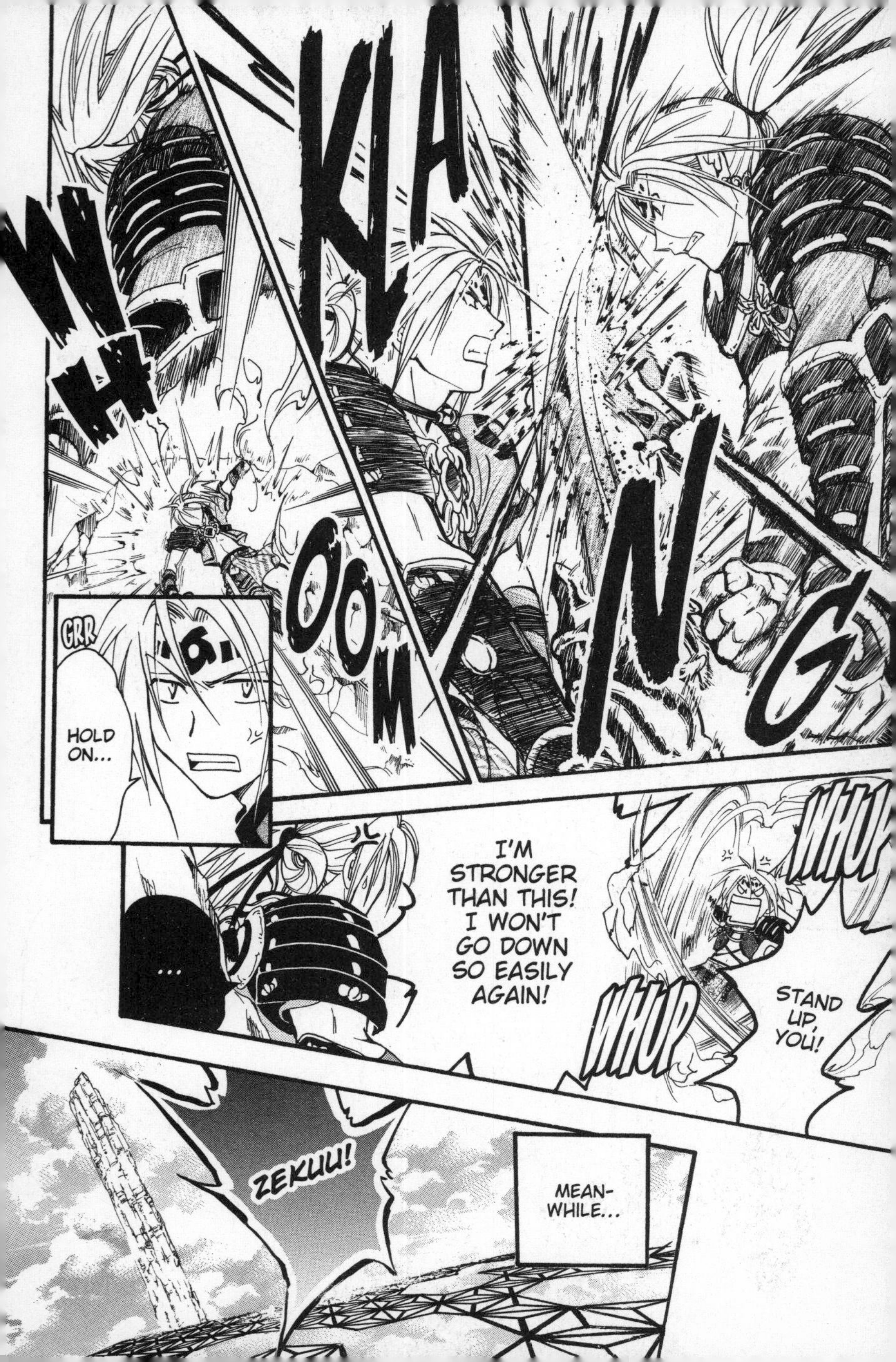
KLANG
WHH
OOM
GRR
HOLD ON...
WHUP
STAND UP, YOU!
WHUP
I'M STRONGER THAN THIS! I WON'T GO DOWN SO EASILY AGAIN!
...
MEAN-WHILE...
ZEKUU!

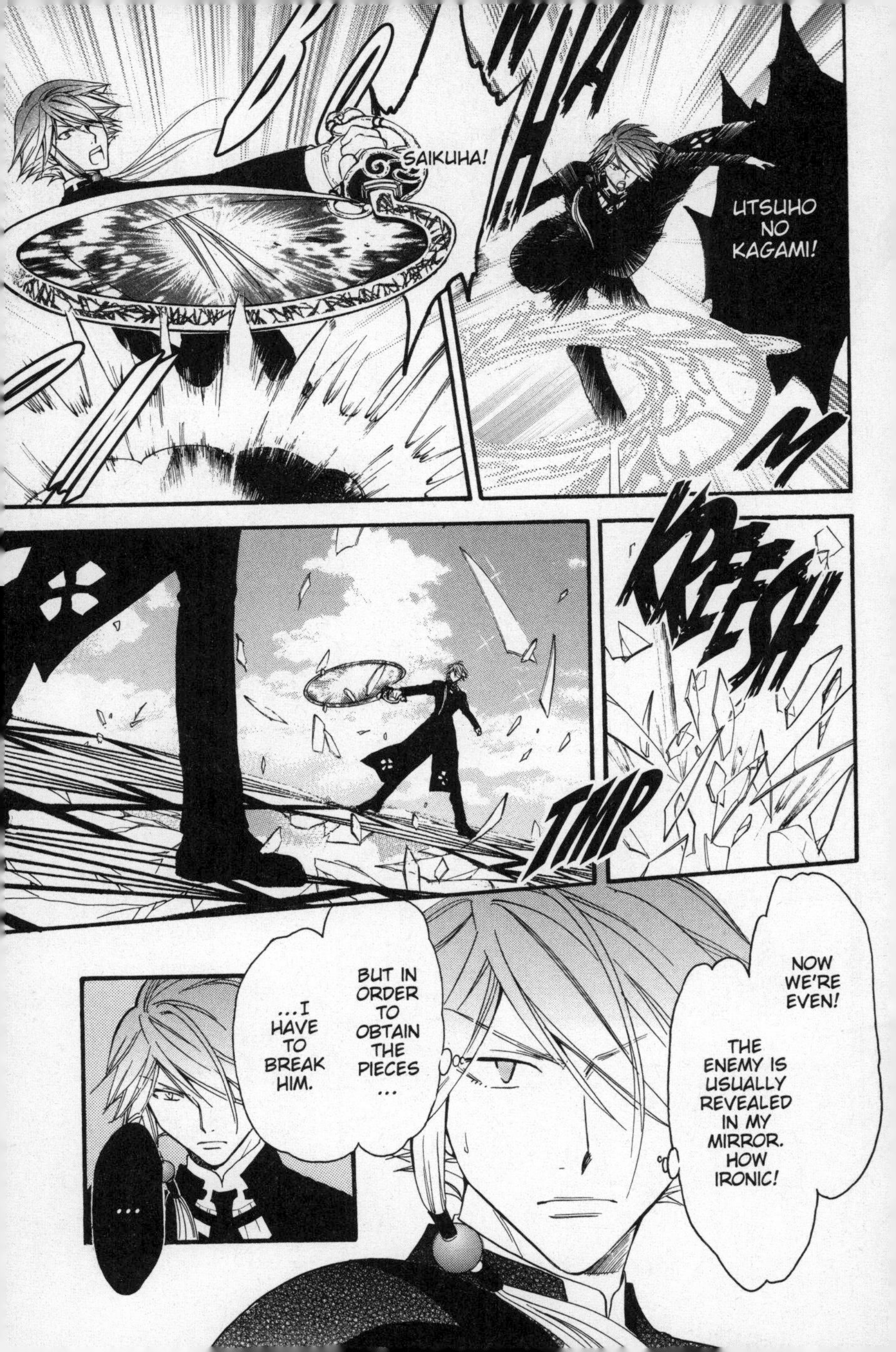
UTSUHO NO KAGAMI!
SAIKUHA!
TMP
NOW WE'RE EVEN!
THE ENEMY IS USUALLY REVEALED IN MY MIRROR. HOW IRONIC!
BUT IN ORDER TO OBTAIN THE PIECES ...
...I HAVE TO BREAK HIM.
...

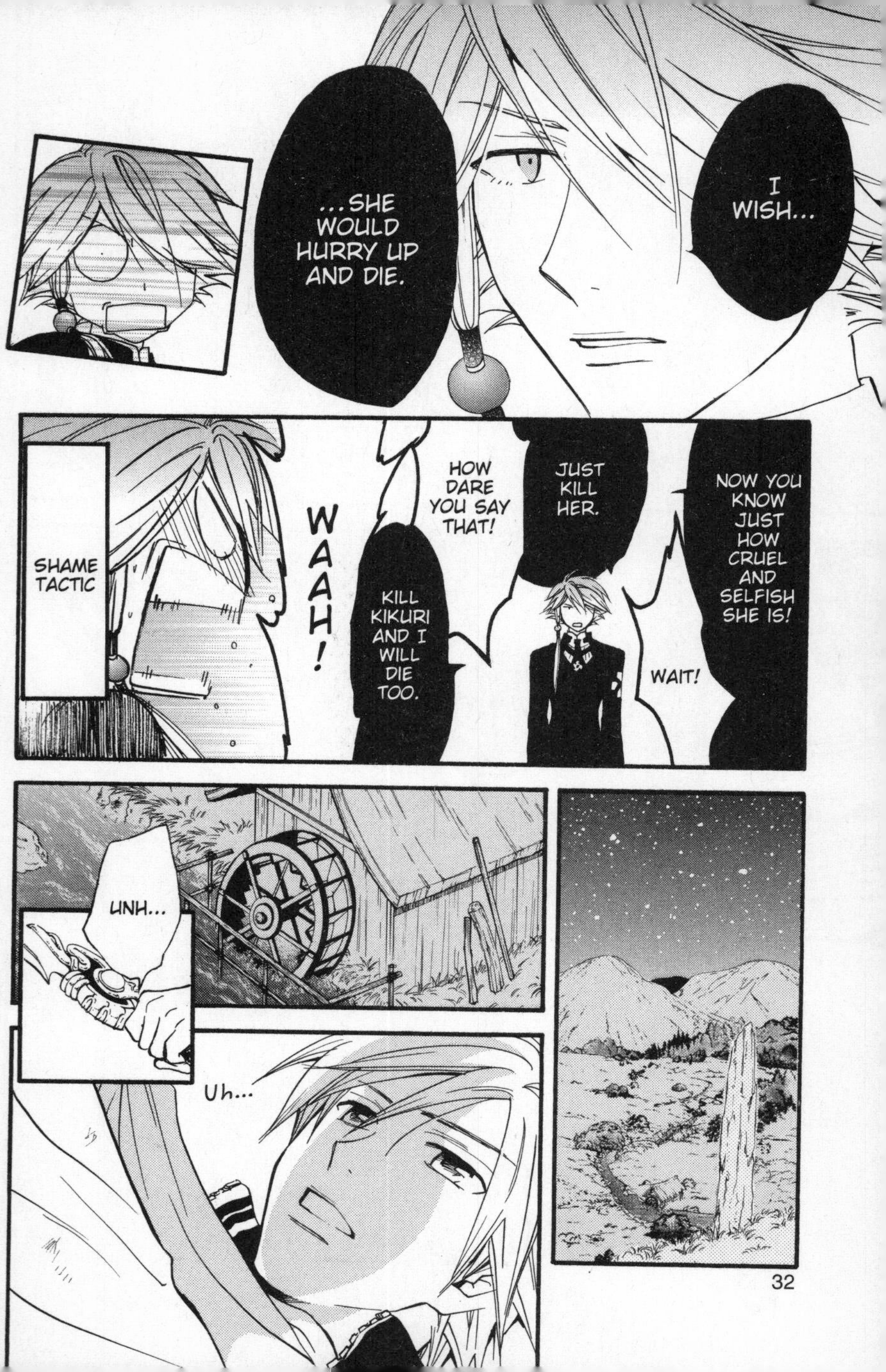
I WISH...
...SHE WOULD HURRY UP AND DIE.
NOW YOU KNOW JUST HOW CRUEL AND SELFISH SHE IS!
WAIT!
JUST KILL HER.
HOW DARE YOU SAY THAT!
KILL KIKURI AND I WILL DIE TOO.
WAAAH!
SHAME TACTIC
UNH...
Uh...

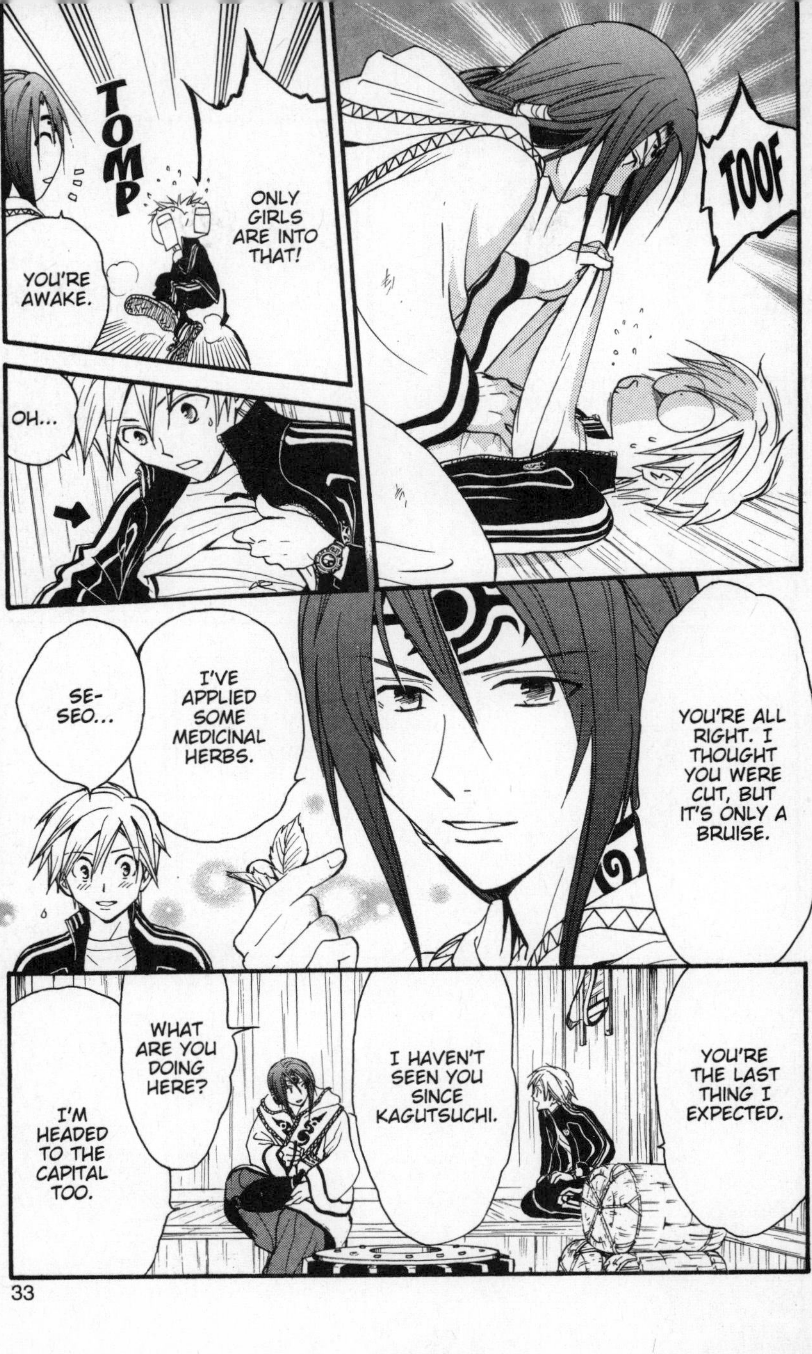
TOOF
ONLY GIRLS ARE INTO THAT!
TOMP
YOU'RE AWAKE.
OH...
YOU'RE ALL RIGHT. I THOUGHT YOU WERE CUT, BUT IT'S ONLY A BRUISE.
I'VE APPLIED SOME MEDICINAL HERBS.
SE-SEO...
YOU'RE THE LAST THING I EXPECTED.
I HAVEN'T SEEN YOU SINCE KAGUTSUCHI.
WHAT ARE YOU DOING HERE?
I'M HEADED TO THE CAPITAL TOO.

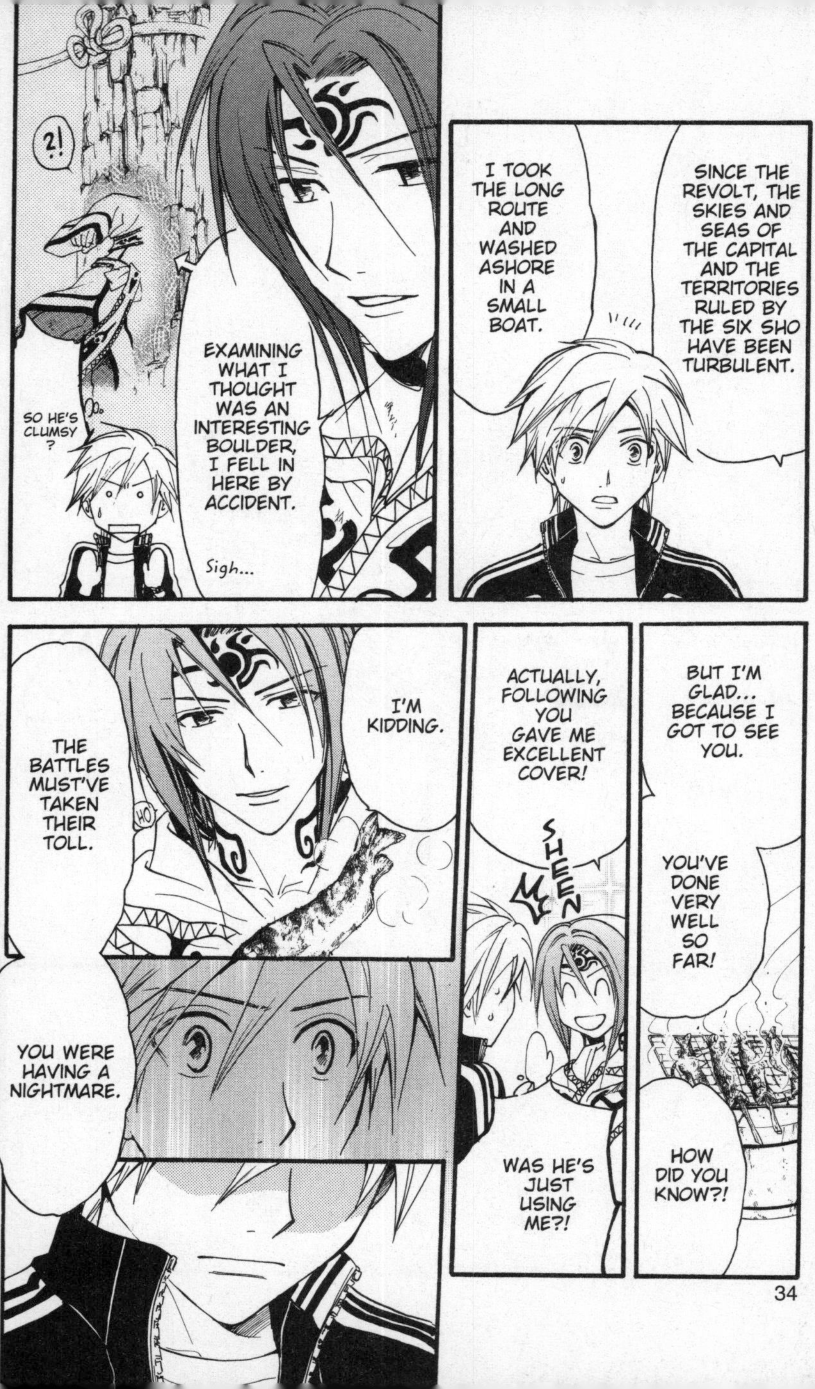
SINCE THE REVOLT, THE SKIES AND SEAS OF THE CAPITAL AND THE TERRITORIES RULED BY THE SIX SHO HAVE BEEN TURBULENT.
I TOOK THE LONG ROUTE AND WASHED ASHORE IN A SMALL BOAT.
?!
EXAMINING WHAT I THOUGHT WAS AN INTERESTING BOULDER, I FELL IN HERE BY ACCIDENT.
SO HE'S CLUMSY?
Sigh...
BUT I'M GLAD... BECAUSE I GOT TO SEE YOU.
YOU'VE DONE VERY WELL SO FAR!
HOW DID YOU KNOW?!
ACTUALLY, FOLLOWING YOU GAVE ME EXCELLENT COVER!
SHEEN
WAS HE'S JUST USING ME?!
I'M KIDDING.
HO
THE BATTLES MUST'VE TAKEN THEIR TOLL.
YOU WERE HAVING A NIGHTMARE.

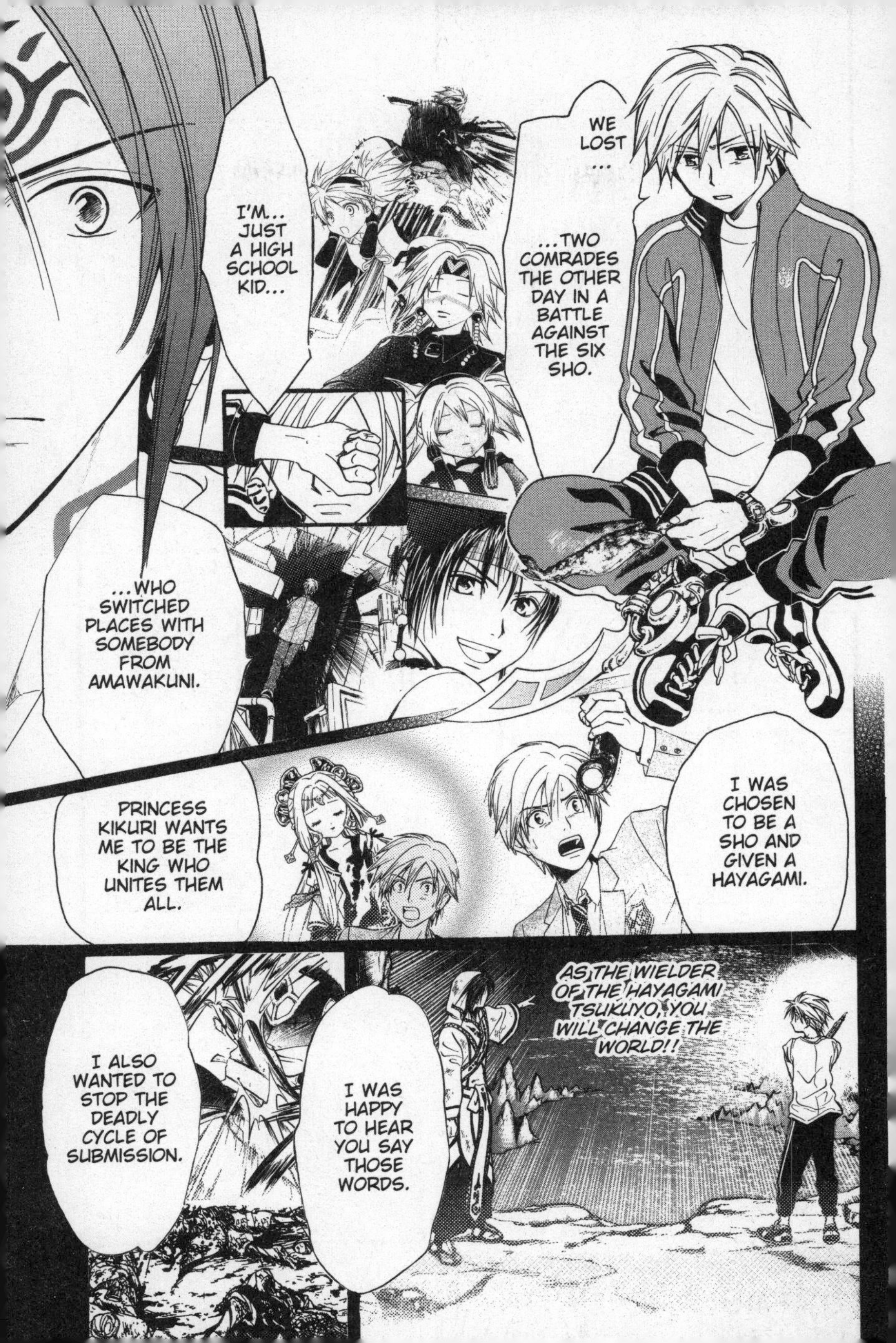
WE LOST ...
...TWO COMRADES THE OTHER DAY IN A BATTLE AGAINST THE SIX SHO.
I'M... JUST A HIGH SCHOOL KID...
...WHO SWITCHED PLACES WITH SOMEBODY FROM AMAWAKUNI.
I WAS CHOSEN TO BE A SHO AND GIVEN A HAYAGAMI.
PRINCESS KIKURI WANTS ME TO BE THE KING WHO UNITES THEM ALL.
AS THE WIELDER OF THE HAYAGAMI TSUKUYO, YOU WILL CHANGE THE WORLD!!
I WAS HAPPY TO HEAR YOU SAY THOSE WORDS.
I ALSO WANTED TO STOP THE DEADLY CYCLE OF SUBMISSION.

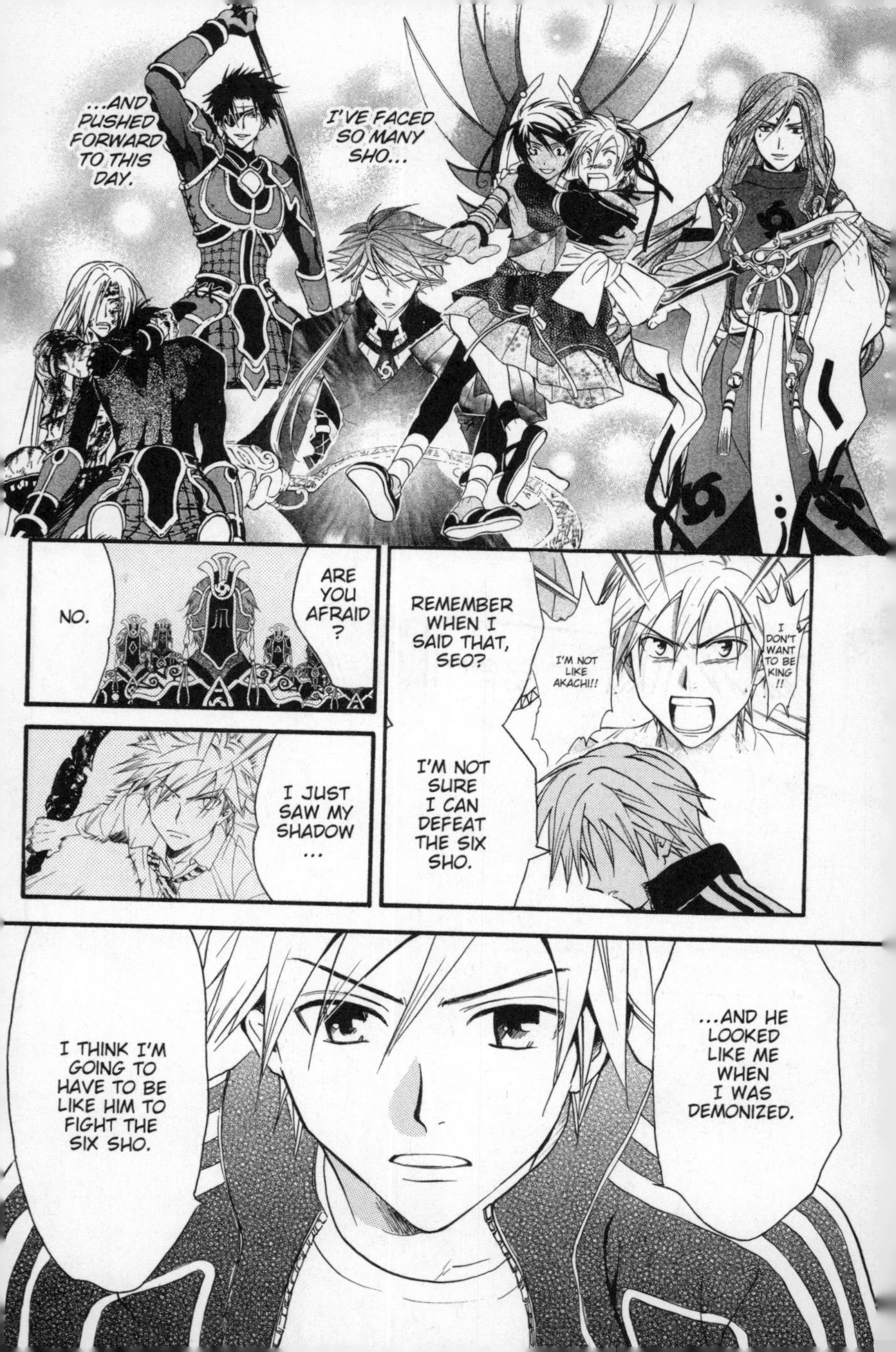
I'VE FACED SO MANY SHO...
...AND PUSHED FORWARD TO THIS DAY.
I DON'T WANT TO BE KING!!
I'M NOT LIKE AKACHI!!
REMEMBER WHEN I SAID THAT, SEO?
I'M NOT SURE I CAN DEFEAT THE SIX SHO.
ARE YOU AFRAID?
NO.
I JUST SAW MY SHADOW...
...AND HE LOOKED LIKE ME WHEN I WAS DEMONIZED.
I THINK I'M GOING TO HAVE TO BE LIKE HIM TO FIGHT THE SIX SHO.

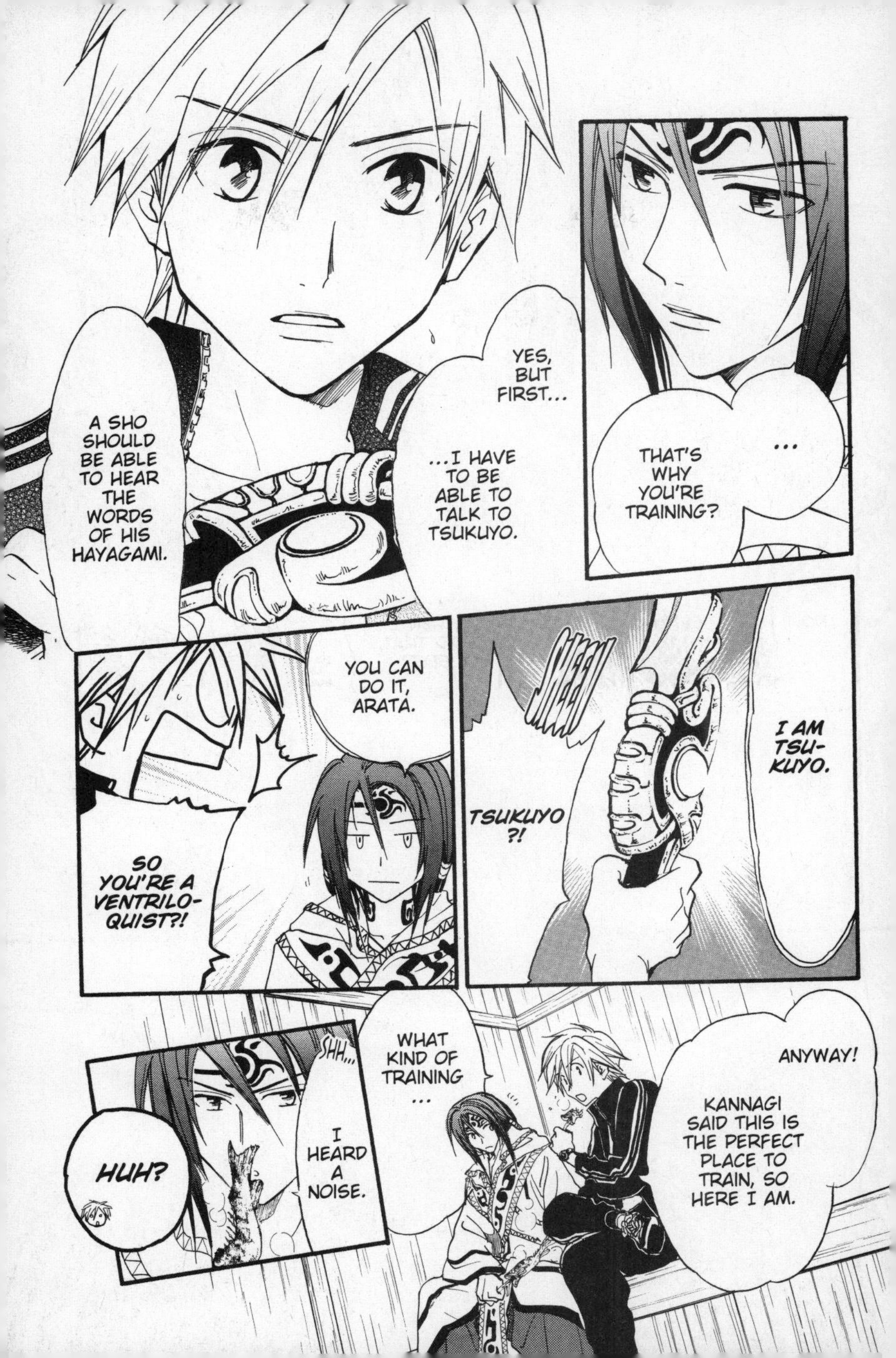
...
THAT'S WHY YOU'RE TRAINING?
YES, BUT FIRST...
...I HAVE TO BE ABLE TO TALK TO TSUKUYO.
A SHO SHOULD BE ABLE TO HEAR THE WORDS OF HIS HAYAGAMI.
I AM TSUKUYO.
TSUKUYO?!
YOU CAN DO IT, ARATA.
SO YOU'RE A VENTRILOQUIST?!
ANYWAY!
KANNAGI SAID THIS IS THE PERFECT PLACE TO TRAIN, SO HERE I AM.
WHAT KIND OF TRAINING ...
SHH...
I HEARD A NOISE.
HUH?

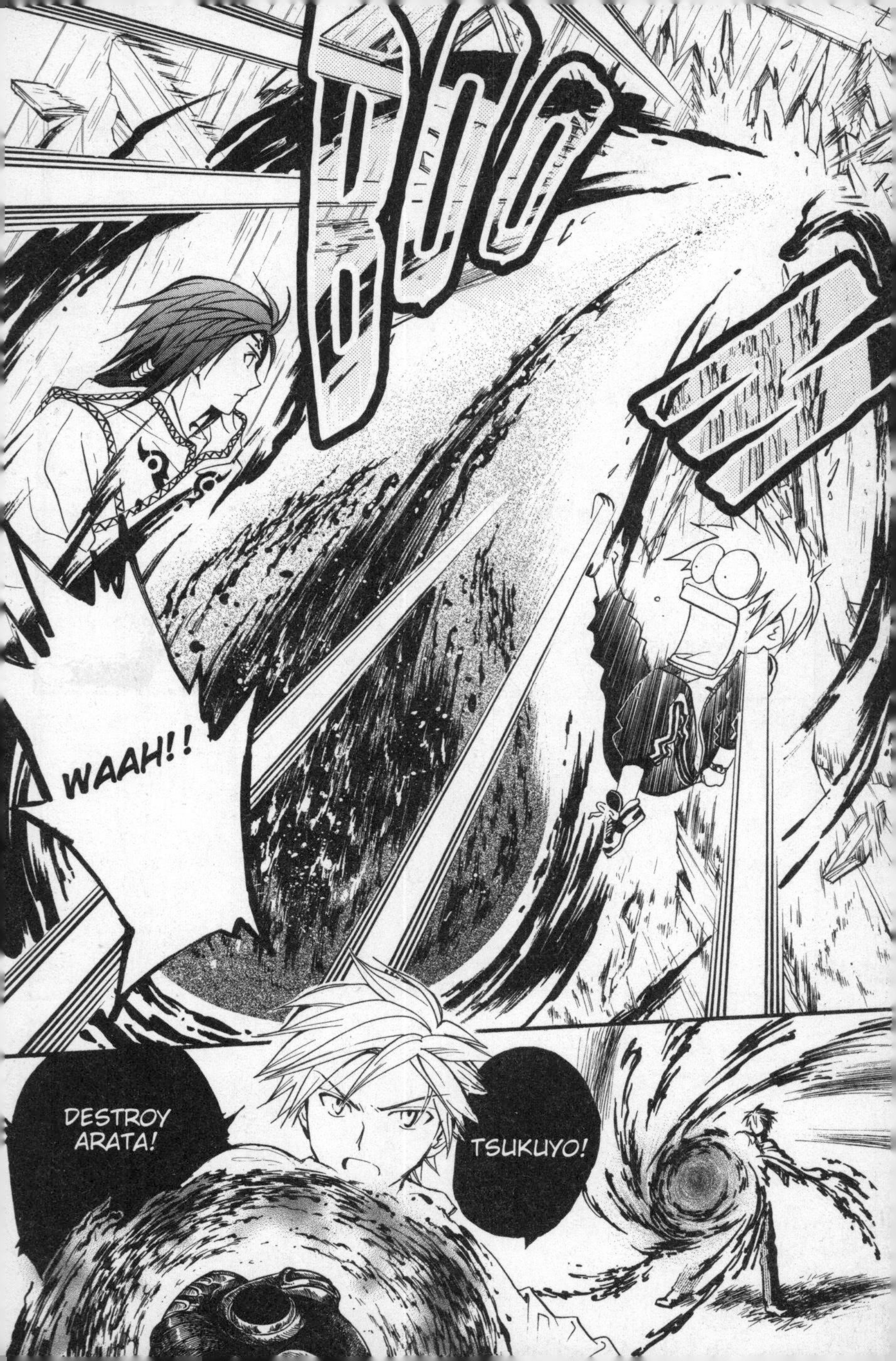
WAAH!!
TSUKUYO!
DESTROY ARATA!

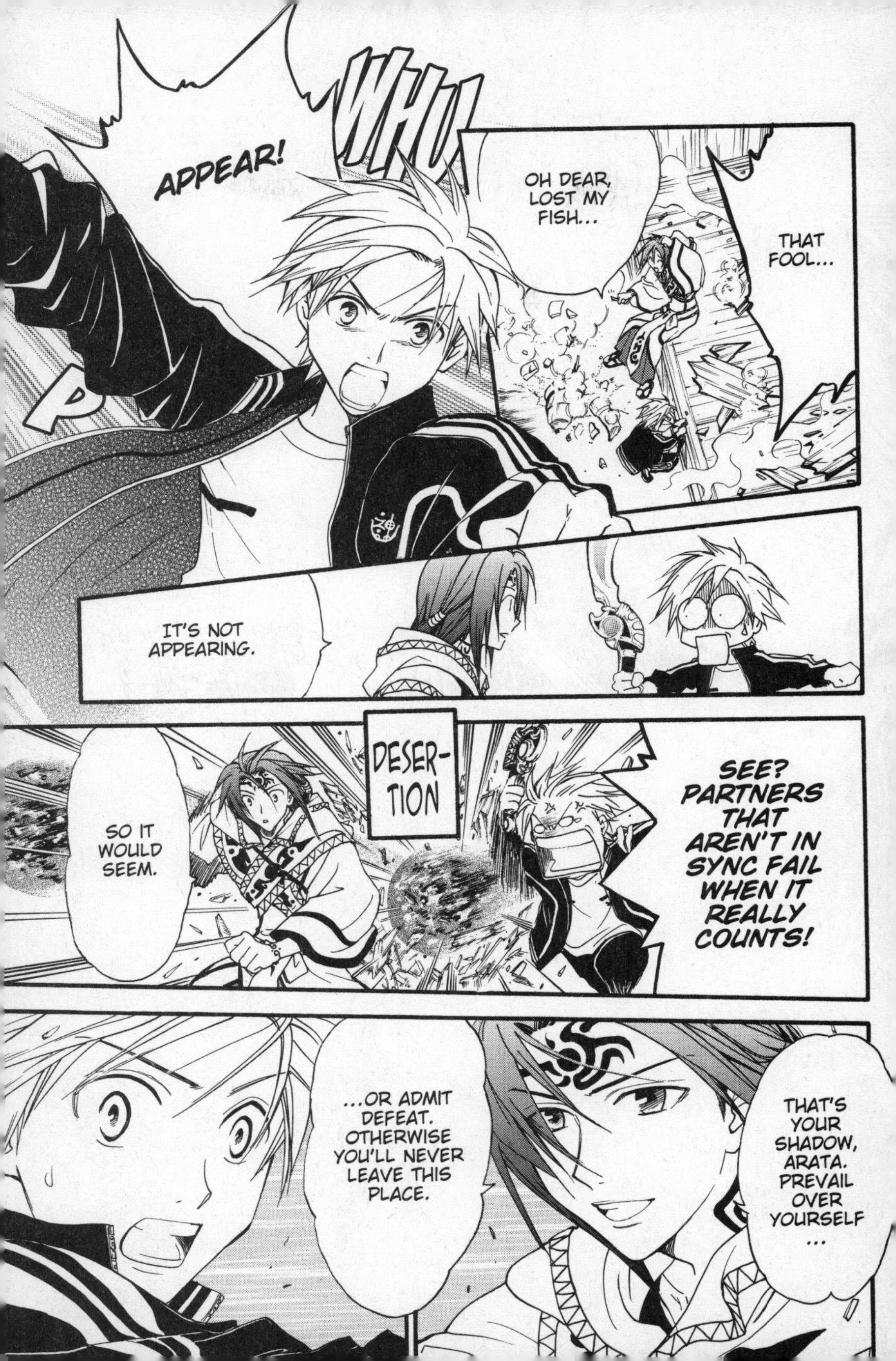
THAT FOOL...
OH DEAR, LOST MY FISH...
WHU
APPEAR!
IT'S NOT APPEARING.
SEE? PARTNERS THAT AREN'T IN SYNC FAIL WHEN IT REALLY COUNTS!
DESER-TION
SO IT WOULD SEEM.
THAT'S YOUR SHADOW, ARATA. PREVAIL OVER YOURSELF...
...OR ADMIT DEFEAT. OTHERWISE YOU'LL NEVER LEAVE THIS PLACE.

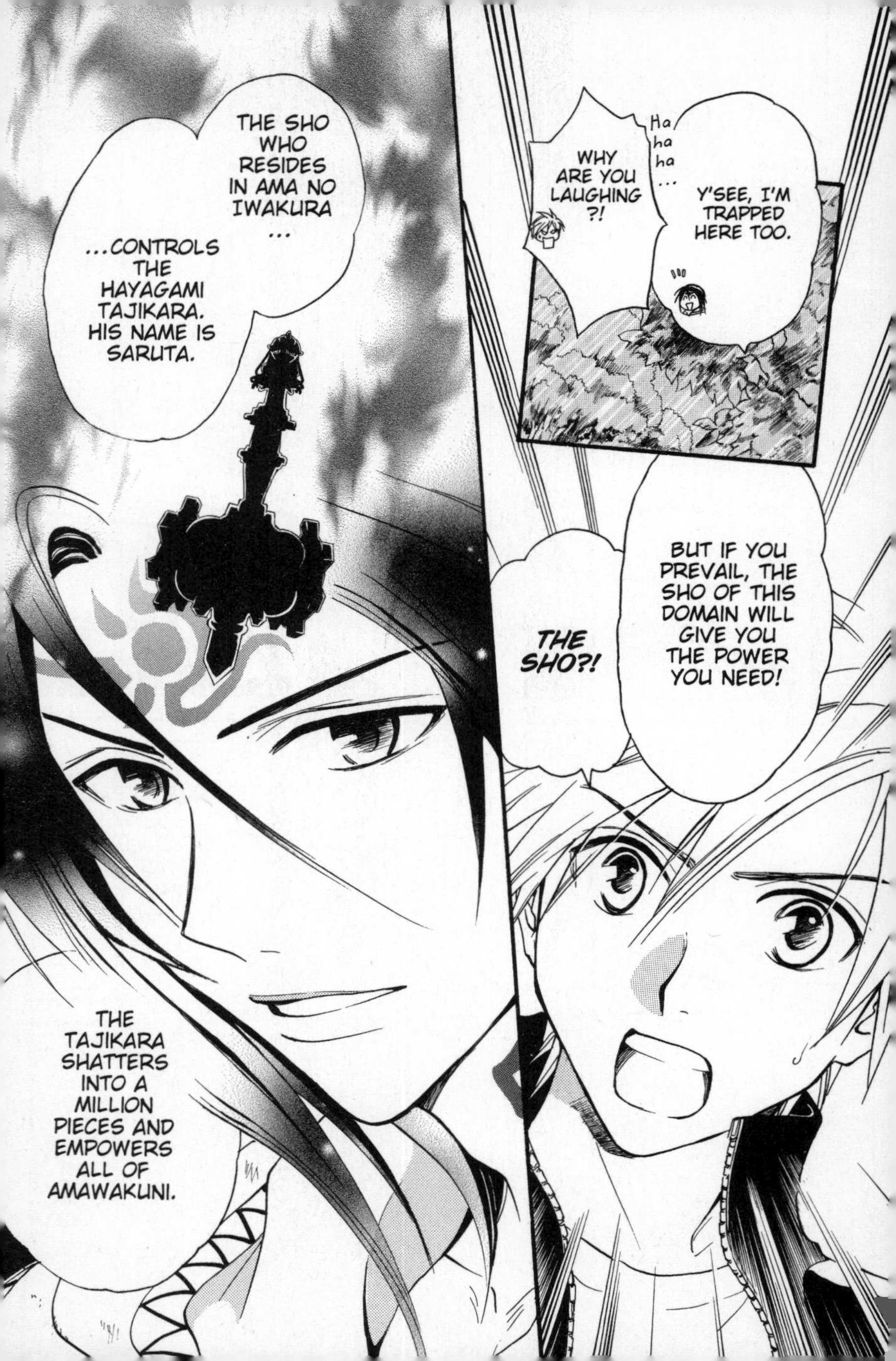
Ha ha ha...
WHY ARE YOU LAUGHING?!
Y'SEE, I'M TRAPPED HERE TOO.
BUT IF YOU PREVAIL, THE SHO OF THIS DOMAIN WILL GIVE YOU THE POWER YOU NEED!
THE SHO?!
THE SHO WHO RESIDES IN AMA NO IWAKURA...
...CONTROLS THE HAYAGAMI TAJIKARA. HIS NAME IS SARUTA.
THE TAJIKARA SHATTERS INTO A MILLION PIECES AND EMPOWERS ALL OF AMAWAKUNI.

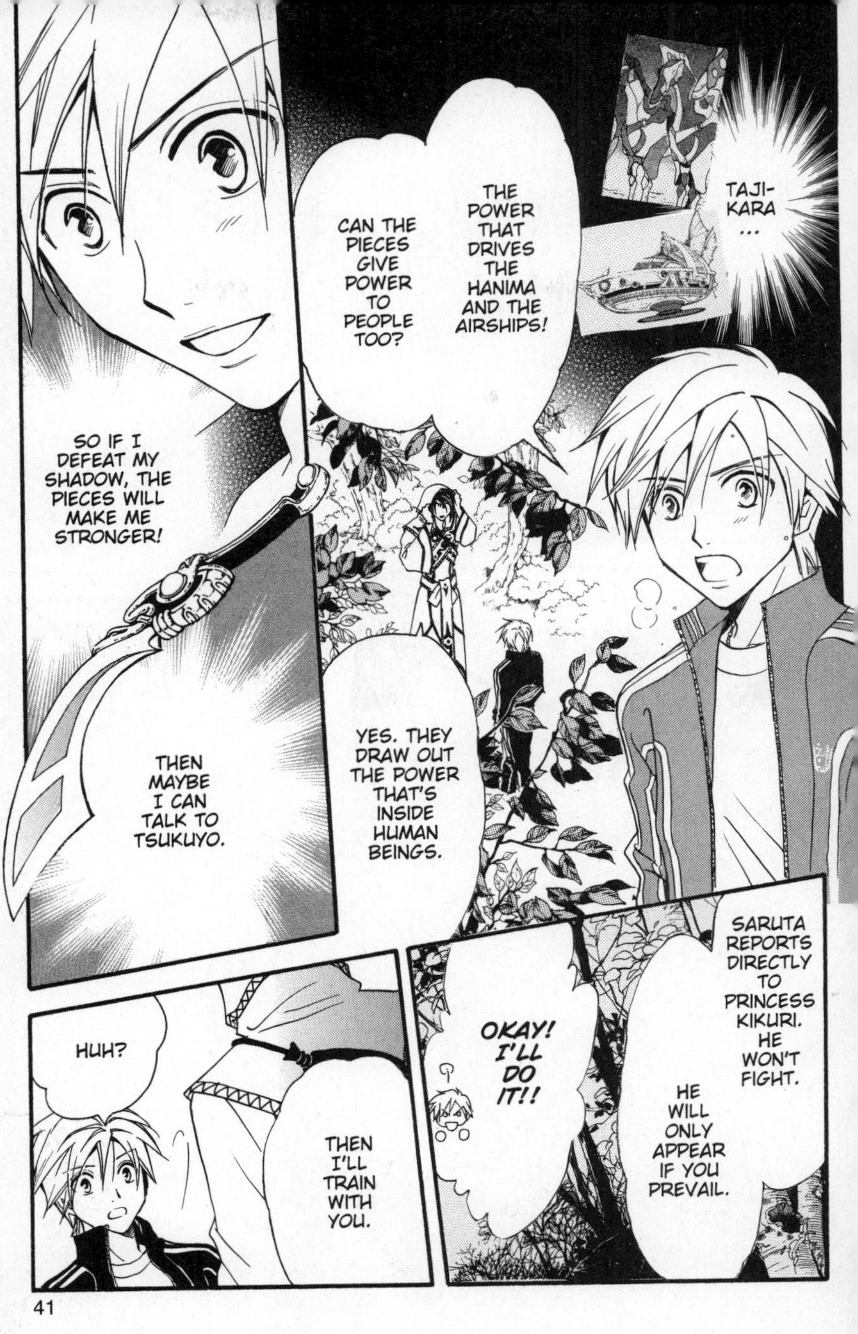
TAJI-KARA...
THE POWER THAT DRIVES THE HANIMA AND THE AIRSHIPS!
CAN THE PIECES GIVE POWER TO PEOPLE TOO?
YES. THEY DRAW OUT THE POWER THAT'S INSIDE HUMAN BEINGS.
SO IF I DEFEAT MY SHADOW, THE PIECES WILL MAKE ME STRONGER!
THEN MAYBE I CAN TALK TO TSUKUYO.
SARUTA REPORTS DIRECTLY TO PRINCESS KIKURI. HE WON'T FIGHT.
HE WILL ONLY APPEAR IF YOU PREVAIL.
OKAY! I'LL DO IT!!
THEN I'LL TRAIN WITH YOU.
HUH?

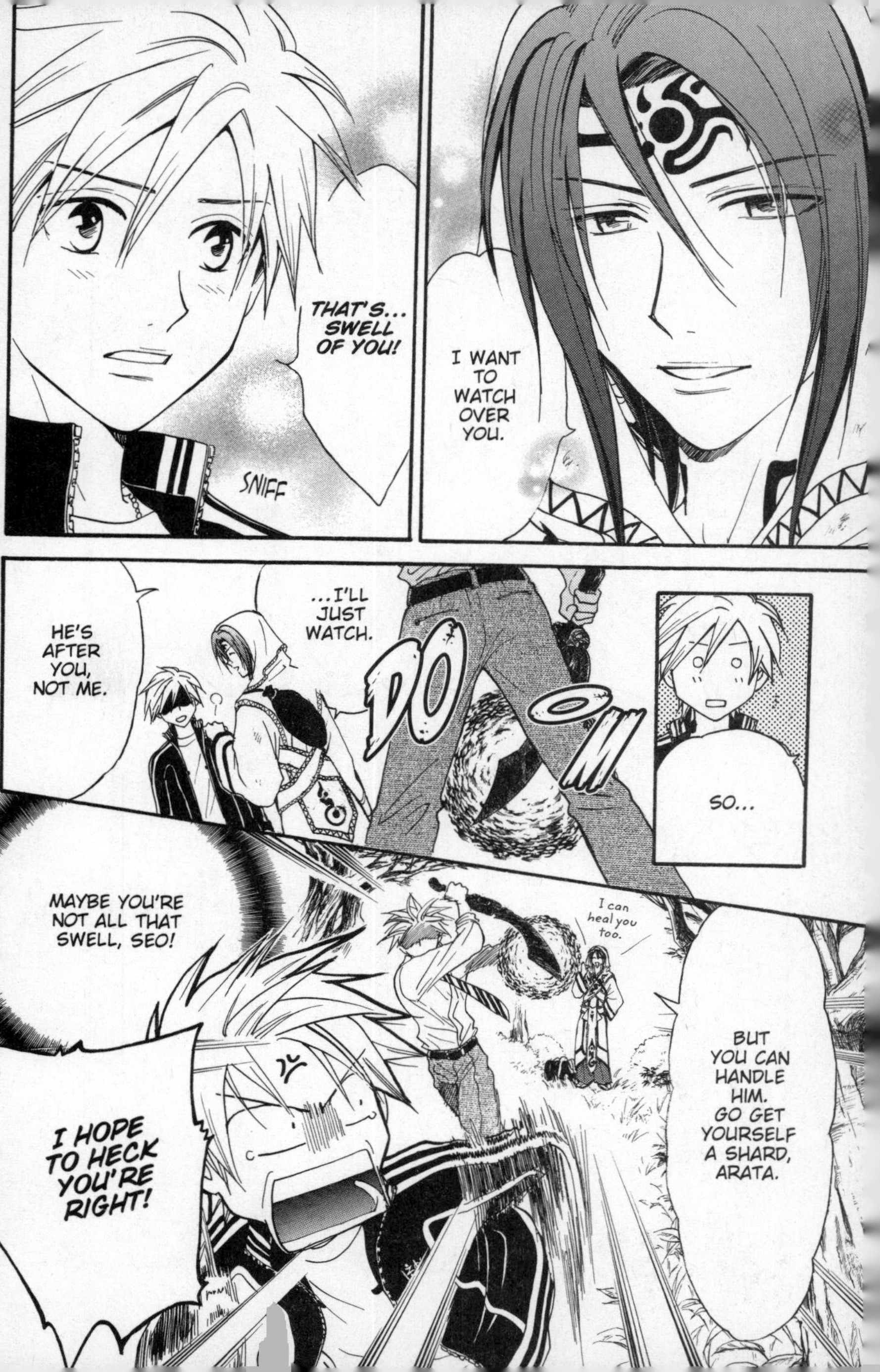
I WANT TO WATCH OVER YOU.
THAT'S... SWELL OF YOU!
SNIFF
SO...
...I'LL JUST WATCH.
HE'S AFTER YOU, NOT ME.
BUT YOU CAN HANDLE HIM. GO GET YOURSELF A SHARD, ARATA.
I can heal you too.
MAYBE YOU'RE NOT ALL THAT SWELL, SEO!
I HOPE TO HECK YOU'RE RIGHT!

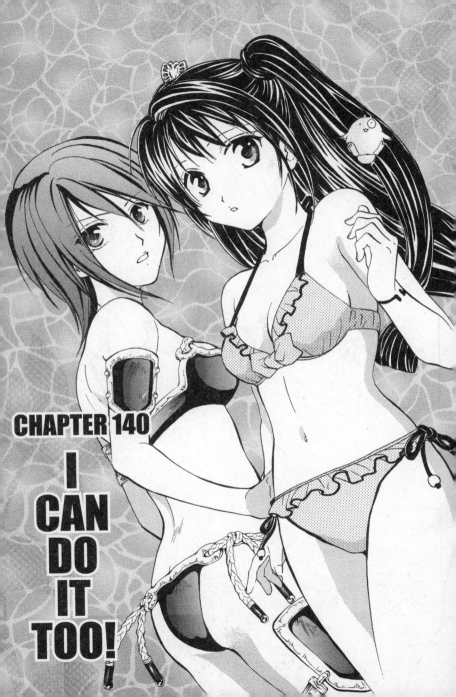

CHAPTER 140

I CAN DO IT TOO!

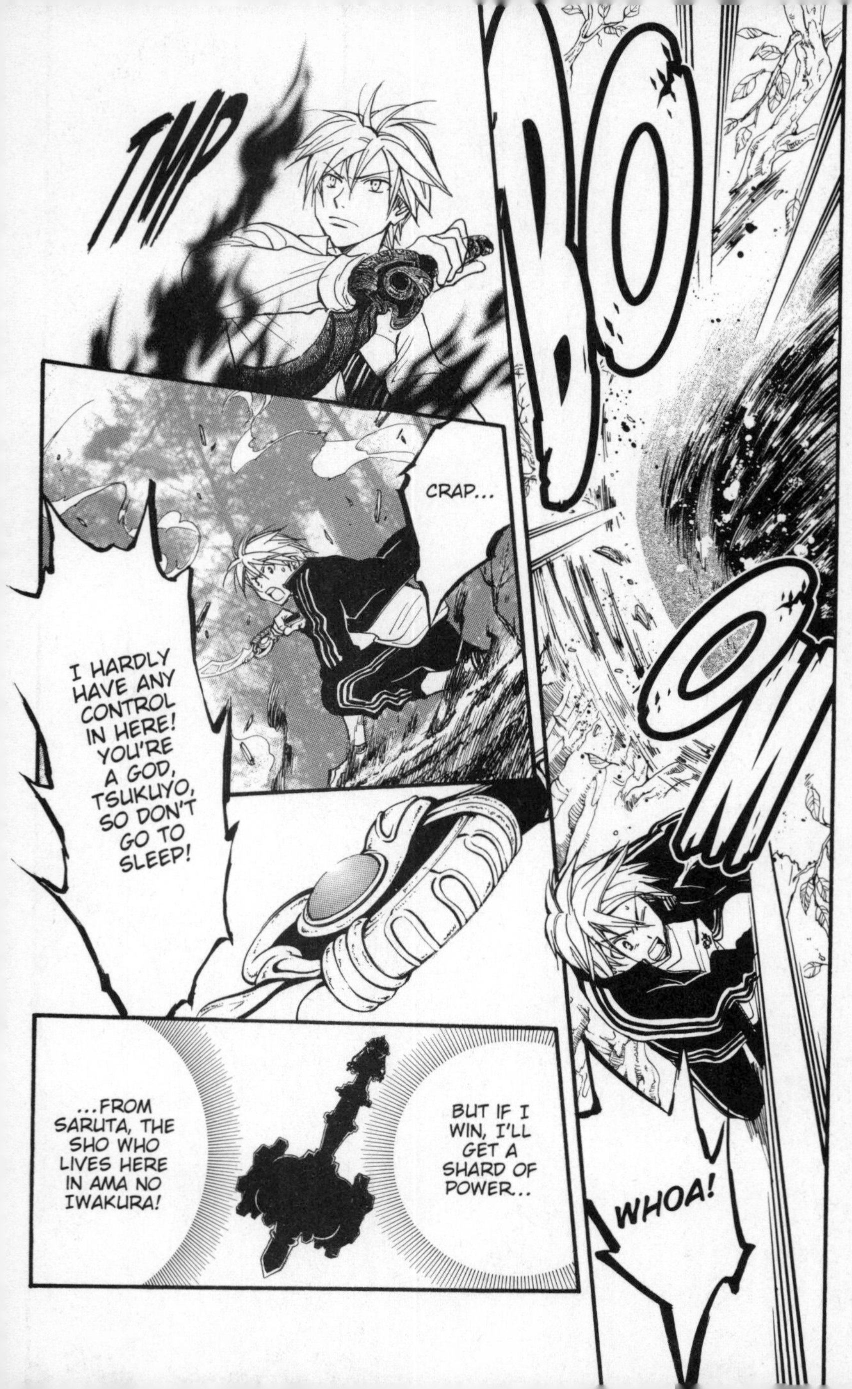
WHOA!
TMP
CRAP...
I HARDLY HAVE ANY CONTROL IN HERE! YOU'RE A GOD, TSUKUYO, SO DON'T GO TO SLEEP!
BUT IF I WIN, I'LL GET A SHARD OF POWER...
...FROM SARUTA, THE SHO WHO LIVES HERE IN AMA NO IWAKURA!

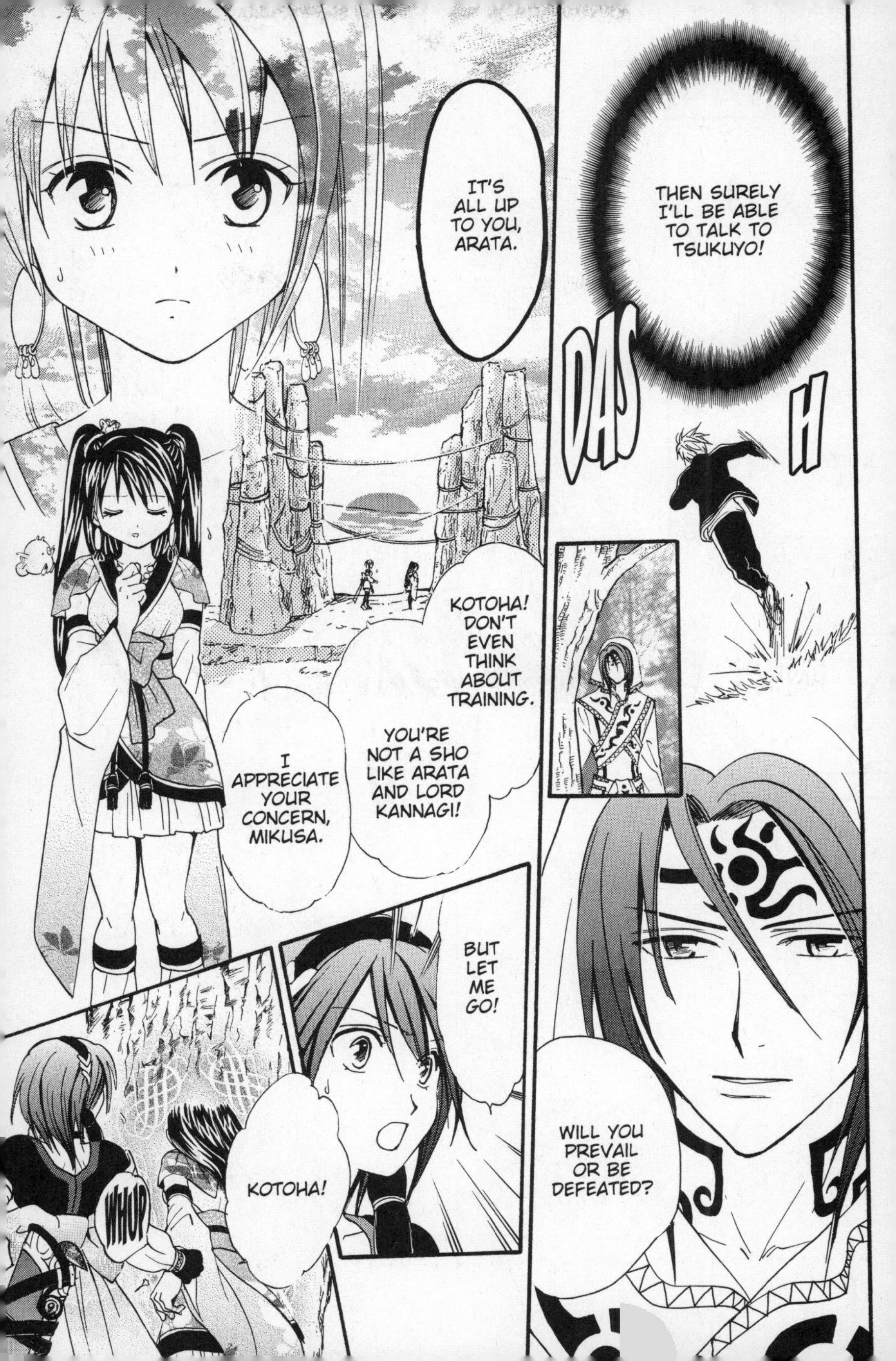
THEN SURELY I'LL BE ABLE TO TALK TO TSUKUYO!
DASH
IT'S ALL UP TO YOU, ARATA.
KOTOHA! DON'T EVEN THINK ABOUT TRAINING.
YOU'RE NOT A SHO LIKE ARATA AND LORD KANNAGI!
I APPRECIATE YOUR CONCERN, MIKUSA.
BUT LET ME GO!
KOTOHA!
WHUP
WILL YOU PREVAIL OR BE DEFEATED?

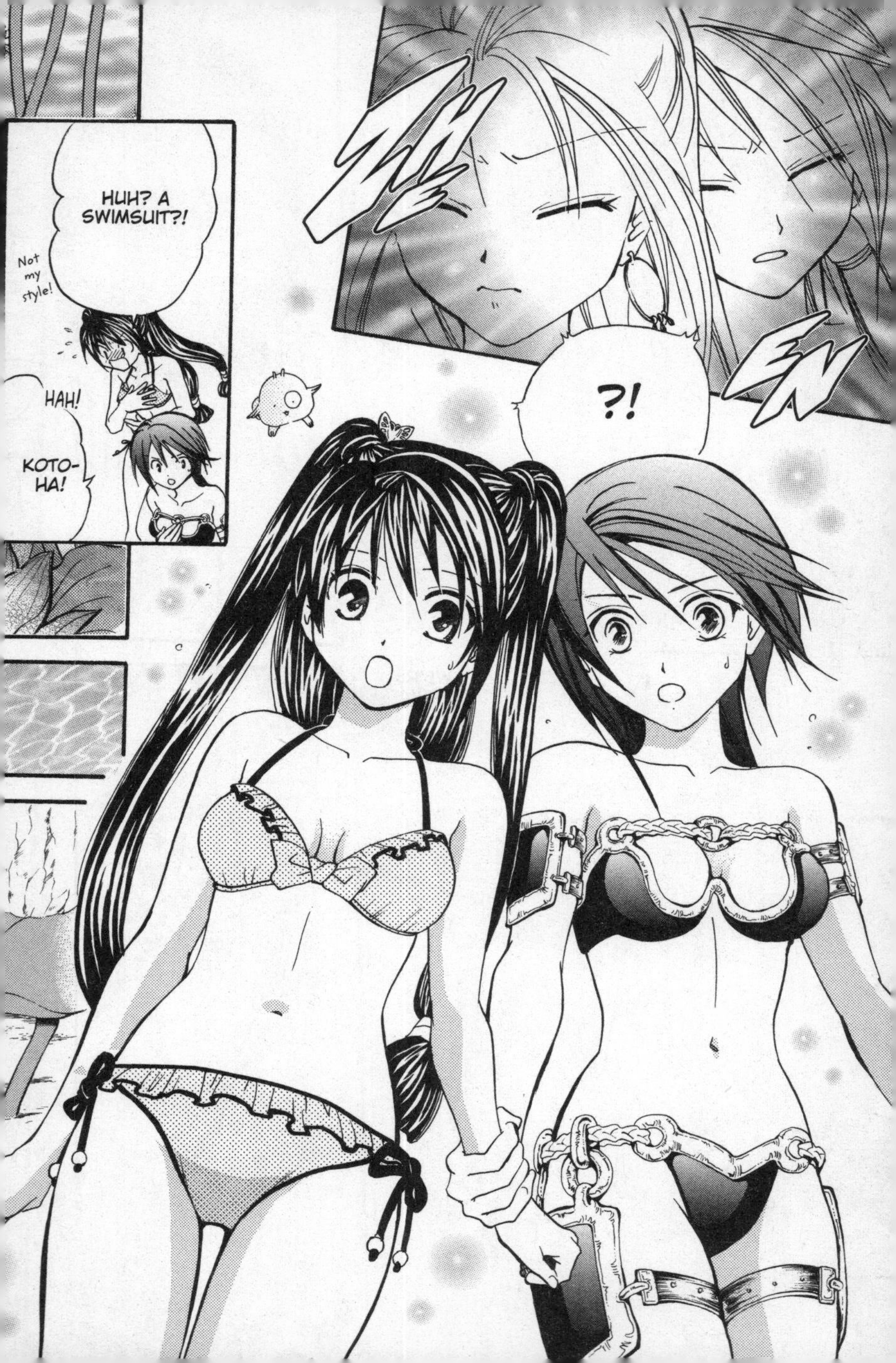
HUH? A SWIMSUIT?!
Not my style!
HAH!
KOTO-HA!
?!

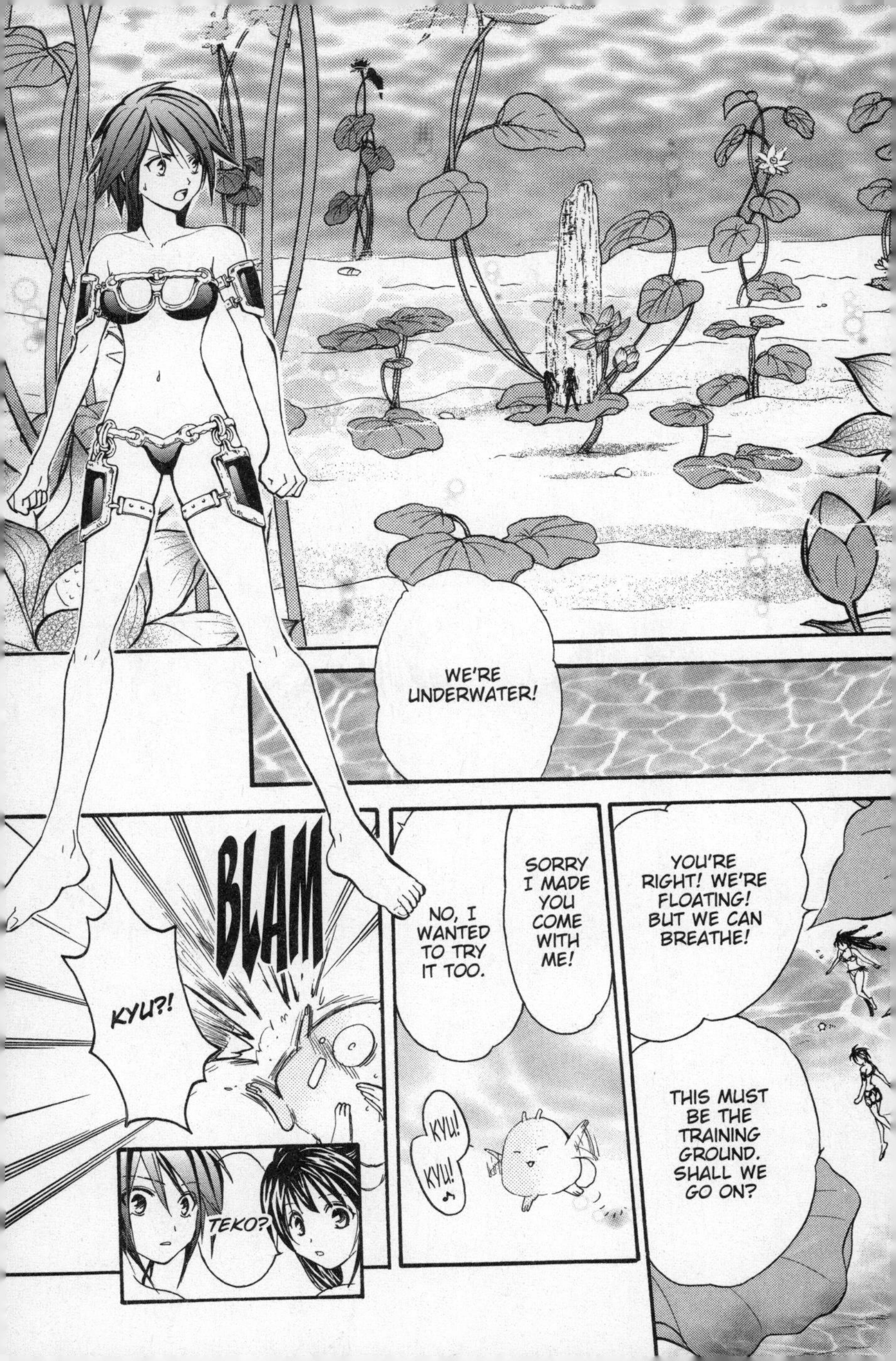
WE'RE UNDERWATER!
YOU'RE RIGHT! WE'RE FLOATING! BUT WE CAN BREATHE!
THIS MUST BE THE TRAINING GROUND. SHALL WE GO ON?
SORRY I MADE YOU COME WITH ME!
NO, I WANTED TO TRY IT TOO.
KYU! KYU! ♪
BLAM
KYU?!
TEKO?

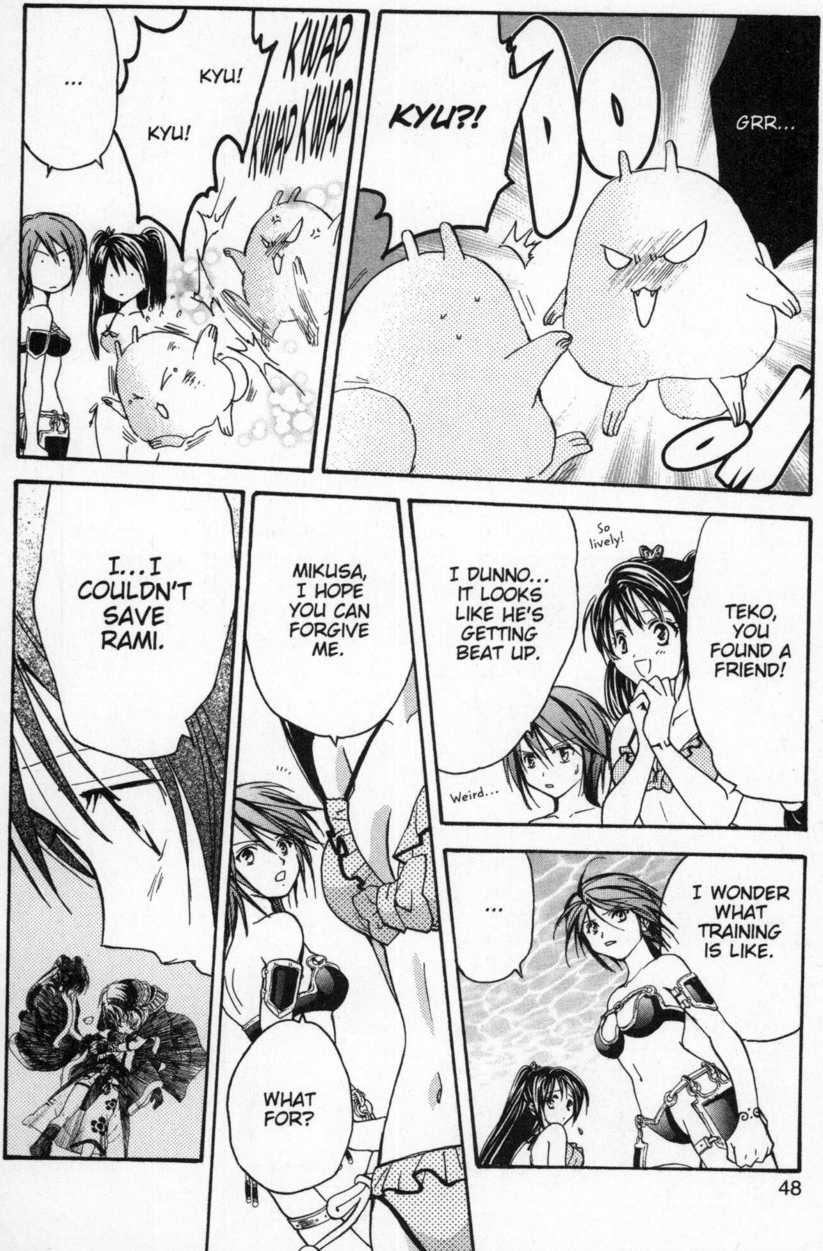
GRR...
KYU?!
KWAP KWAP KWAP
KYU!
...
KYU!
TEKO, YOU FOUND A FRIEND!
So lively!
I DUNNO... IT LOOKS LIKE HE'S GETTING BEAT UP.
Weird...
I WONDER WHAT TRAINING IS LIKE.
...
MIKUSA, I HOPE YOU CAN FORGIVE ME.
WHAT FOR?
I... I COULDN'T SAVE RAMI.

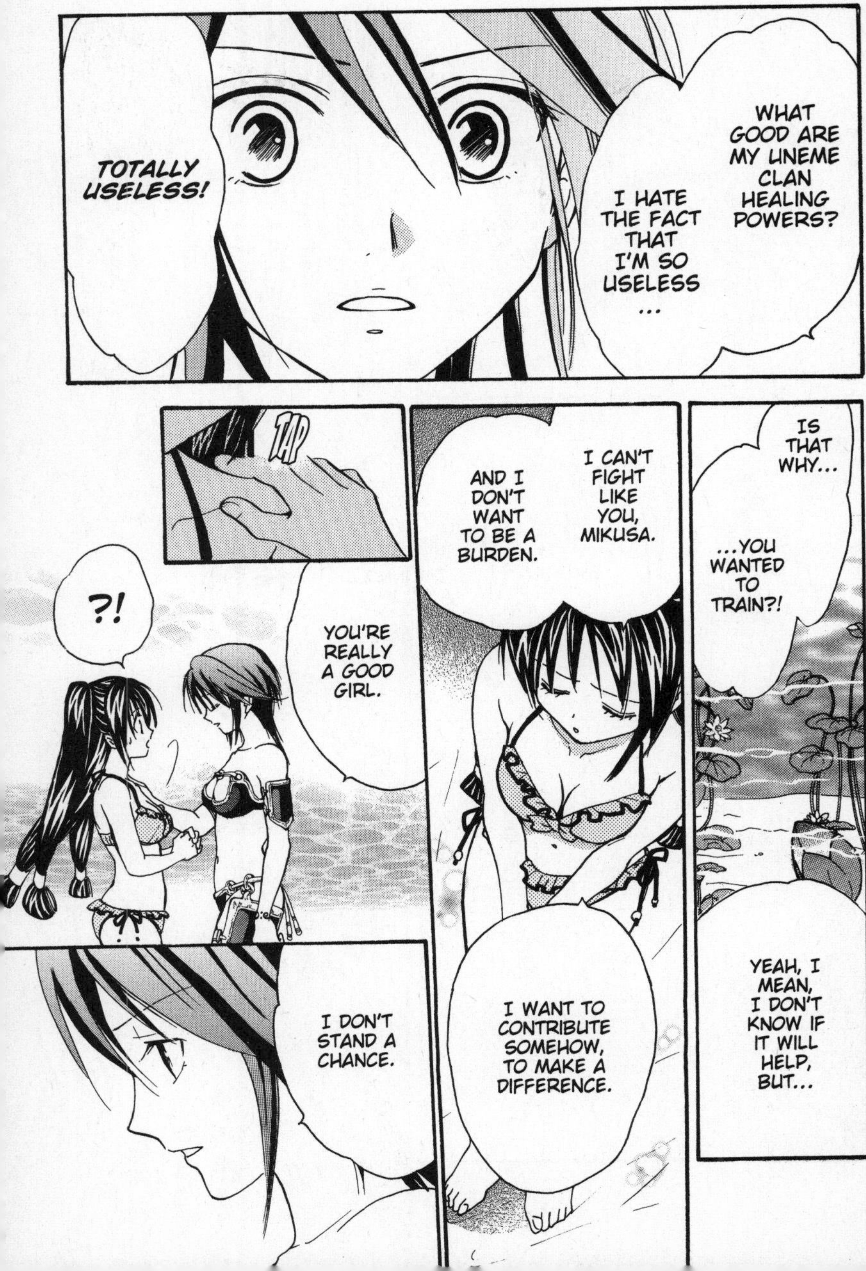
WHAT GOOD ARE MY UNEME CLAN HEALING POWERS?
I HATE THE FACT THAT I'M SO USELESS ...
TOTALLY USELESS!
IS THAT WHY...
...YOU WANTED TO TRAIN?!
YEAH, I MEAN, I DON'T KNOW IF IT WILL HELP, BUT...
I CAN'T FIGHT LIKE YOU, MIKUSA.
AND I DON'T WANT TO BE A BURDEN.
I WANT TO CONTRIBUTE SOMEHOW, TO MAKE A DIFFERENCE.
TAP
YOU'RE REALLY A GOOD GIRL.
?!
I DON'T STAND A CHANCE.

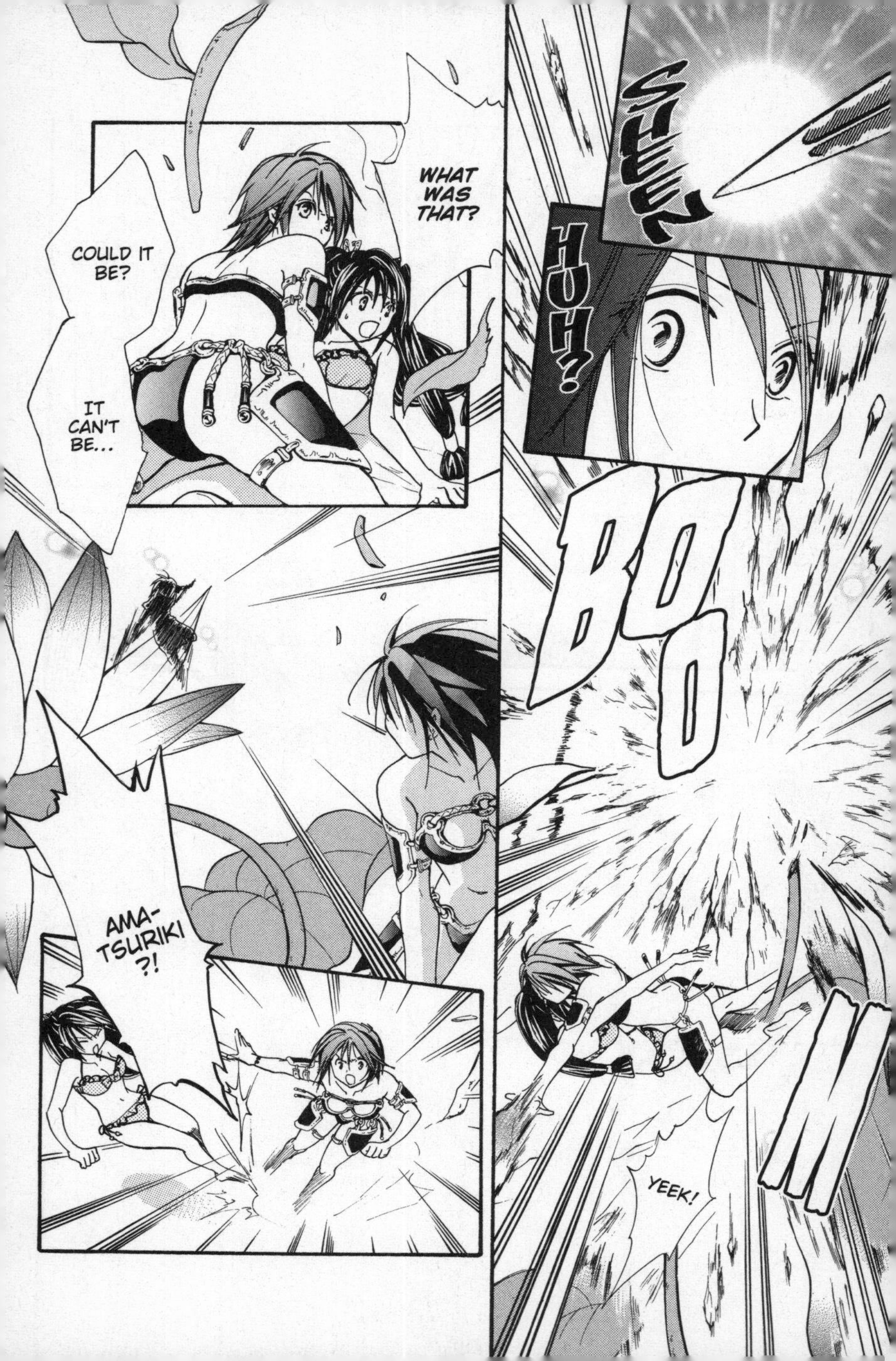
SHEEN
HUH?
BOOM
YEEK!
WHAT WAS THAT?
COULD IT BE?
IT CAN'T BE...
AMA-TSURIKI ?!

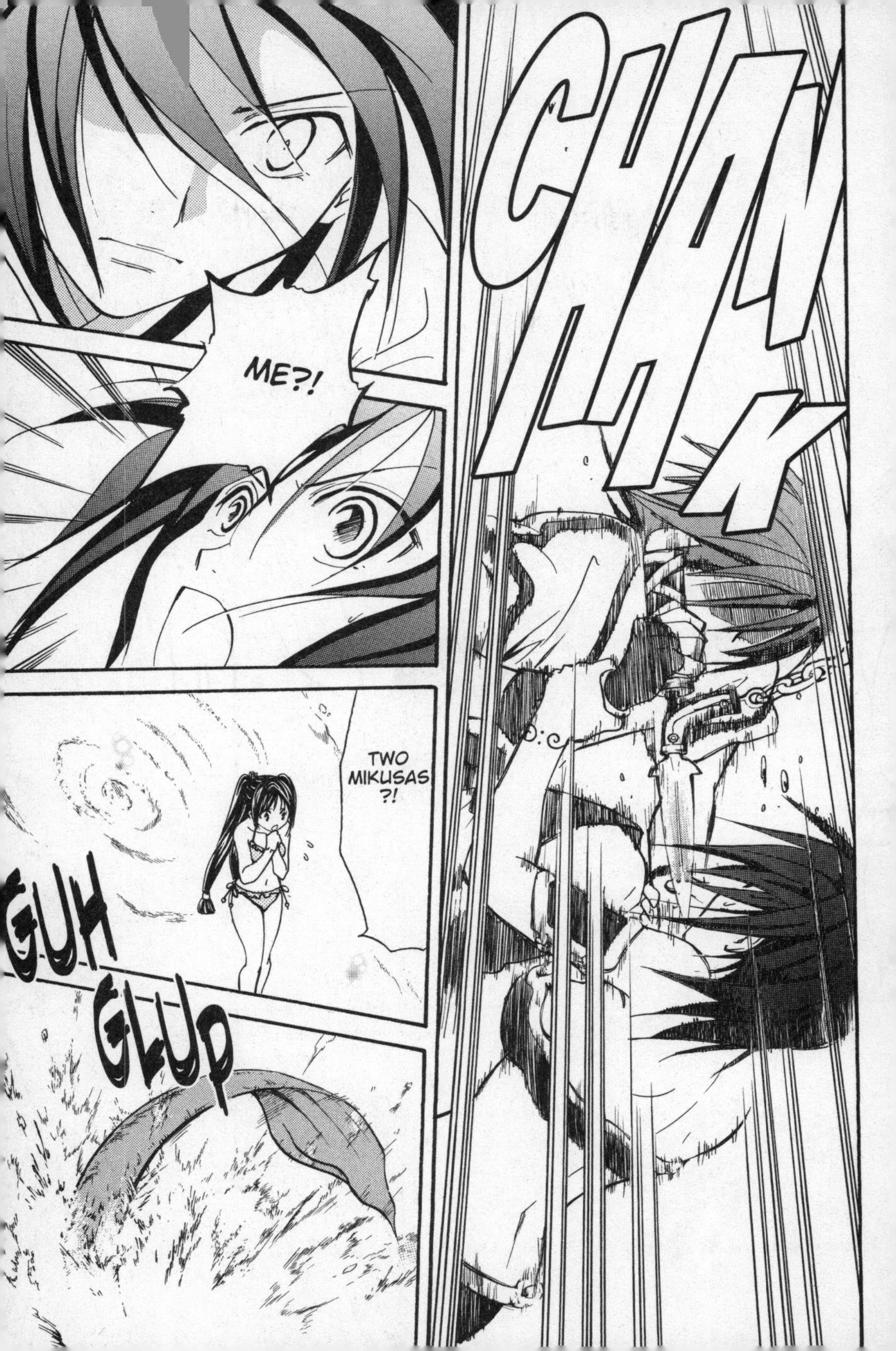
ME?!
TWO MIKUSAS ?!
GUH GLUP

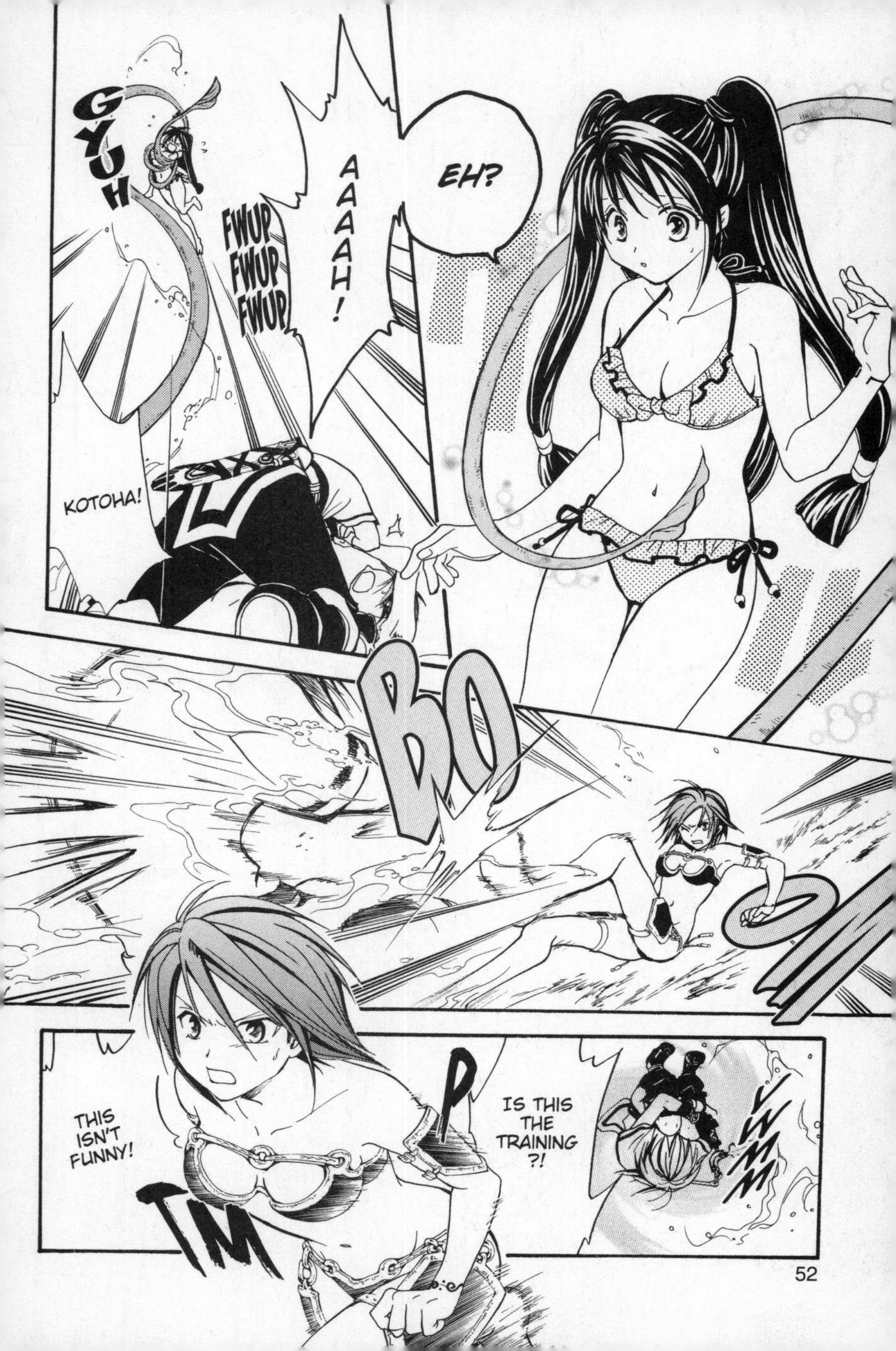
EH?
AAAAAH!
FWUP FWUP FWUP
GYUH
KOTOHA!
BO
OM
VWMM
IS THIS THE TRAINING ?!
THIS ISN'T FUNNY!
P
TM

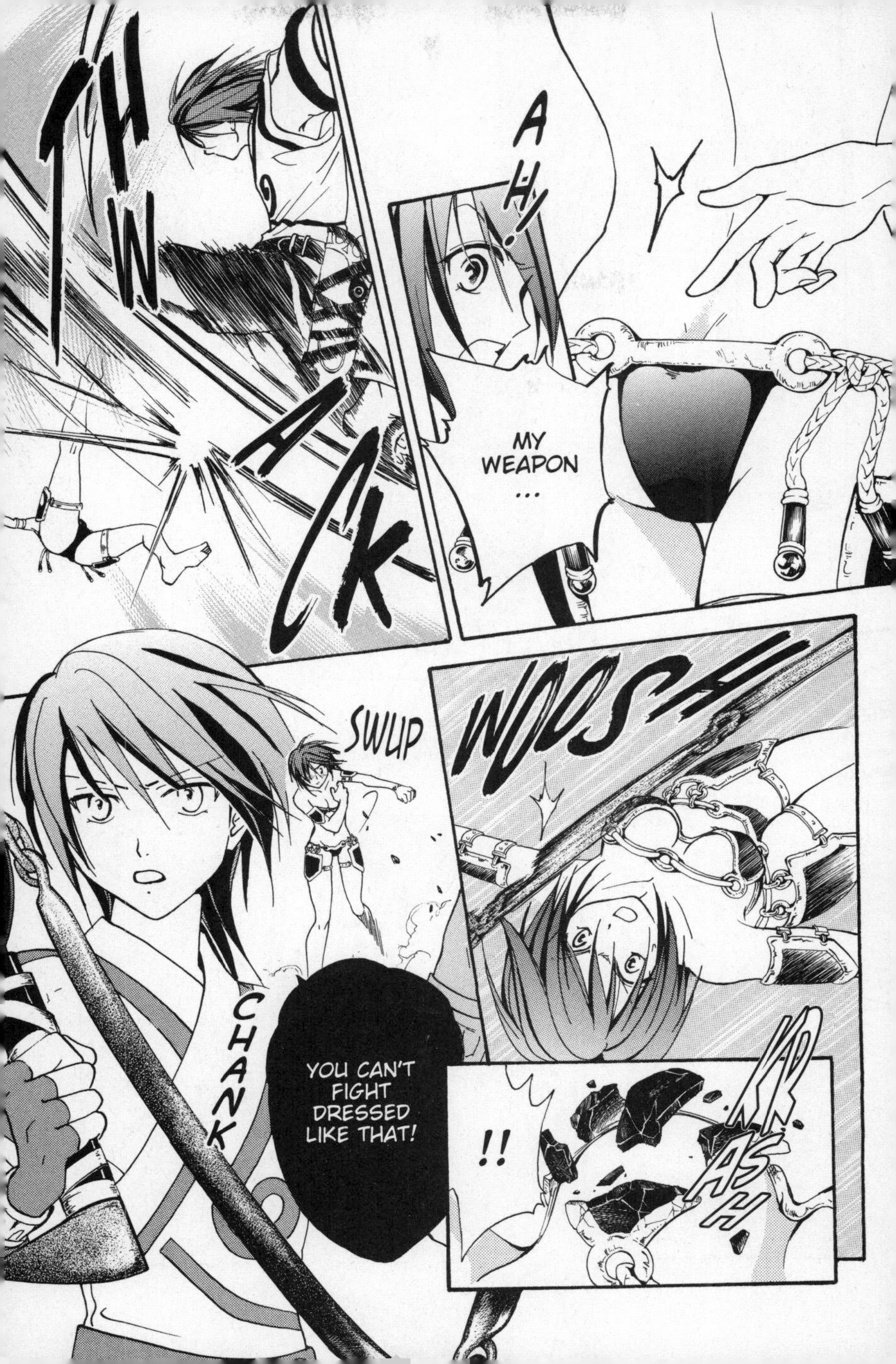
AH!!
MY WEAPON ...
THWACK
WOOSH
!!
KRASH
SWUP
CHANK
YOU CAN'T FIGHT DRESSED LIKE THAT!

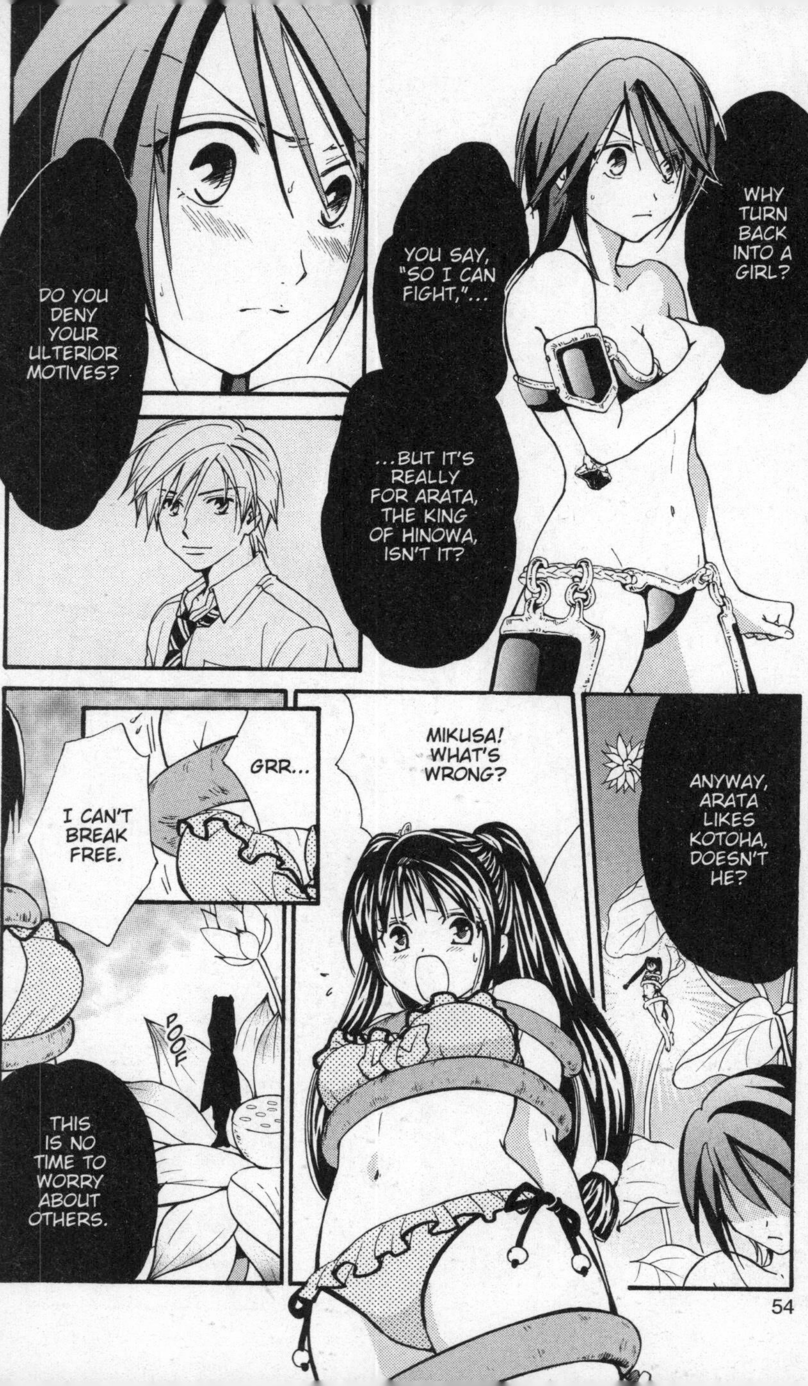

WHY TURN BACK INTO A GIRL?
YOU SAY, "SO I CAN FIGHT,"...
...BUT IT'S REALLY FOR ARATA, THE KING OF HINOWA, ISN'T IT?
DO YOU DENY YOUR ULTERIOR MOTIVES?
ANYWAY, ARATA LIKES KOTOHA, DOESN'T HE?
MIKUSA! WHAT'S WRONG?
GRR...
I CAN'T BREAK FREE.
POOF
THIS IS NO TIME TO WORRY ABOUT OTHERS.

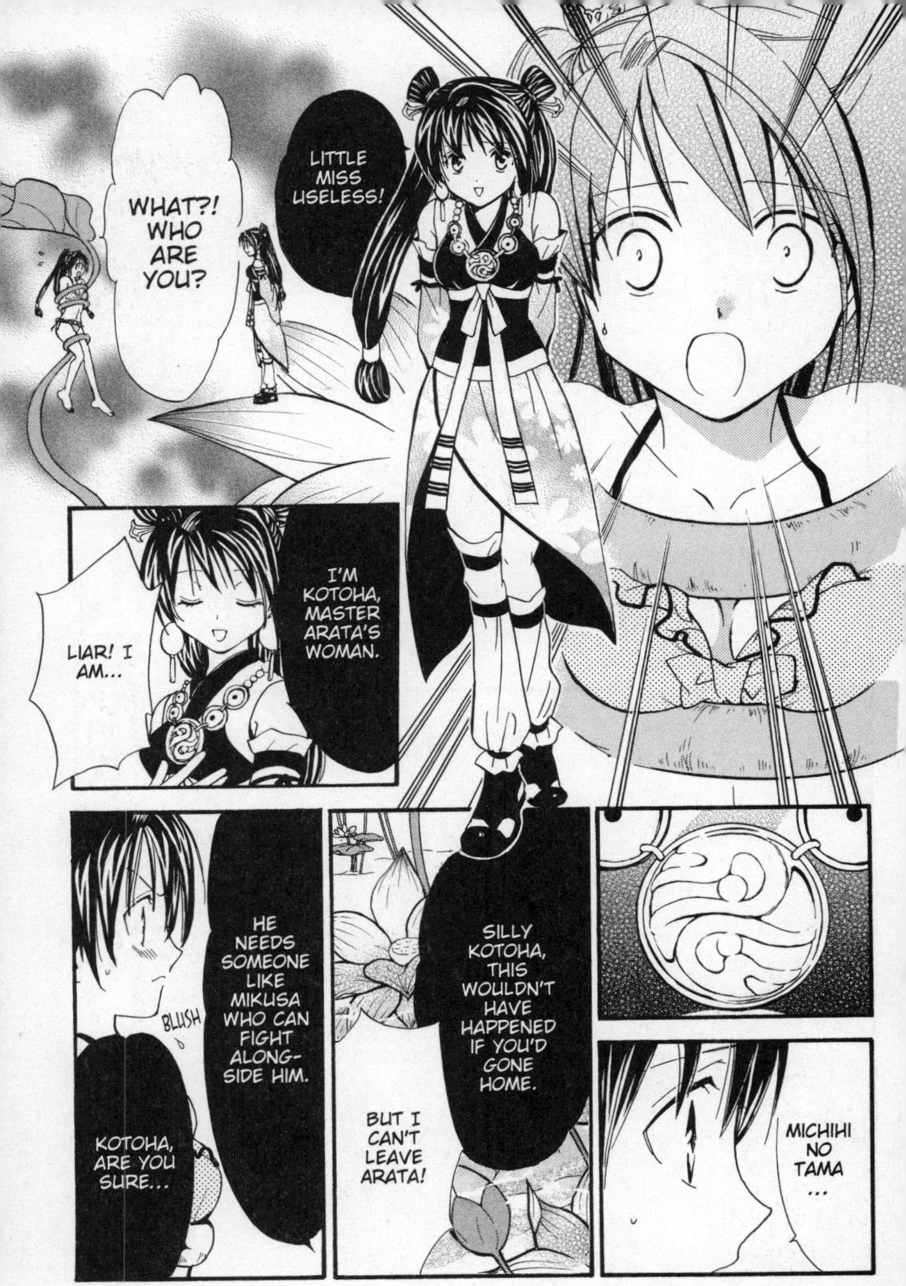
LITTLE MISS USELESS!
WHAT?! WHO ARE YOU?
I'M KOTOHA, MASTER ARATA'S WOMAN.
LIAR! I AM...
MICHIHI NO TAMA...
SILLY KOTOHA, THIS WOULDN'T HAVE HAPPENED IF YOU'D GONE HOME.
BUT I CAN'T LEAVE ARATA!
HE NEEDS SOMEONE LIKE MIKUSA WHO CAN FIGHT ALONG-SIDE HIM.
BLUSH
KOTOHA, ARE YOU SURE...

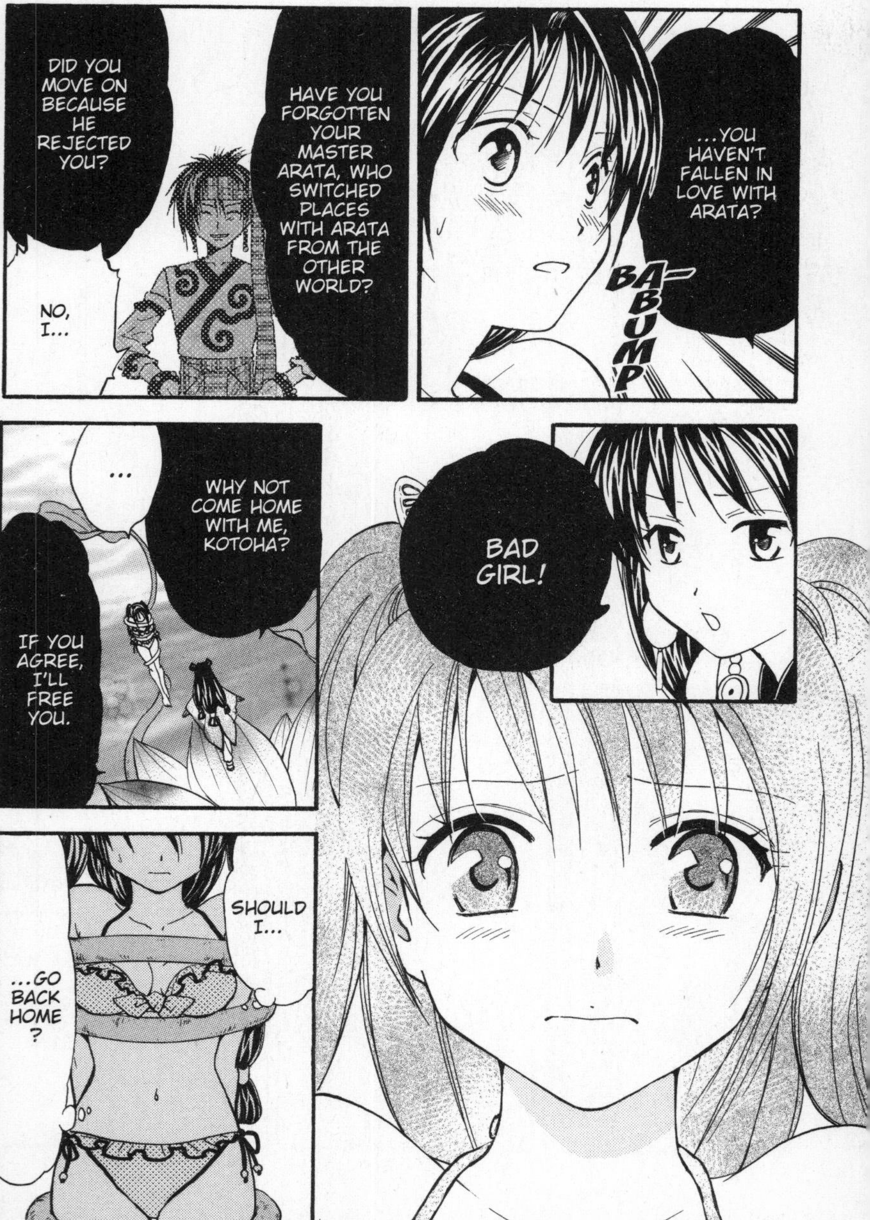
...YOU HAVEN'T FALLEN IN LOVE WITH ARATA?
BA-BUMP
HAVE YOU FORGOTTEN YOUR MASTER ARATA, WHO SWITCHED PLACES WITH ARATA FROM THE OTHER WORLD?
DID YOU MOVE ON BECAUSE HE REJECTED YOU?
NO, I...
BAD GIRL!
WHY NOT COME HOME WITH ME, KOTOHA?
...
IF YOU AGREE, I'LL FREE YOU.
SHOULD I...
...GO BACK HOME?

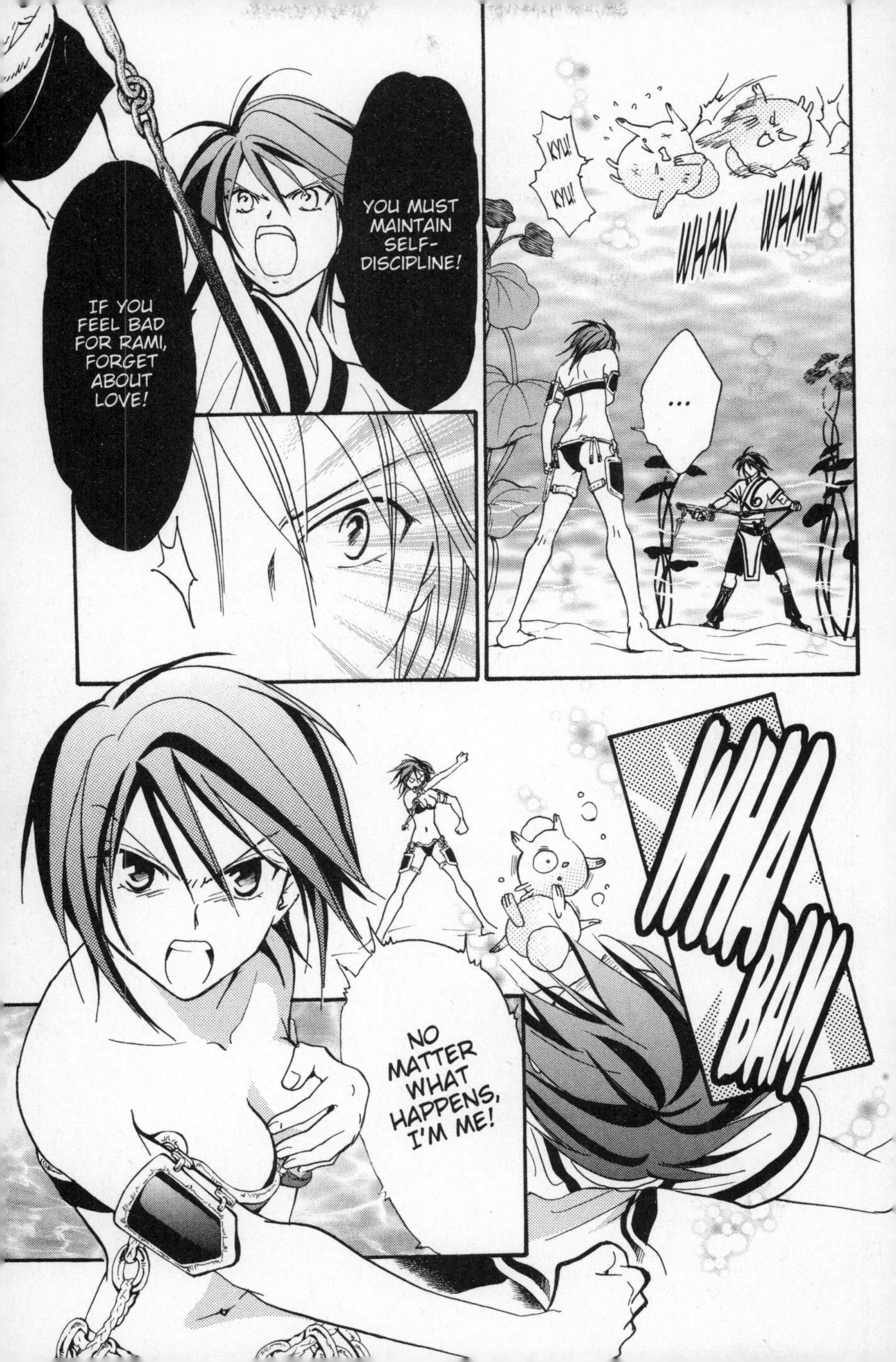
KYU! KYU!
WHAK
WHAM
...
YOU MUST MAINTAIN SELF-DISCIPLINE!
IF YOU FEEL BAD FOR RAMI, FORGET ABOUT LOVE!
WHAM BAM
NO MATTER WHAT HAPPENS, I'M ME!

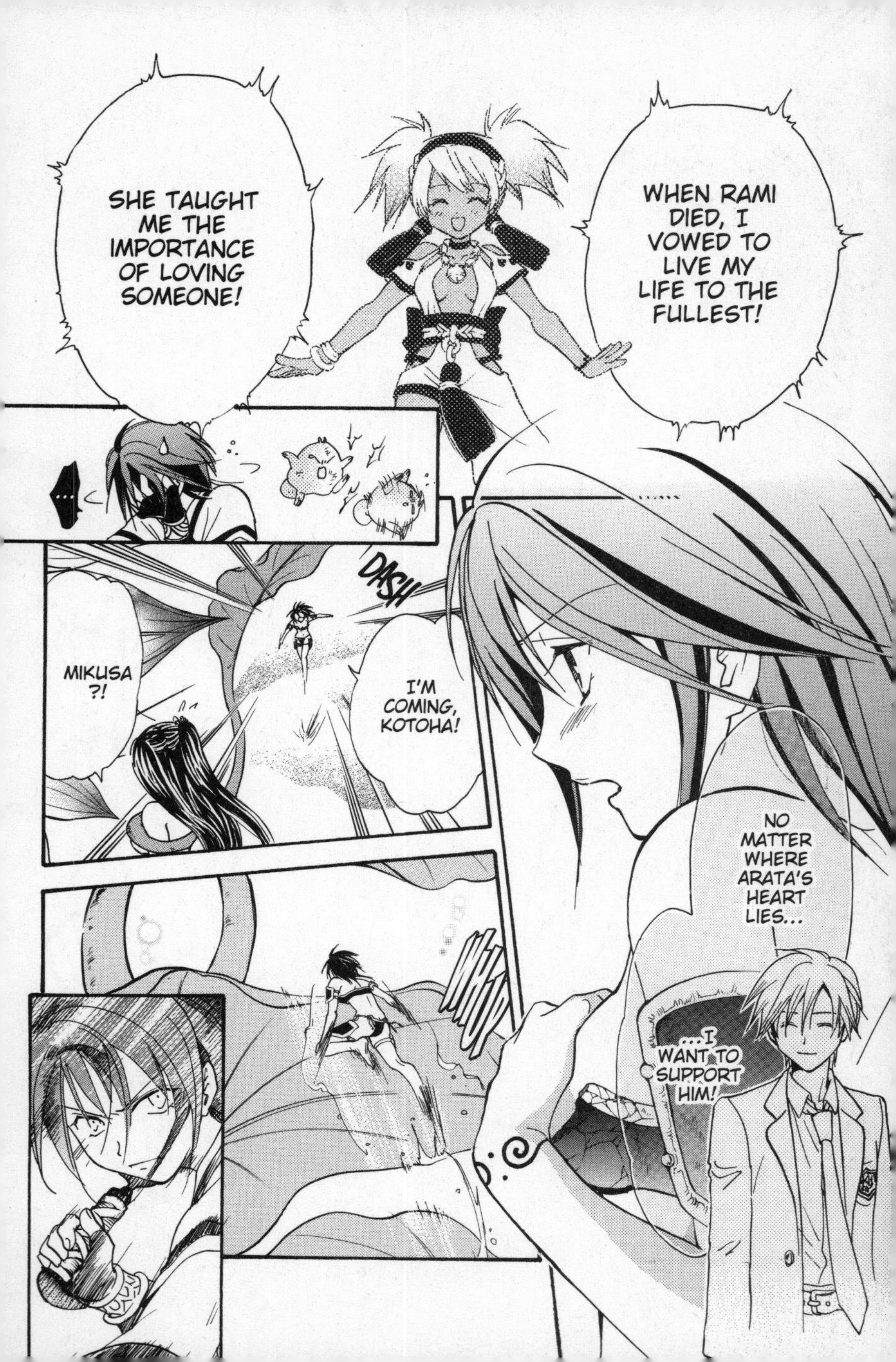

WHEN RAMI DIED, I VOWED TO LIVE MY LIFE TO THE FULLEST!
SHE TAUGHT ME THE IMPORTANCE OF LOVING SOMEONE!
......
NO MATTER WHERE ARATA'S HEART LIES...
...I WANT TO SUPPORT HIM!
...
DASH
I'M COMING, KOTOHA!
MIKUSA ?!

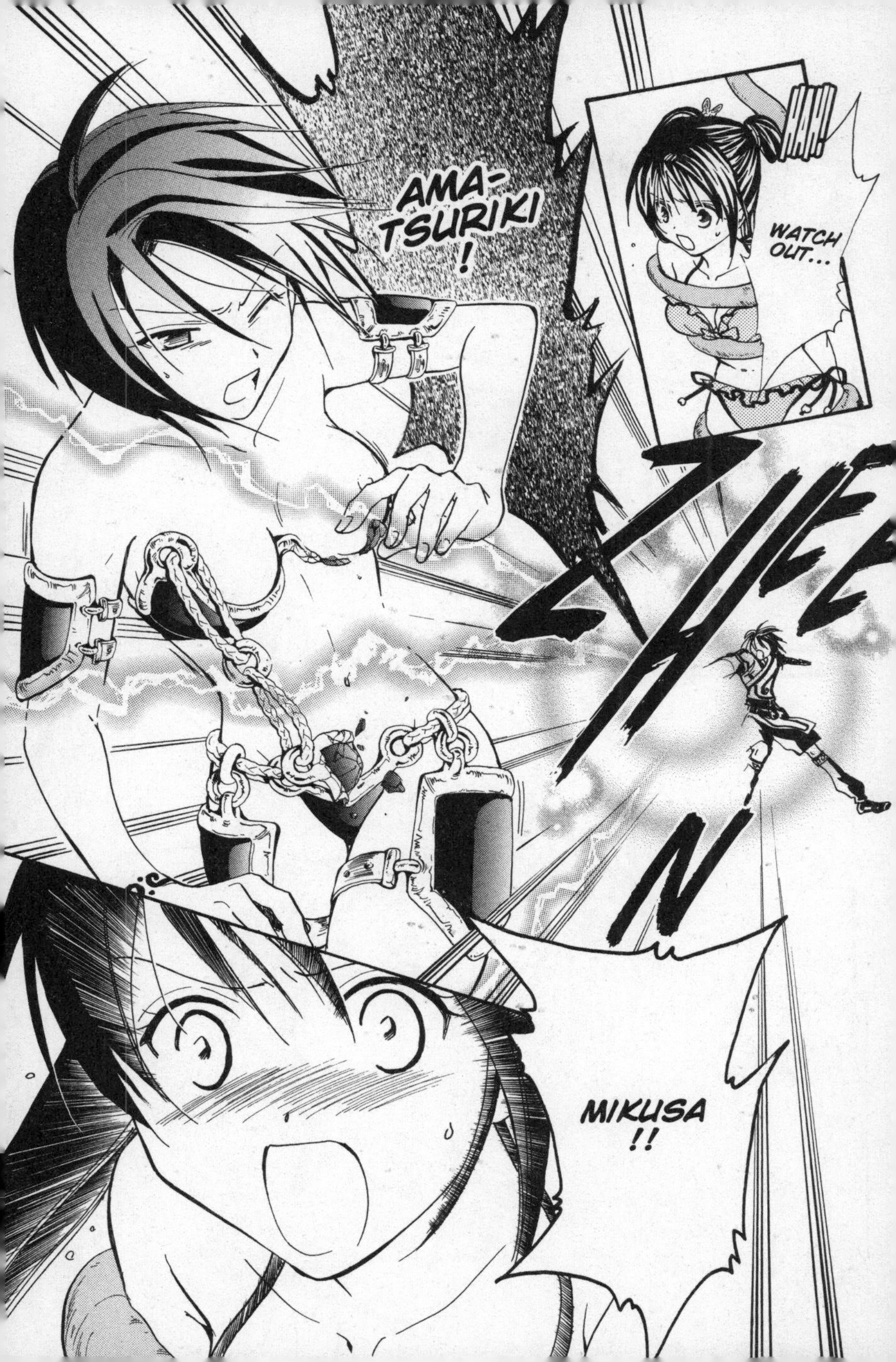
HAH
WATCH OUT...
AMA-TSURIKI!
MIKUSA!!

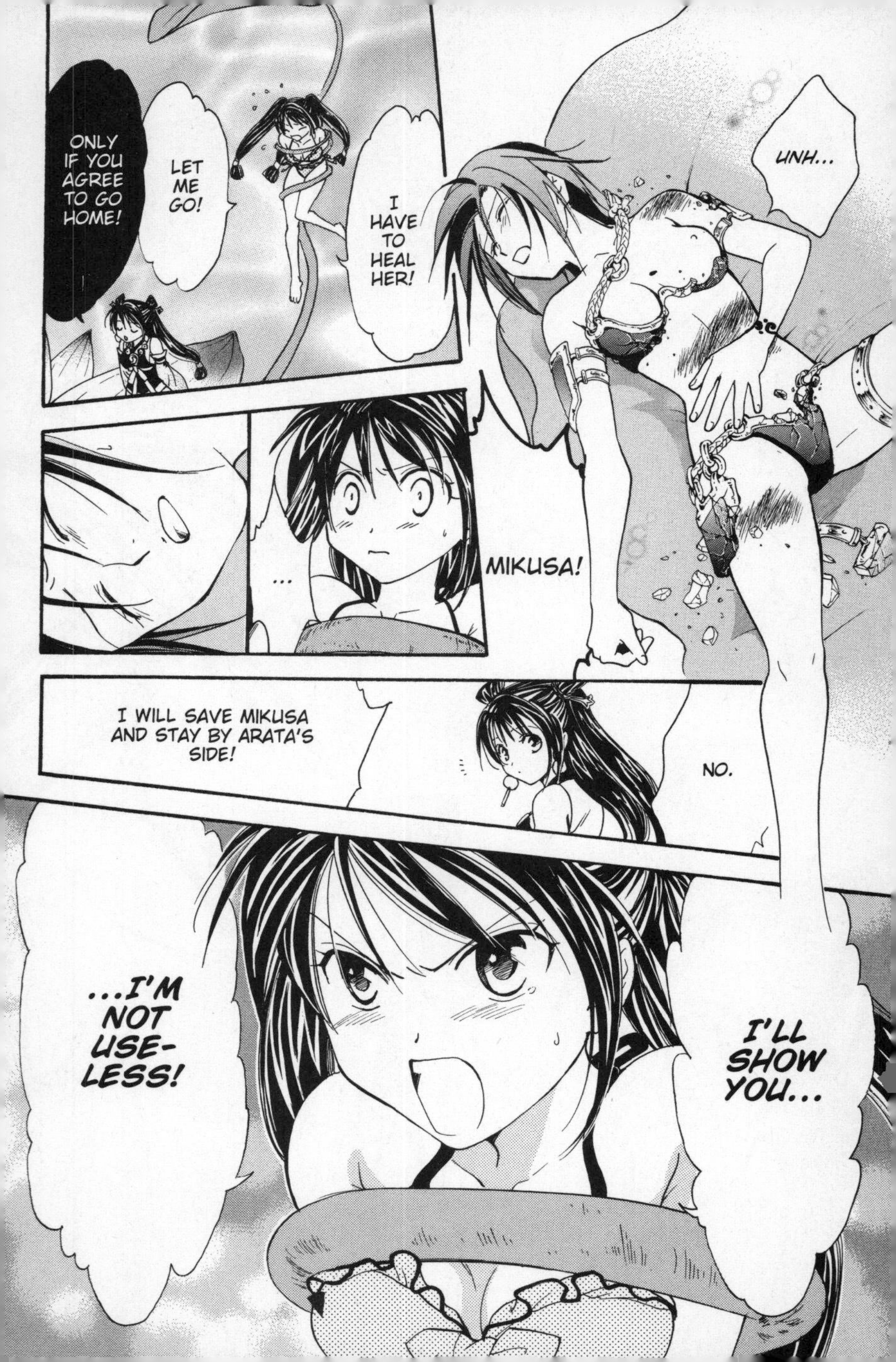
UNH...
I HAVE TO HEAL HER!
LET ME GO!
ONLY IF YOU AGREE TO GO HOME!
MIKUSA!
...
NO.
I WILL SAVE MIKUSA AND STAY BY ARATA'S SIDE!
I'LL SHOW YOU...
...I'M NOT USELESS!

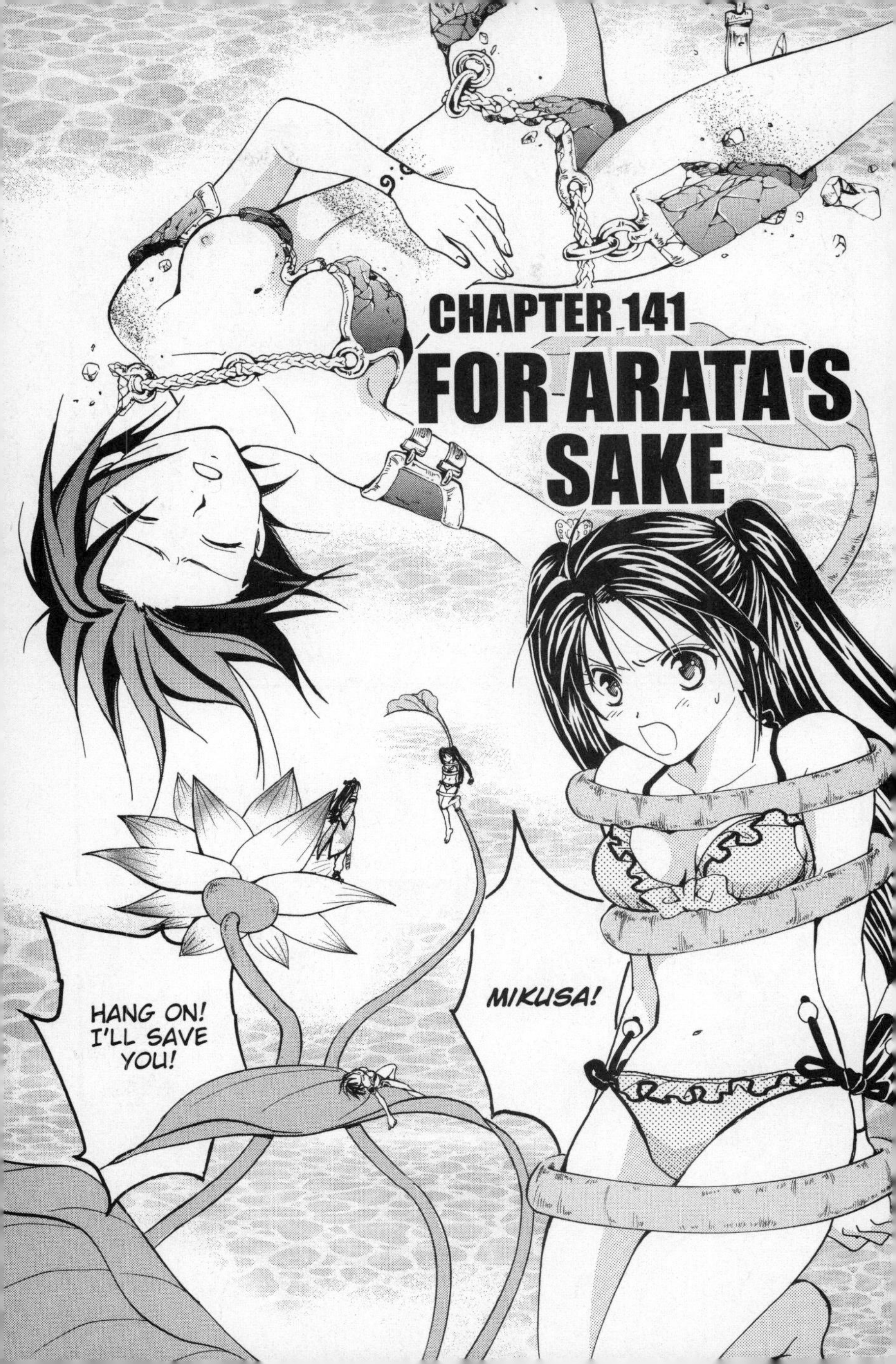
CHAPTER 141
FOR ARATA'S SAKE
MIKUSA!
HANG ON! I'LL SAVE YOU!

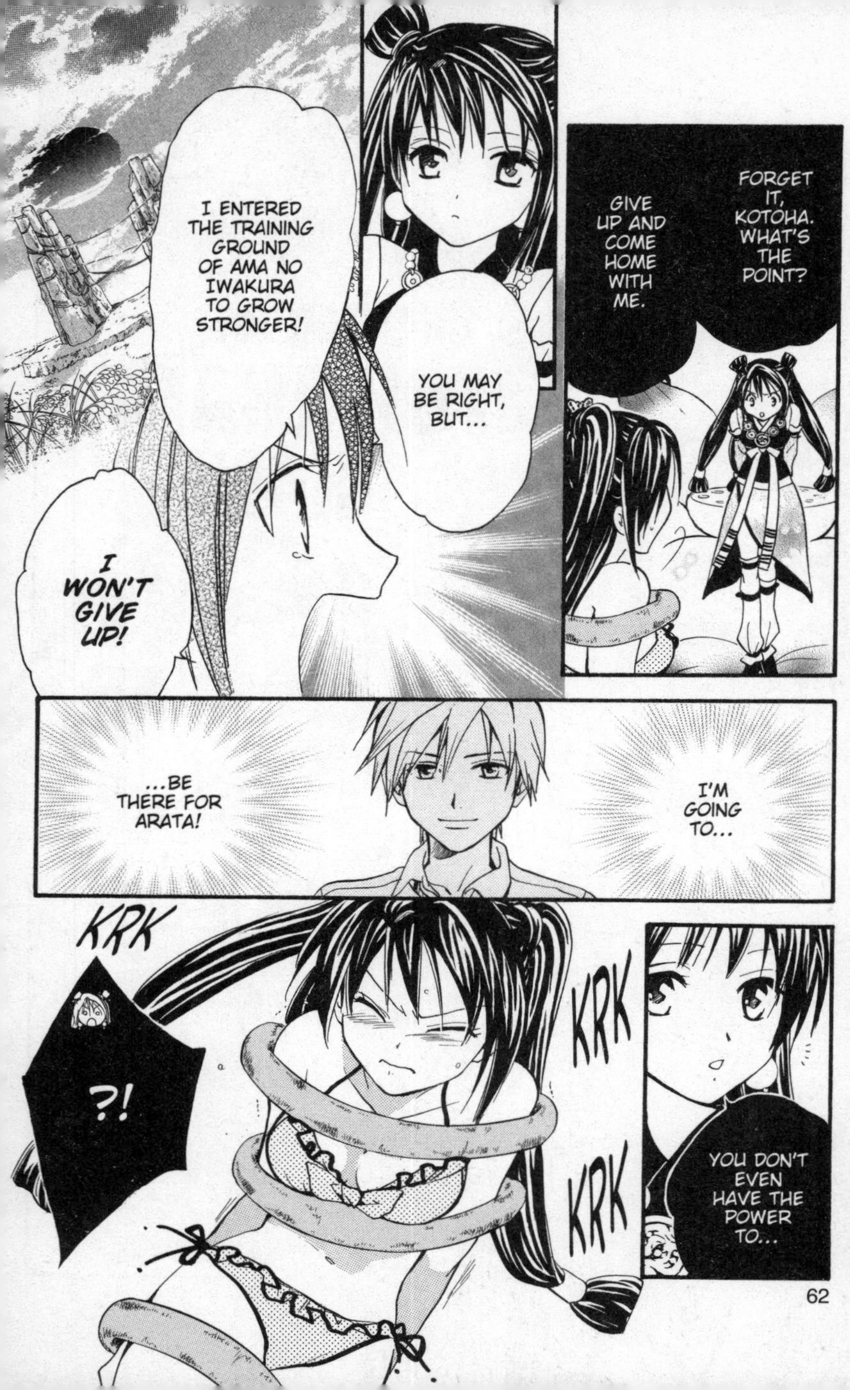
FORGET IT, KOTOHA. WHAT'S THE POINT?
GIVE UP AND COME HOME WITH ME.
YOU MAY BE RIGHT, BUT...
I ENTERED THE TRAINING GROUND OF AMA NO IWAKURA TO GROW STRONGER!
I WON'T GIVE UP!
I'M GOING TO...
...BE THERE FOR ARATA!
YOU DON'T EVEN HAVE THE POWER TO...
KRK
KRK
KRK
?!

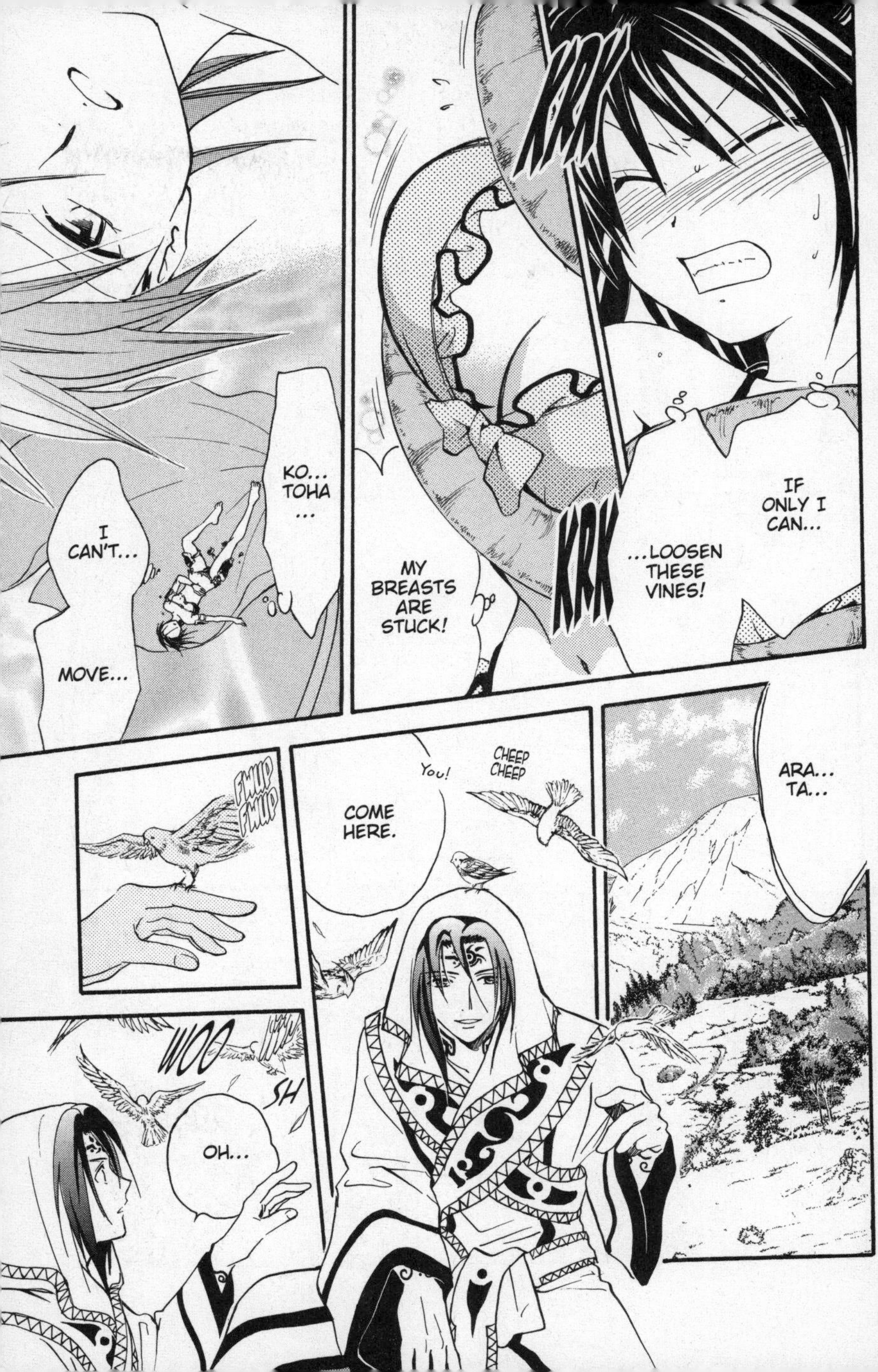
IF ONLY I CAN...
...LOOSEN THESE VINES!
KRK
MY BREASTS ARE STUCK!
KO... TOHA ...
I CAN'T...
MOVE...
ARA... TA...
CHEEP CHEEP
You!
COME HERE.
FWUP FWUP
WOO
SH
OH...

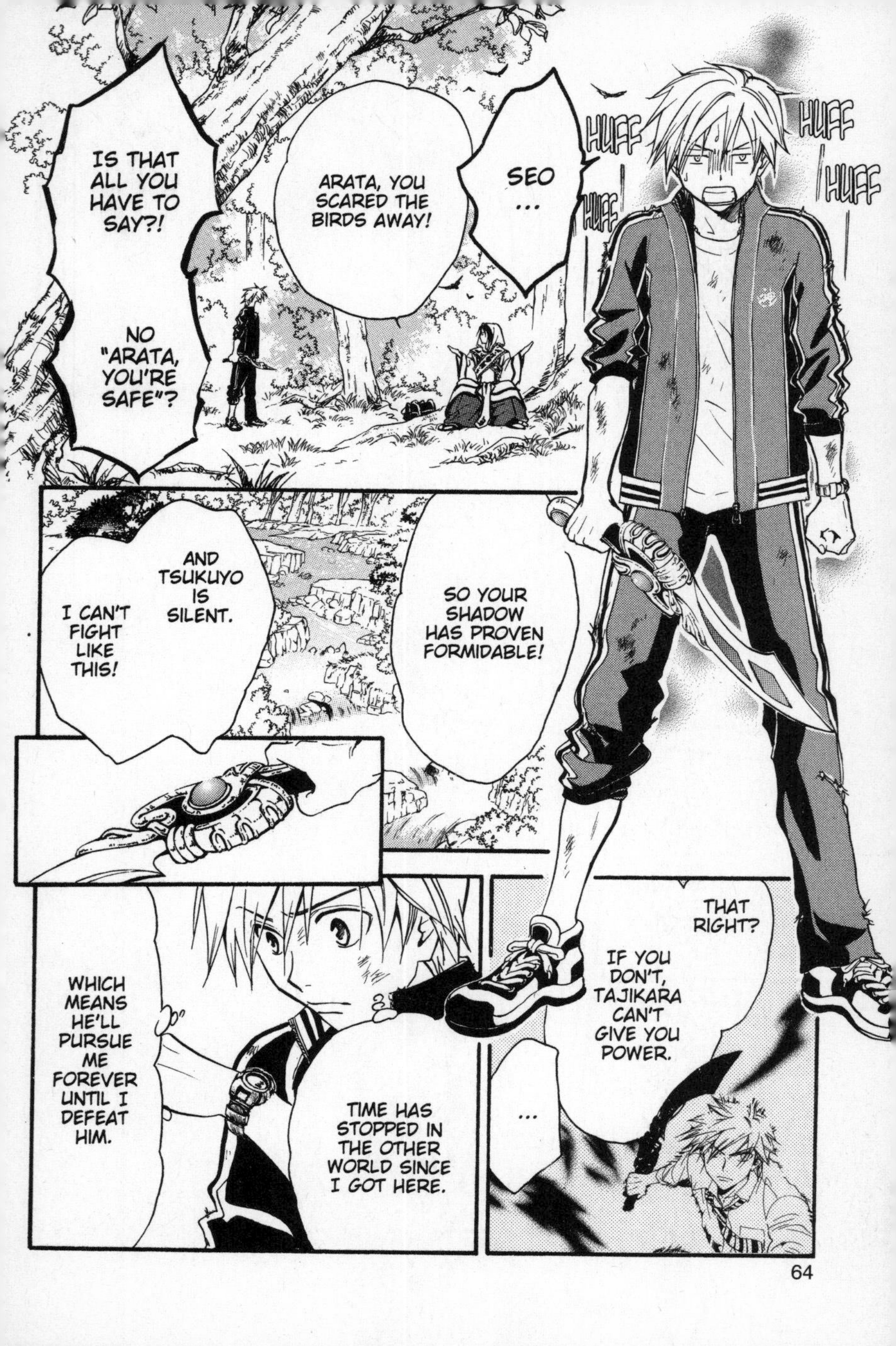
HUFF
HUFF
HUFF
HUFF
SEO ...
ARATA, YOU SCARED THE BIRDS AWAY!
IS THAT ALL YOU HAVE TO SAY?!
NO "ARATA, YOU'RE SAFE"?
SO YOUR SHADOW HAS PROVEN FORMIDABLE!
AND TSUKUYO IS SILENT.
I CAN'T FIGHT LIKE THIS!
THAT RIGHT?
IF YOU DON'T, TAJIKARA CAN'T GIVE YOU POWER.
...
TIME HAS STOPPED IN THE OTHER WORLD SINCE I GOT HERE.
WHICH MEANS HE'LL PURSUE ME FOREVER UNTIL I DEFEAT HIM.

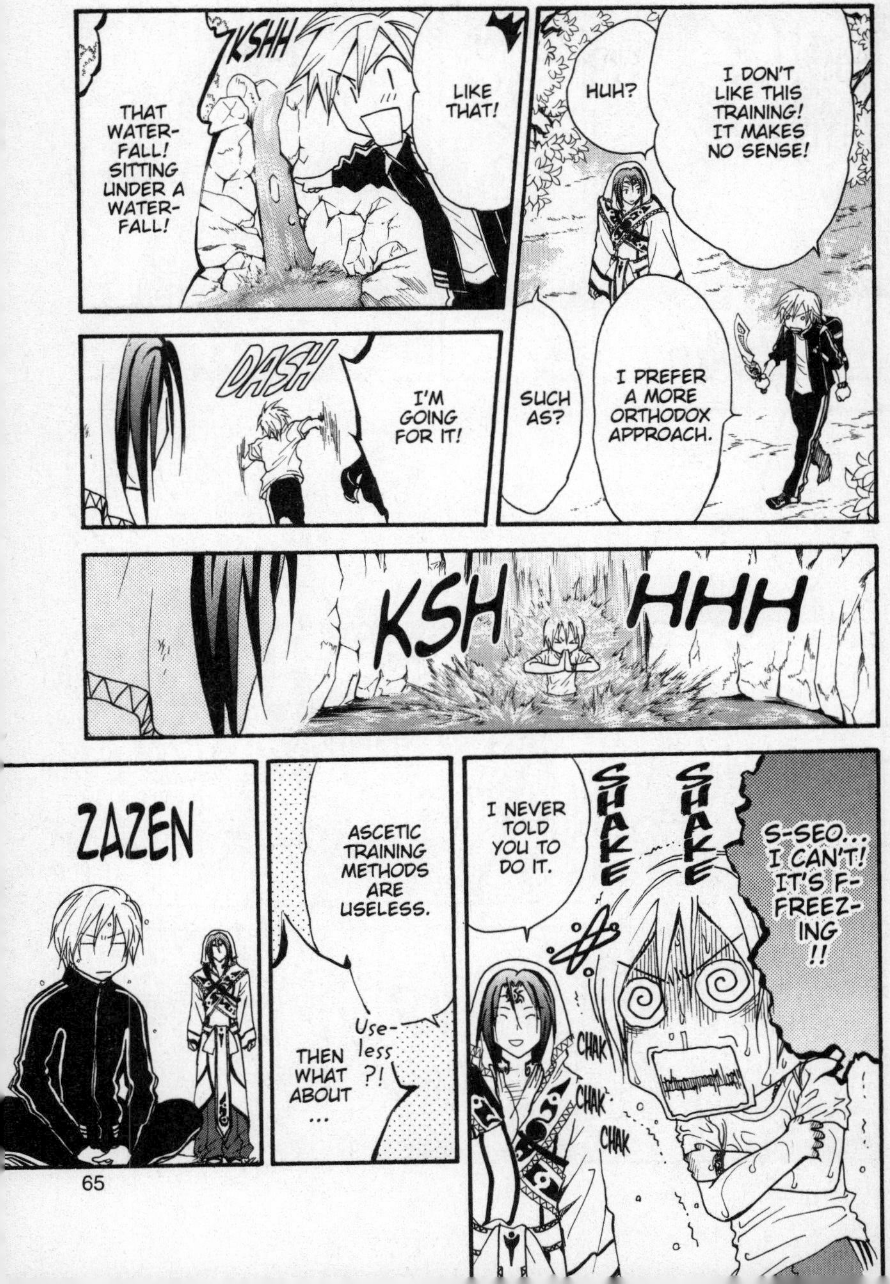
I DON'T LIKE THIS TRAINING! IT MAKES NO SENSE!
HUH?
I PREFER A MORE ORTHODOX APPROACH.
SUCH AS?
KSHH
LIKE THAT!
THAT WATERFALL! SITTING UNDER A WATERFALL!
DASH
I'M GOING FOR IT!
KSH HHH
S-SEO... I CAN'T! IT'S F-FREEZING!!
SHAKE SHAKE
I NEVER TOLD YOU TO DO IT.
CHAK CHAK CHAK
ASCETIC TRAINING METHODS ARE USELESS.
Useless?!
THEN WHAT ABOUT...
ZAZEN

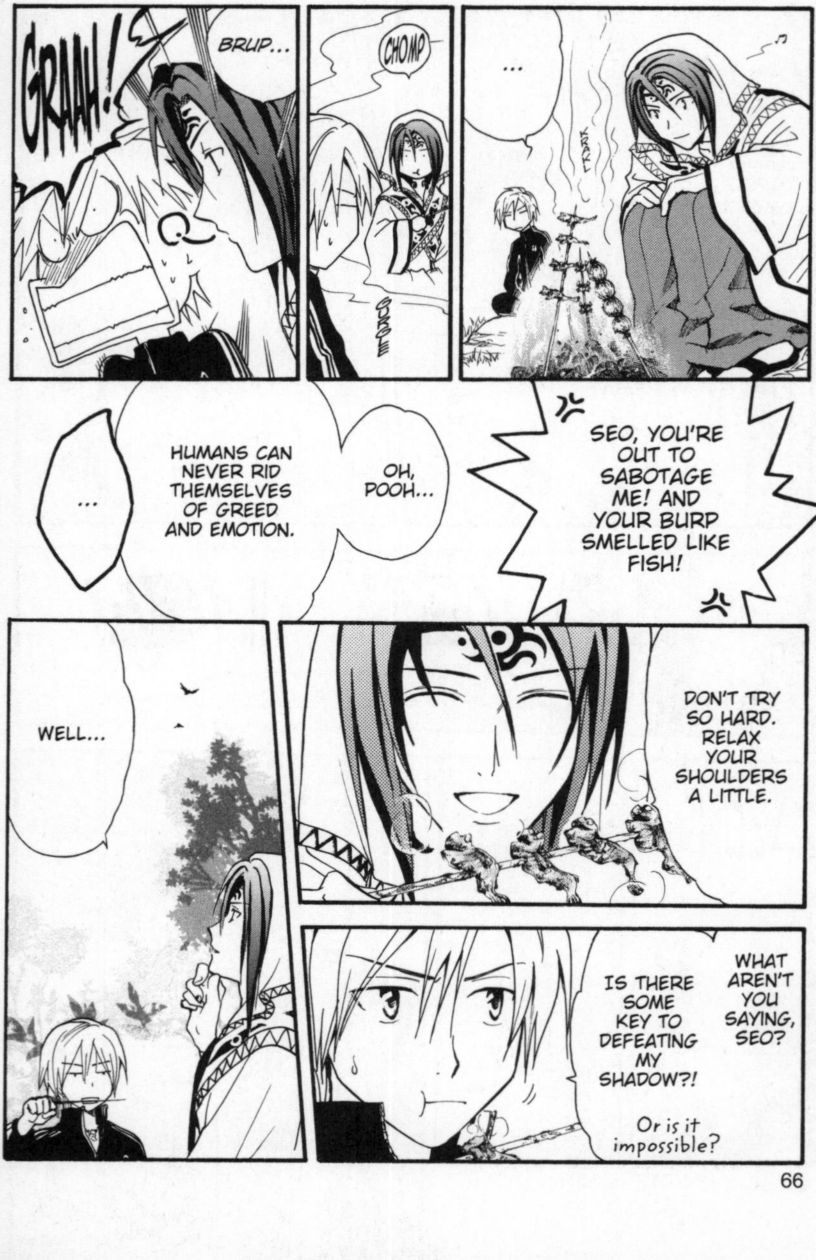
...
KRAKL
CHOMP
GURGLE
BRUP...
GRAAH!
SEO, YOU'RE OUT TO SABOTAGE ME! AND YOUR BURP SMELLED LIKE FISH!
OH, POOH...
HUMANS CAN NEVER RID THEMSELVES OF GREED AND EMOTION.
...
DON'T TRY SO HARD. RELAX YOUR SHOULDERS A LITTLE.
WHAT AREN'T YOU SAYING, SEO?
IS THERE SOME KEY TO DEFEATING MY SHADOW?!
Or is it impossible?
WELL...

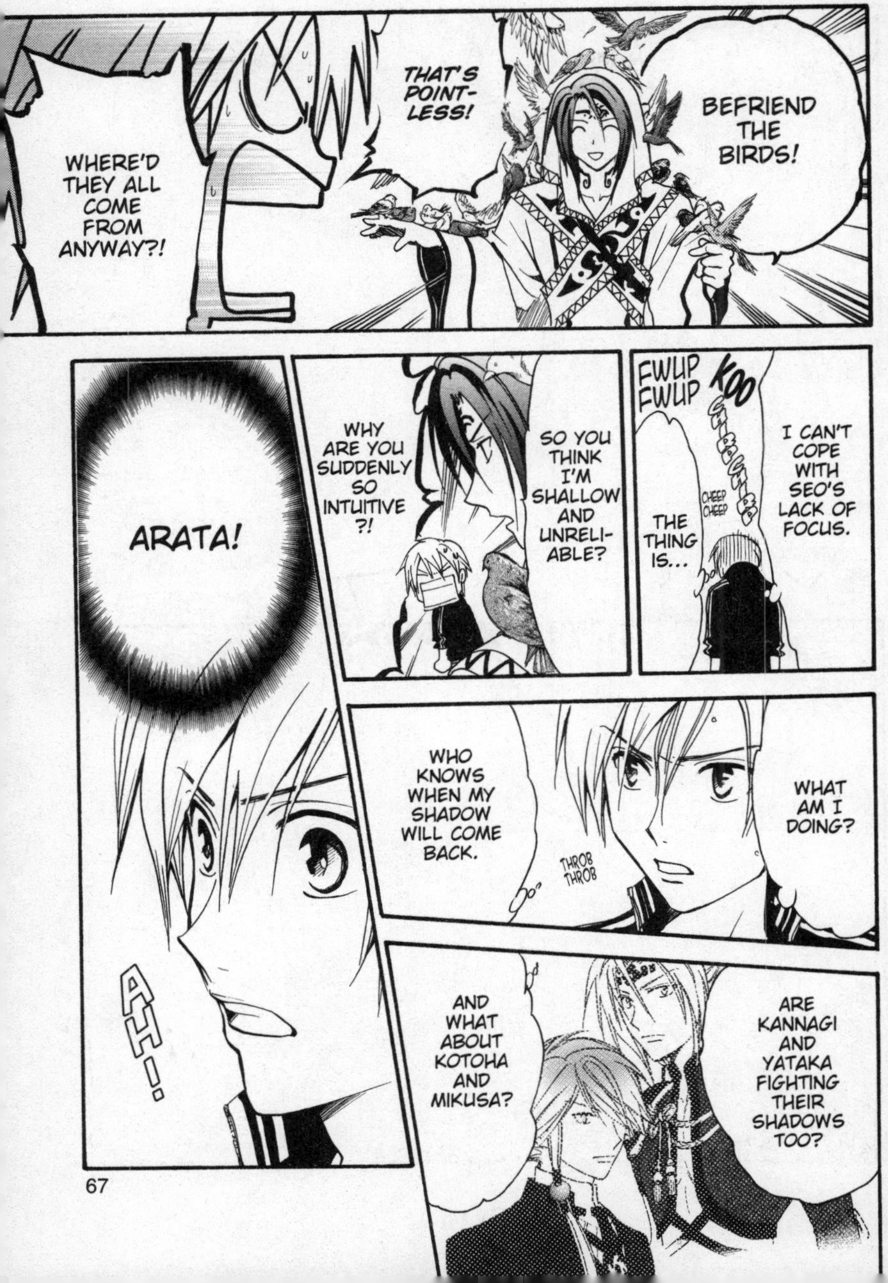
BEFRIEND THE BIRDS!
THAT'S POINT-LESS!
WHERE'D THEY ALL COME FROM ANYWAY?!
FWUP FWUP
KOO
I CAN'T COPE WITH SEO'S LACK OF FOCUS.
CHEEP CHEEP
THE THING IS...
SO YOU THINK I'M SHALLOW AND UNRELI-ABLE?
WHY ARE YOU SUDDENLY SO INTUITIVE?!
WHAT AM I DOING?
WHO KNOWS WHEN MY SHADOW WILL COME BACK.
THROB THROB
ARE KANNAGI AND YATAKA FIGHTING THEIR SHADOWS TOO?
AND WHAT ABOUT KOTOHA AND MIKUSA?
ARATA!
AHH!

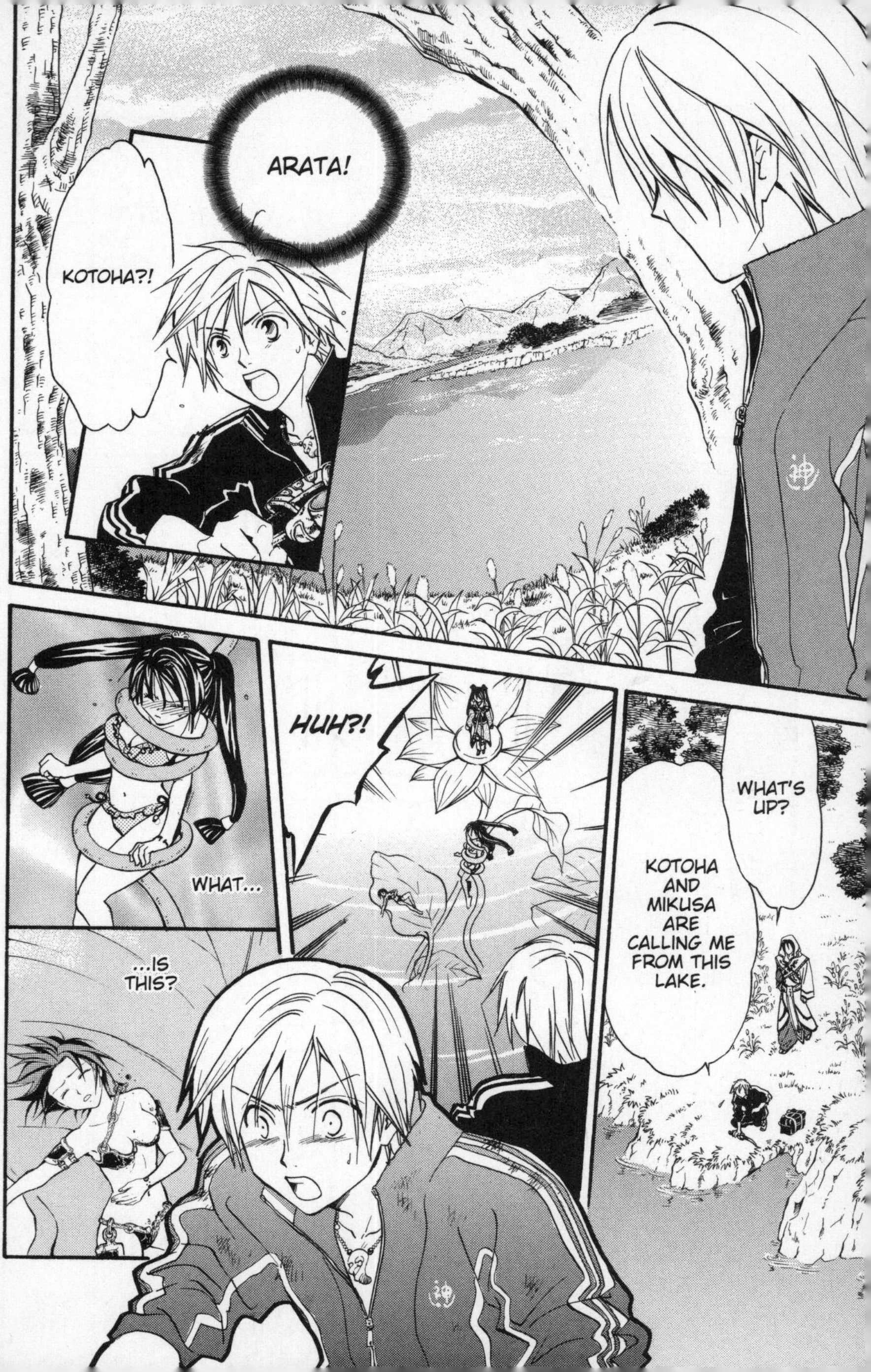
ARATA!
KOTOHA?!
WHAT'S UP?
KOTOHA AND MIKUSA ARE CALLING ME FROM THIS LAKE.
HUH?!
WHAT...
...IS THIS?

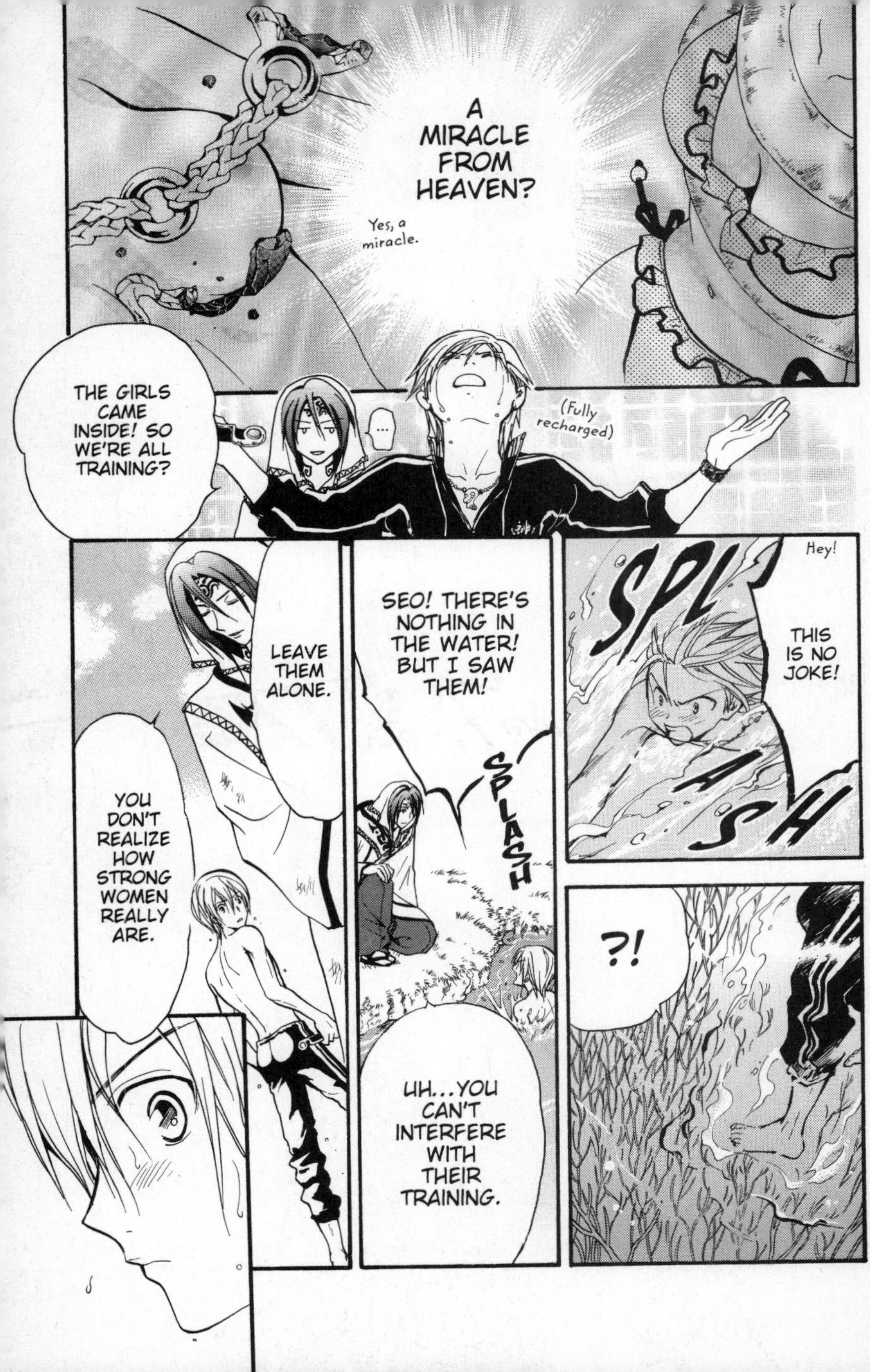
A MIRACLE FROM HEAVEN?
Yes, a miracle.
(Fully recharged)
...
THE GIRLS CAME INSIDE! SO WE'RE ALL TRAINING?
Hey!
SPLASH
THIS IS NO JOKE!
?!
SEO! THERE'S NOTHING IN THE WATER! BUT I SAW THEM!
SPLASH
UH...YOU CAN'T INTERFERE WITH THEIR TRAINING.
LEAVE THEM ALONE.
YOU DON'T REALIZE HOW STRONG WOMEN REALLY ARE.

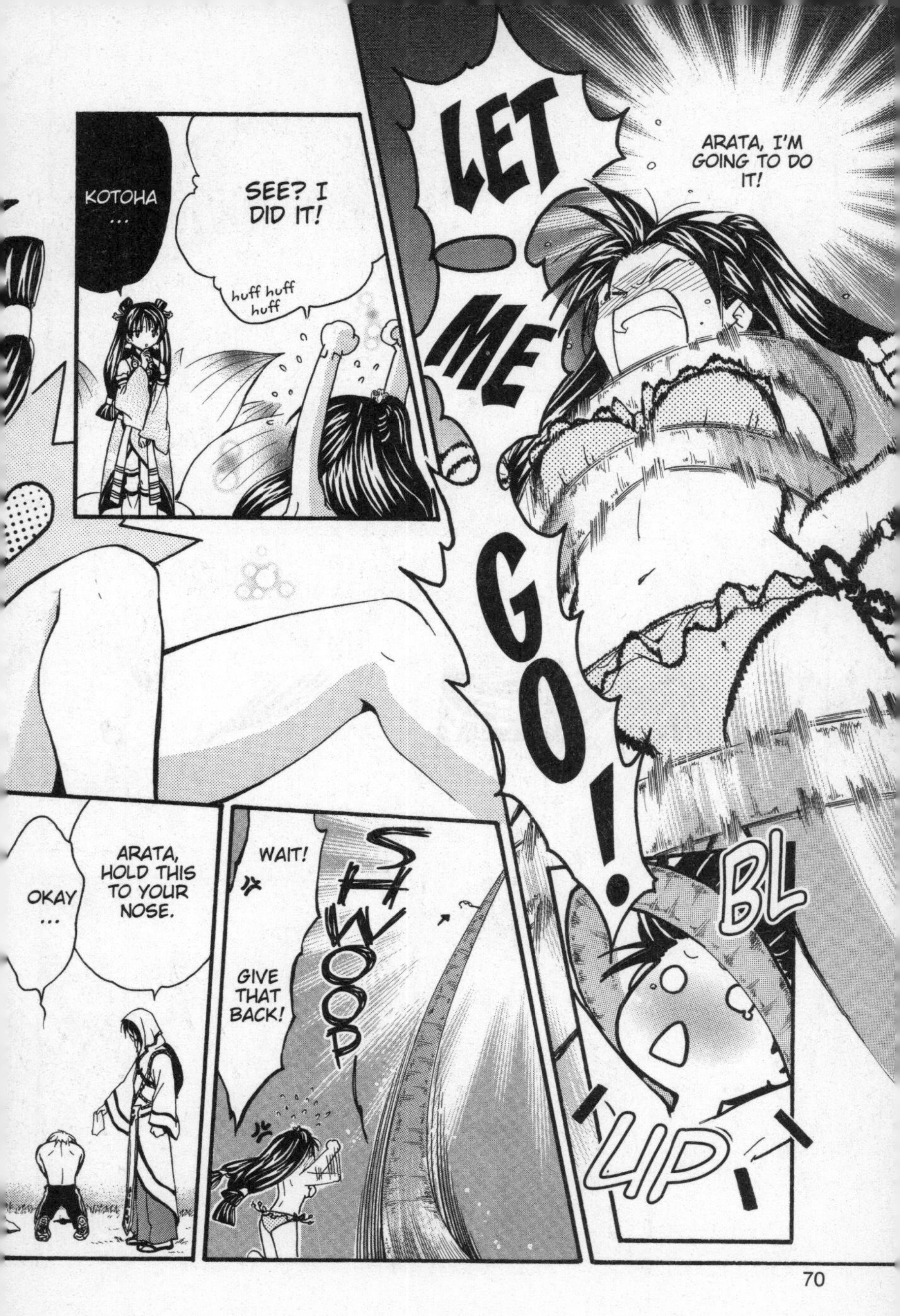
ARATA, I'M GOING TO DO IT!
LET ME GO!
BL
UP
SEE? I DID IT!
huff huff huff
KOTOHA ...
WAIT!
SHWOOP
GIVE THAT BACK!
ARATA, HOLD THIS TO YOUR NOSE.
OKAY ...

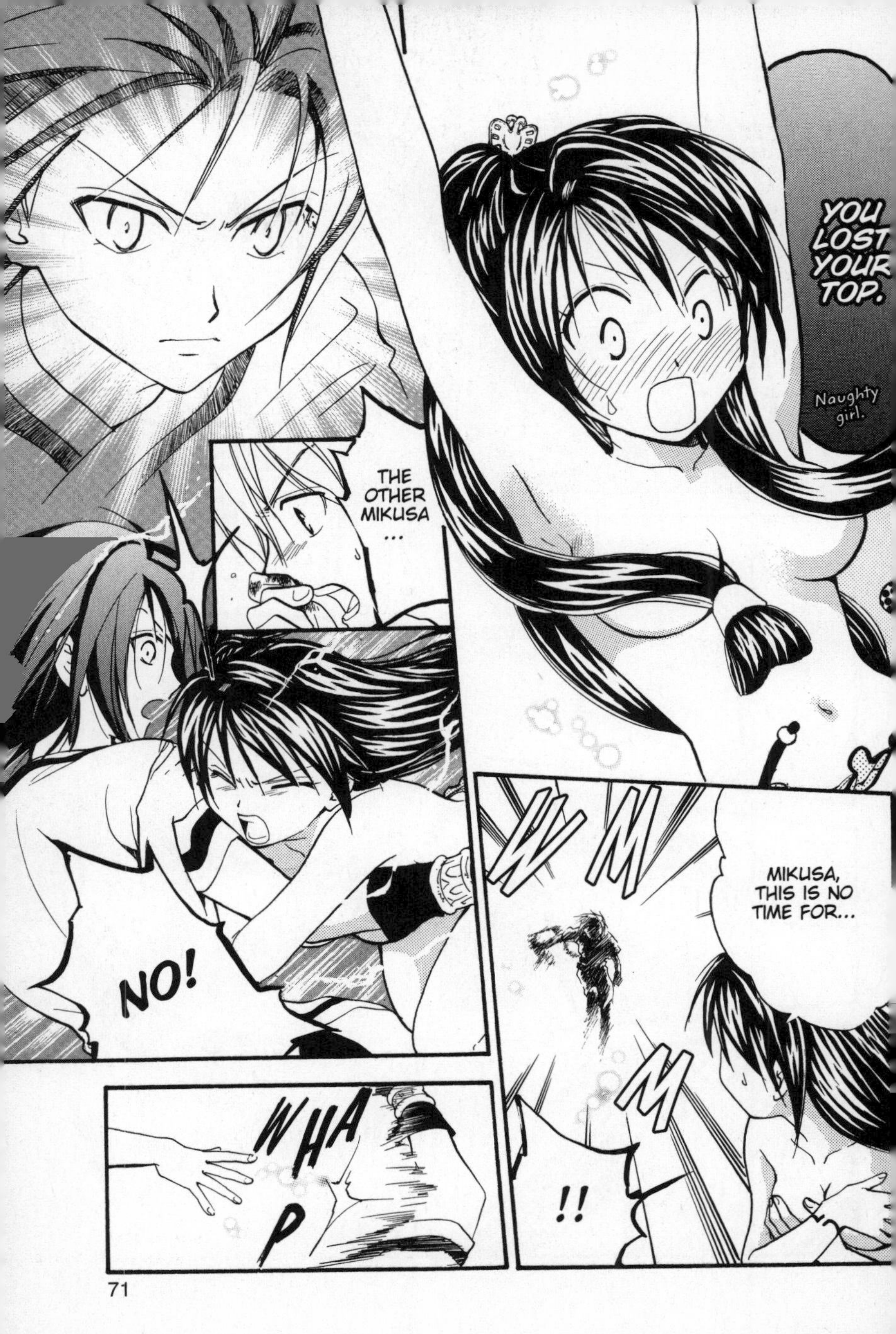
YOU LOST YOUR TOP.
Naughty girl.
THE OTHER MIKUSA ...
NO!
WMM
MIKUSA, THIS IS NO TIME FOR...
M
!!
WHAP

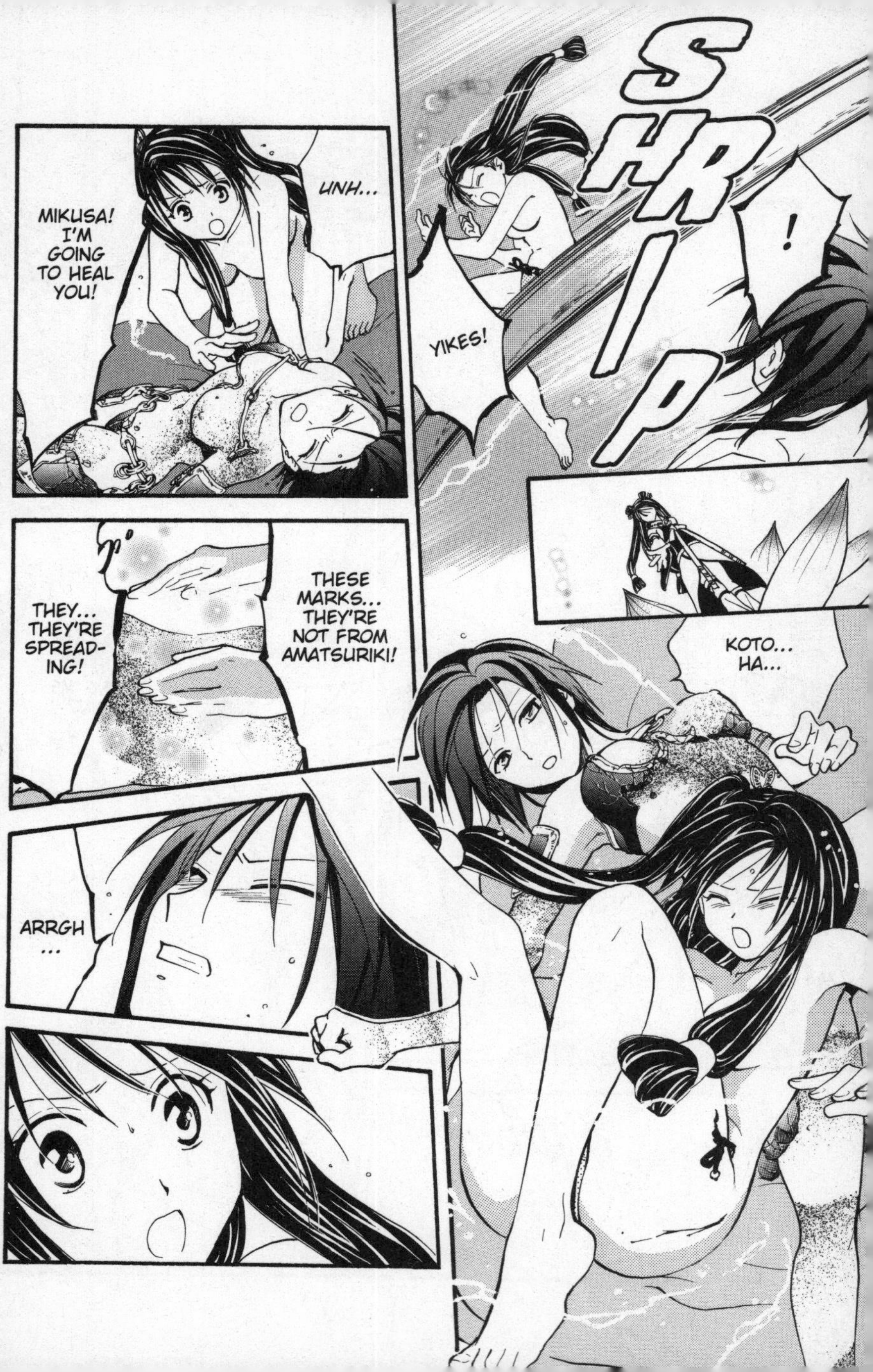
SHRIP
!
YIKES!
UNH...
MIKUSA! I'M GOING TO HEAL YOU!
KOTO... HA...
THESE MARKS... THEY'RE NOT FROM AMATSURIKI!
THEY... THEY'RE SPREAD-ING!
ARRGH...

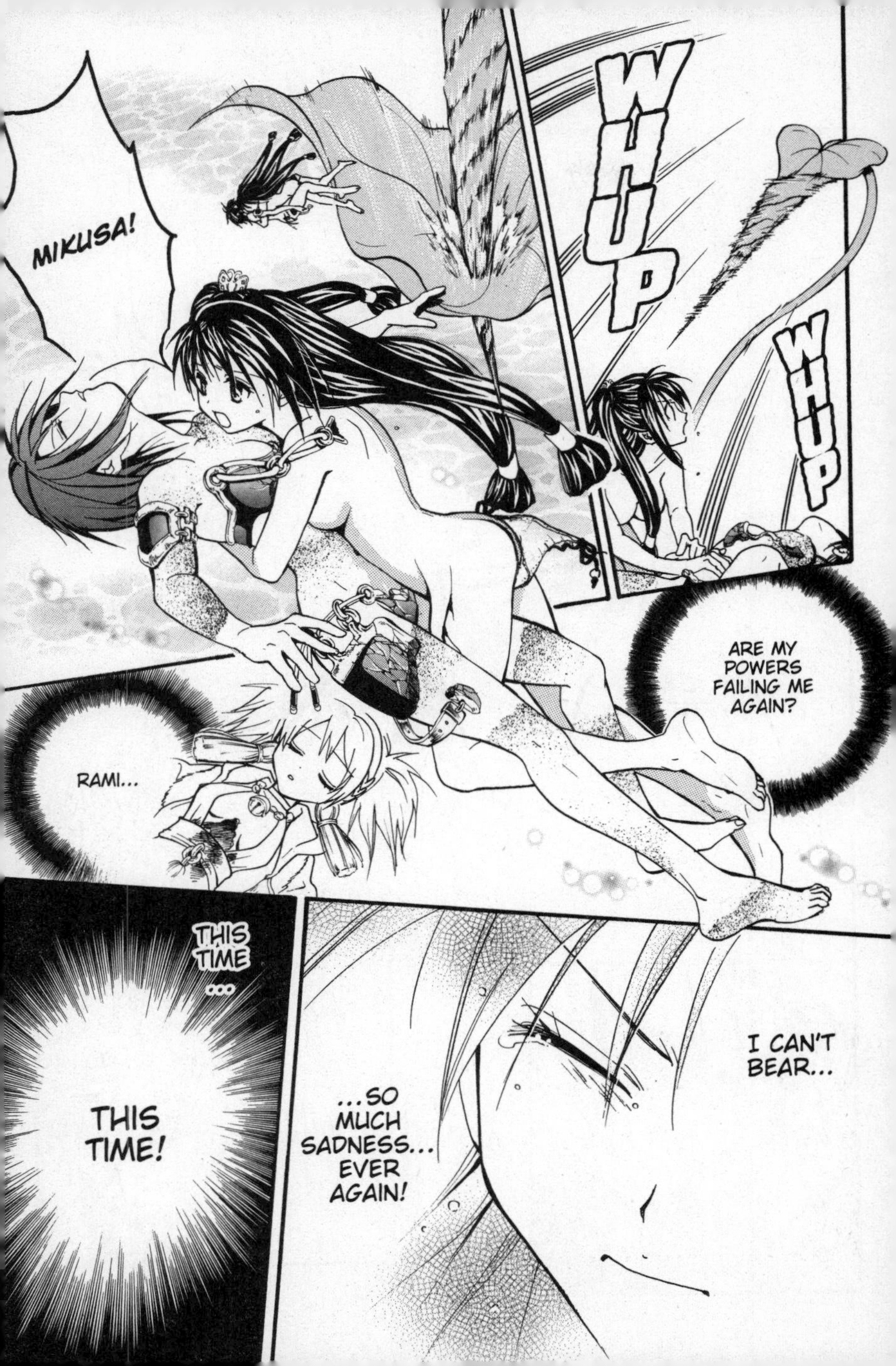
WHUP
WHUP
MIKUSA!
ARE MY POWERS FAILING ME AGAIN?
RAMI...
I CAN'T BEAR...
...SO MUCH SADNESS... EVER AGAIN!
THIS TIME...
THIS TIME!

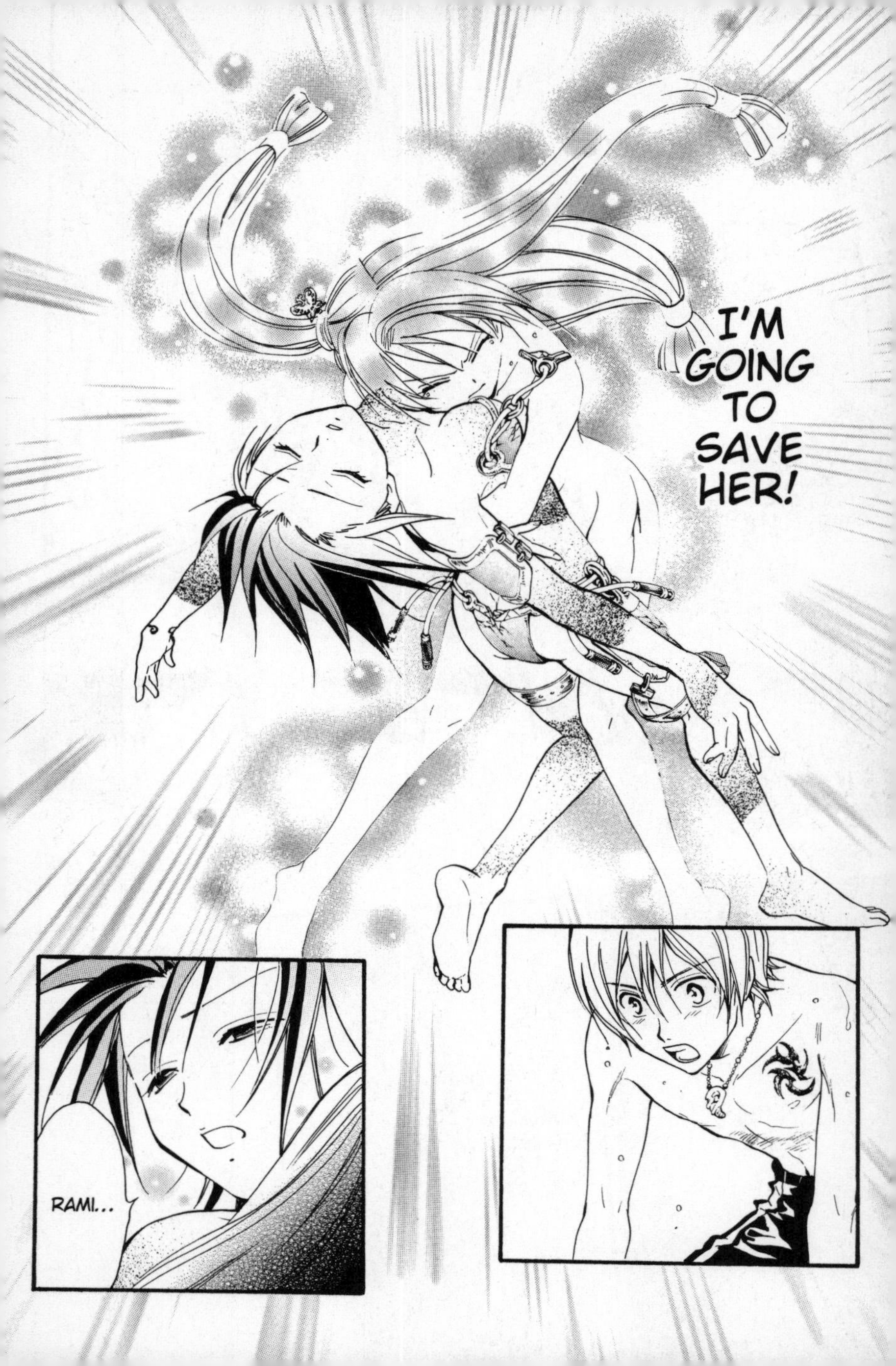
I'M GOING TO SAVE HER!
RAMI...

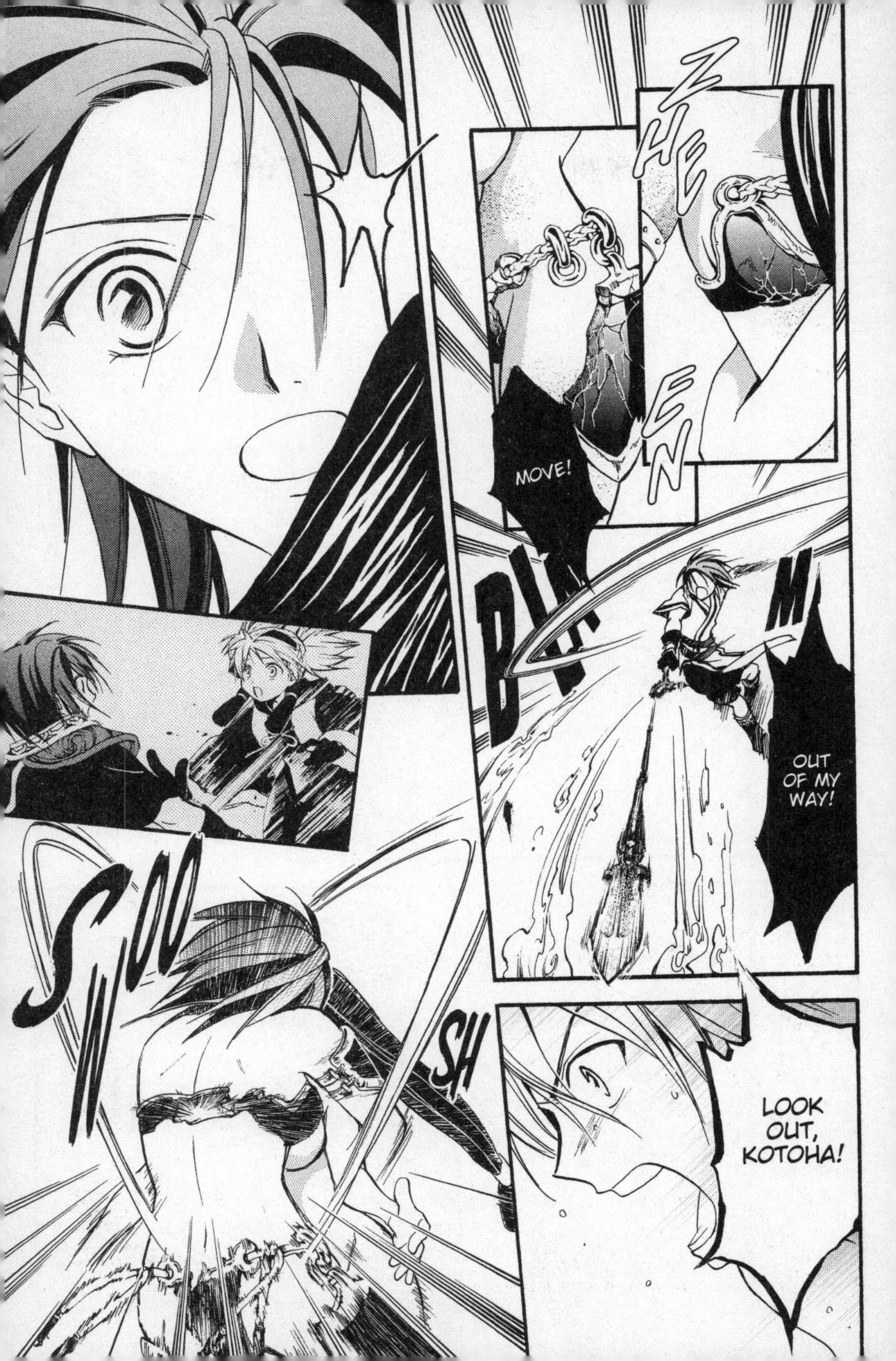
MOVE!
OUT OF MY WAY!
LOOK OUT, KOTOHA!

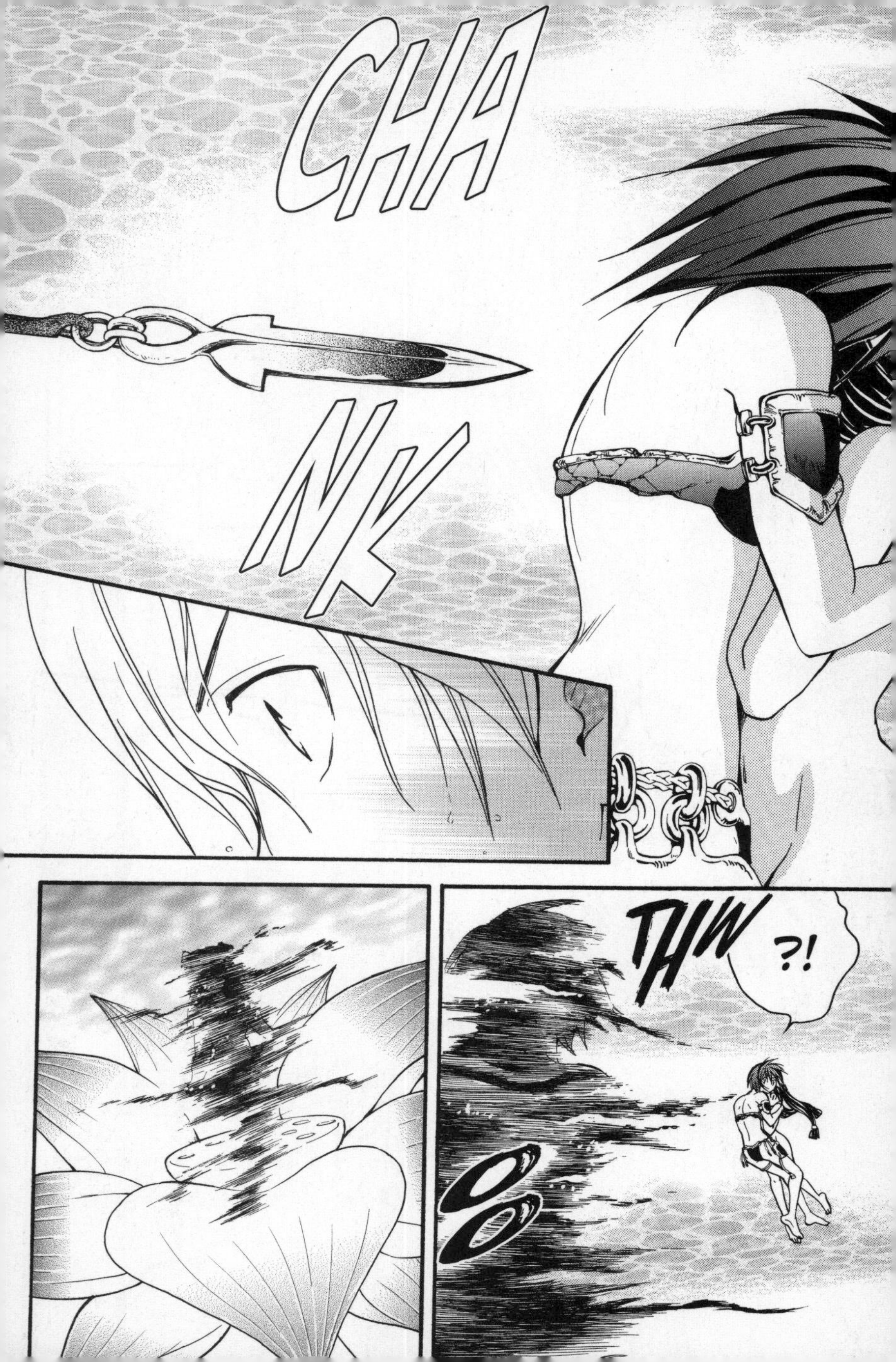
CHA
NK
THW
?!

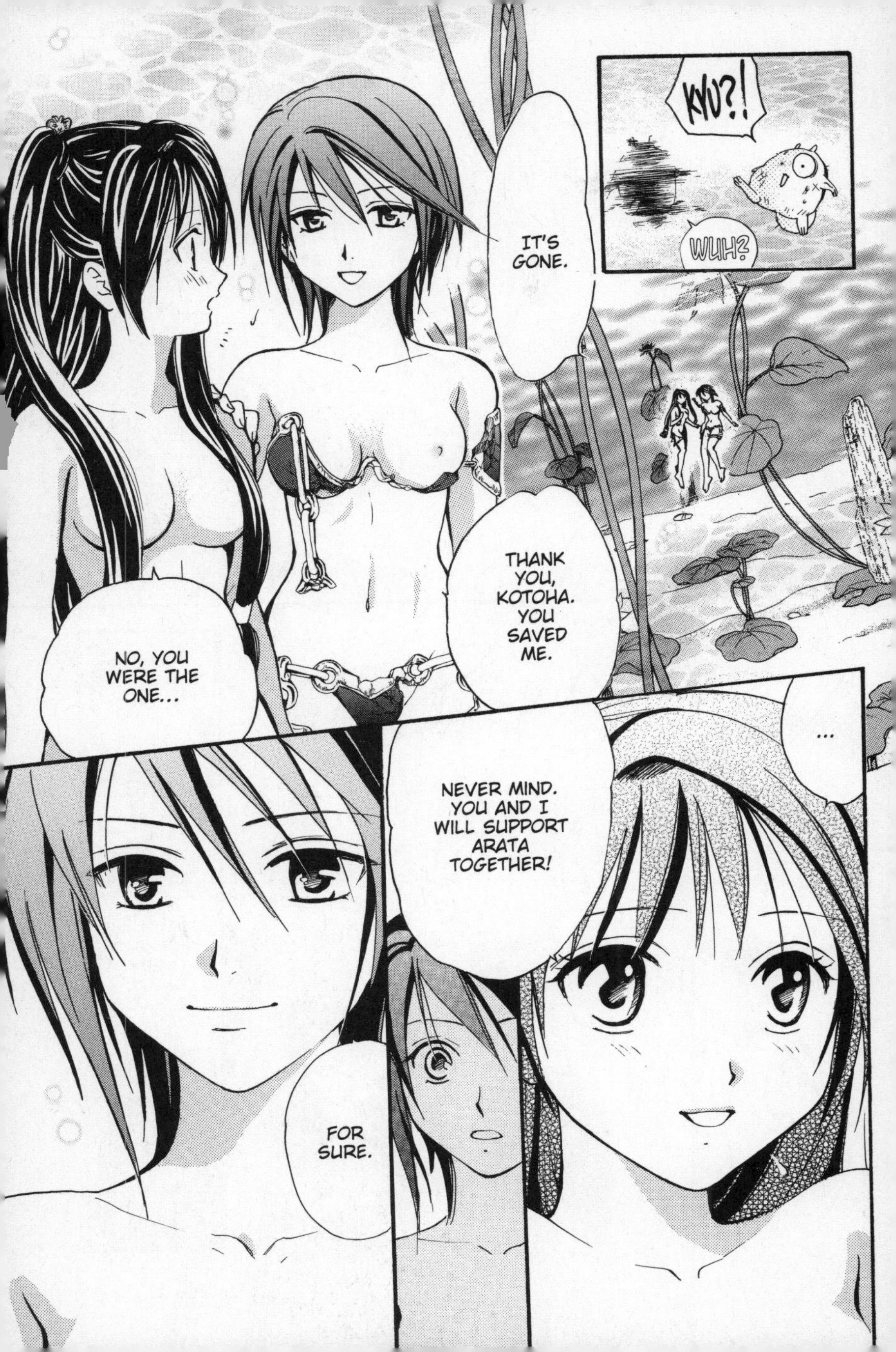
KYU?!
WUH?
IT'S GONE.
THANK YOU, KOTOHA. YOU SAVED ME.
NO, YOU WERE THE ONE...
...
NEVER MIND. YOU AND I WILL SUPPORT ARATA TOGETHER!
FOR SURE.

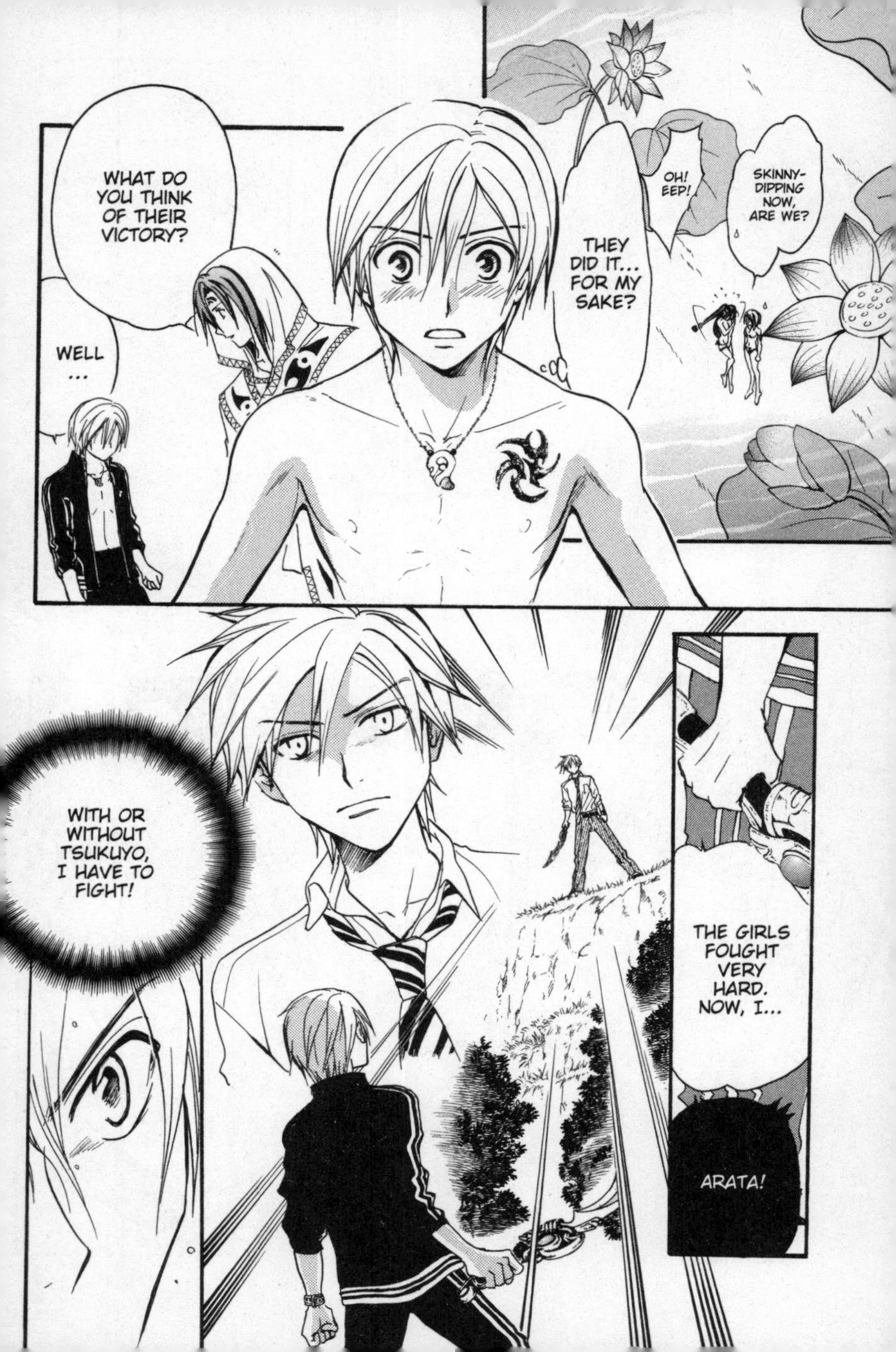
SKINNY-DIPPING NOW, ARE WE?
OH! EEP!
THEY DID IT... FOR MY SAKE?
WHAT DO YOU THINK OF THEIR VICTORY?
WELL ...
THE GIRLS FOUGHT VERY HARD. NOW, I...
ARATA!
WITH OR WITHOUT TSUKUYO, I HAVE TO FIGHT!

CHAPTER 142
REALIZATION

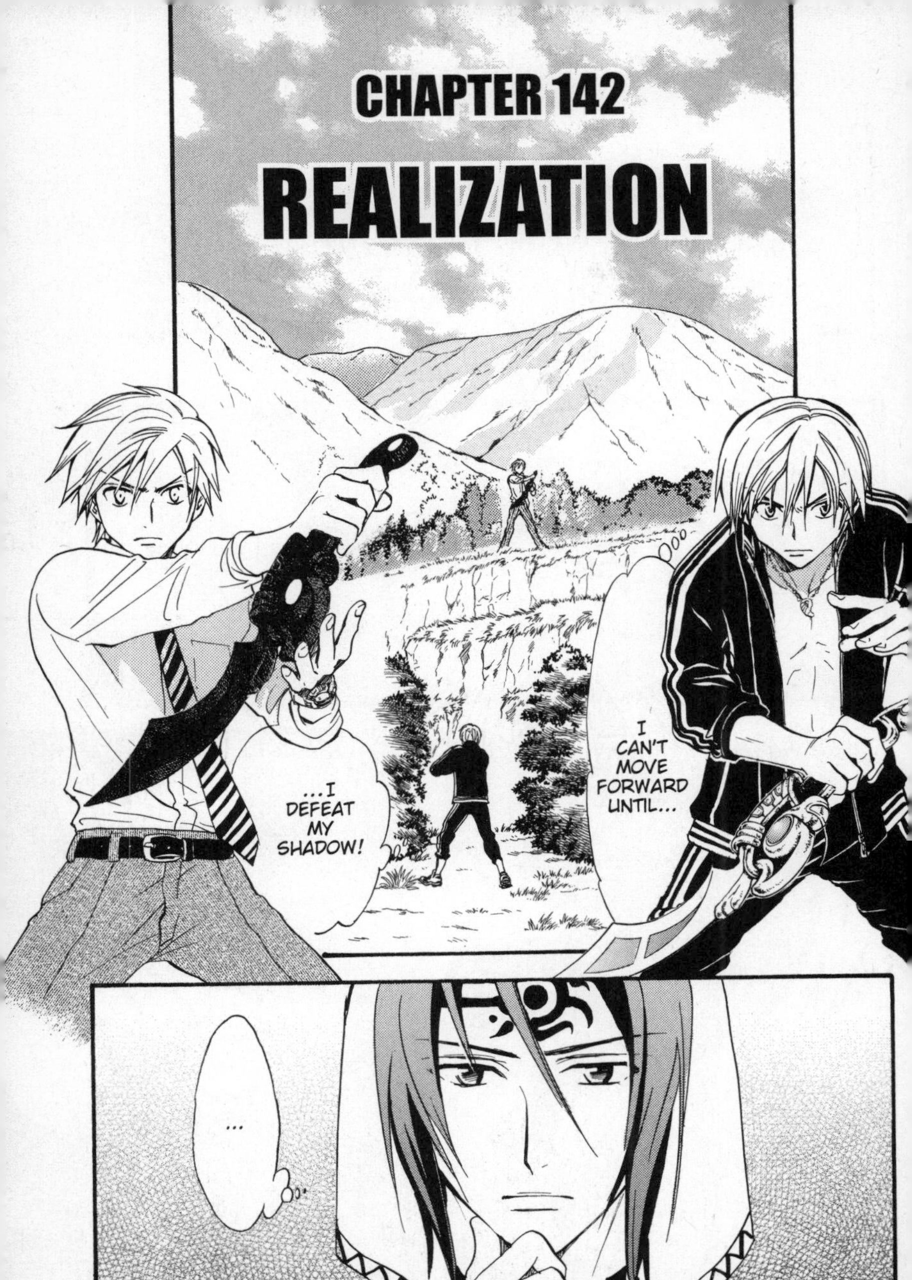
I CAN'T MOVE FORWARD UNTIL...
...I DEFEAT MY SHADOW!
...

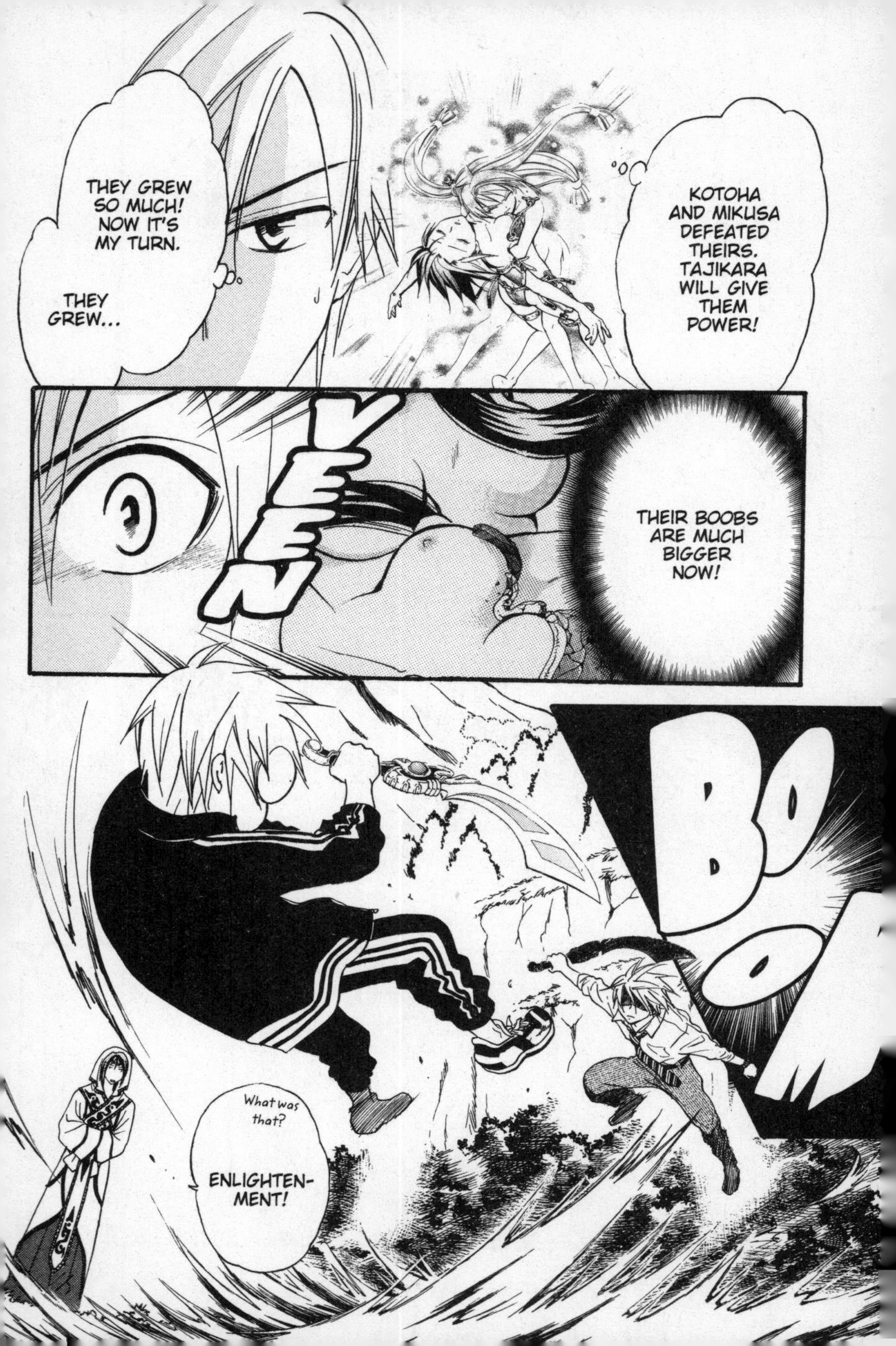
KOTOHA AND MIKUSA DEFEATED THEIRS. TAJIKARA WILL GIVE THEM POWER!
THEY GREW SO MUCH! NOW IT'S MY TURN.
THEY GREW...
THEIR BOOBS ARE MUCH BIGGER NOW!
VEEN
BOOOM
What was that?
ENLIGHTEN-MENT!

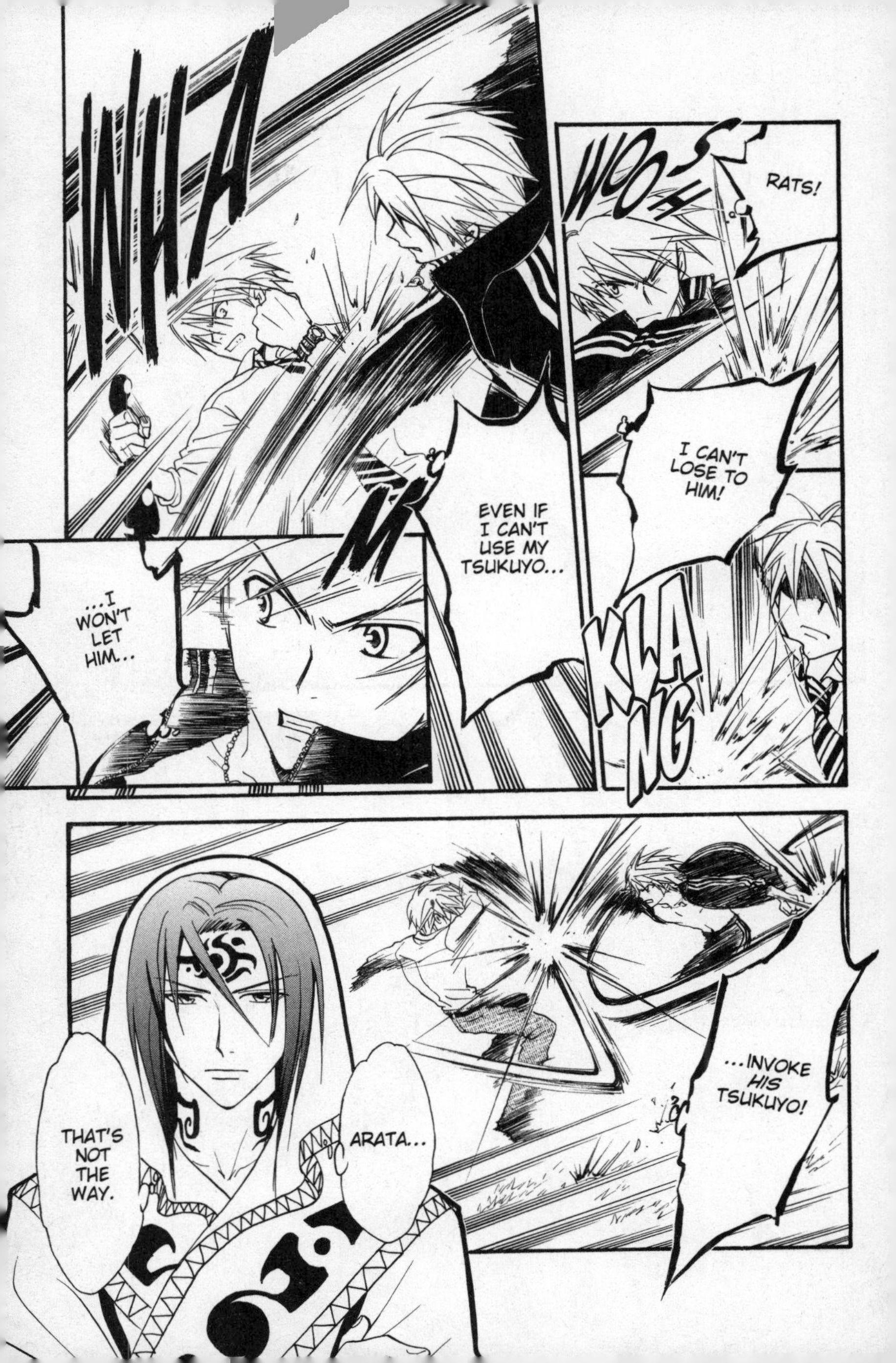
WOOSH
RATS!
I CAN'T LOSE TO HIM!
KLANG
WHA
M
EVEN IF I CAN'T USE MY TSUKUYO...
...I WON'T LET HIM...
...INVOKE HIS TSUKUYO!
ARATA...
THAT'S NOT THE WAY.

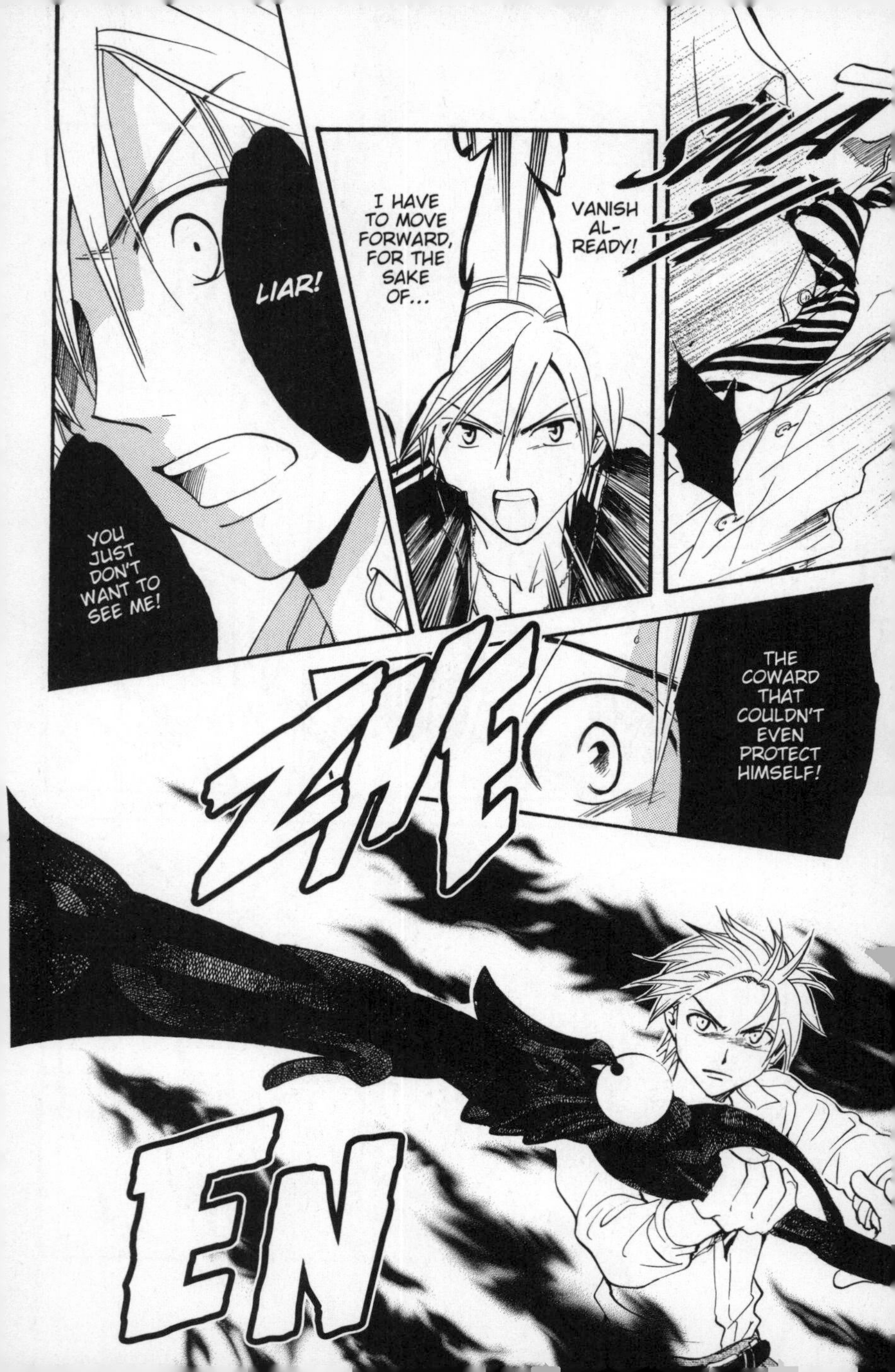
VANISH AL-READY!
I HAVE TO MOVE FORWARD, FOR THE SAKE OF...
LIAR!
YOU JUST DON'T WANT TO SEE ME!
THE COWARD THAT COULDN'T EVEN PROTECT HIMSELF!
ZHE
EN

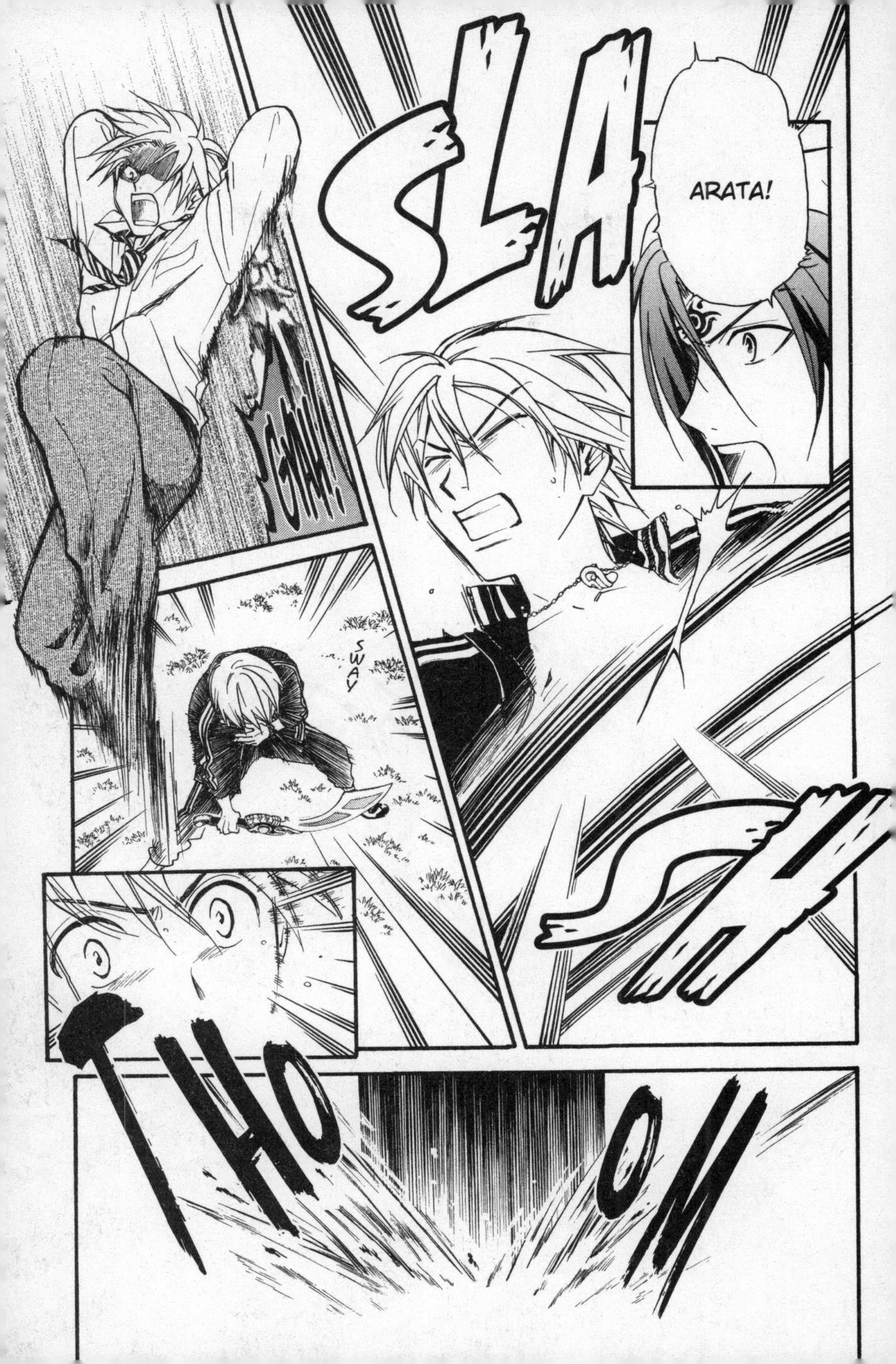
ARATA!
SLA
SH
GYAH!
SWAY
THO
OM

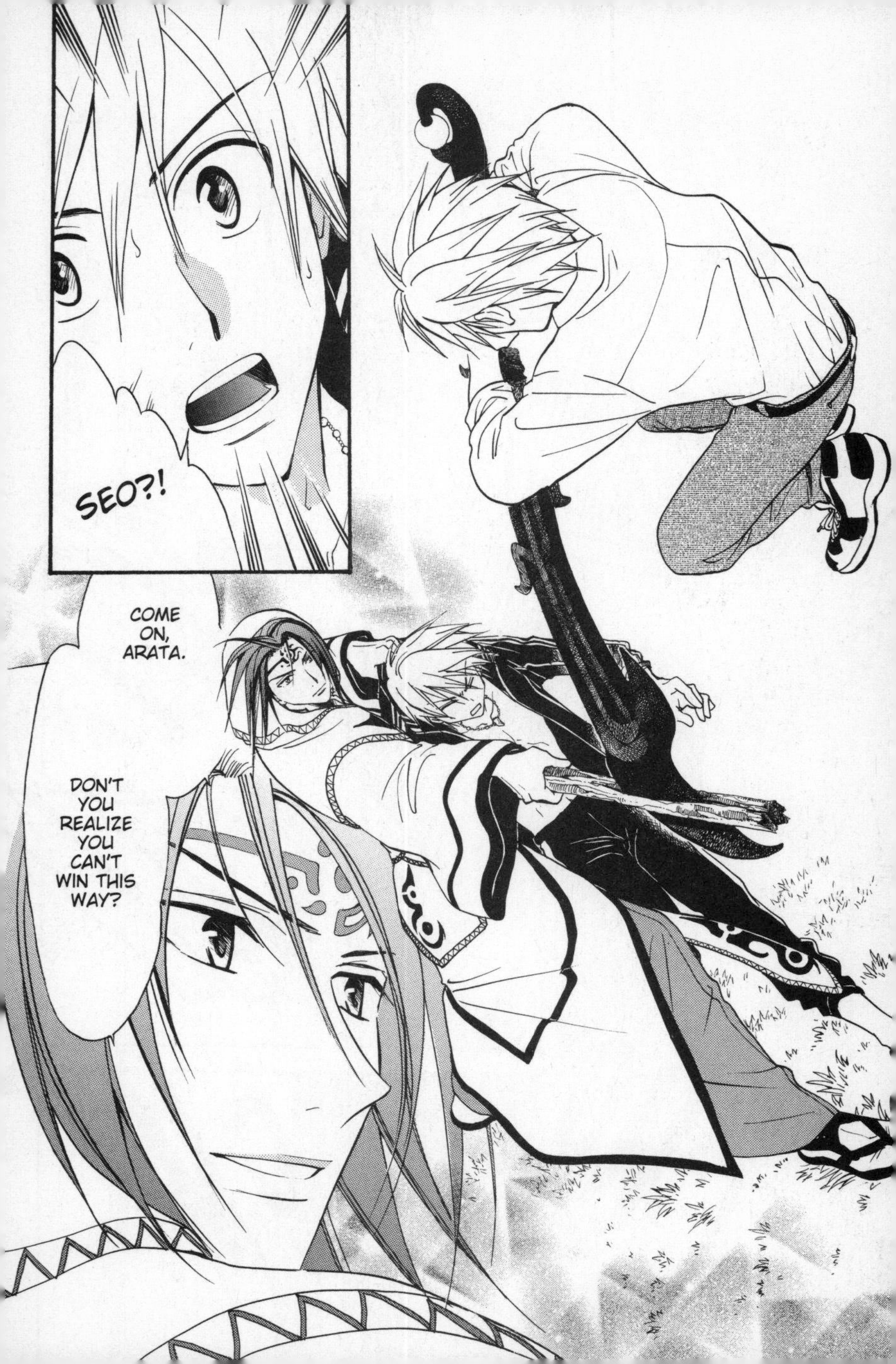
SEO?!
COME ON, ARATA.
DON'T YOU REALIZE YOU CAN'T WIN THIS WAY?

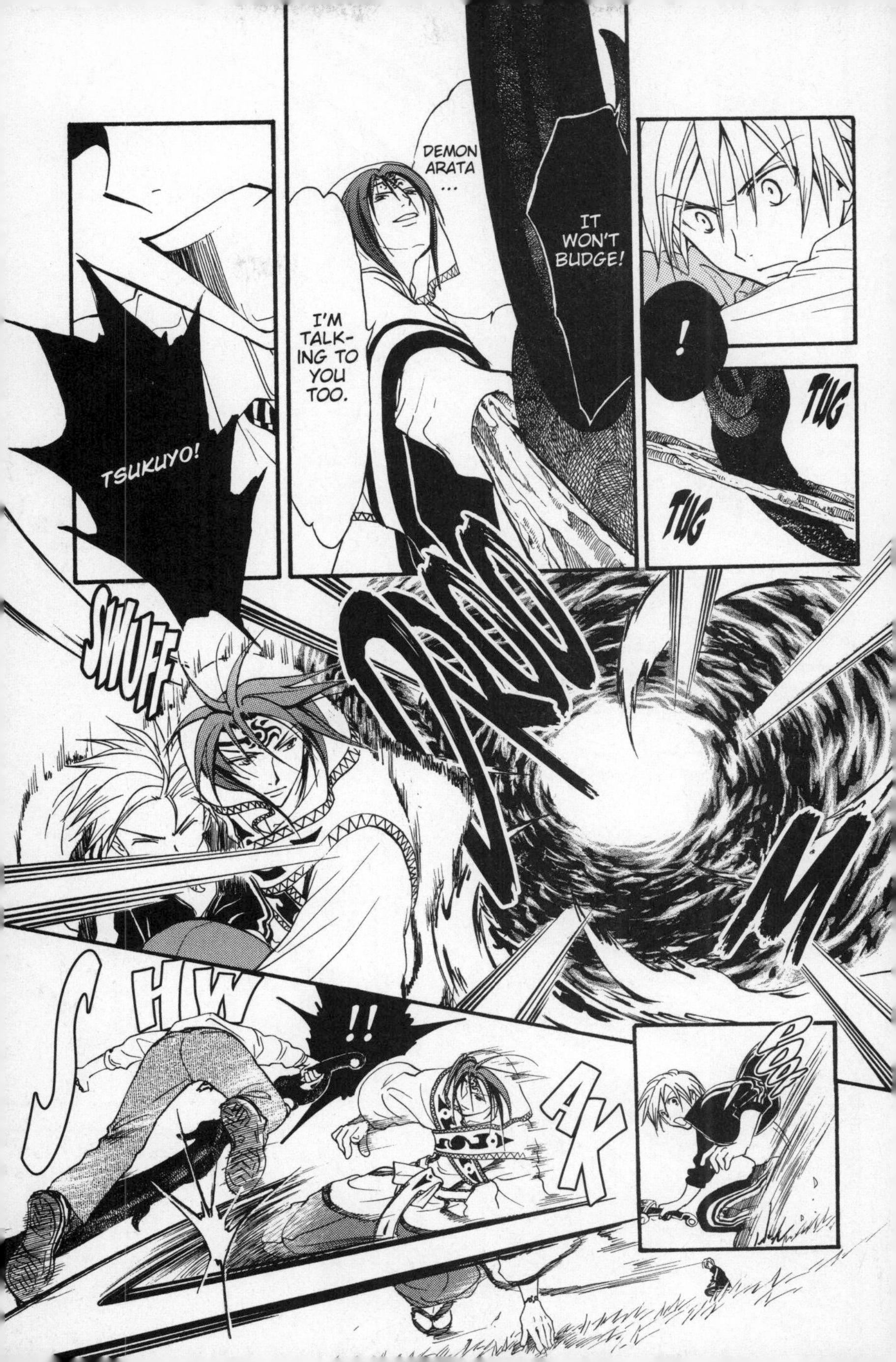

!
TUG
TUG
IT WON'T BUDGE!
DEMON ARATA ...
I'M TALKING TO YOU TOO.
TSUKUYO!
SWUFF
SHW
AK
!!

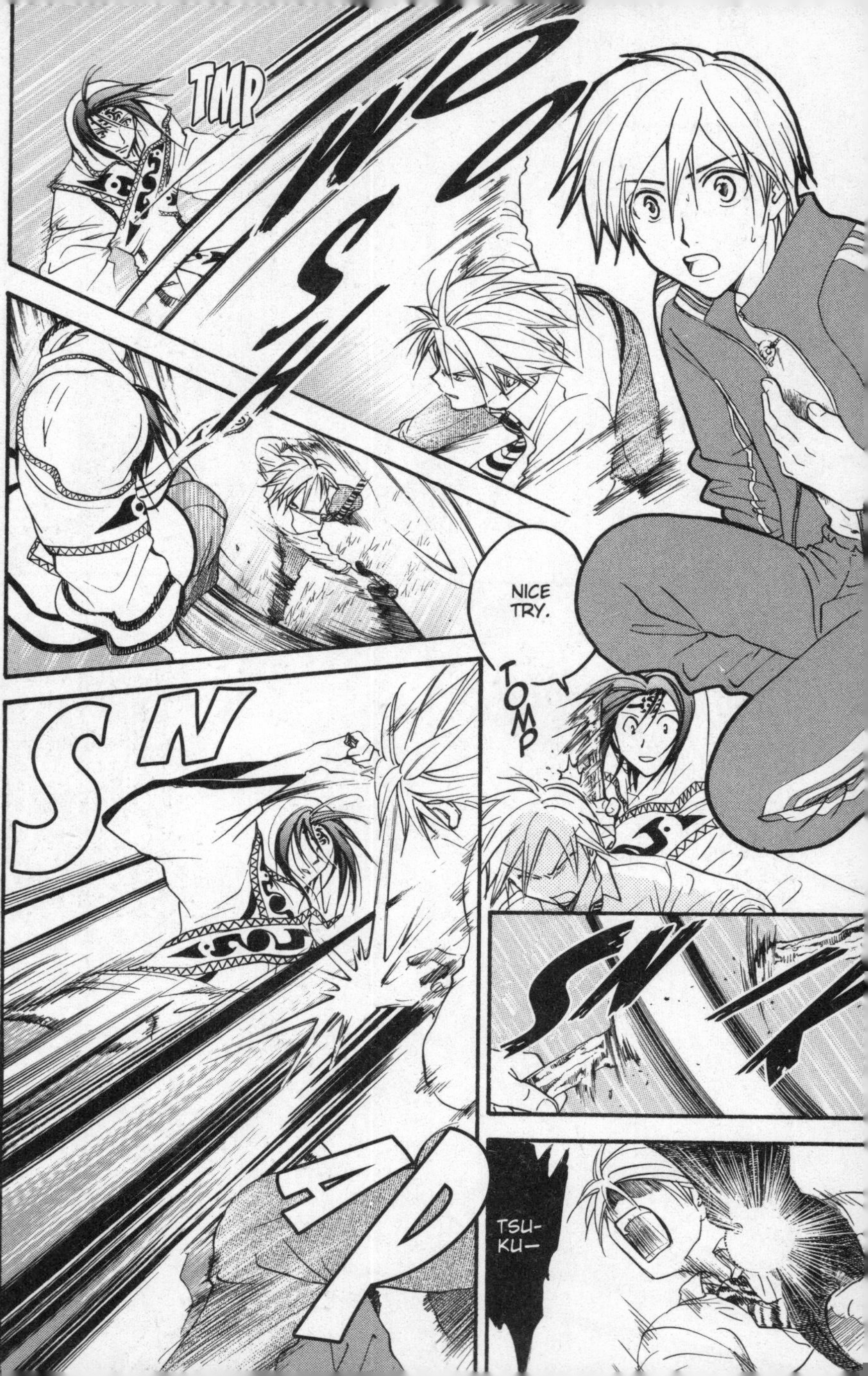
WOOSH
TMP
NICE TRY.
TOMP
TSUKU—
SN
AP

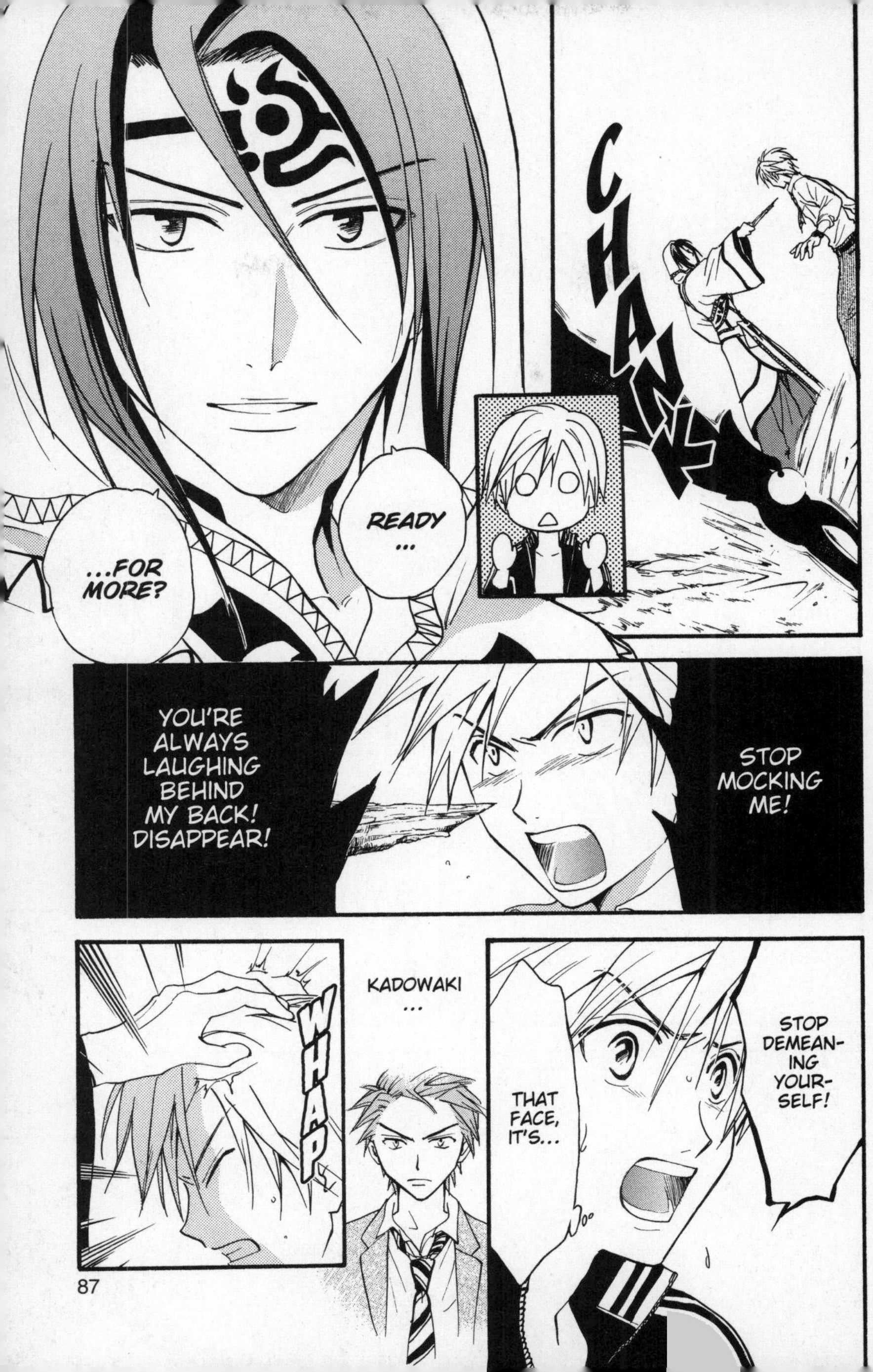
CHANK
READY ...
...FOR MORE?
STOP MOCKING ME!
YOU'RE ALWAYS LAUGHING BEHIND MY BACK! DISAPPEAR!
STOP DEMEANING YOURSELF!
THAT FACE, IT'S...
KADOWAKI ...
WHAP

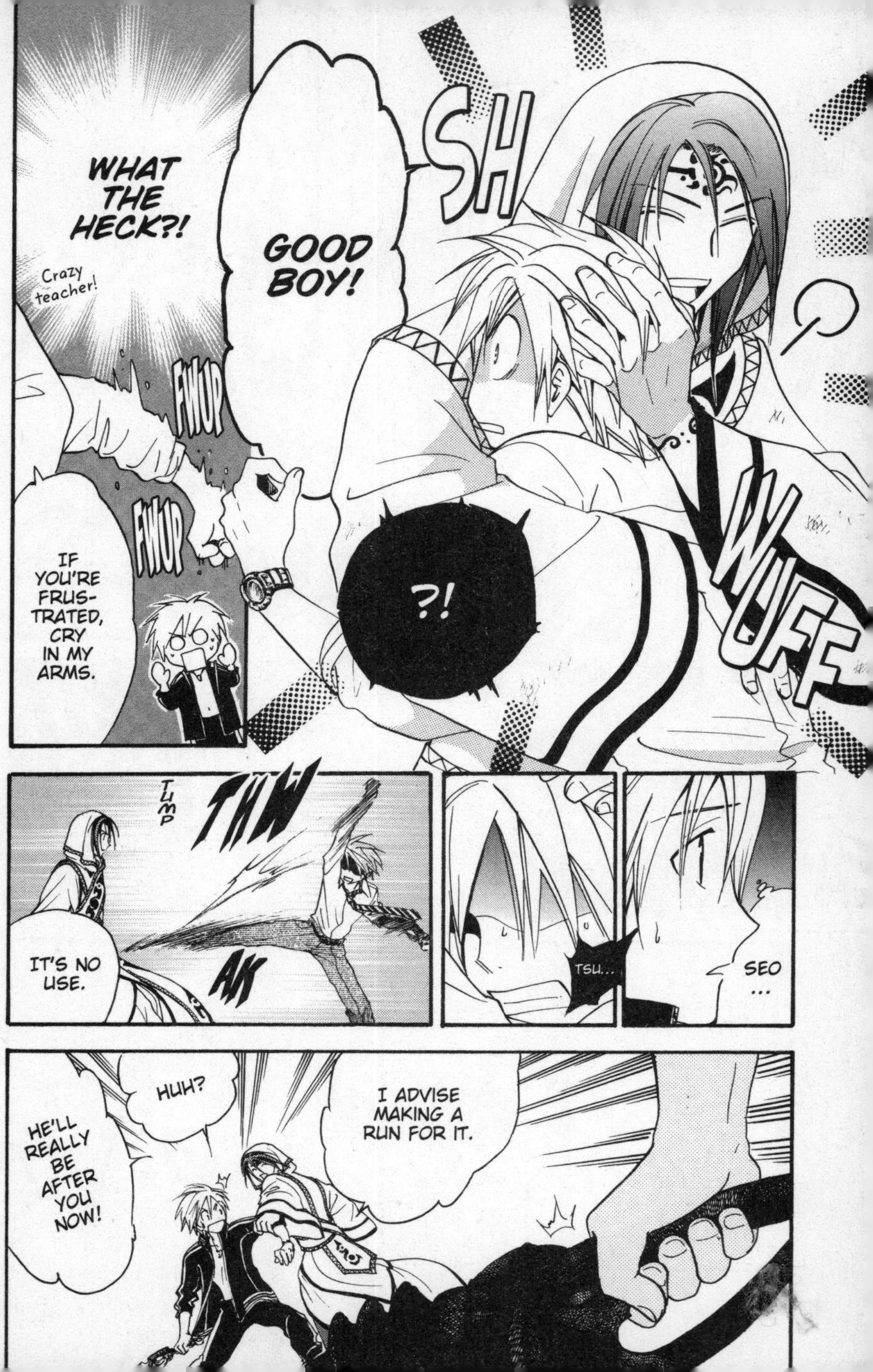
SH
GOOD BOY!
?
WUFF
?!
WHAT THE HECK?!
Crazy teacher!
FWUP
FWUP
IF YOU'RE FRUS-TRATED, CRY IN MY ARMS.
SEO ...
TSU...
THW
AK
TUMP
IT'S NO USE.
I ADVISE MAKING A RUN FOR IT.
HUH?
HE'LL REALLY BE AFTER YOU NOW!

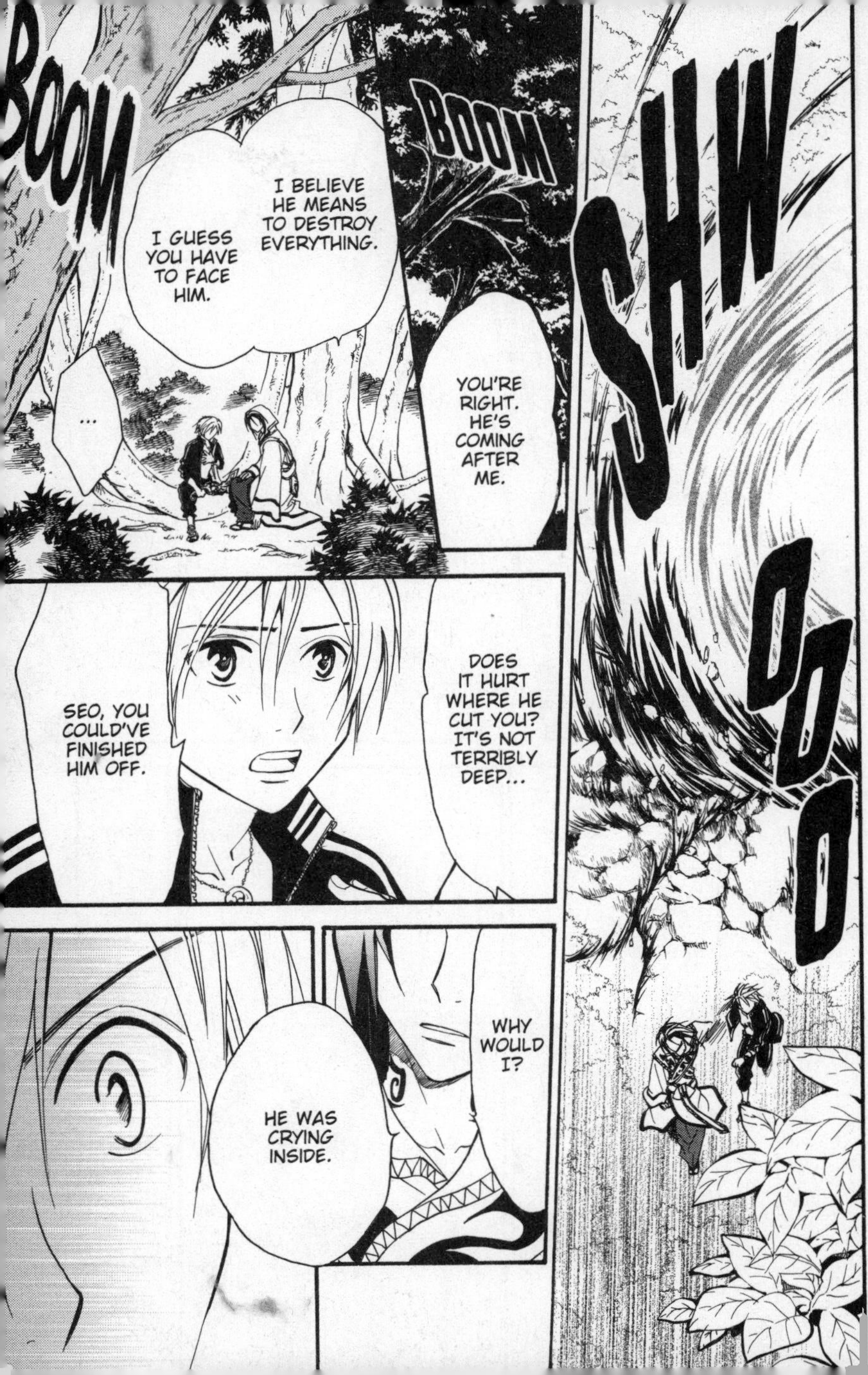
SHW
SSO
BOOM
YOU'RE RIGHT. HE'S COMING AFTER ME.
BOOM
I BELIEVE HE MEANS TO DESTROY EVERYTHING.
I GUESS YOU HAVE TO FACE HIM.
...
DOES IT HURT WHERE HE CUT YOU? IT'S NOT TERRIBLY DEEP...
SEO, YOU COULD'VE FINISHED HIM OFF.
WHY WOULD I?
HE WAS CRYING INSIDE.

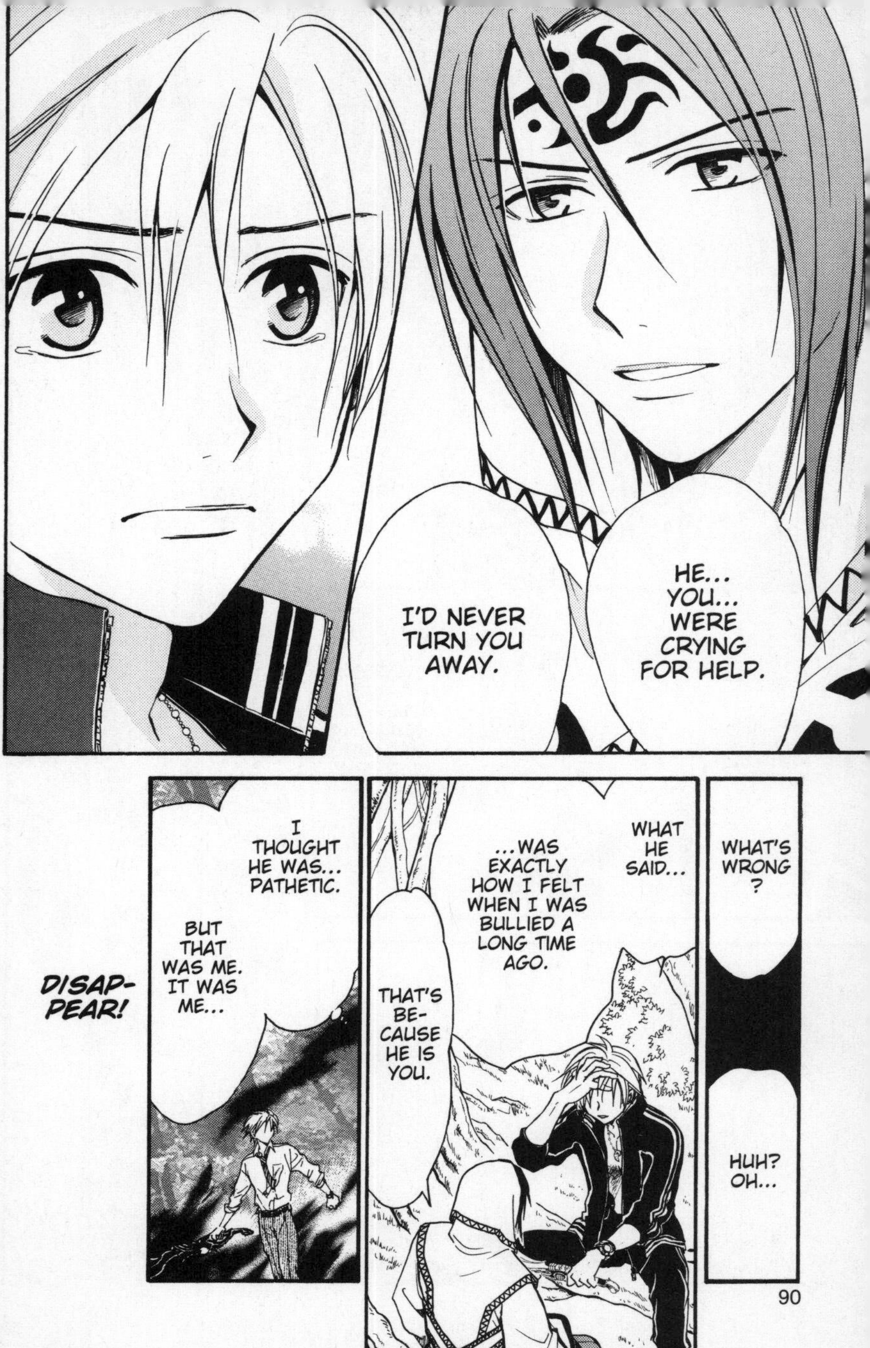
HE... YOU... WERE CRYING FOR HELP.
I'D NEVER TURN YOU AWAY.
WHAT'S WRONG ?
HUH? OH...
WHAT HE SAID...
...WAS EXACTLY HOW I FELT WHEN I WAS BULLIED A LONG TIME AGO.
THAT'S BE-CAUSE HE IS YOU.
I THOUGHT HE WAS... PATHETIC.
BUT THAT WAS ME. IT WAS ME...
DISAP-PEAR!

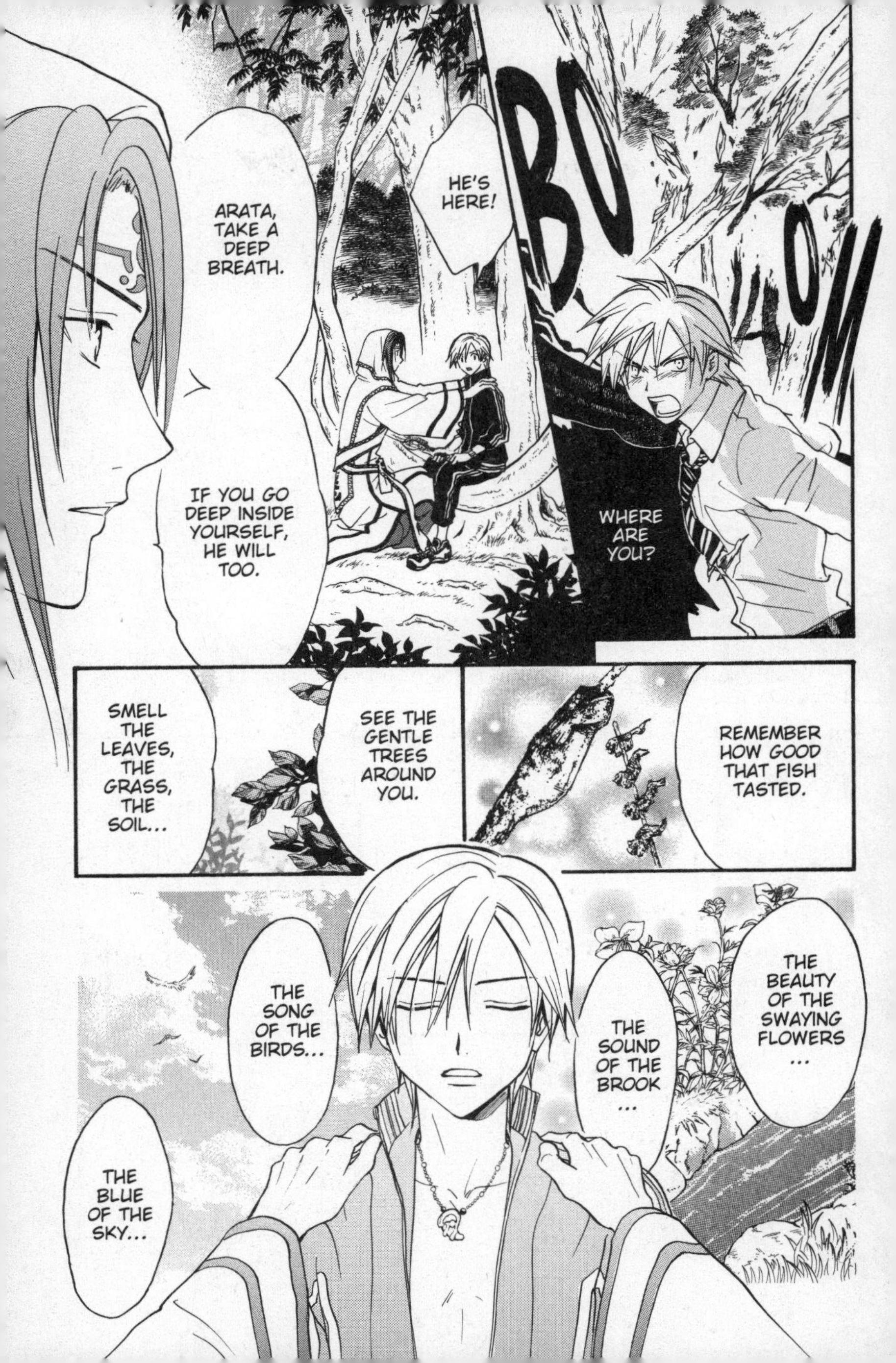
BOOM
HE'S HERE!
WHERE ARE YOU?
ARATA, TAKE A DEEP BREATH.
IF YOU GO DEEP INSIDE YOURSELF, HE WILL TOO.
REMEMBER HOW GOOD THAT FISH TASTED.
SEE THE GENTLE TREES AROUND YOU.
SMELL THE LEAVES, THE GRASS, THE SOIL...
THE BEAUTY OF THE SWAYING FLOWERS ...
THE SOUND OF THE BROOK ...
THE SONG OF THE BIRDS...
THE BLUE OF THE SKY...

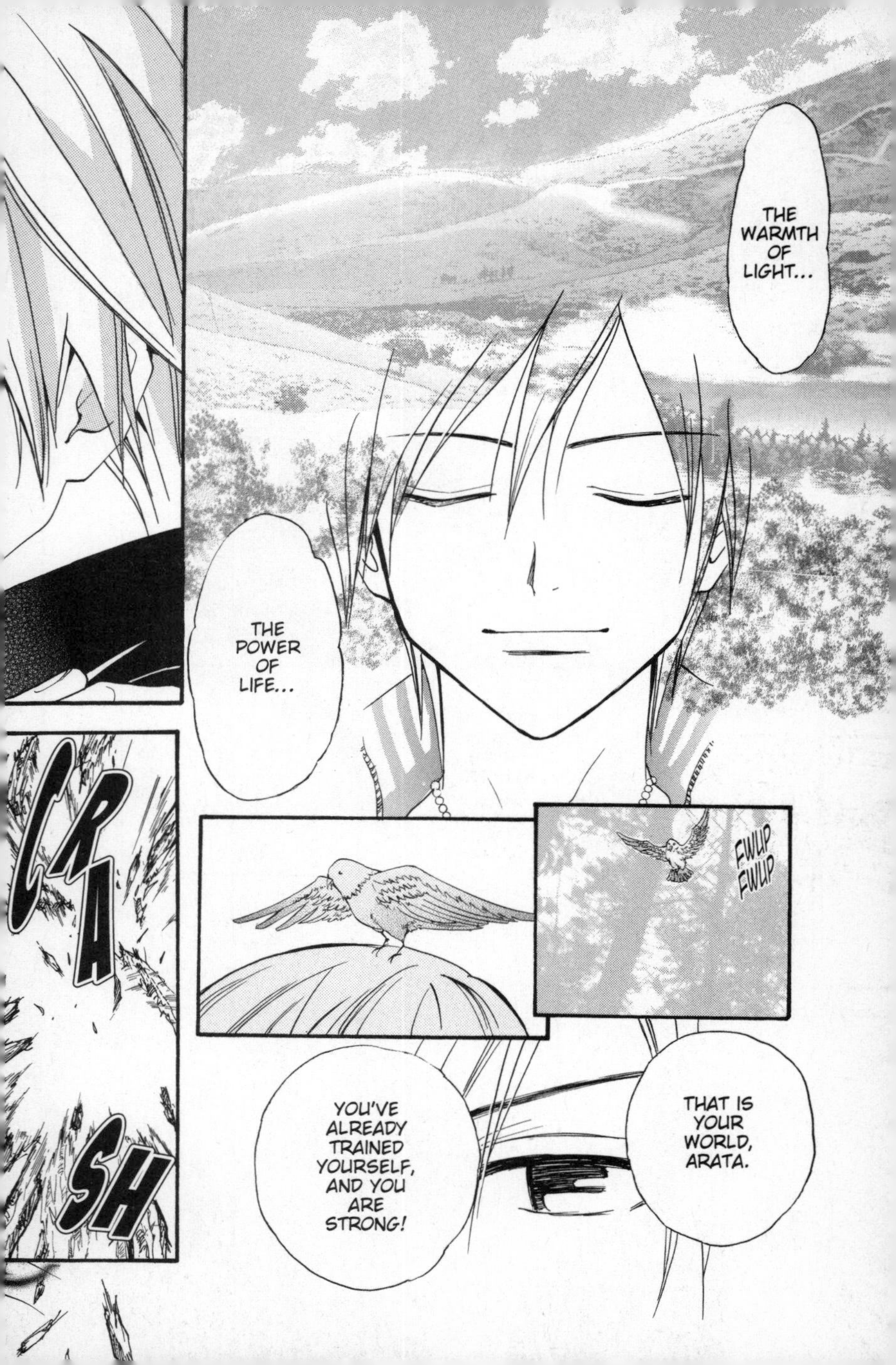
THE WARMTH OF LIGHT...
THE POWER OF LIFE...
FWUP FWUP
THAT IS YOUR WORLD, ARATA.
YOU'VE ALREADY TRAINED YOURSELF, AND YOU ARE STRONG!
CRASH

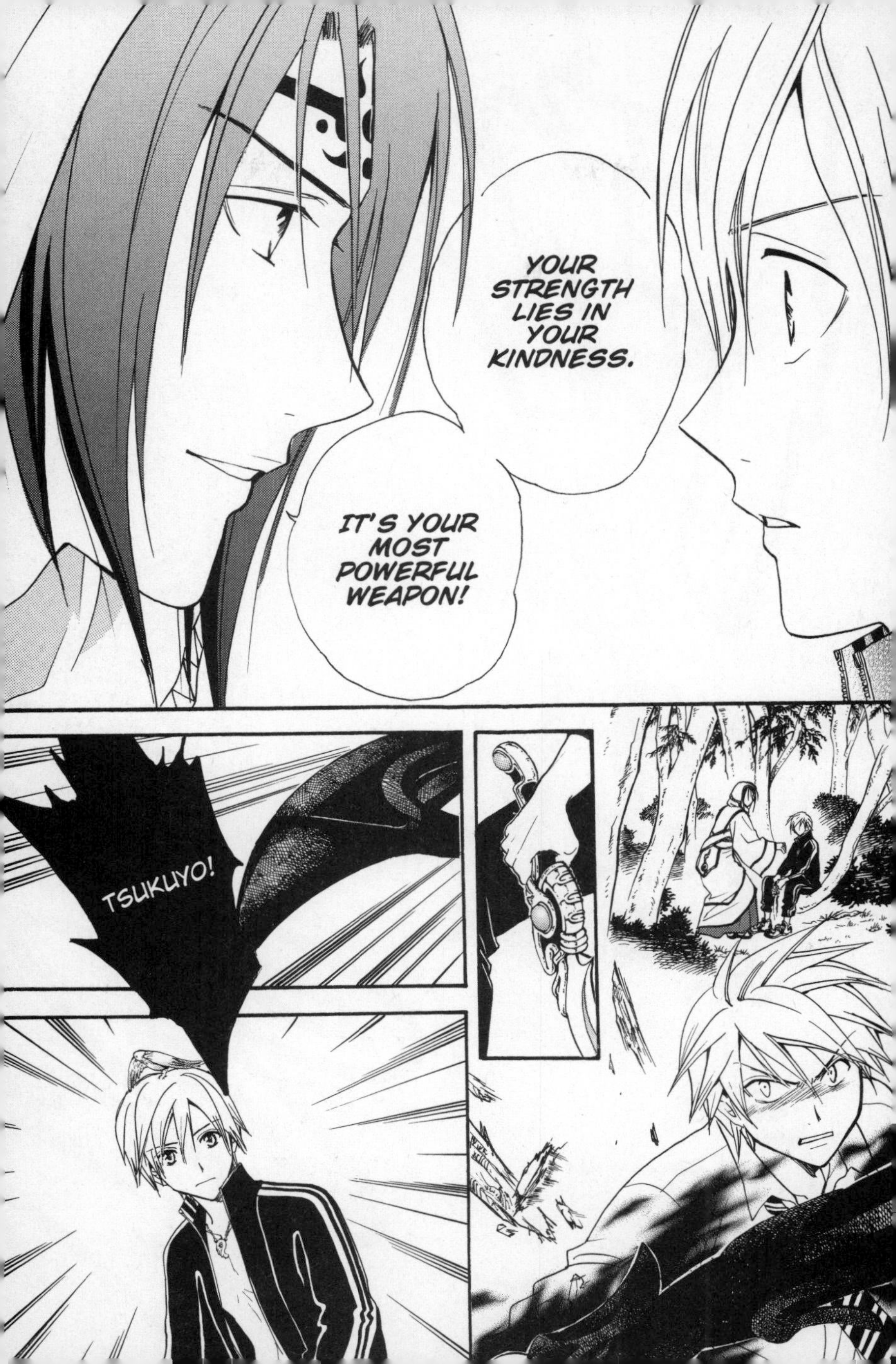
YOUR STRENGTH LIES IN YOUR KINDNESS.
IT'S YOUR MOST POWERFUL WEAPON!
TSUKUYO!

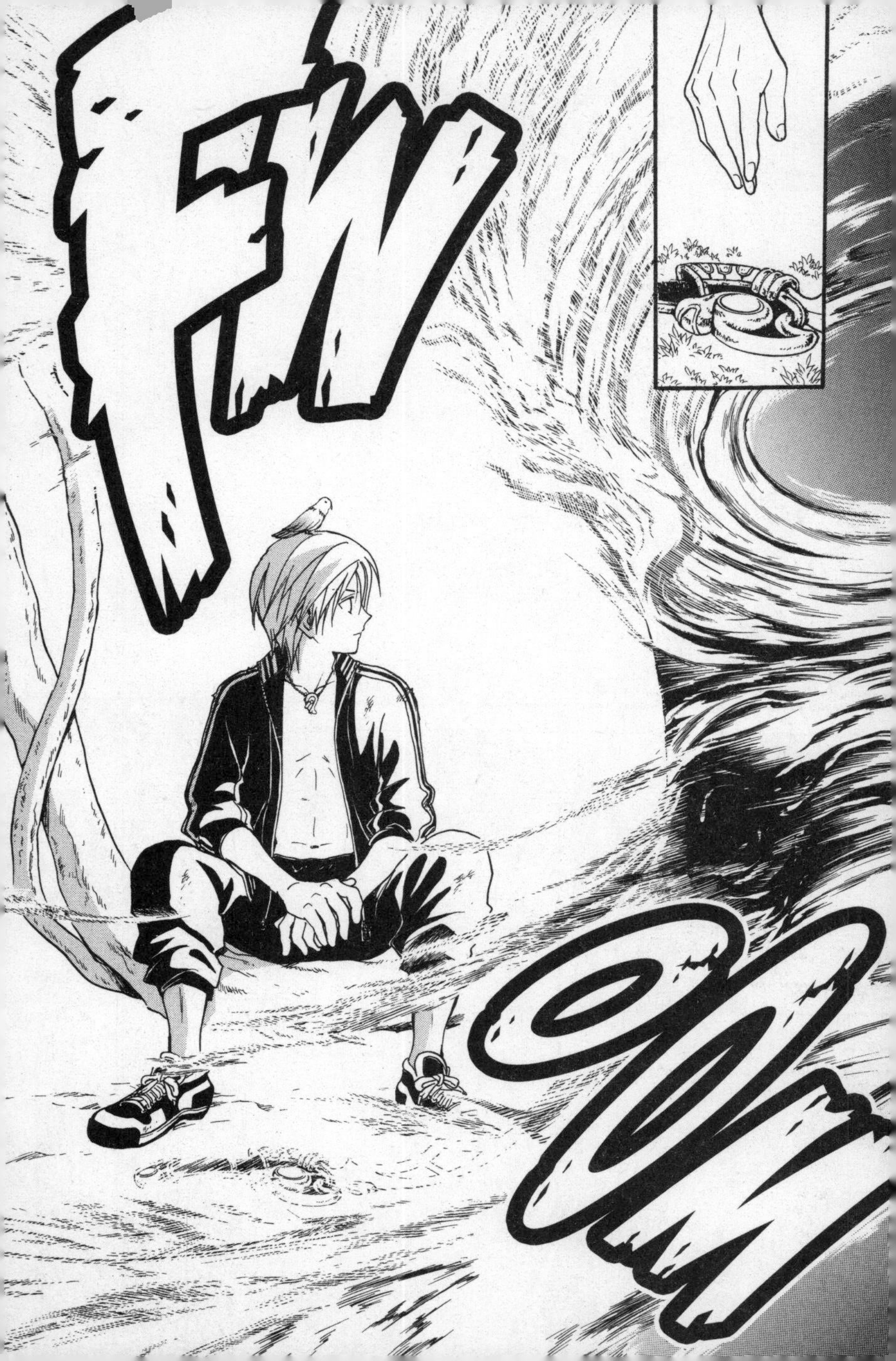
FW
OOM

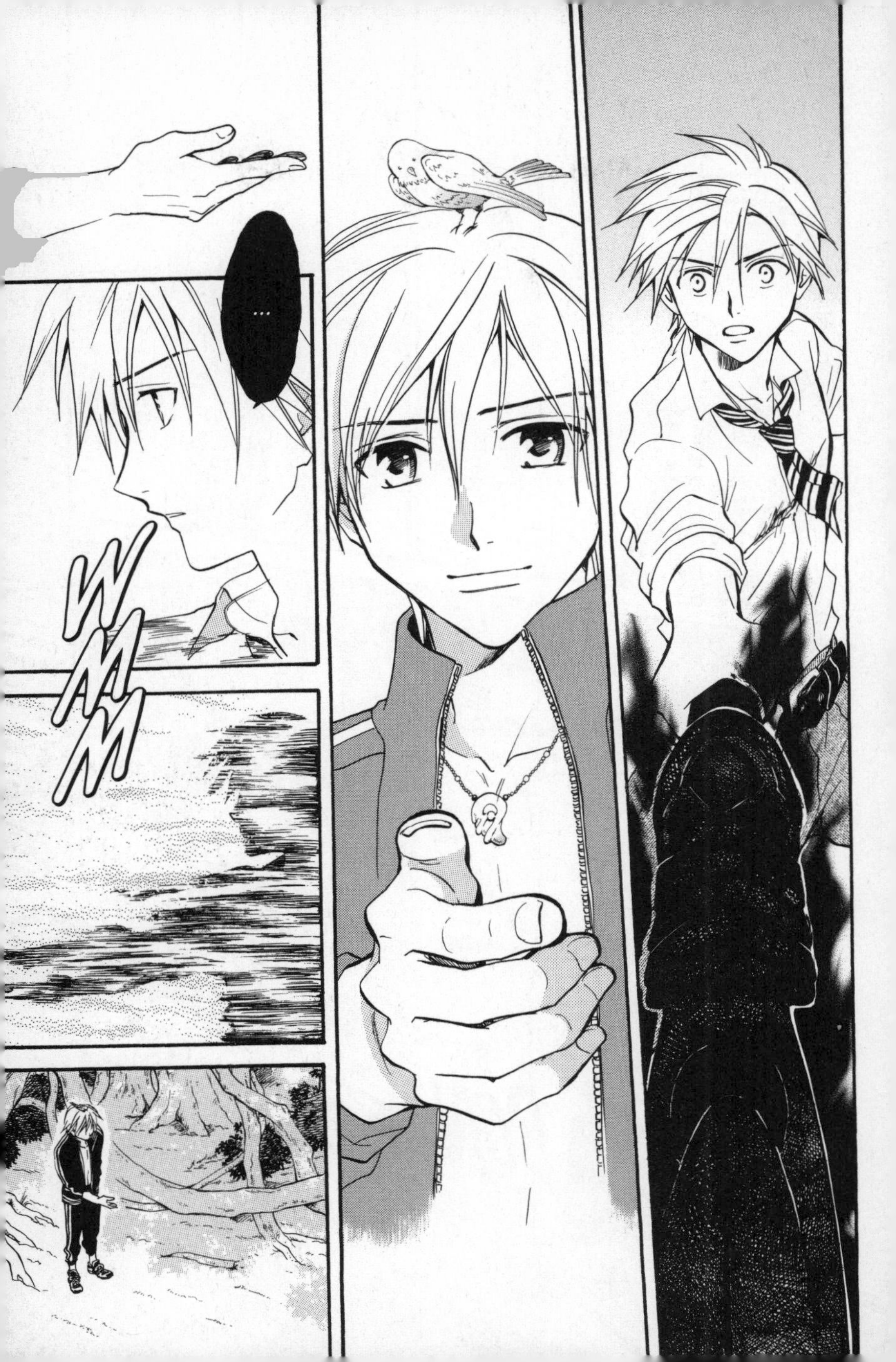
...
WHAM

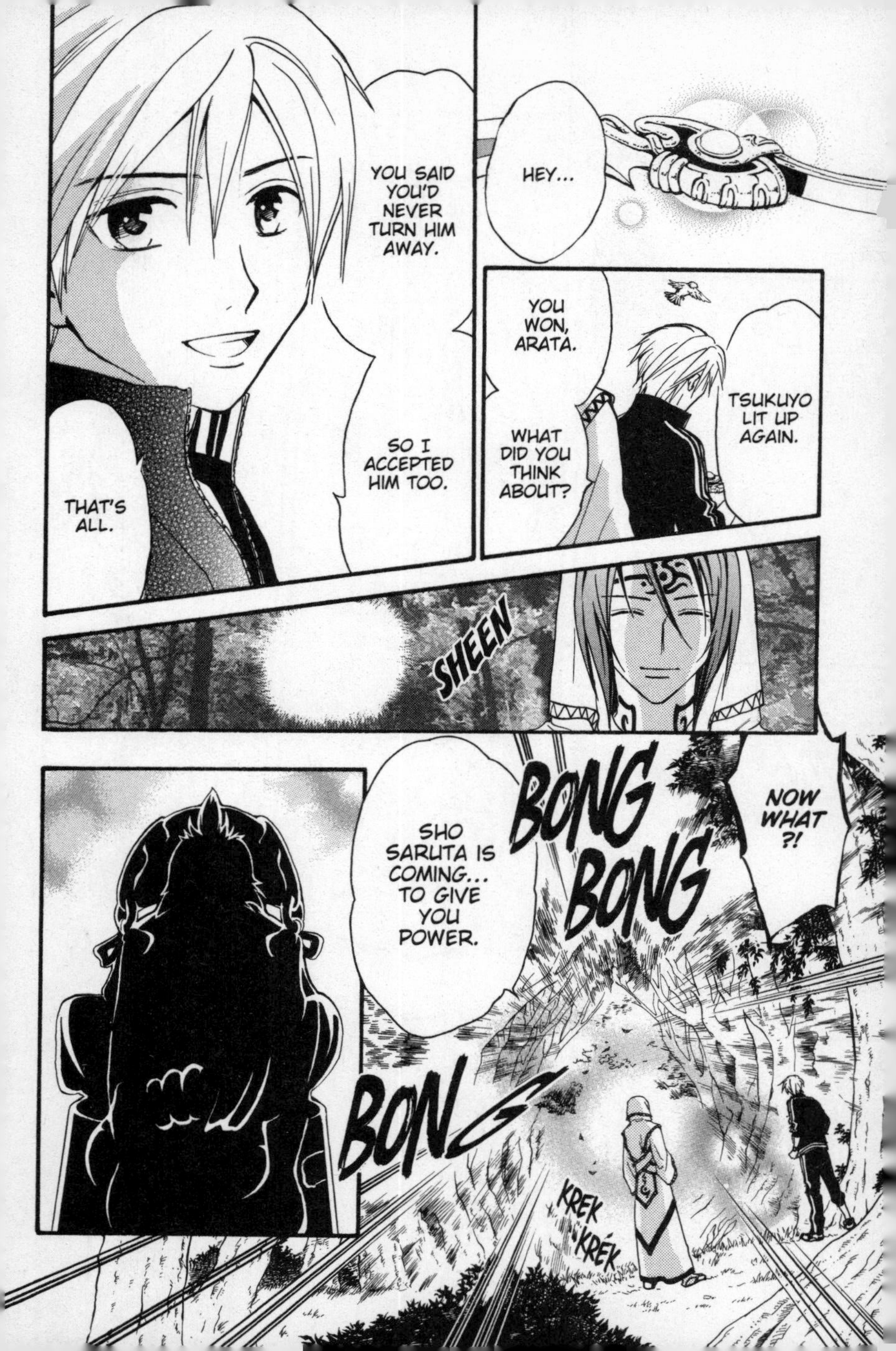
HEY...
TSUKUYO LIT UP AGAIN.
YOU WON, ARATA.
WHAT DID YOU THINK ABOUT?
YOU SAID YOU'D NEVER TURN HIM AWAY.
SO I ACCEPTED HIM TOO.
THAT'S ALL.
SHEEN
NOW WHAT?!
BONG BONG
SHO SARUTA IS COMING... TO GIVE YOU POWER.
BONG
KREK KREK

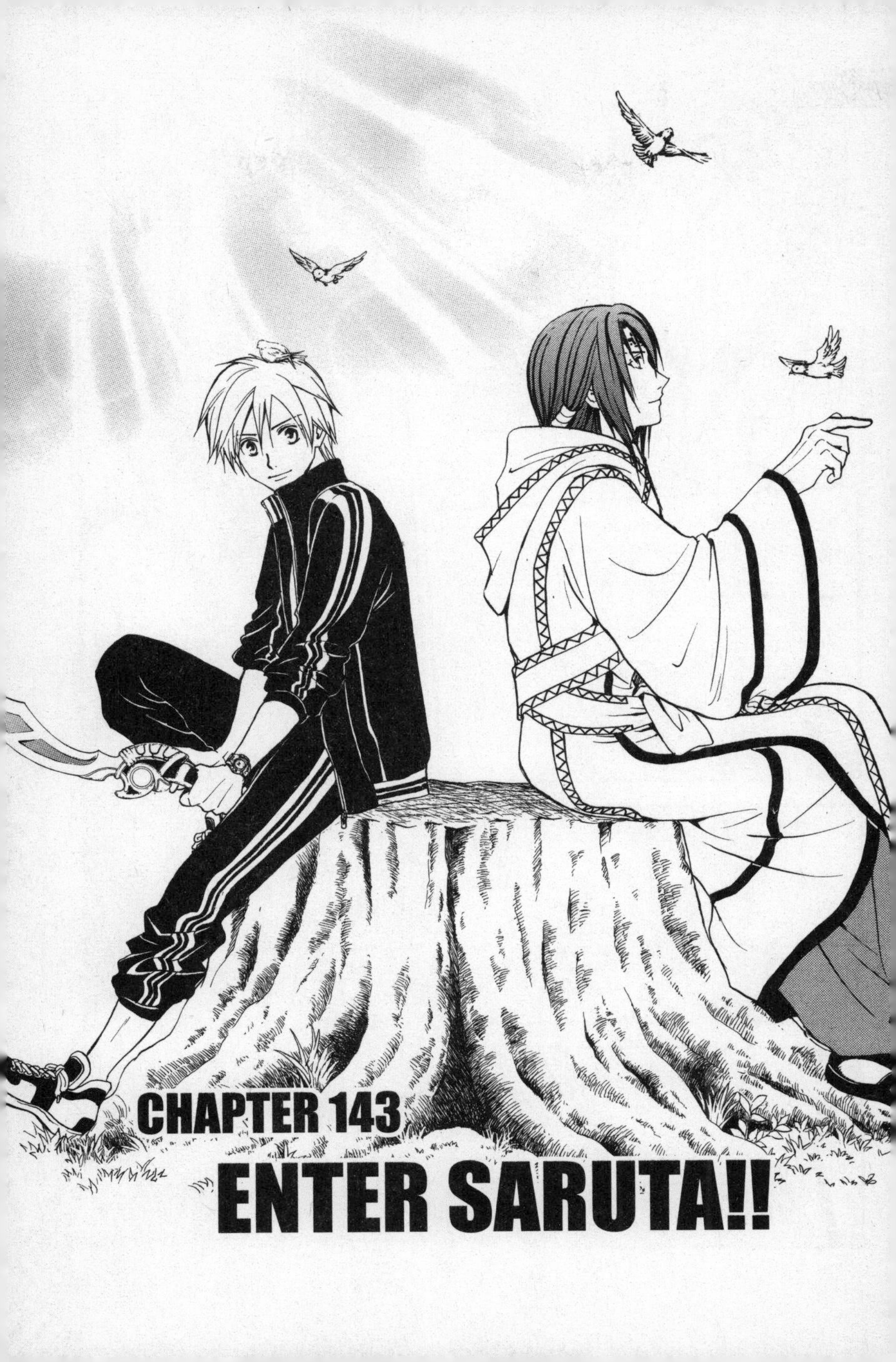
CHAPTER 143
ENTER SARUTA!!

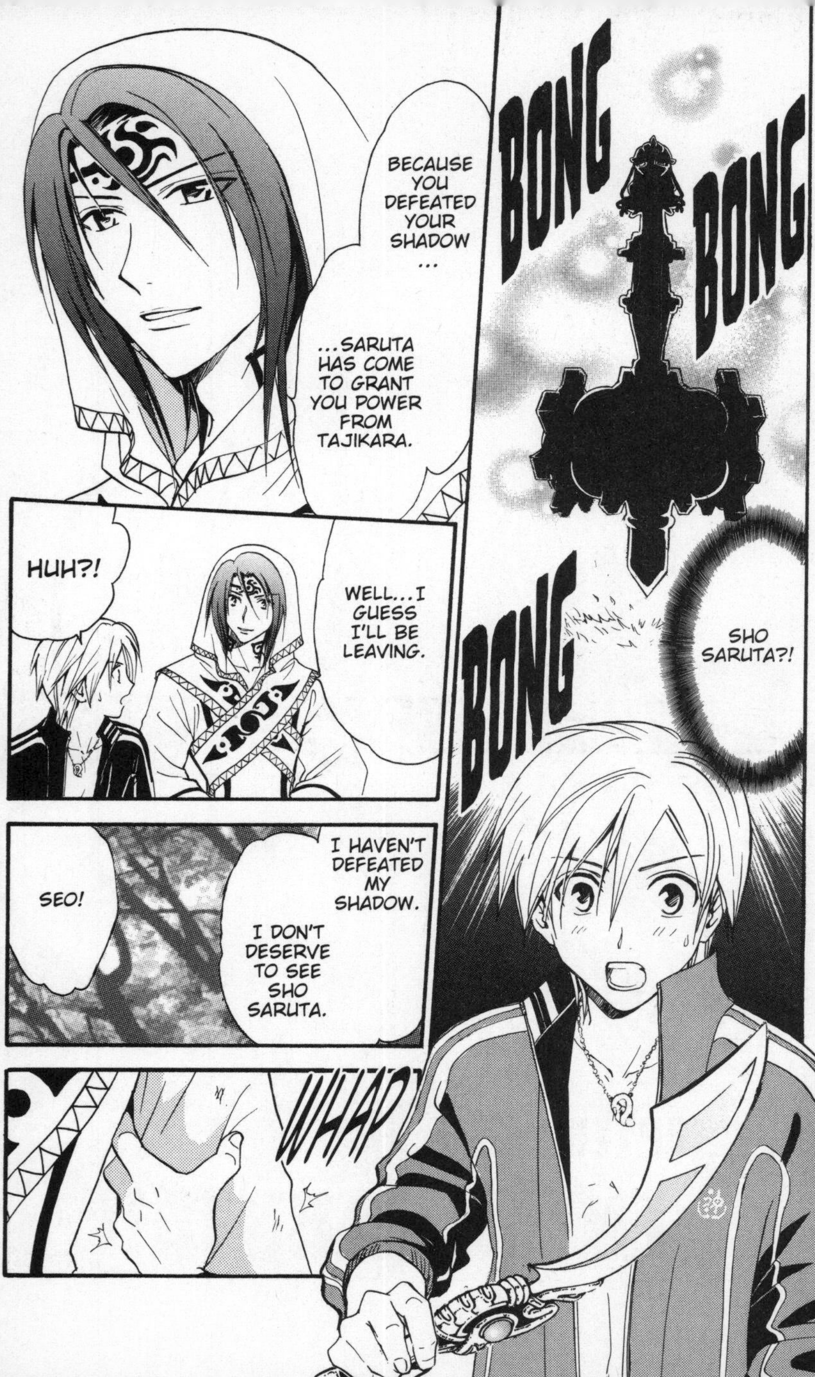
BONG
BONG
BONG
SHO SARUTA?!
BECAUSE YOU DEFEATED YOUR SHADOW ...
...SARUTA HAS COME TO GRANT YOU POWER FROM TAJIKARA.
WELL...I GUESS I'LL BE LEAVING.
HUH?!
I HAVEN'T DEFEATED MY SHADOW.
I DON'T DESERVE TO SEE SHO SARUTA.
SEO!
WHAP

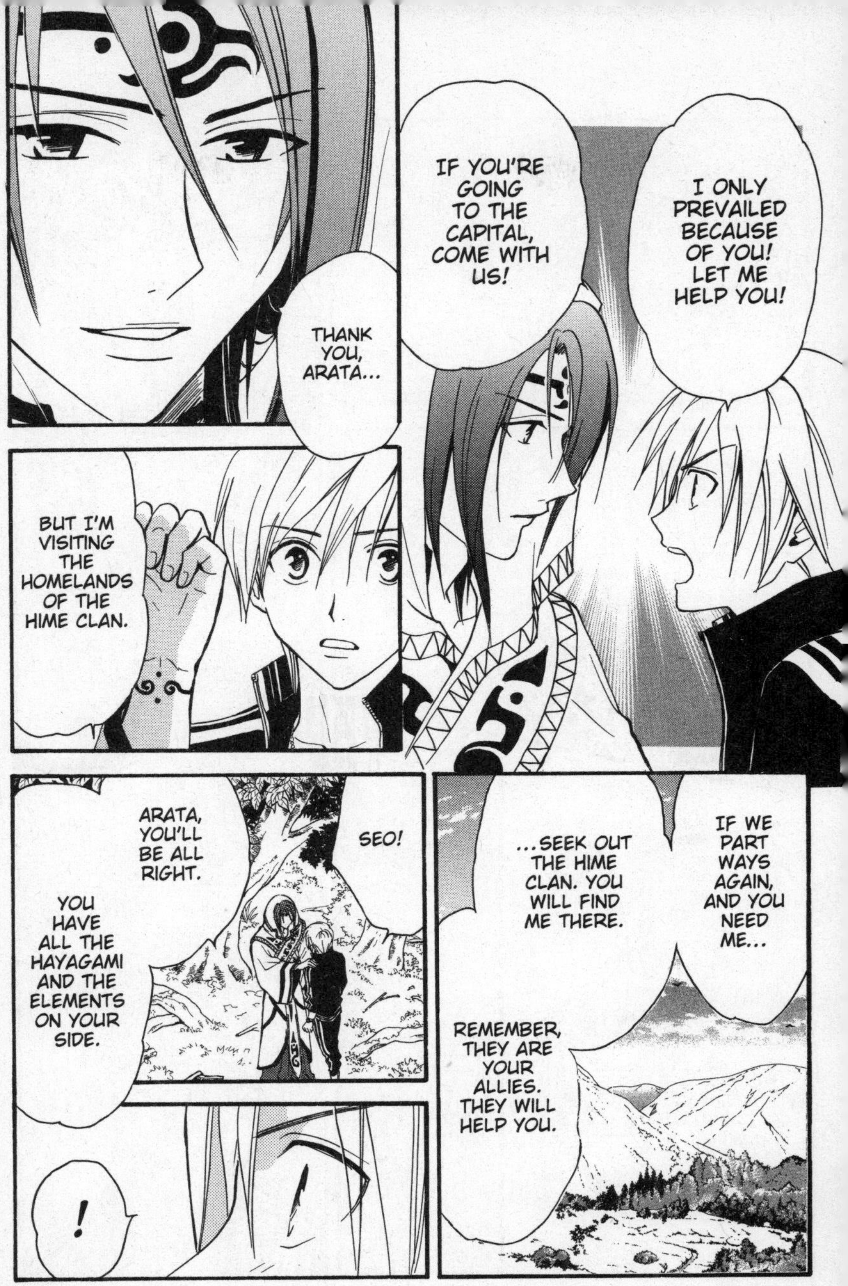
I ONLY PREVAILED BECAUSE OF YOU! LET ME HELP YOU!
IF YOU'RE GOING TO THE CAPITAL, COME WITH US!
THANK YOU, ARATA...
BUT I'M VISITING THE HOMELANDS OF THE HIME CLAN.
IF WE PART WAYS AGAIN, AND YOU NEED ME...
...SEEK OUT THE HIME CLAN. YOU WILL FIND ME THERE.
REMEMBER, THEY ARE YOUR ALLIES. THEY WILL HELP YOU.
SEO!
ARATA, YOU'LL BE ALL RIGHT.
YOU HAVE ALL THE HAYAGAMI AND THE ELEMENTS ON YOUR SIDE.
!

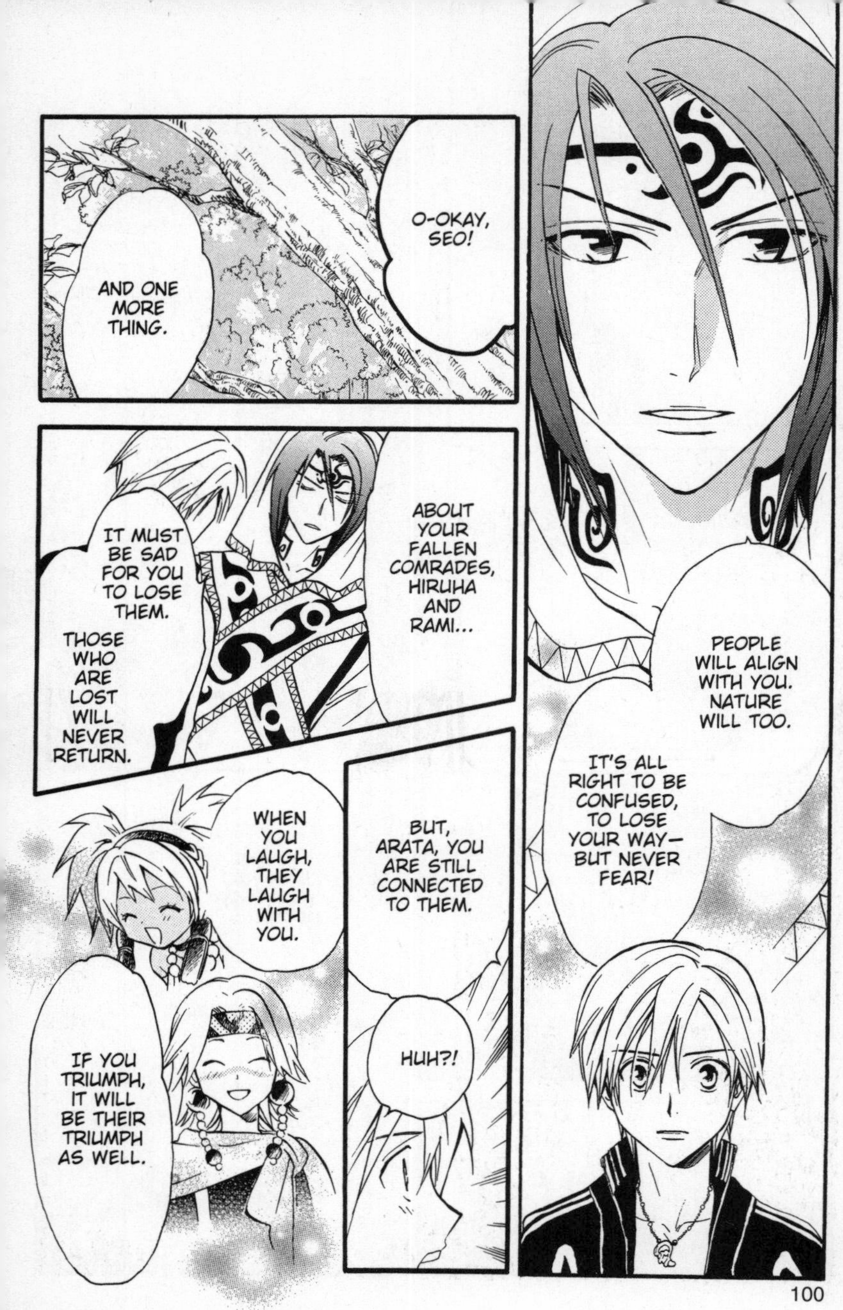

PEOPLE WILL ALIGN WITH YOU. NATURE WILL TOO.
IT'S ALL RIGHT TO BE CONFUSED, TO LOSE YOUR WAY— BUT NEVER FEAR!
O-OKAY, SEO!
AND ONE MORE THING.
ABOUT YOUR FALLEN COMRADES, HIRUHA AND RAMI...
IT MUST BE SAD FOR YOU TO LOSE THEM.
THOSE WHO ARE LOST WILL NEVER RETURN.
BUT, ARATA, YOU ARE STILL CONNECTED TO THEM.
HUH?!
WHEN YOU LAUGH, THEY LAUGH WITH YOU.
IF YOU TRIUMPH, IT WILL BE THEIR TRIUMPH AS WELL.

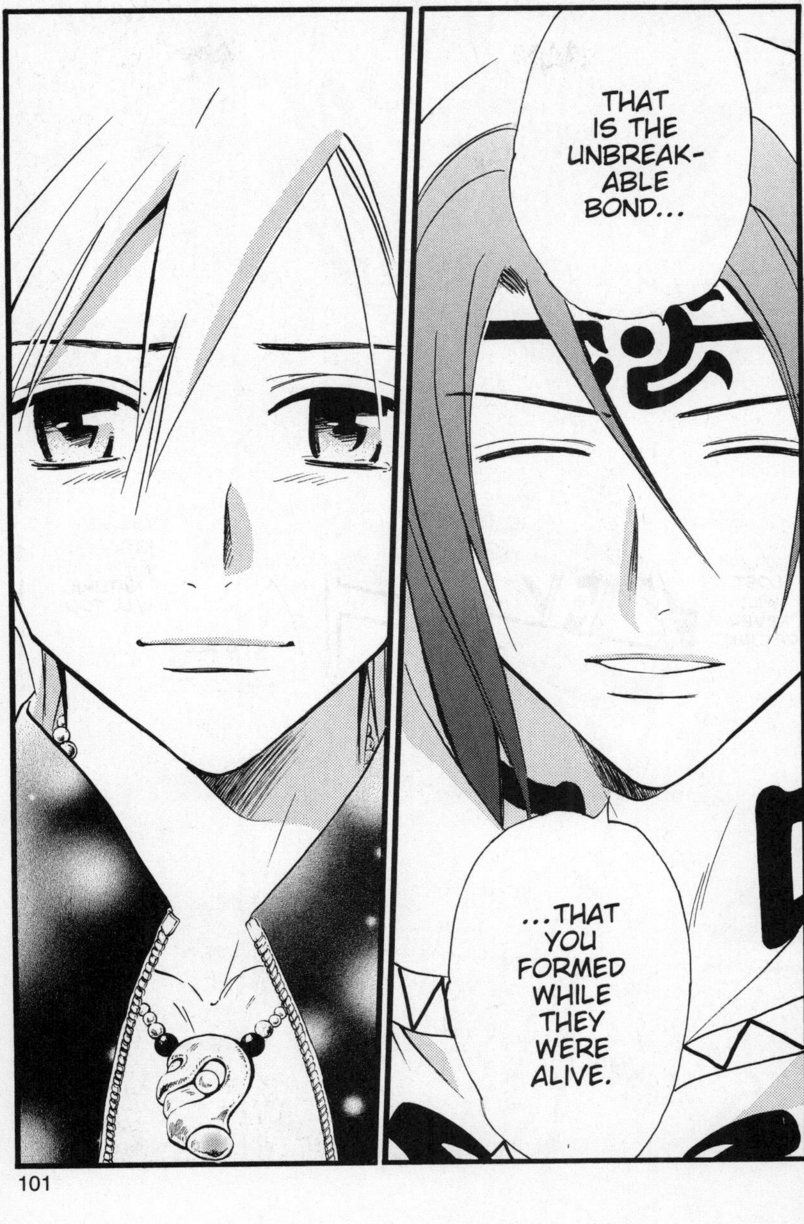
THAT IS THE UNBREAK-ABLE BOND...
...THAT YOU FORMED WHILE THEY WERE ALIVE.

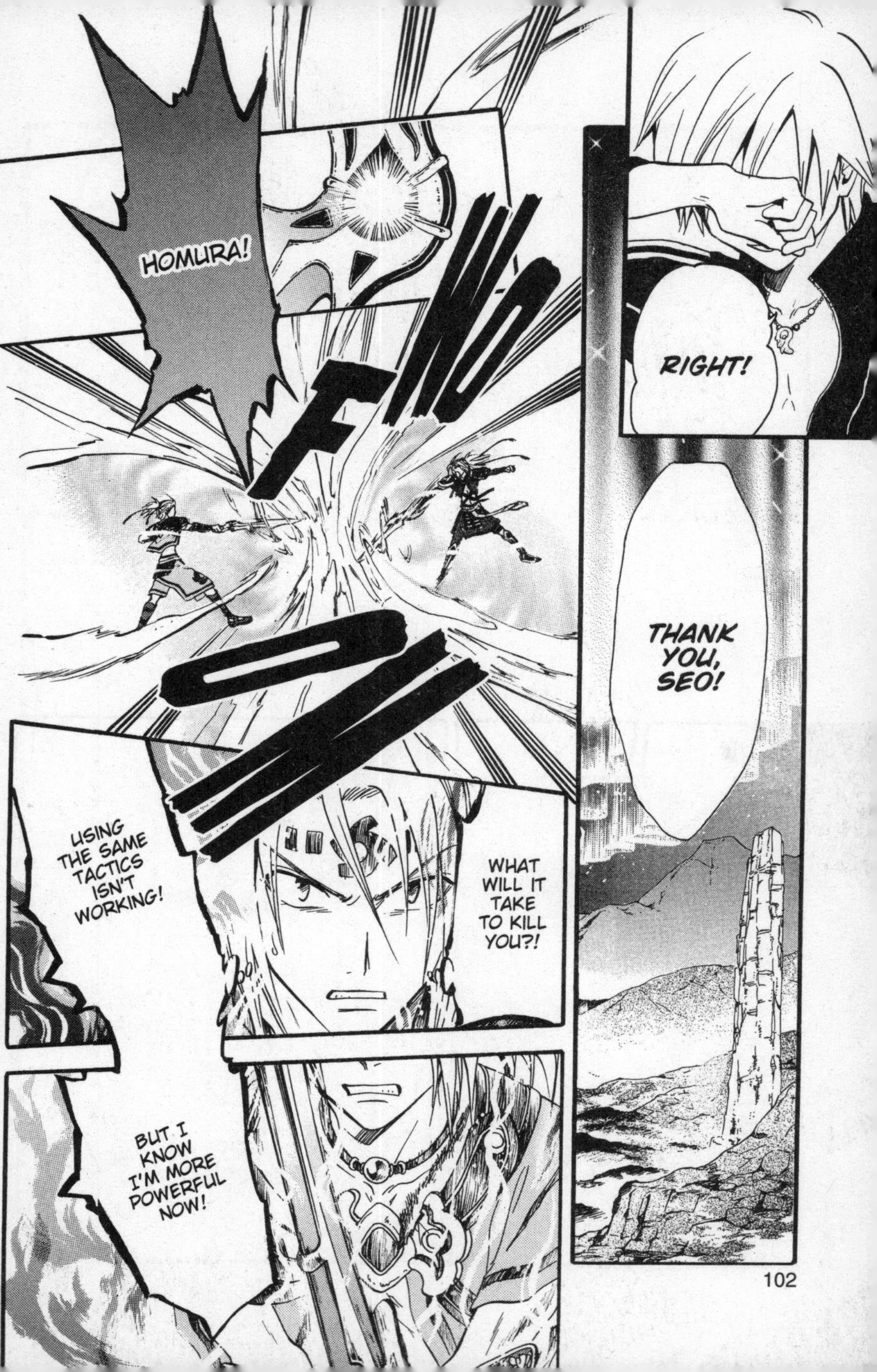

RIGHT!
THANK YOU, SEO!
HOMURA!
FWOOM
WHAT WILL IT TAKE TO KILL YOU?!
USING THE SAME TACTICS ISN'T WORKING!
BUT I KNOW I'M MORE POWERFUL NOW!

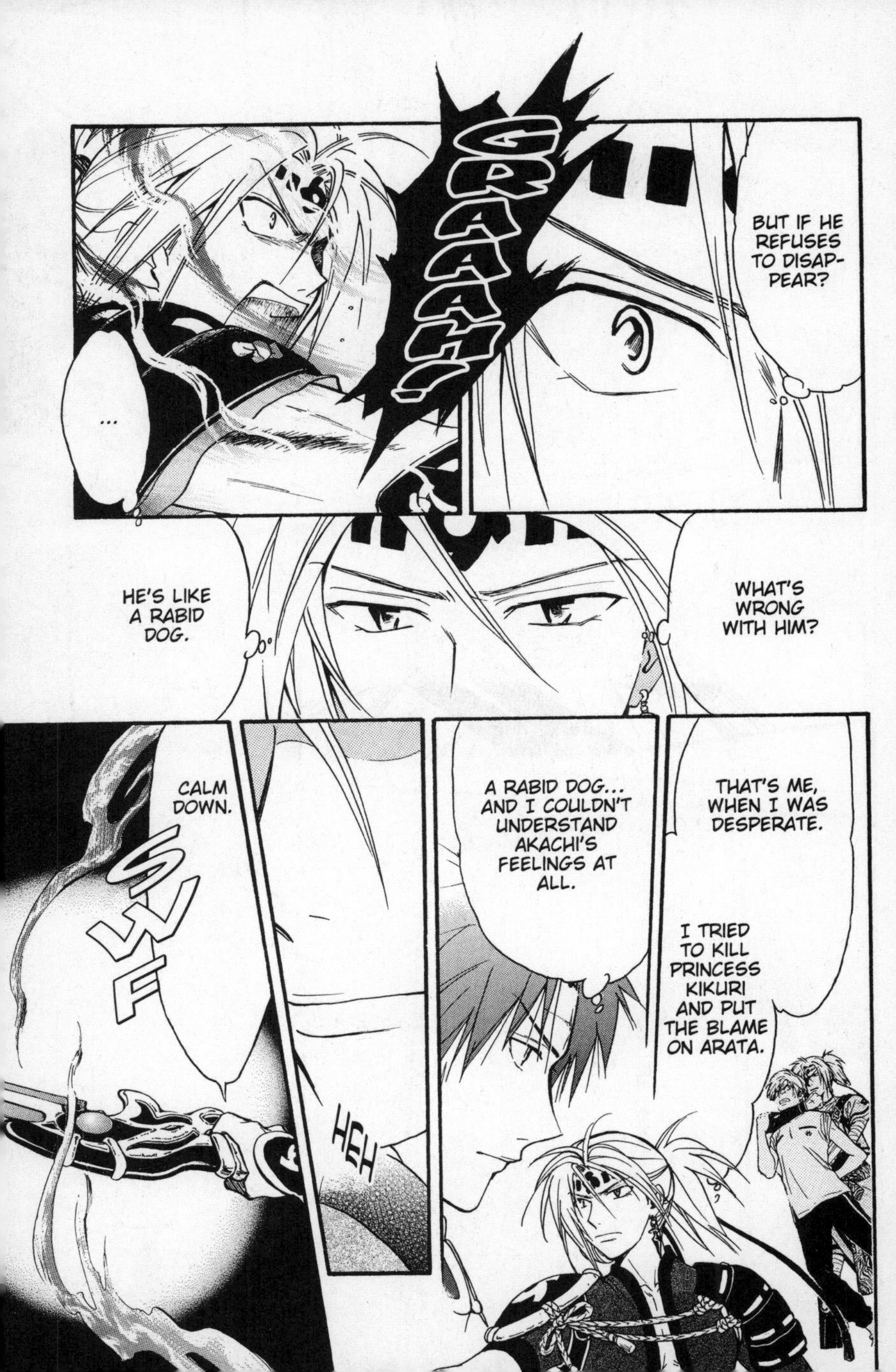
BUT IF HE REFUSES TO DISAP-PEAR?
GRAAAH!
...
WHAT'S WRONG WITH HIM?
HE'S LIKE A RABID DOG.
THAT'S ME, WHEN I WAS DESPERATE.
I TRIED TO KILL PRINCESS KIKURI AND PUT THE BLAME ON ARATA.
A RABID DOG... AND I COULDN'T UNDERSTAND AKACHI'S FEELINGS AT ALL.
HEH
CALM DOWN.
SWF

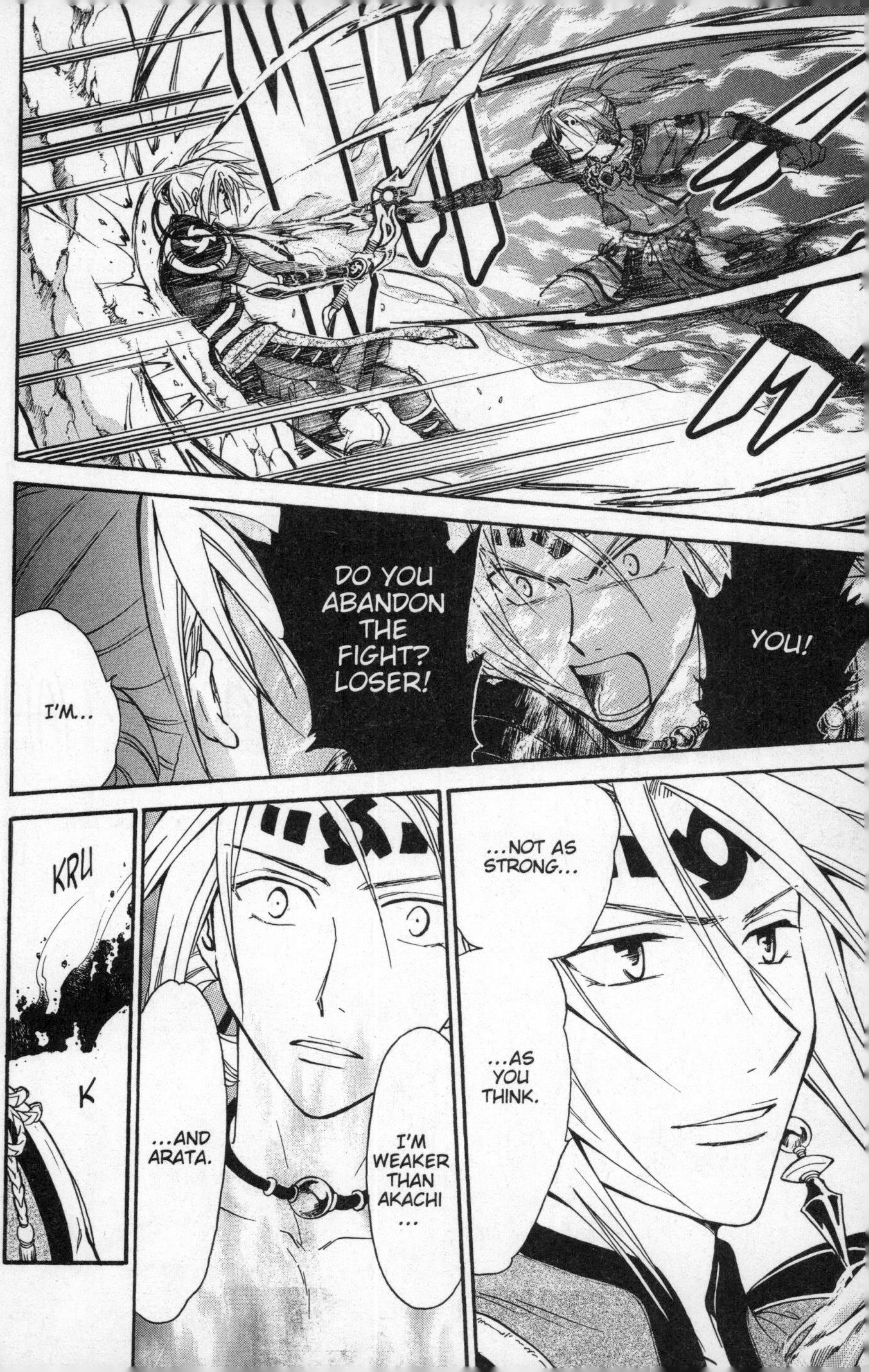
YOU!
DO YOU ABANDON THE FIGHT? LOSER!
I'M...
...NOT AS STRONG...
...AS YOU THINK.
I'M WEAKER THAN AKACHI ...
...AND ARATA.
KRU
K

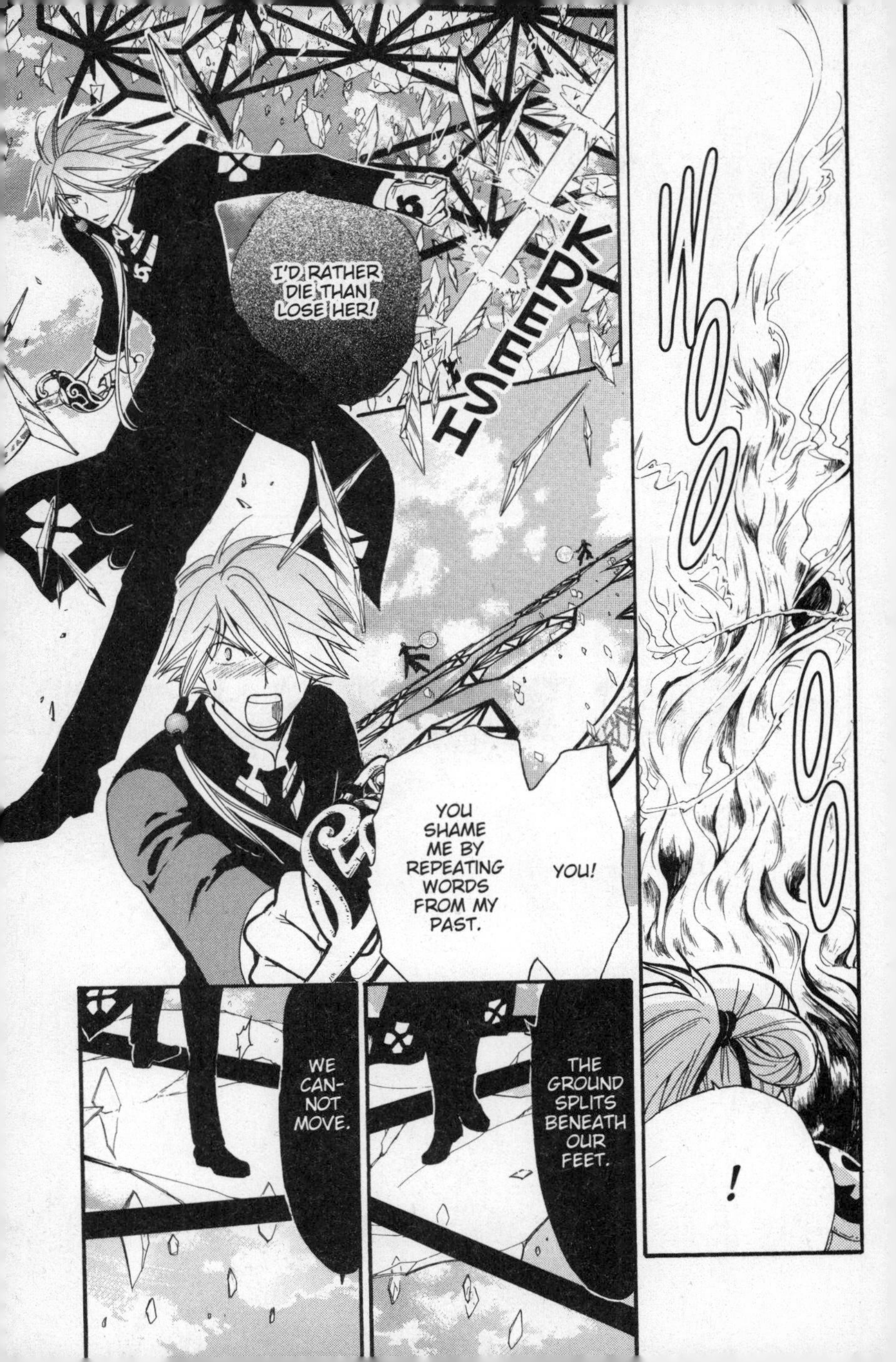

WOOOOOO
!
KREEESH
I'D RATHER DIE THAN LOSE HER!
YOU!
YOU SHAME ME BY REPEATING WORDS FROM MY PAST.
THE GROUND SPLITS BENEATH OUR FEET.
WE CAN-NOT MOVE.

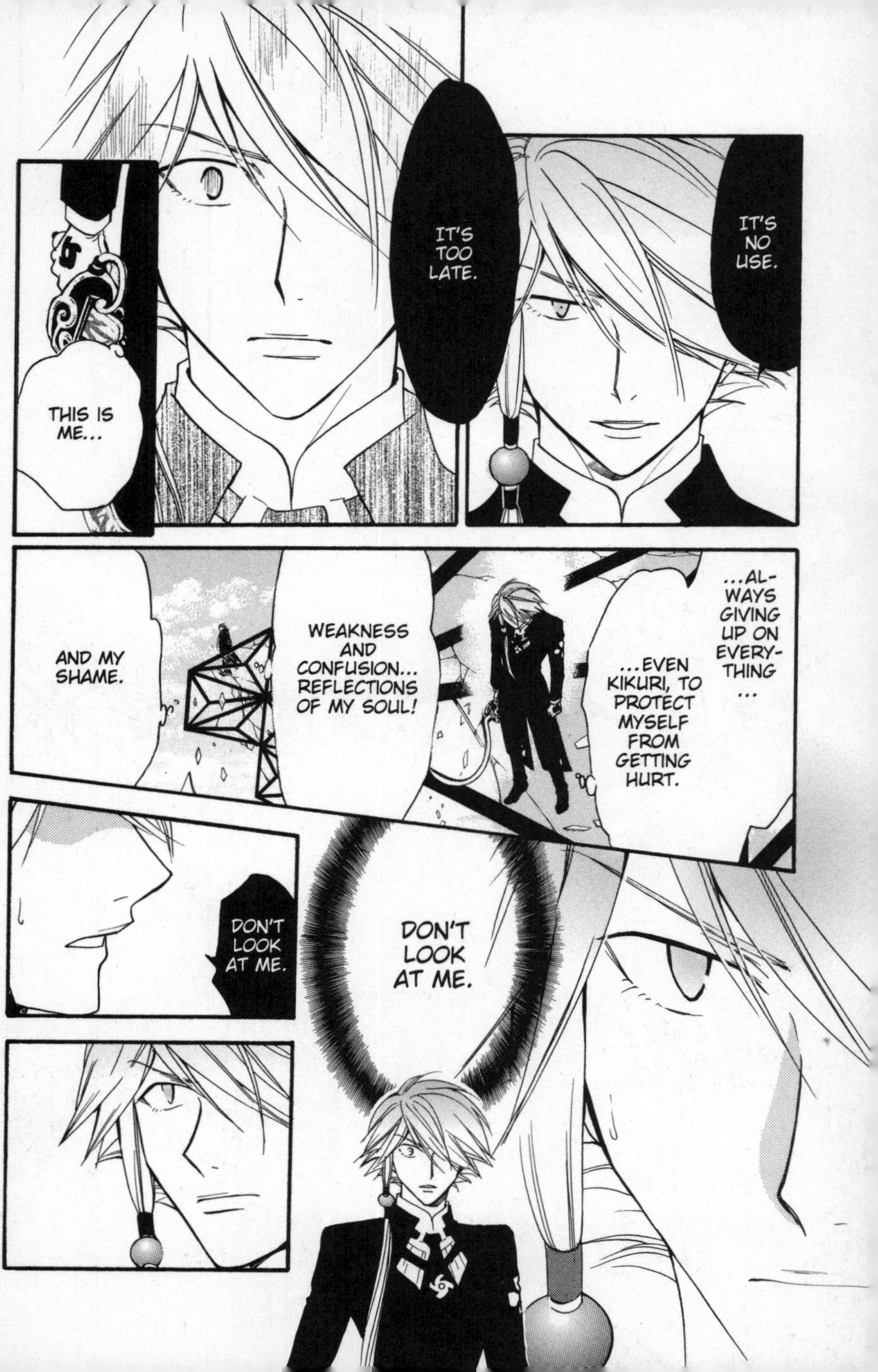
IT'S NO USE.
IT'S TOO LATE.
THIS IS ME...
...AL-WAYS GIVING UP ON EVERY-THING ...
...EVEN KIKURI, TO PROTECT MYSELF FROM GETTING HURT.
WEAKNESS AND CONFUSION... REFLECTIONS OF MY SOUL!
AND MY SHAME.
DON'T LOOK AT ME.
DON'T LOOK AT ME.

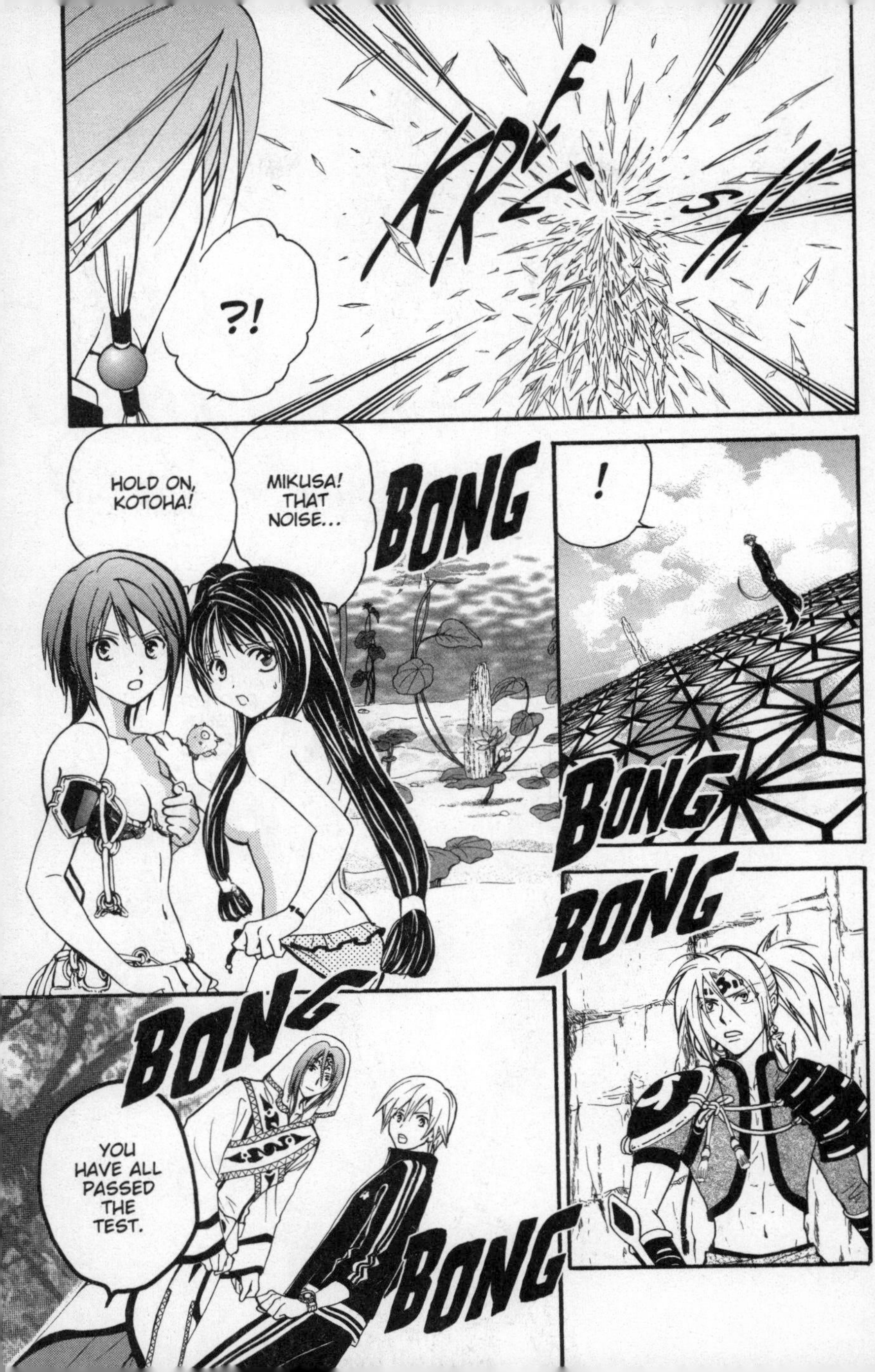
KREESH
?!
!
BONG
MIKUSA! THAT NOISE...
HOLD ON, KOTOHA!
BONG
BONG
BONG
YOU HAVE ALL PASSED THE TEST.
BONG

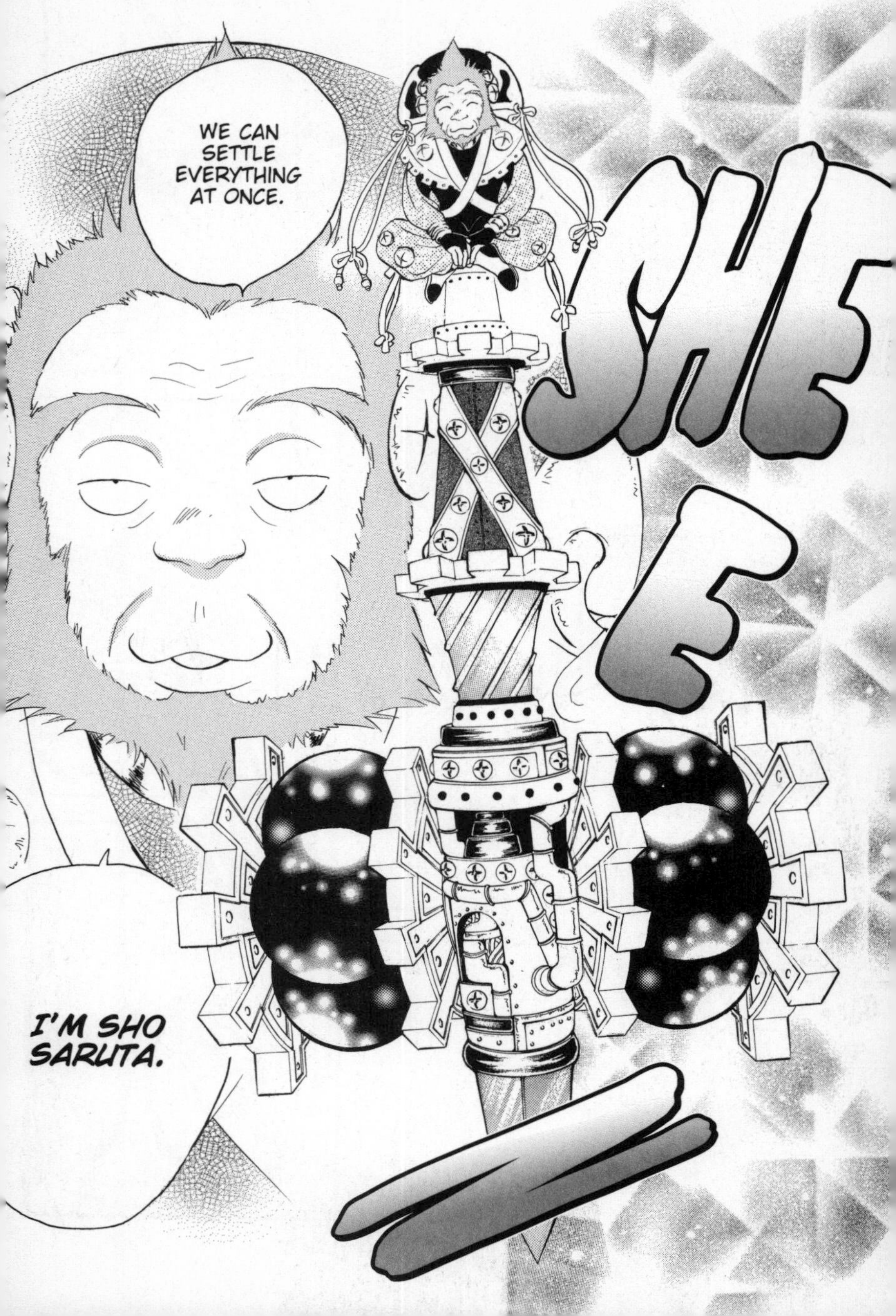
WE CAN SETTLE EVERYTHING AT ONCE.
SHEEN
I'M SHO SARUTA.

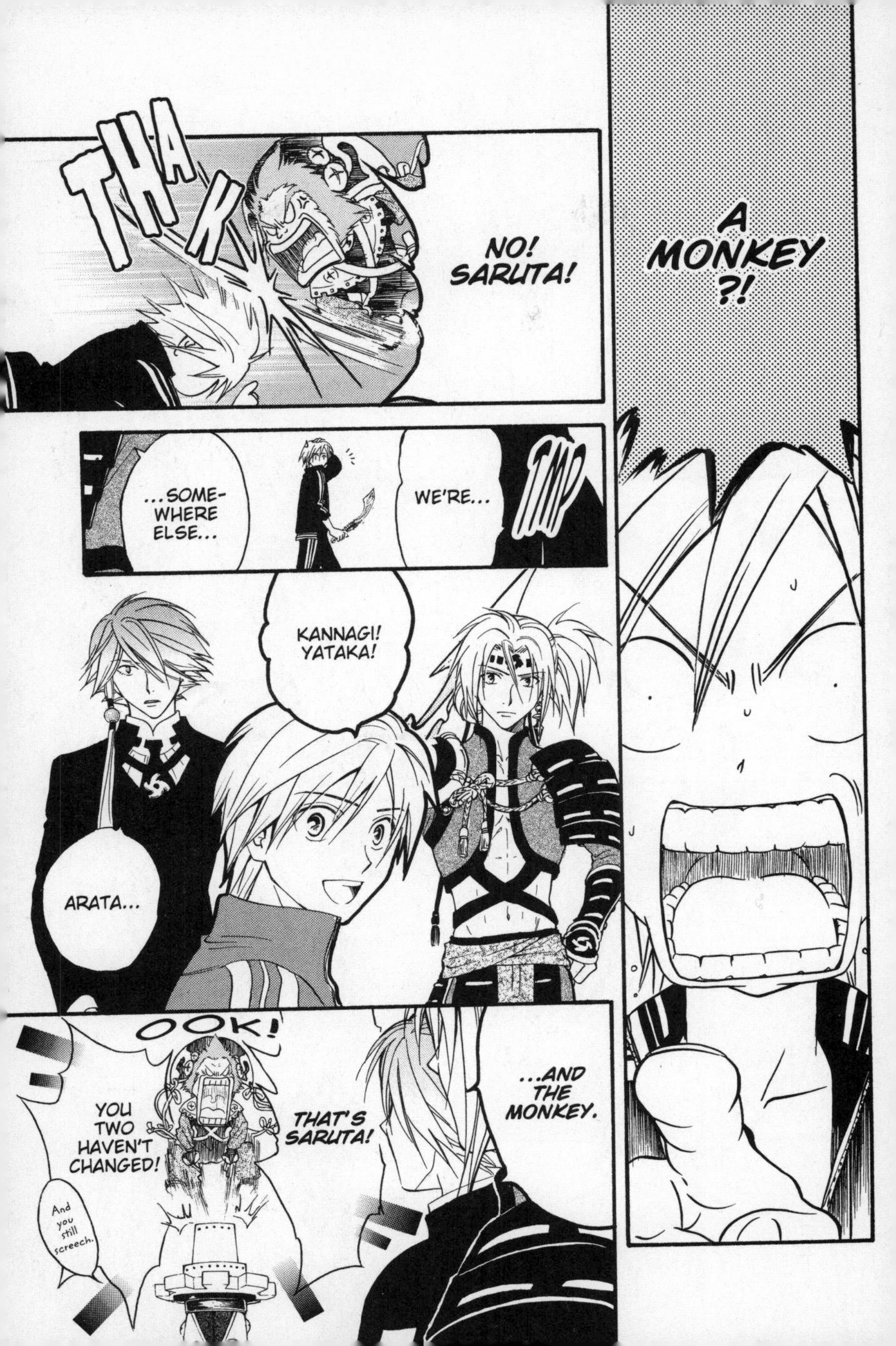
A MONKEY?!
NO! SARUTA!
THAK
TMP
WE'RE...
...SOME-WHERE ELSE...
KANNAGI! YATAKA!
ARATA...
...AND THE MONKEY.
THAT'S SARUTA!
OOK!
YOU TWO HAVEN'T CHANGED!
And you still screech.

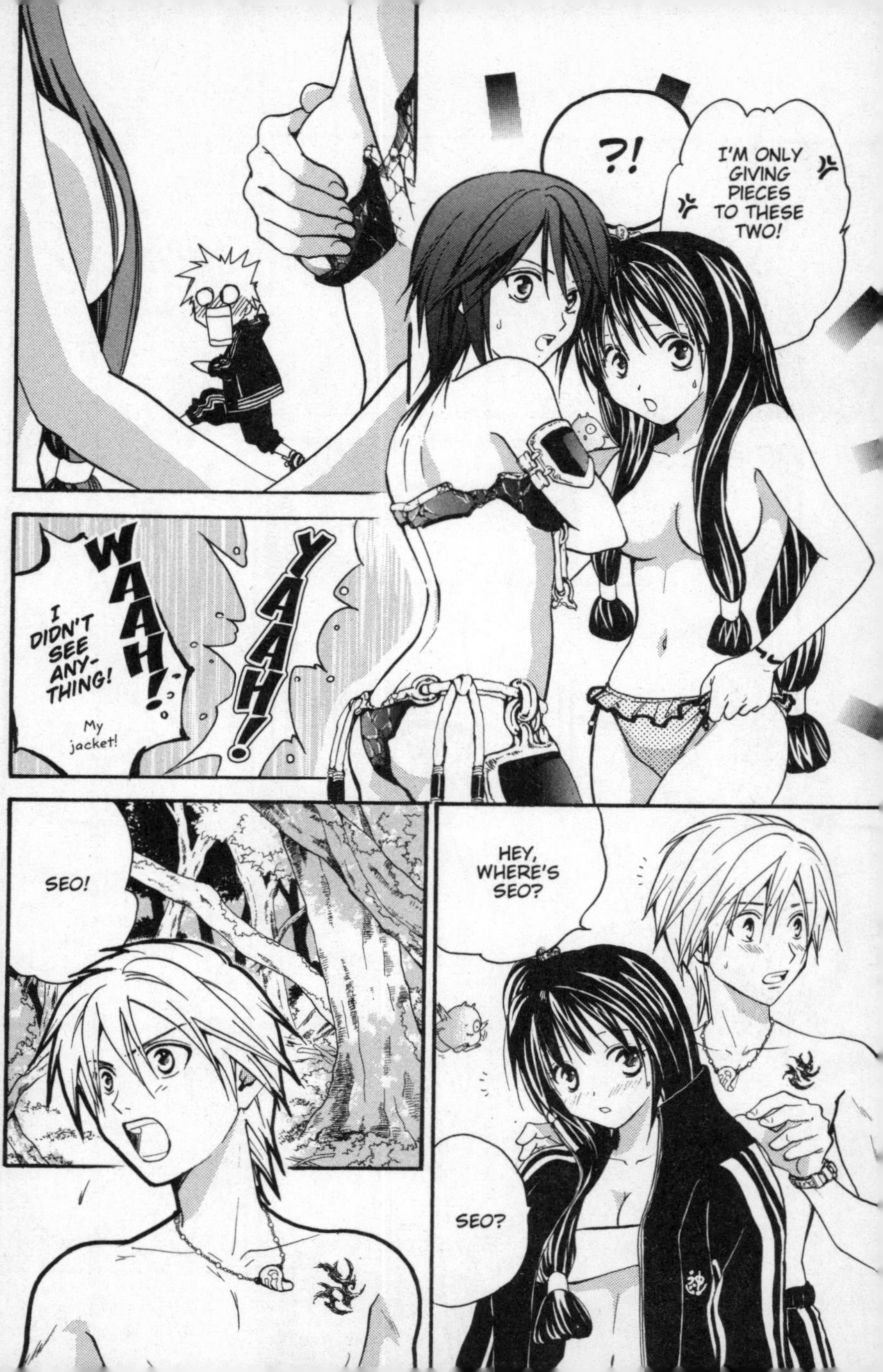
I'M ONLY GIVING PIECES TO THESE TWO!
?!
YAAAH!
WAAH!
I DIDN'T SEE ANY-THING!
My jacket!
HEY, WHERE'S SEO?
SEO?
SEO!

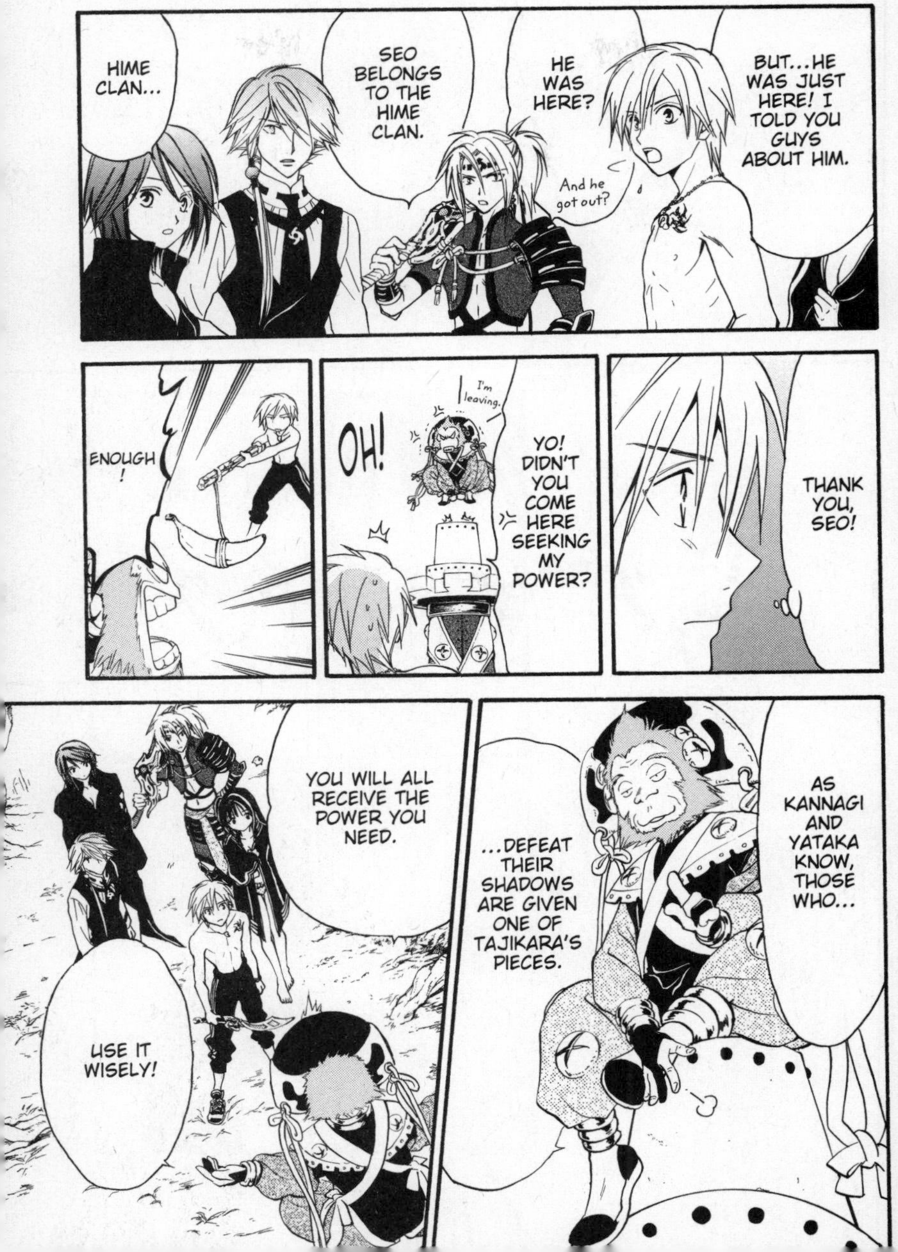
BUT...HE WAS JUST HERE! I TOLD YOU GUYS ABOUT HIM.
HE WAS HERE?
And he got out?
SEO BELONGS TO THE HIME CLAN.
HIME CLAN...
THANK YOU, SEO!
YO! DIDN'T YOU COME HERE SEEKING MY POWER?
I'm leaving.
OH!
ENOUGH!
AS KANNAGI AND YATAKA KNOW, THOSE WHO...
...DEFEAT THEIR SHADOWS ARE GIVEN ONE OF TAJIKARA'S PIECES.
YOU WILL ALL RECEIVE THE POWER YOU NEED.
USE IT WISELY!

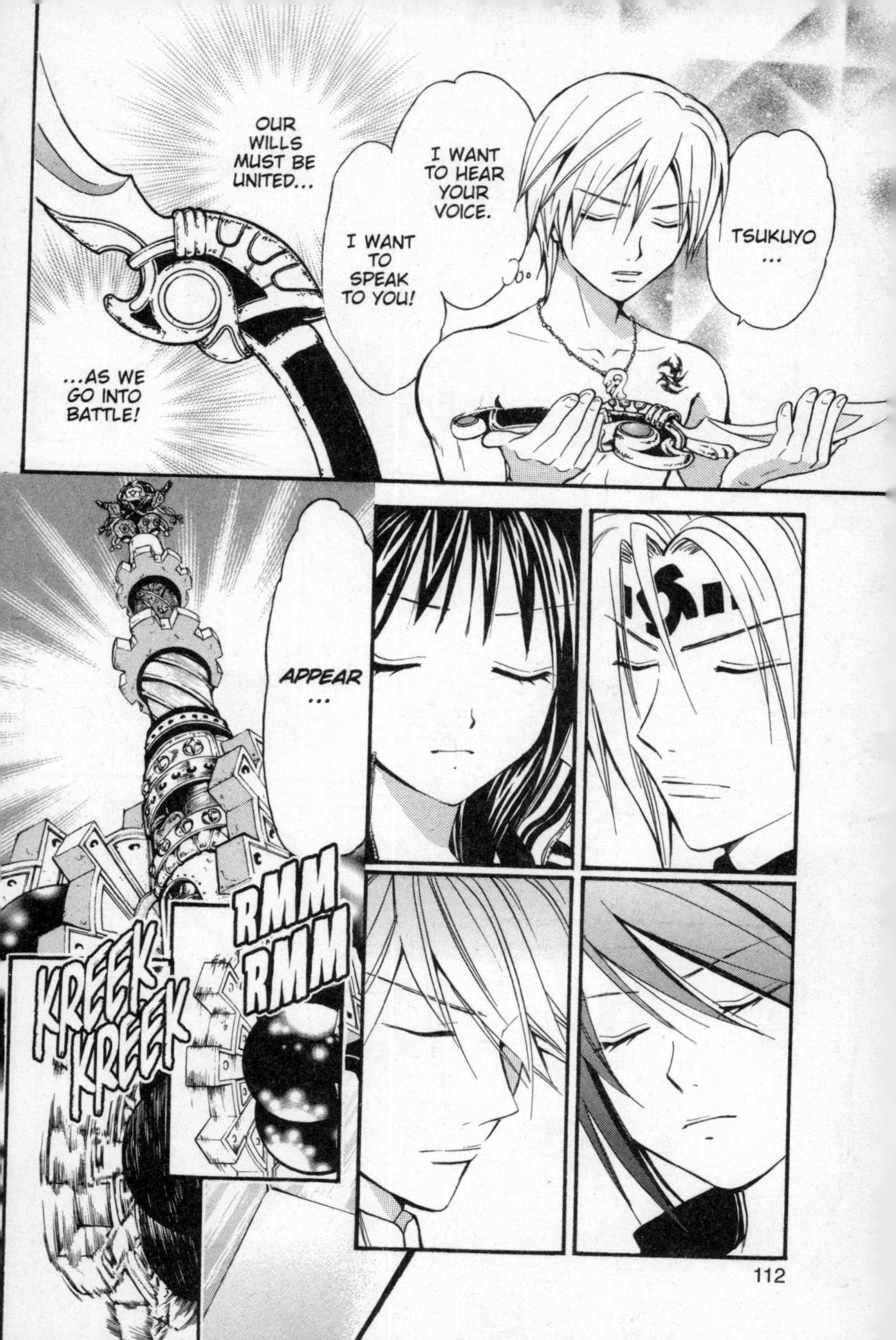
TSUKUYO ...
I WANT TO HEAR YOUR VOICE.
I WANT TO SPEAK TO YOU!
OUR WILLS MUST BE UNITED...
...AS WE GO INTO BATTLE!
APPEAR ...
RMM RMM
KREEK KREEK

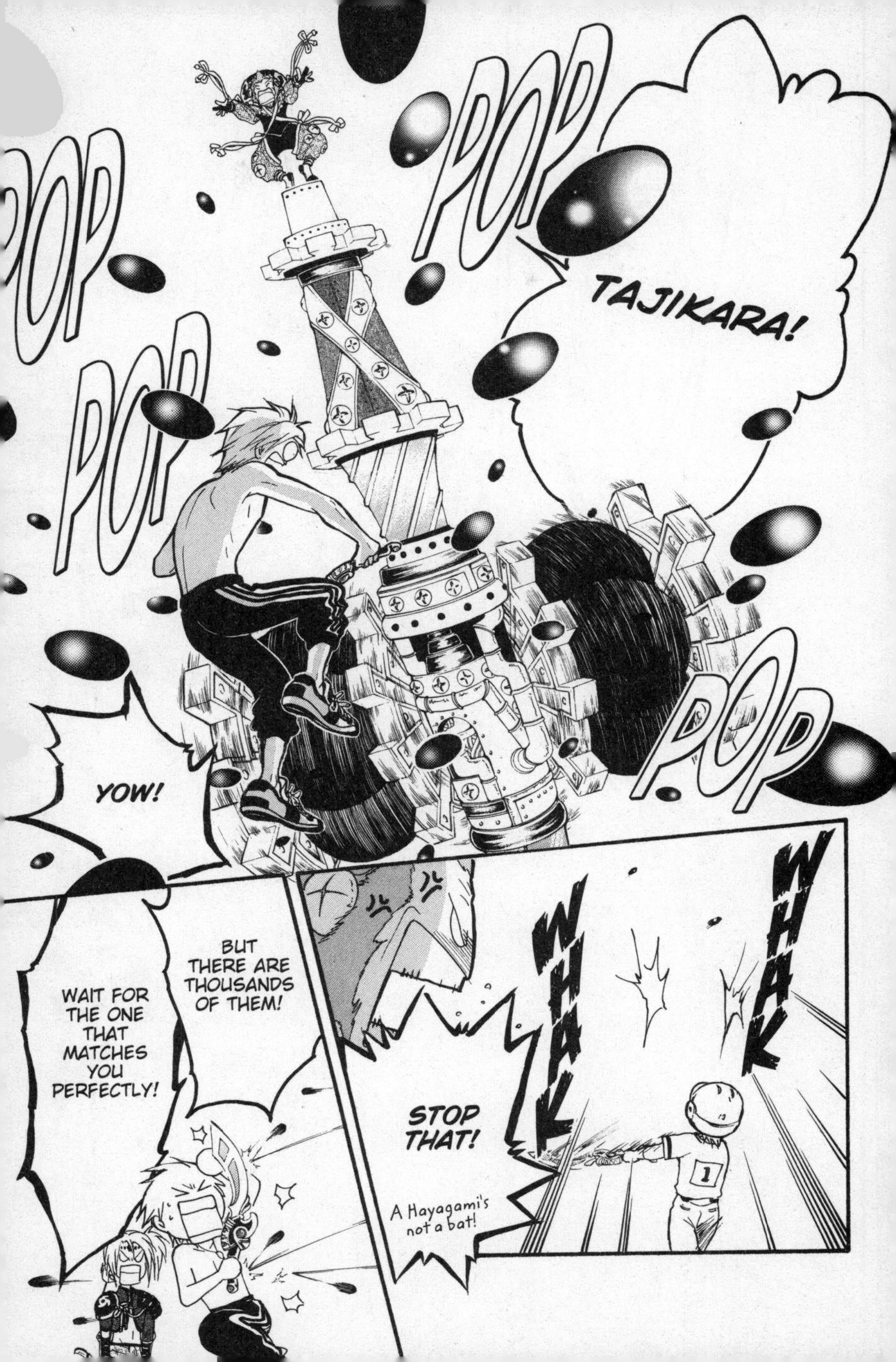

POP POP
TAJIKARA!
POP POP
POP
YOW!
WHAK WHAK
STOP THAT!
A Hayagami's not a bat!
BUT THERE ARE THOUSANDS OF THEM!
WAIT FOR THE ONE THAT MATCHES YOU PERFECTLY!

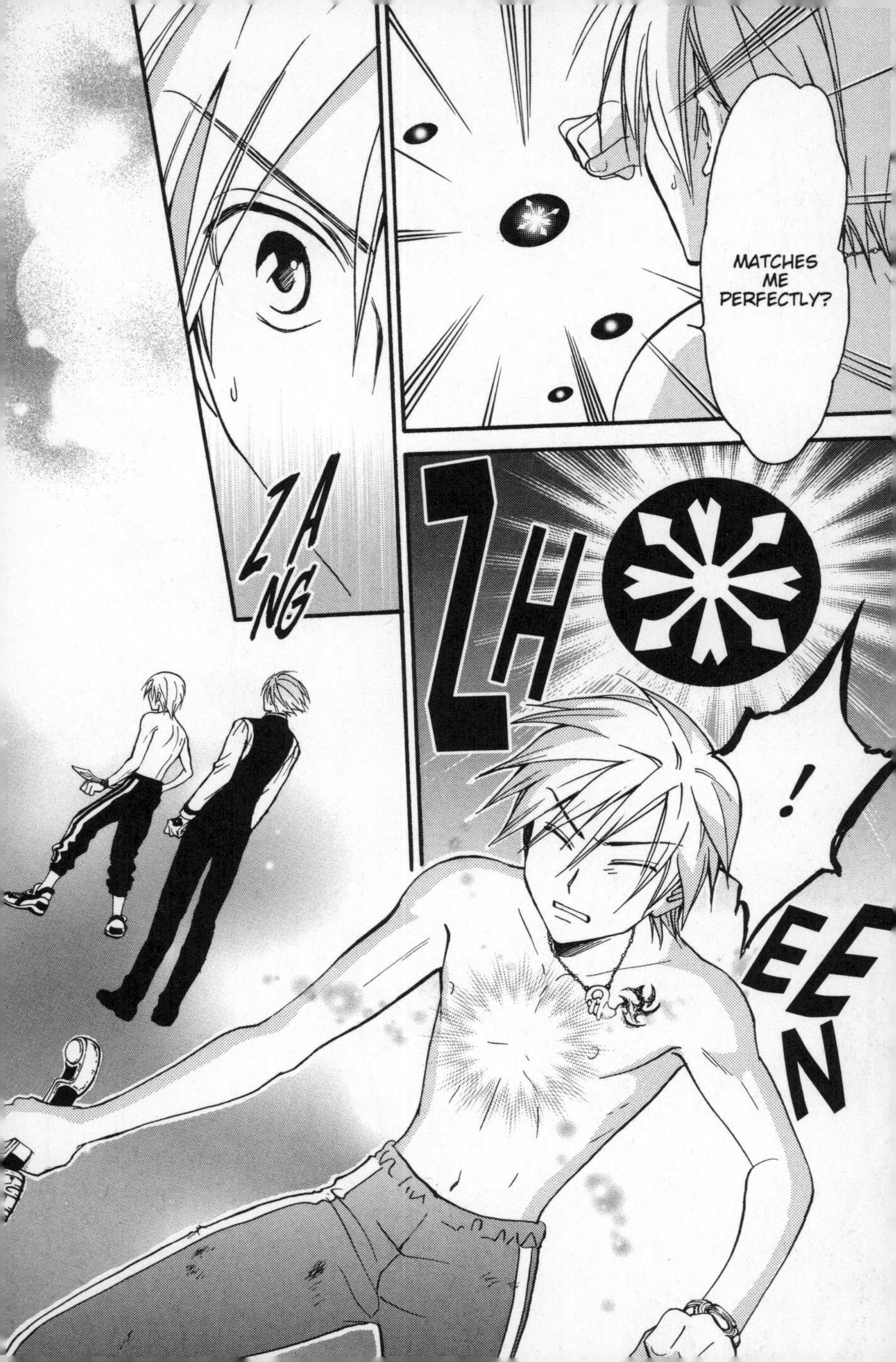
MATCHES ME PERFECTLY?
ZANG
ZH
!
EEN

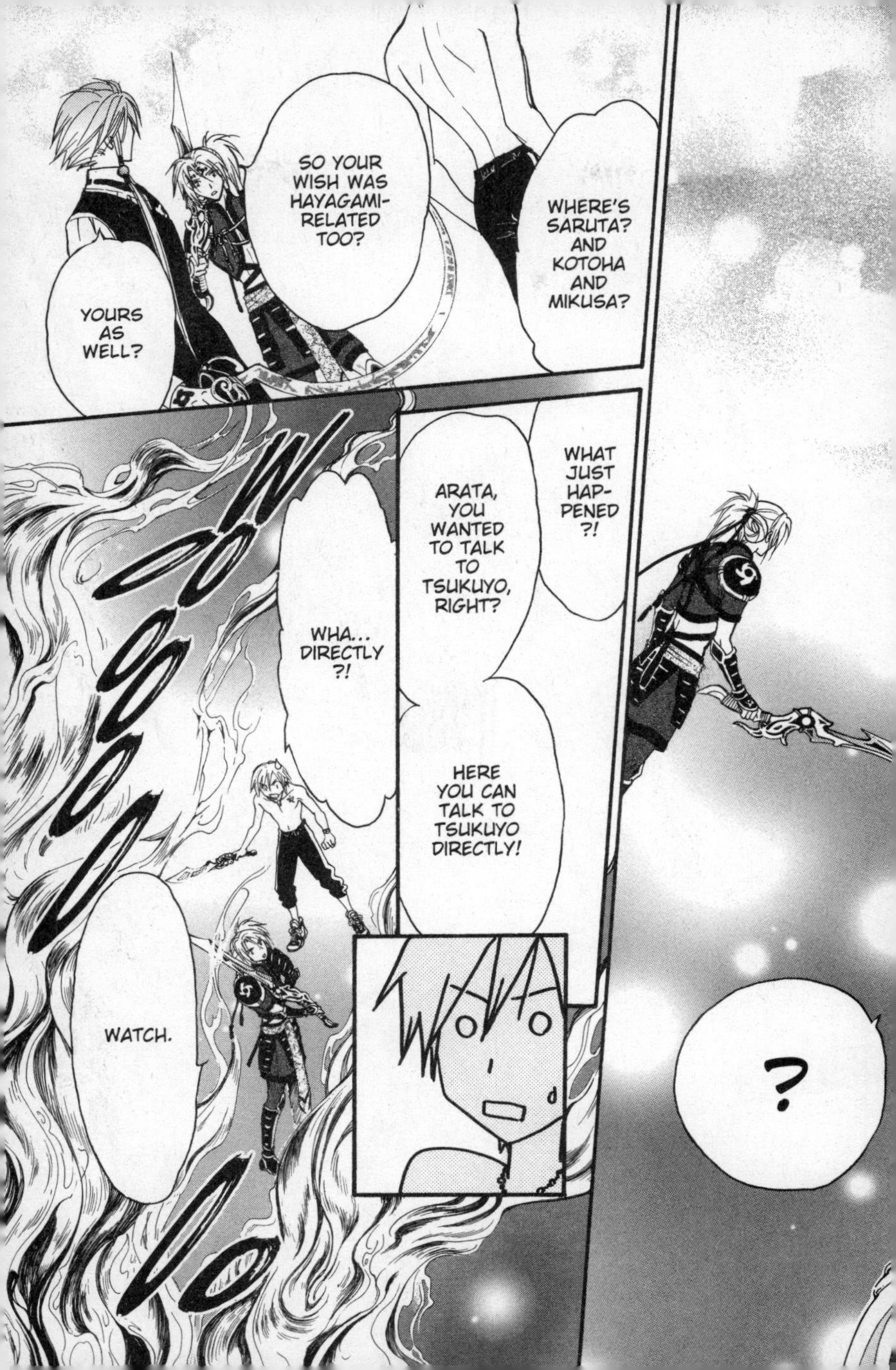
?
WHERE'S SARUTA? AND KOTOHA AND MIKUSA?
SO YOUR WISH WAS HAYAGAMI-RELATED TOO?
YOURS AS WELL?
WHAT JUST HAP-PENED?!
ARATA, YOU WANTED TO TALK TO TSUKUYO, RIGHT?
HERE YOU CAN TALK TO TSUKUYO DIRECTLY!
WHA... DIRECTLY?!
WATCH.

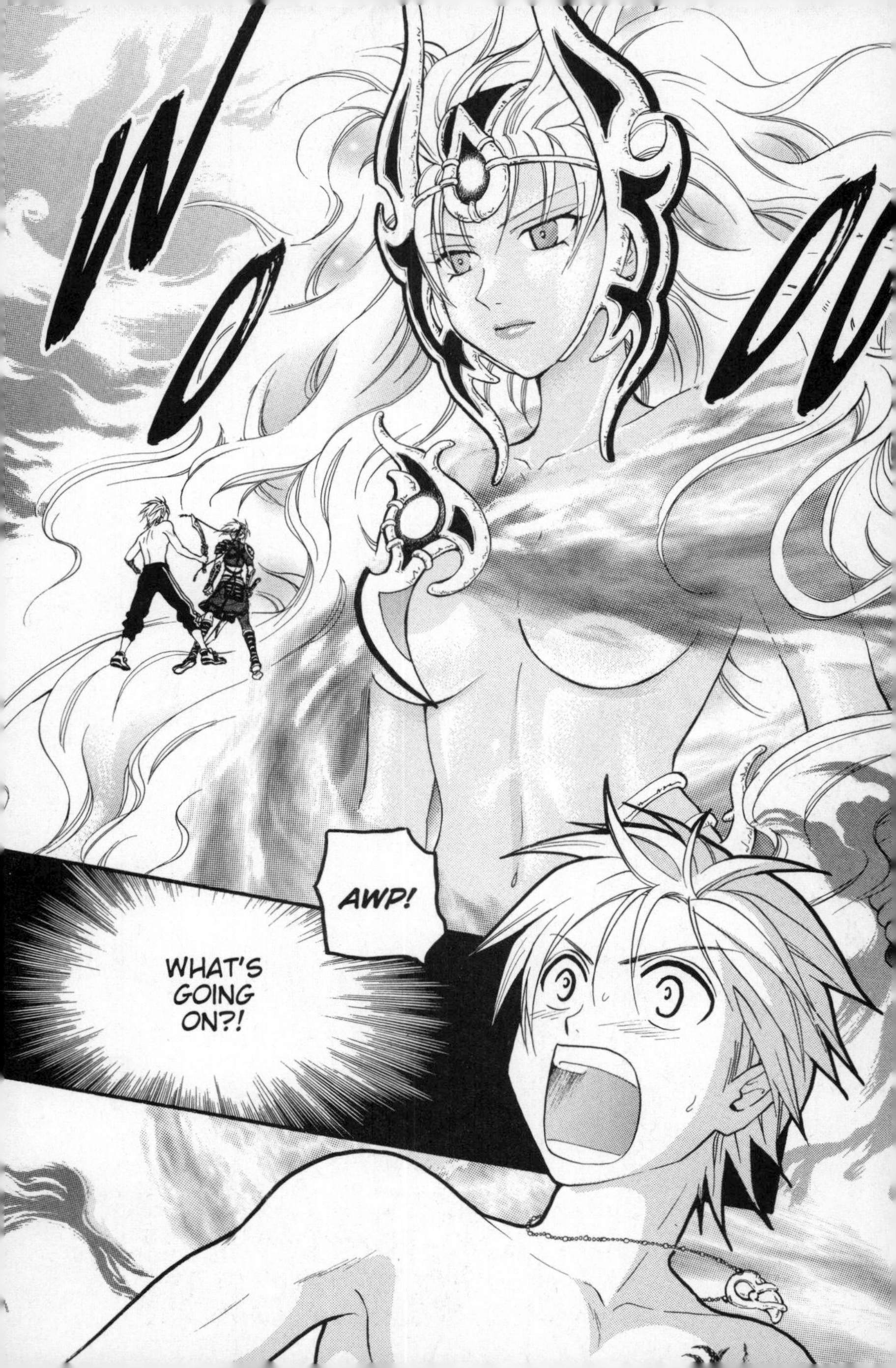
WOOOO
AWP!
WHAT'S GOING ON?!

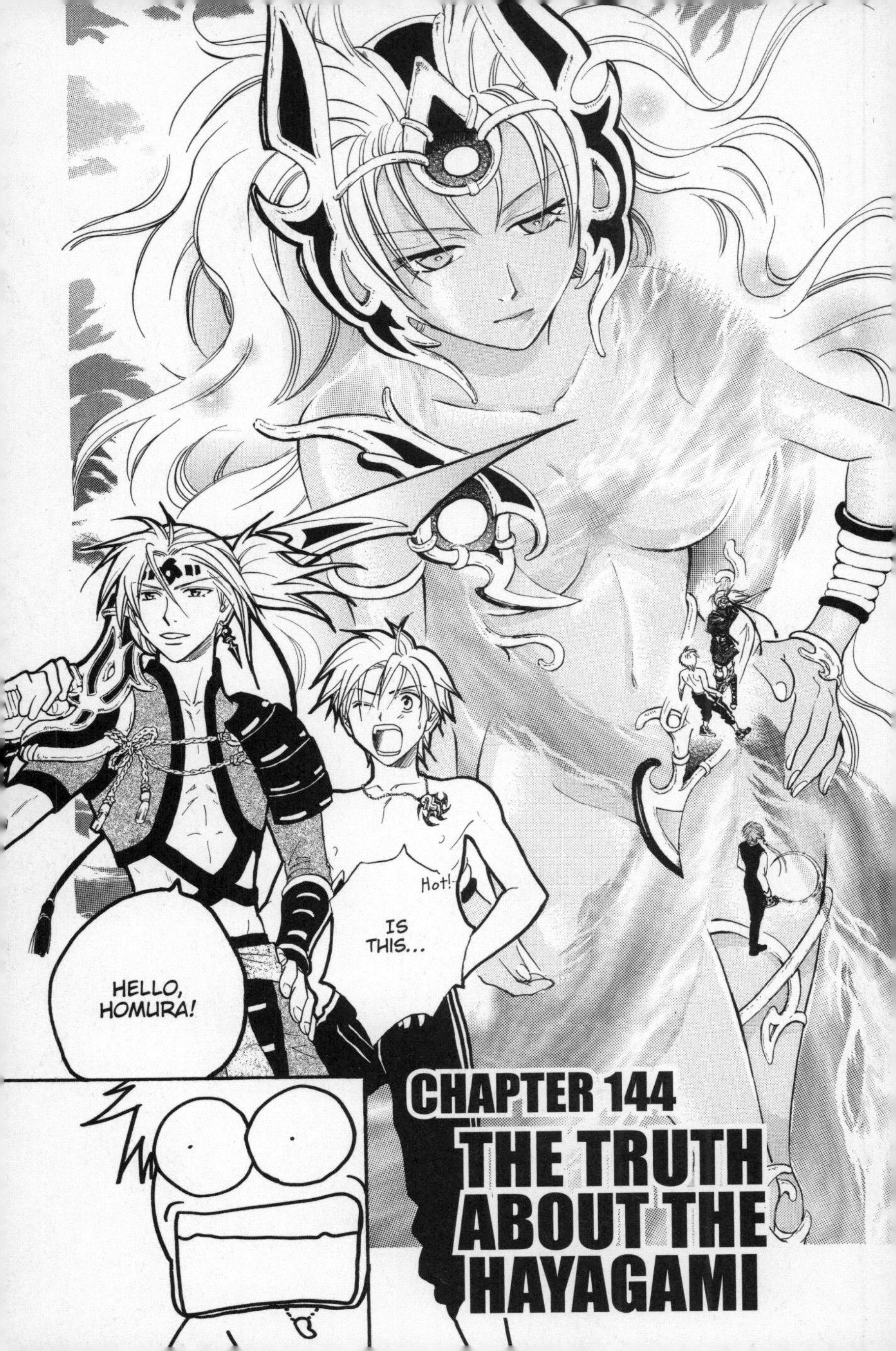
Hot!
IS THIS...
HELLO, HOMURA!
CHAPTER 144
THE TRUTH ABOUT THE HAYAGAMI

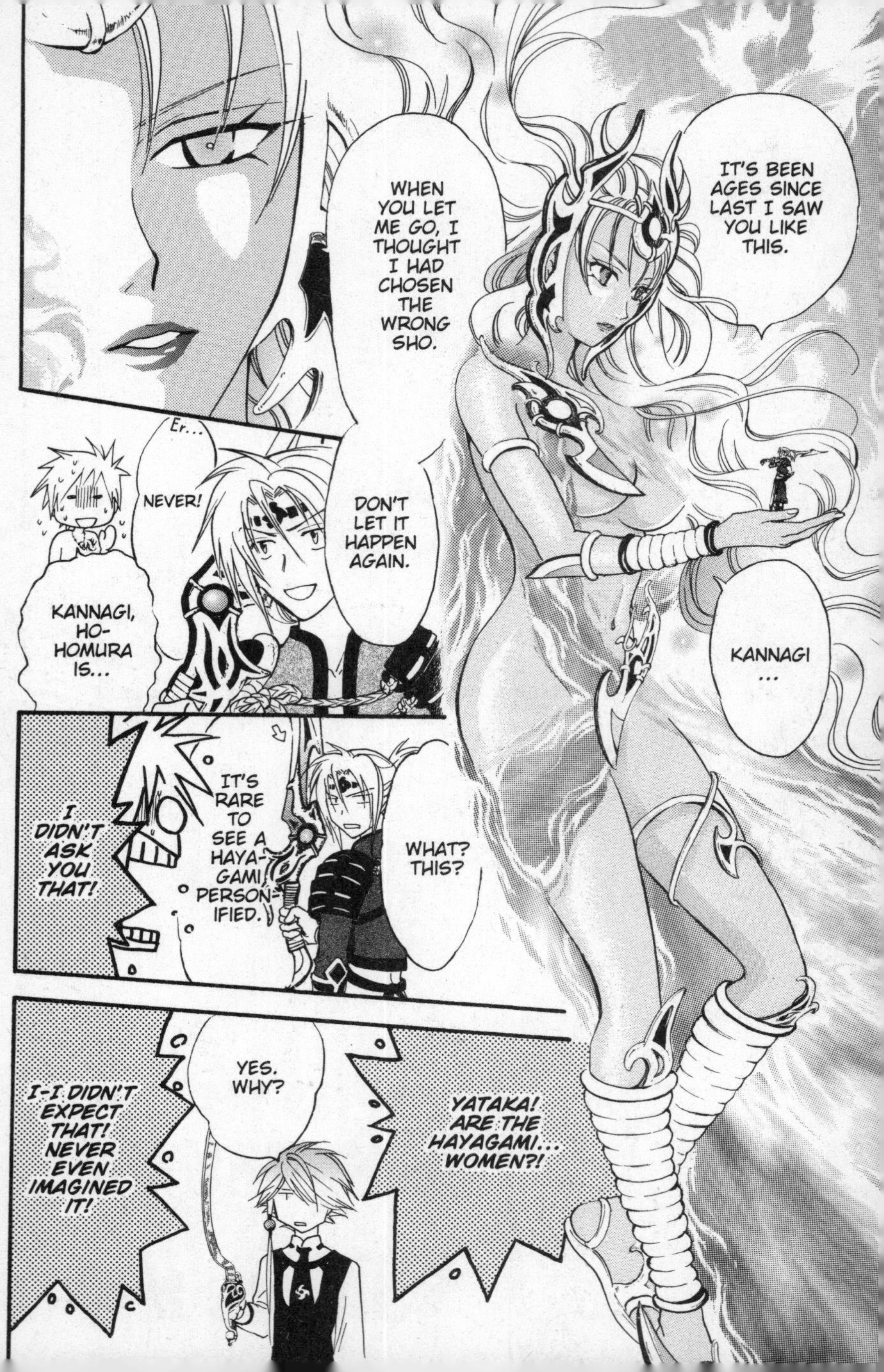
IT'S BEEN AGES SINCE LAST I SAW YOU LIKE THIS.
KANNAGI ...
WHEN YOU LET ME GO, I THOUGHT I HAD CHOSEN THE WRONG SHO.
DON'T LET IT HAPPEN AGAIN.
NEVER!
Er...
KANNAGI, HO-HOMURA IS...
WHAT? THIS?
IT'S RARE TO SEE A HAYAGAMI PERSONIFIED.
I DIDN'T ASK YOU THAT!
YATAKA! ARE THE HAYAGAMI... WOMEN?!
YES. WHY?
I-I DIDN'T EXPECT THAT! NEVER EVEN IMAGINED IT!

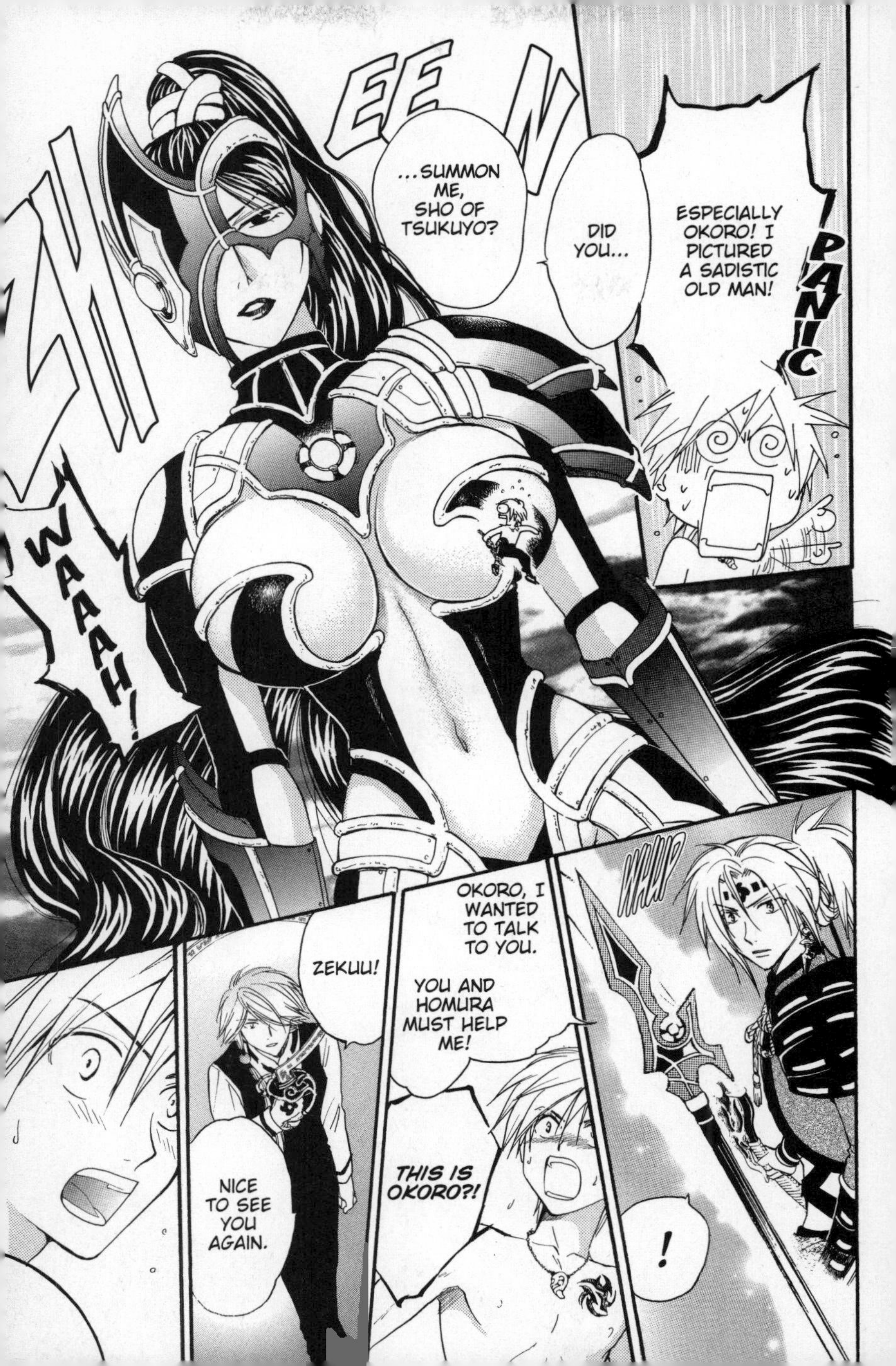
ESPECIALLY OKORO! I PICTURED A SADISTIC OLD MAN!
PANIC
DID YOU...
...SUMMON ME, SHO OF TSUKUYO?
WAAAAH!
!
OKORO, I WANTED TO TALK TO YOU.
YOU AND HOMURA MUST HELP ME!
THIS IS OKORO?!
ZEKUU!
NICE TO SEE YOU AGAIN.

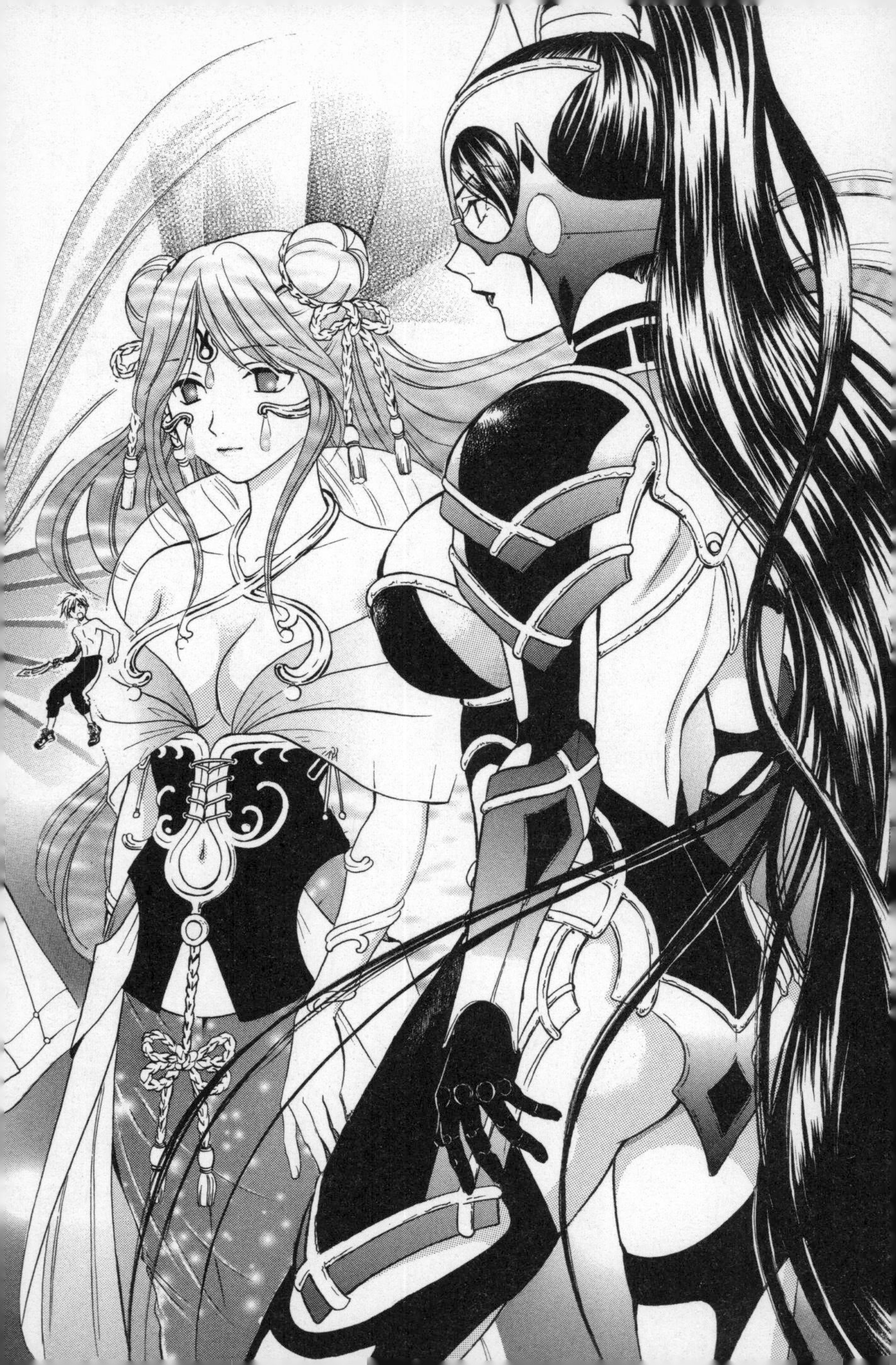

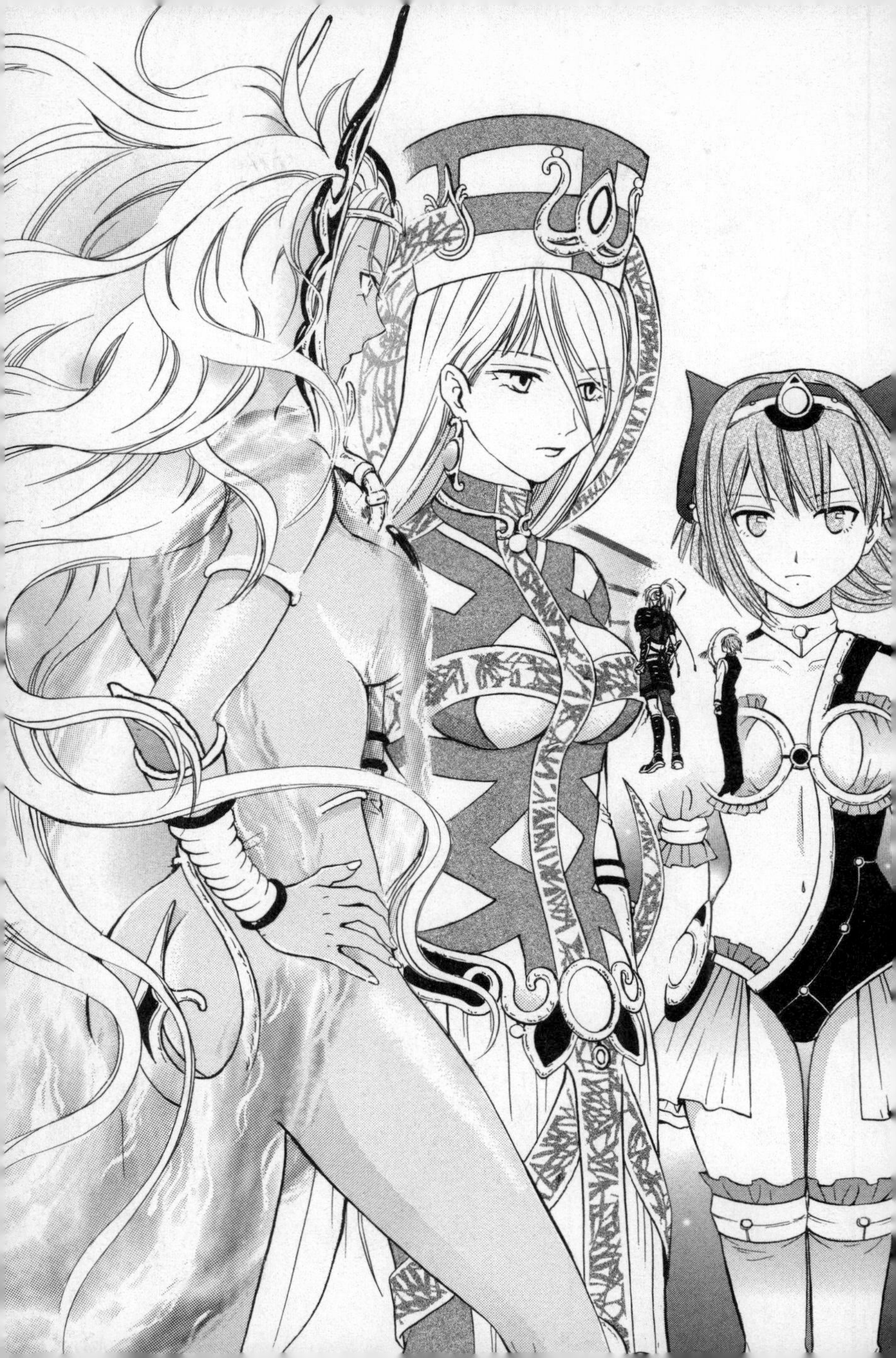

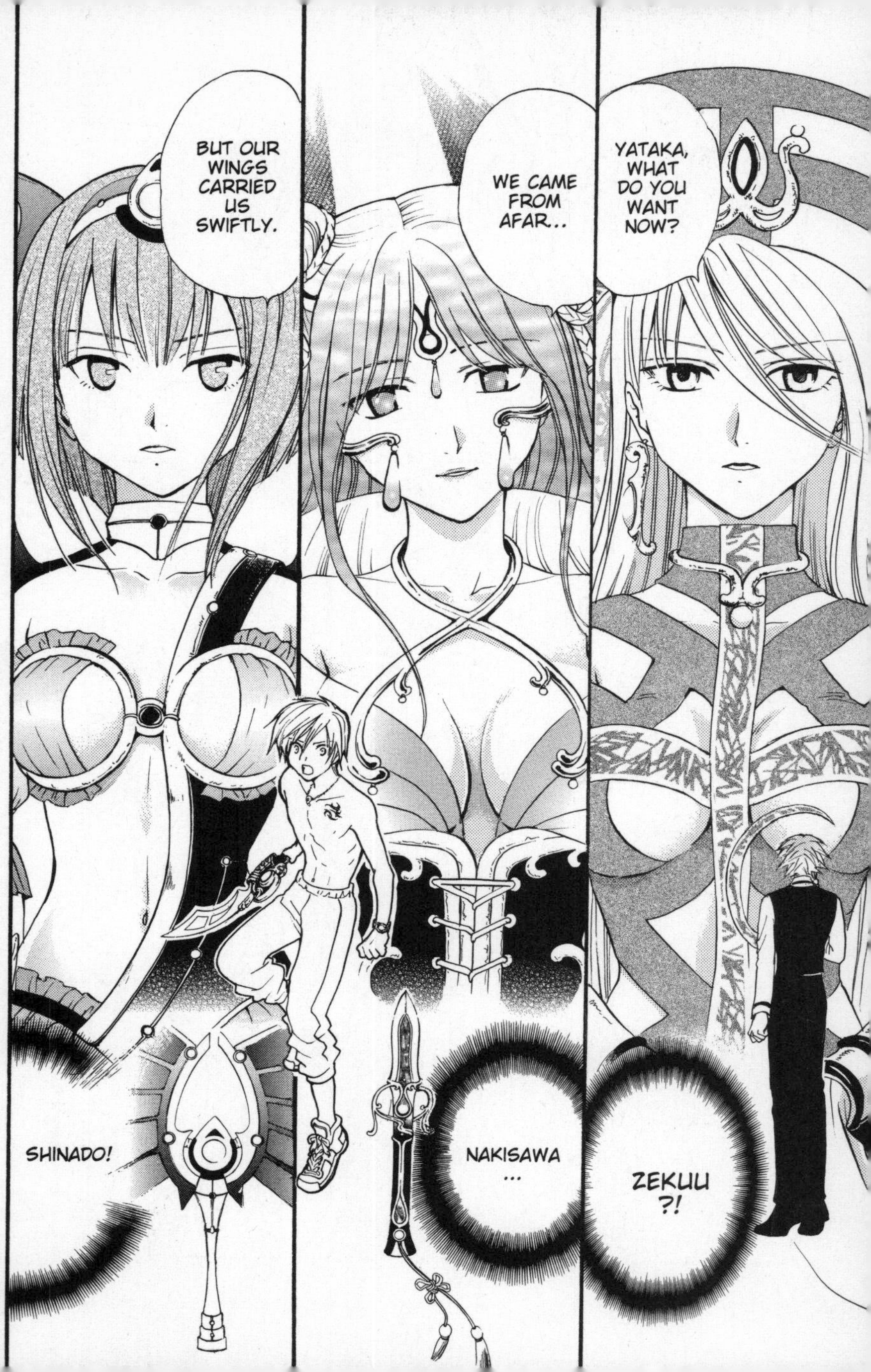
YATAKA, WHAT DO YOU WANT NOW?
ZEKUU ?!
WE CAME FROM AFAR...
NAKISAWA ...
BUT OUR WINGS CARRIED US SWIFTLY.
SHINADO!

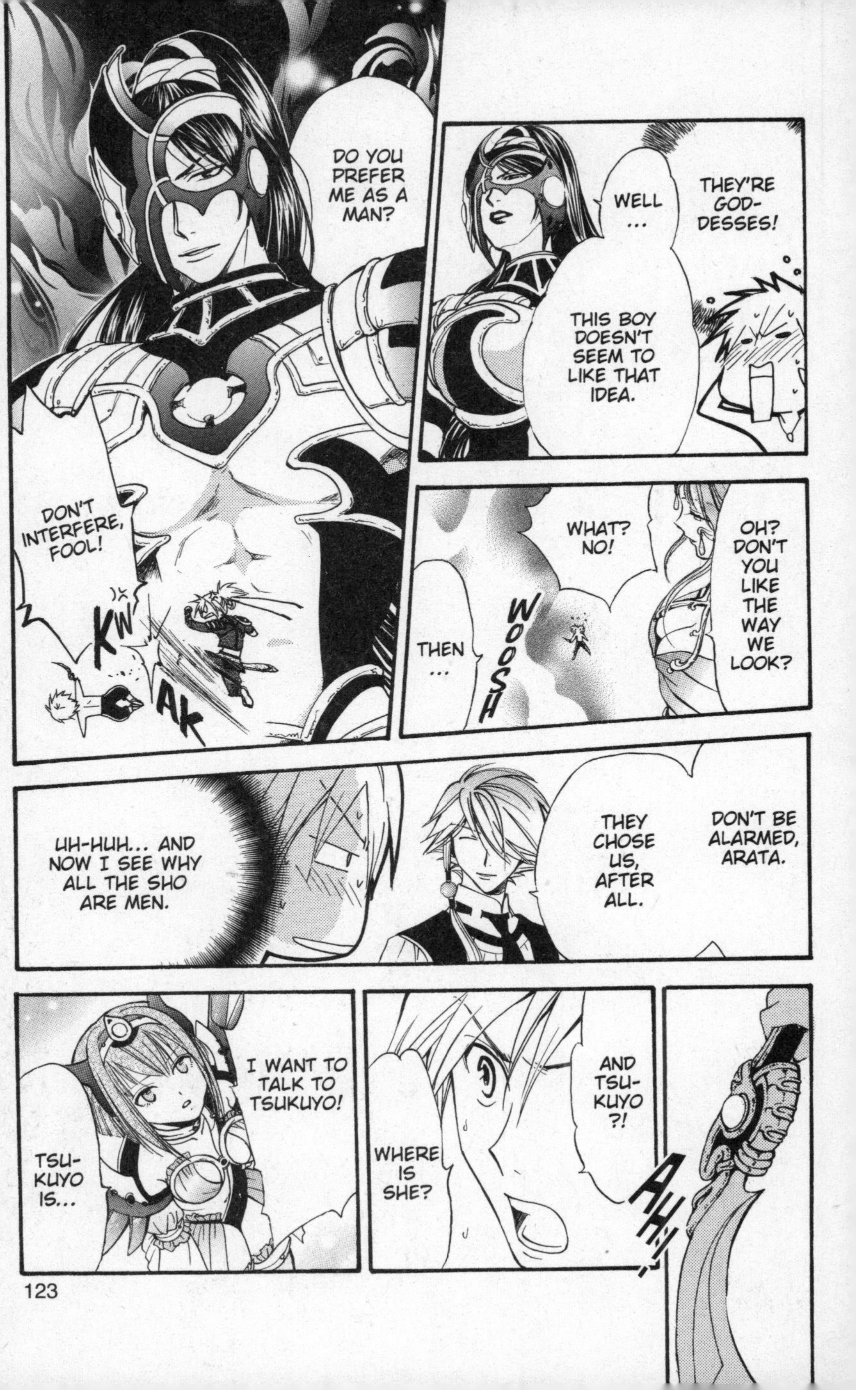
THEY'RE GOD-DESSES!
WELL ...
THIS BOY DOESN'T SEEM TO LIKE THAT IDEA.
OH? DON'T YOU LIKE THE WAY WE LOOK?
WHAT? NO!
WOOOSH
THEN ...
DO YOU PREFER ME AS A MAN?
DON'T INTERFERE, FOOL!
KWAK
DON'T BE ALARMED, ARATA.
THEY CHOSE US, AFTER ALL.
UH-HUH... AND NOW I SEE WHY ALL THE SHO ARE MEN.
AH!!
AND TSU-KUYO?!
WHERE IS SHE?
I WANT TO TALK TO TSUKUYO!
TSU-KUYO IS...

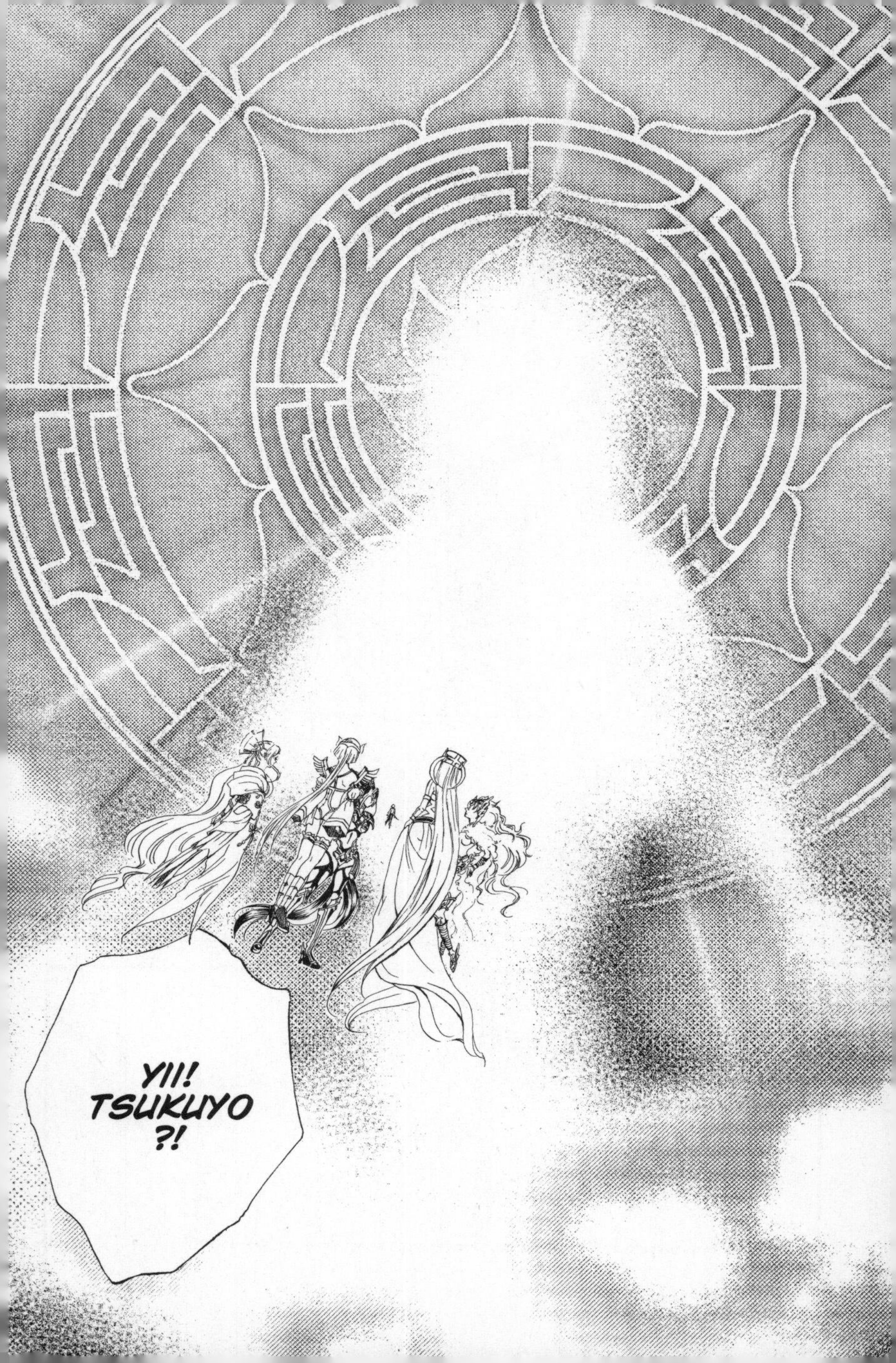
YII! TSUKUYO ?!

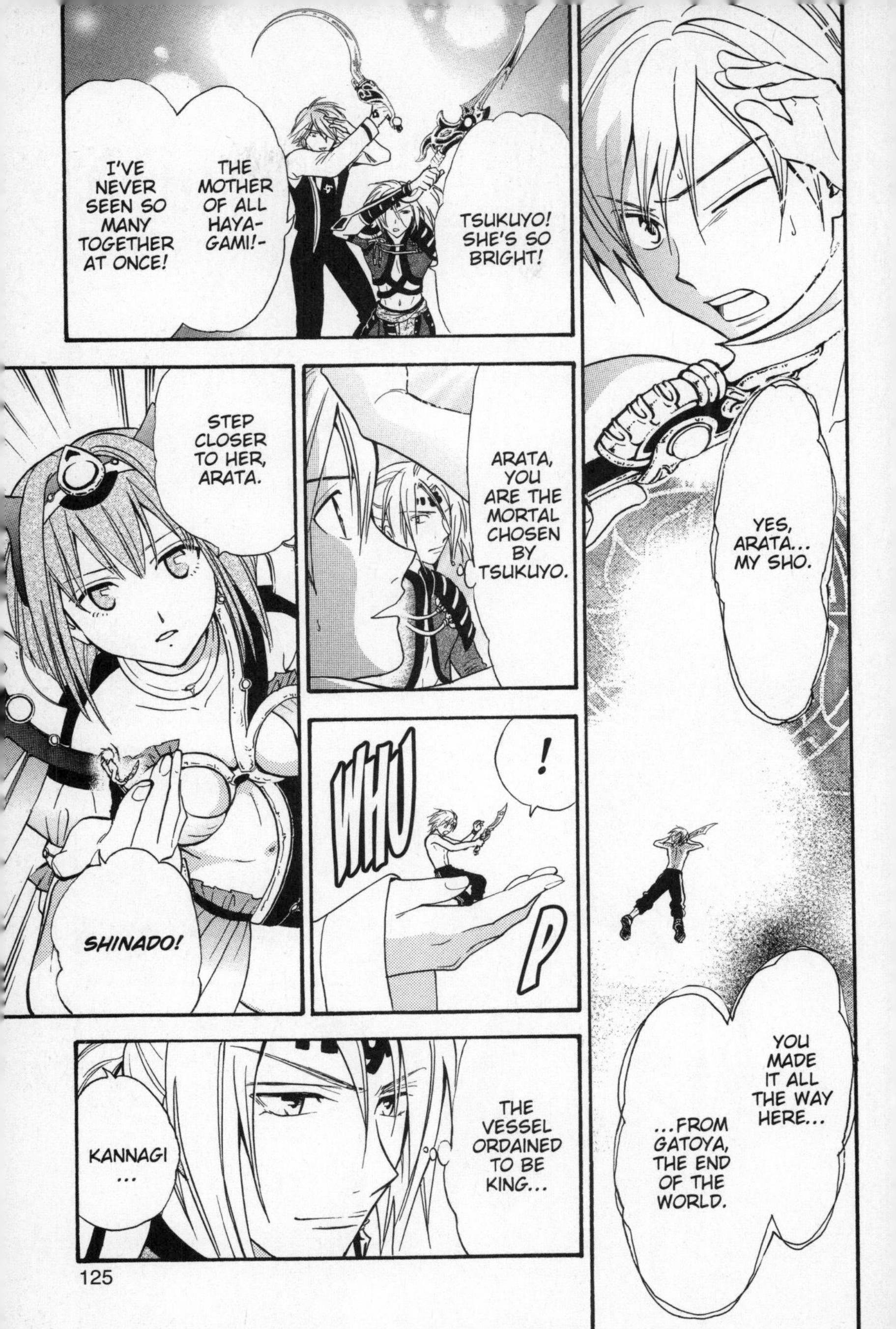
YES, ARATA... MY SHO.
YOU MADE IT ALL THE WAY HERE...
...FROM GATOYA, THE END OF THE WORLD.
TSUKUYO! SHE'S SO BRIGHT!
THE MOTHER OF ALL HAYA-GAMI!-
I'VE NEVER SEEN SO MANY TOGETHER AT ONCE!
ARATA, YOU ARE THE MORTAL CHOSEN BY TSUKUYO.
!
WHUP
STEP CLOSER TO HER, ARATA.
SHINADO!
THE VESSEL ORDAINED TO BE KING...
KANNAGI ...

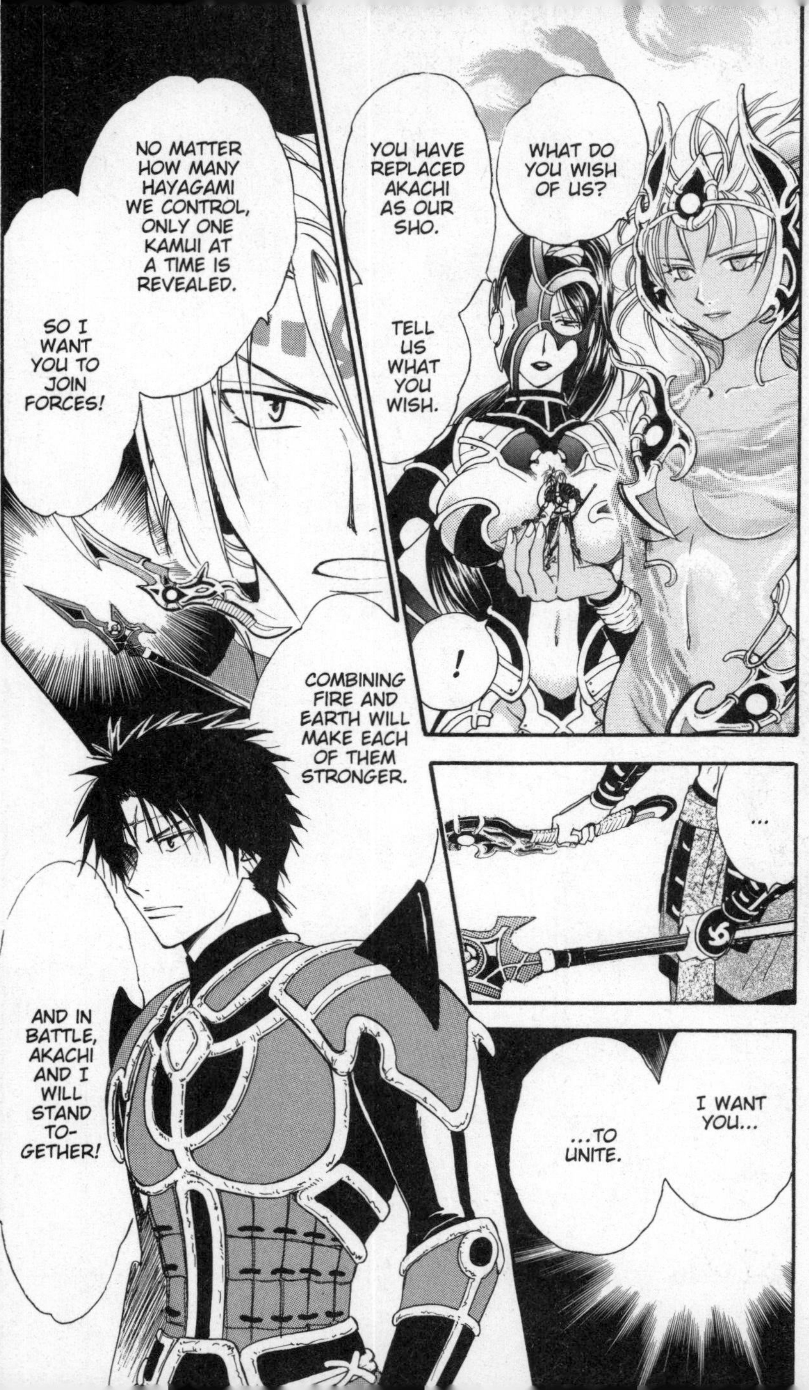
WHAT DO YOU WISH OF US?
YOU HAVE REPLACED AKACHI AS OUR SHO.
TELL US WHAT YOU WISH.
!
NO MATTER HOW MANY HAYAGAMI WE CONTROL, ONLY ONE KAMUI AT A TIME IS REVEALED.
SO I WANT YOU TO JOIN FORCES!
COMBINING FIRE AND EARTH WILL MAKE EACH OF THEM STRONGER.
...
I WANT YOU...
...TO UNITE.
AND IN BATTLE, AKACHI AND I WILL STAND TO-GETHER!

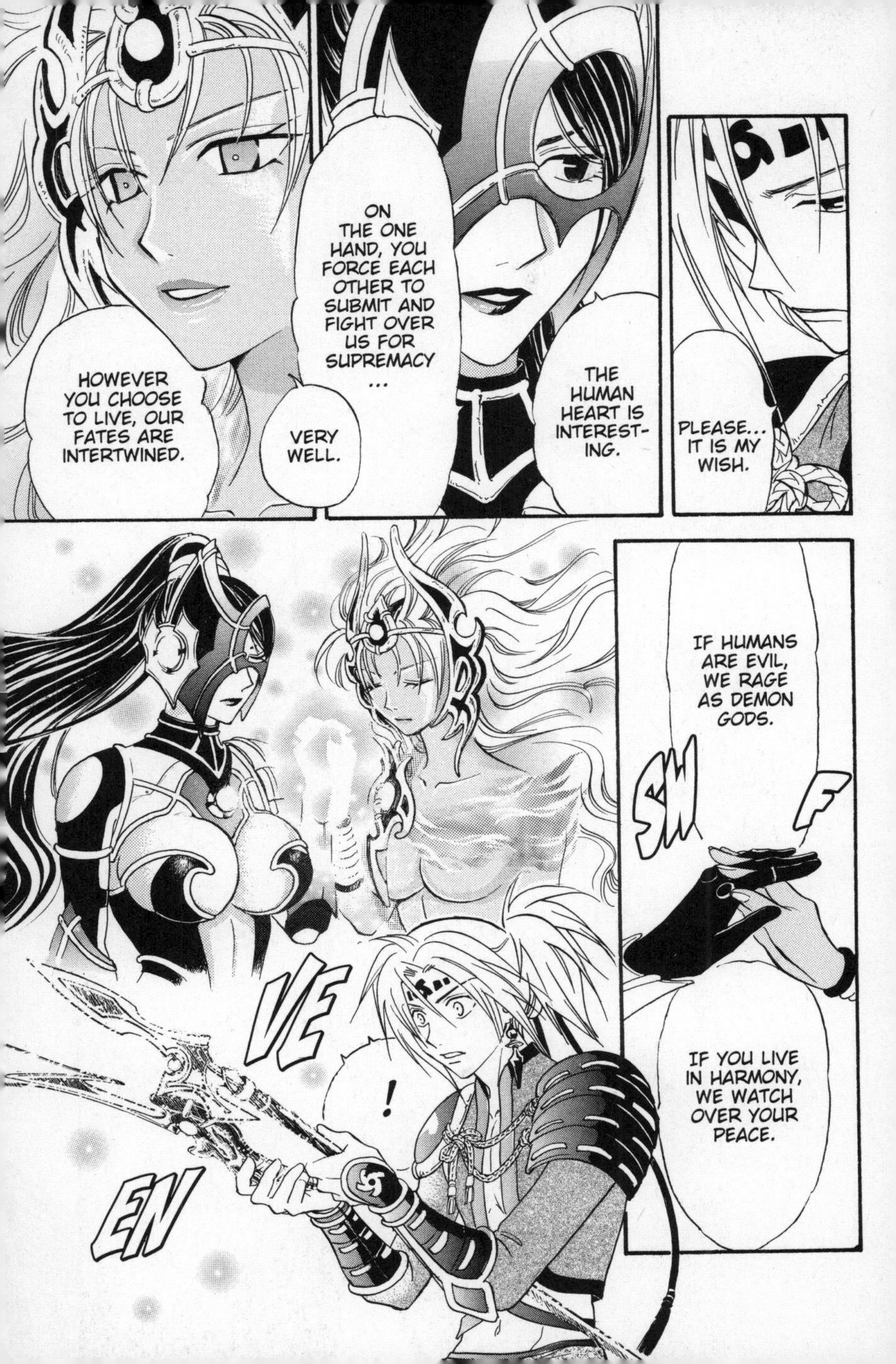
PLEASE... IT IS MY WISH.
THE HUMAN HEART IS INTEREST-ING.
ON THE ONE HAND, YOU FORCE EACH OTHER TO SUBMIT AND FIGHT OVER US FOR SUPREMACY ...
VERY WELL.
HOWEVER YOU CHOOSE TO LIVE, OUR FATES ARE INTERTWINED.
IF HUMANS ARE EVIL, WE RAGE AS DEMON GODS.
SW F
IF YOU LIVE IN HARMONY, WE WATCH OVER YOUR PEACE.
VE
!
EN

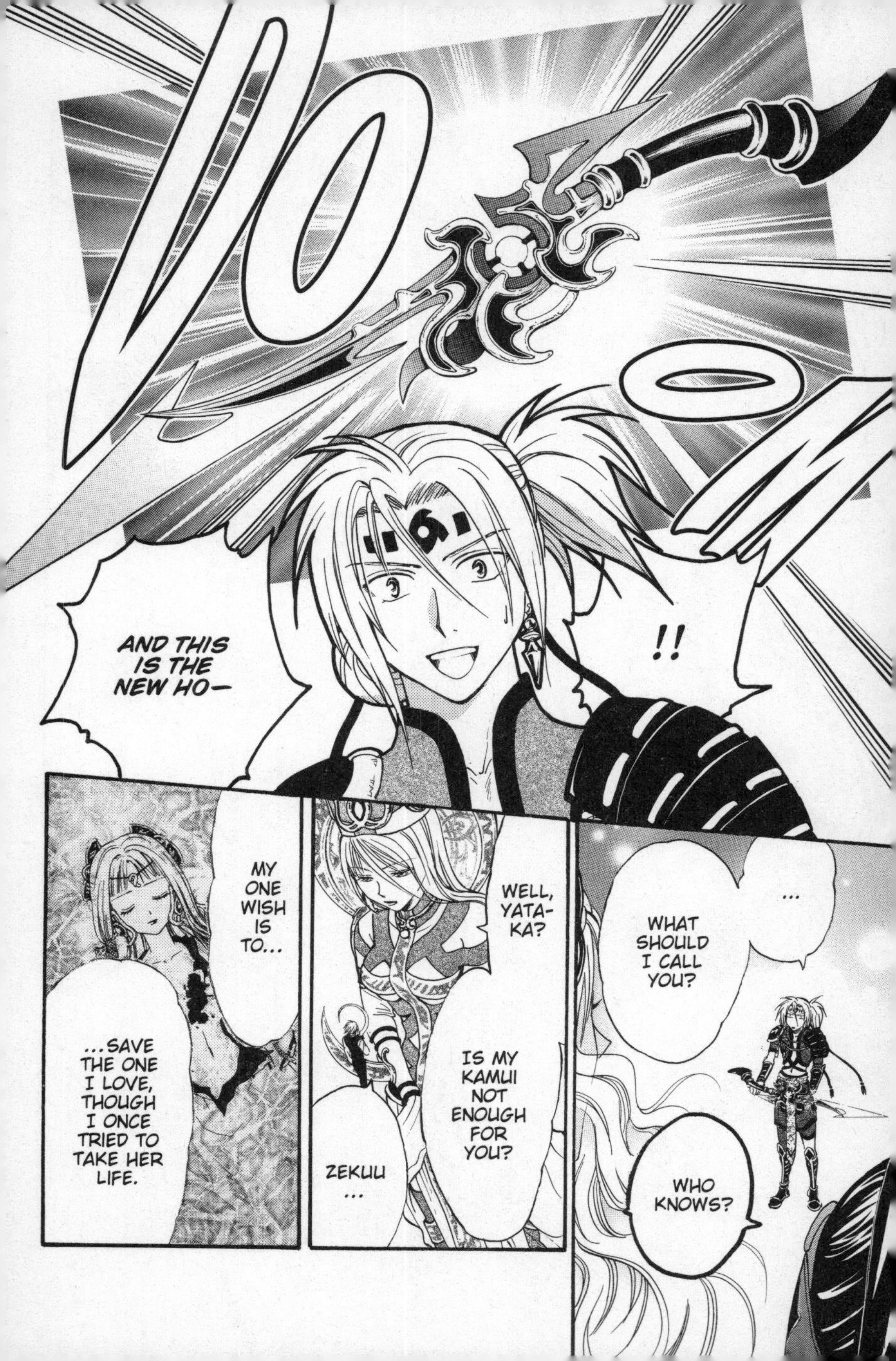
VOOM
AND THIS IS THE NEW HO—
!!
...
WHAT SHOULD I CALL YOU?
WHO KNOWS?
WELL, YATAKA?
IS MY KAMUI NOT ENOUGH FOR YOU?
ZEKUU ...
MY ONE WISH IS TO...
...SAVE THE ONE I LOVE, THOUGH I ONCE TRIED TO TAKE HER LIFE.

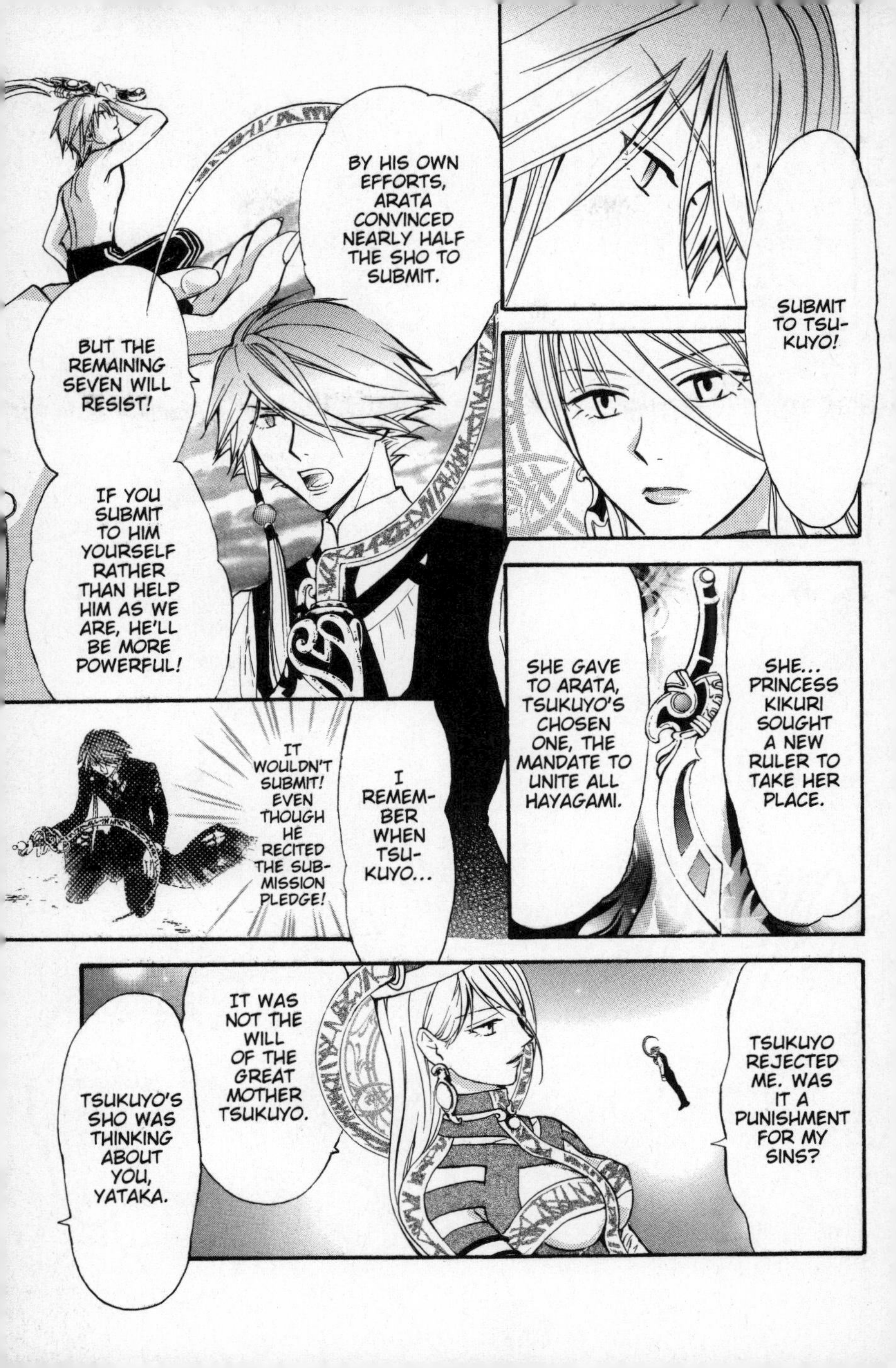
SUBMIT TO TSU-KUYO!
BY HIS OWN EFFORTS, ARATA CONVINCED NEARLY HALF THE SHO TO SUBMIT.
BUT THE REMAINING SEVEN WILL RESIST!
IF YOU SUBMIT TO HIM YOURSELF RATHER THAN HELP HIM AS WE ARE, HE'LL BE MORE POWERFUL!
SHE... PRINCESS KIKURI SOUGHT A NEW RULER TO TAKE HER PLACE.
SHE GAVE TO ARATA, TSUKUYO'S CHOSEN ONE, THE MANDATE TO UNITE ALL HAYAGAMI.
I REMEM-BER WHEN TSU-KUYO...
IT WOULDN'T SUBMIT! EVEN THOUGH HE RECITED THE SUB-MISSION PLEDGE!
TSUKUYO REJECTED ME. WAS IT A PUNISHMENT FOR MY SINS?
IT WAS NOT THE WILL OF THE GREAT MOTHER TSUKUYO.
TSUKUYO'S SHO WAS THINKING ABOUT YOU, YATAKA.

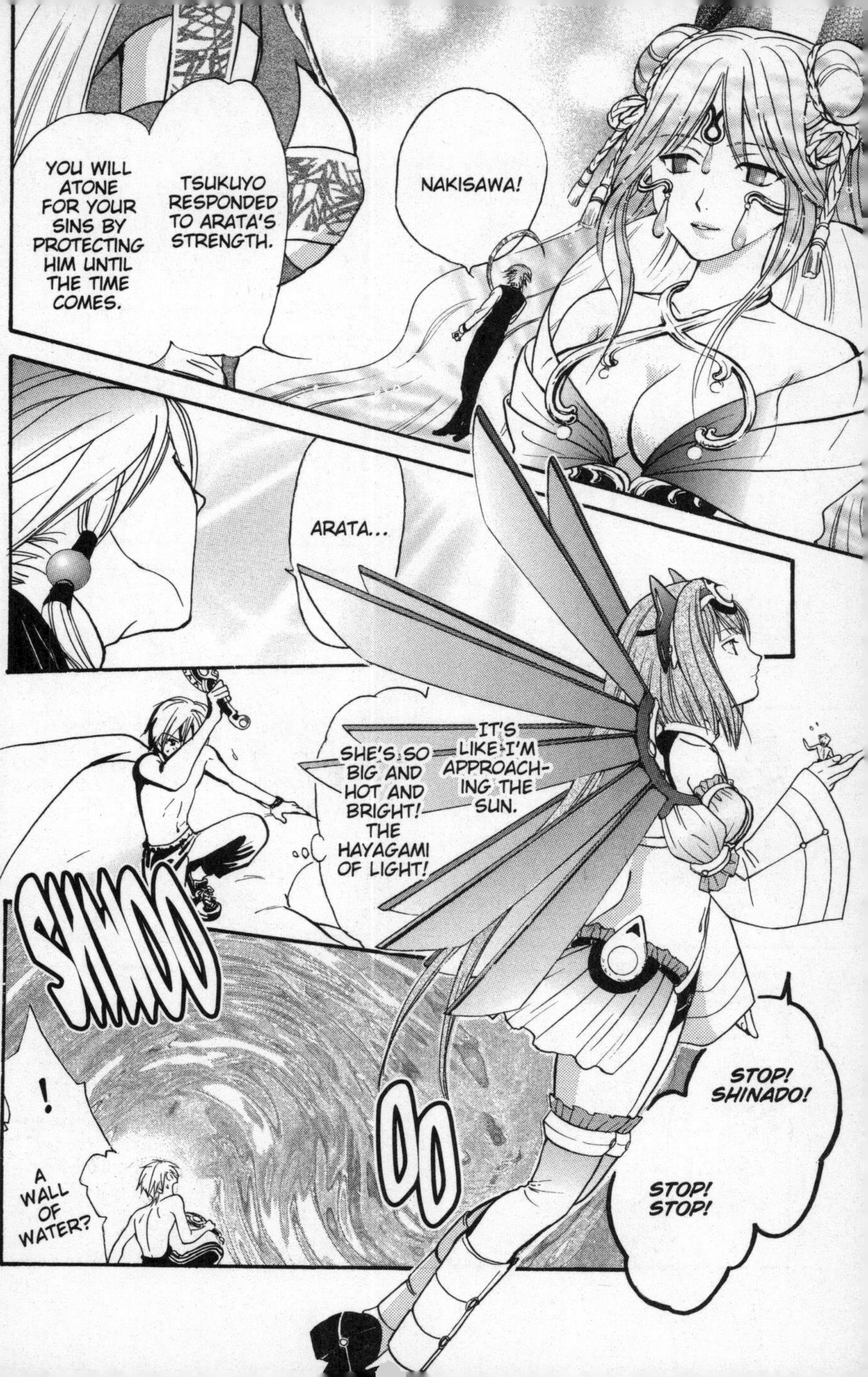
NAKISAWA!
TSUKUYO RESPONDED TO ARATA'S STRENGTH.
YOU WILL ATONE FOR YOUR SINS BY PROTECTING HIM UNTIL THE TIME COMES.
ARATA...
IT'S LIKE I'M APPROACHING THE SUN.
SHE'S SO BIG AND HOT AND BRIGHT! THE HAYAGAMI OF LIGHT!
STOP! SHINADO!
STOP! STOP!
SHWOO
!
A WALL OF WATER?

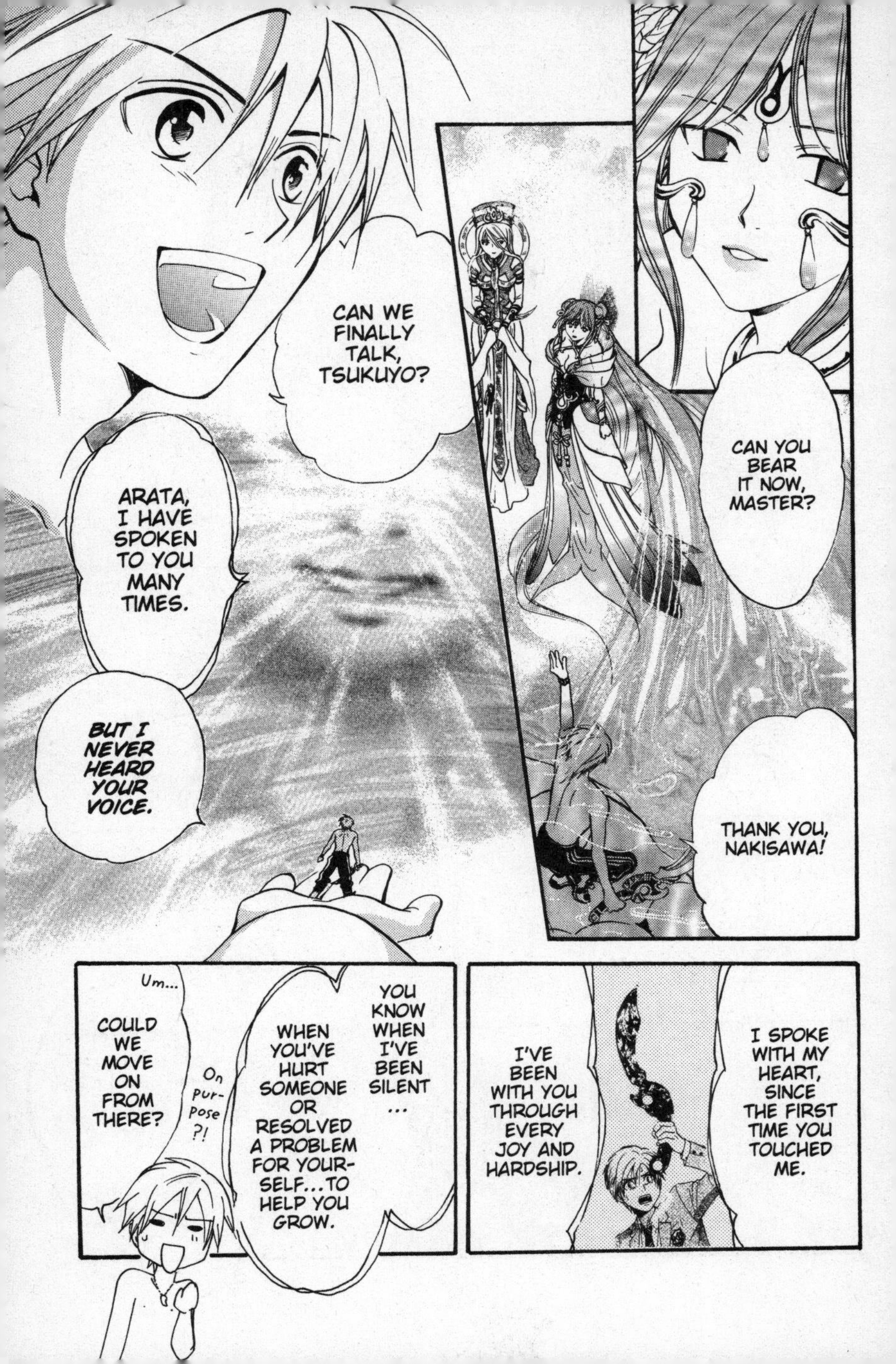
CAN YOU BEAR IT NOW, MASTER?
THANK YOU, NAKISAWA!
CAN WE FINALLY TALK, TSUKUYO?
ARATA, I HAVE SPOKEN TO YOU MANY TIMES.
BUT I NEVER HEARD YOUR VOICE.
I SPOKE WITH MY HEART, SINCE THE FIRST TIME YOU TOUCHED ME.
I'VE BEEN WITH YOU THROUGH EVERY JOY AND HARDSHIP.
YOU KNOW WHEN I'VE BEEN SILENT...
WHEN YOU'VE HURT SOMEONE OR RESOLVED A PROBLEM FOR YOUR-SELF...TO HELP YOU GROW.
On pur-pose?!
Um...
COULD WE MOVE ON FROM THERE?

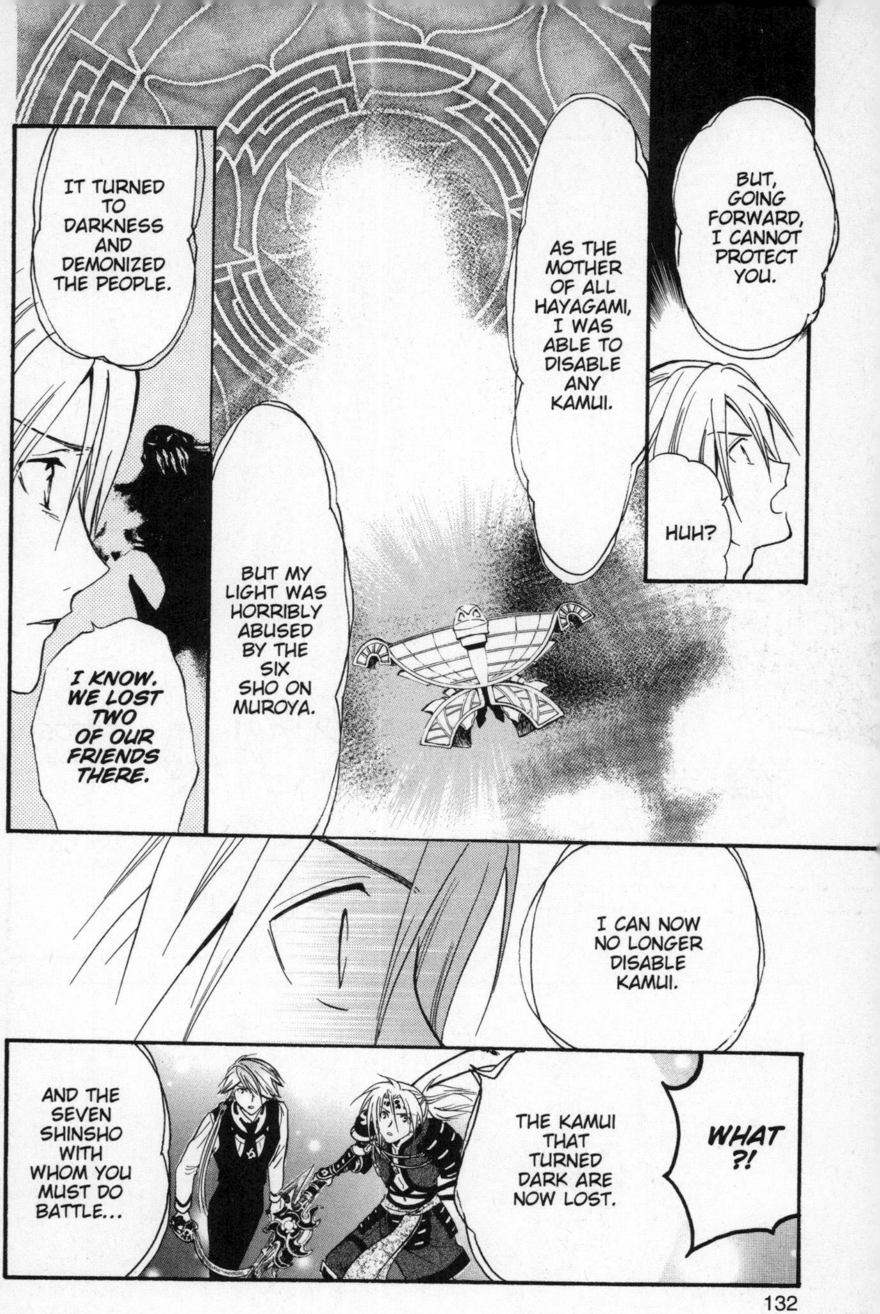
AS THE MOTHER OF ALL HAYAGAMI, I WAS ABLE TO DISABLE ANY KAMUI.
BUT MY LIGHT WAS HORRIBLY ABUSED BY THE SIX SHO ON MUROYA.
IT TURNED TO DARKNESS AND DEMONIZED THE PEOPLE.
I KNOW. WE LOST TWO OF OUR FRIENDS THERE.
BUT, GOING FORWARD, I CANNOT PROTECT YOU.
HUH?
I CAN NOW NO LONGER DISABLE KAMUI.
WHAT?!
THE KAMUI THAT TURNED DARK ARE NOW LOST.
AND THE SEVEN SHINSHO WITH WHOM YOU MUST DO BATTLE...

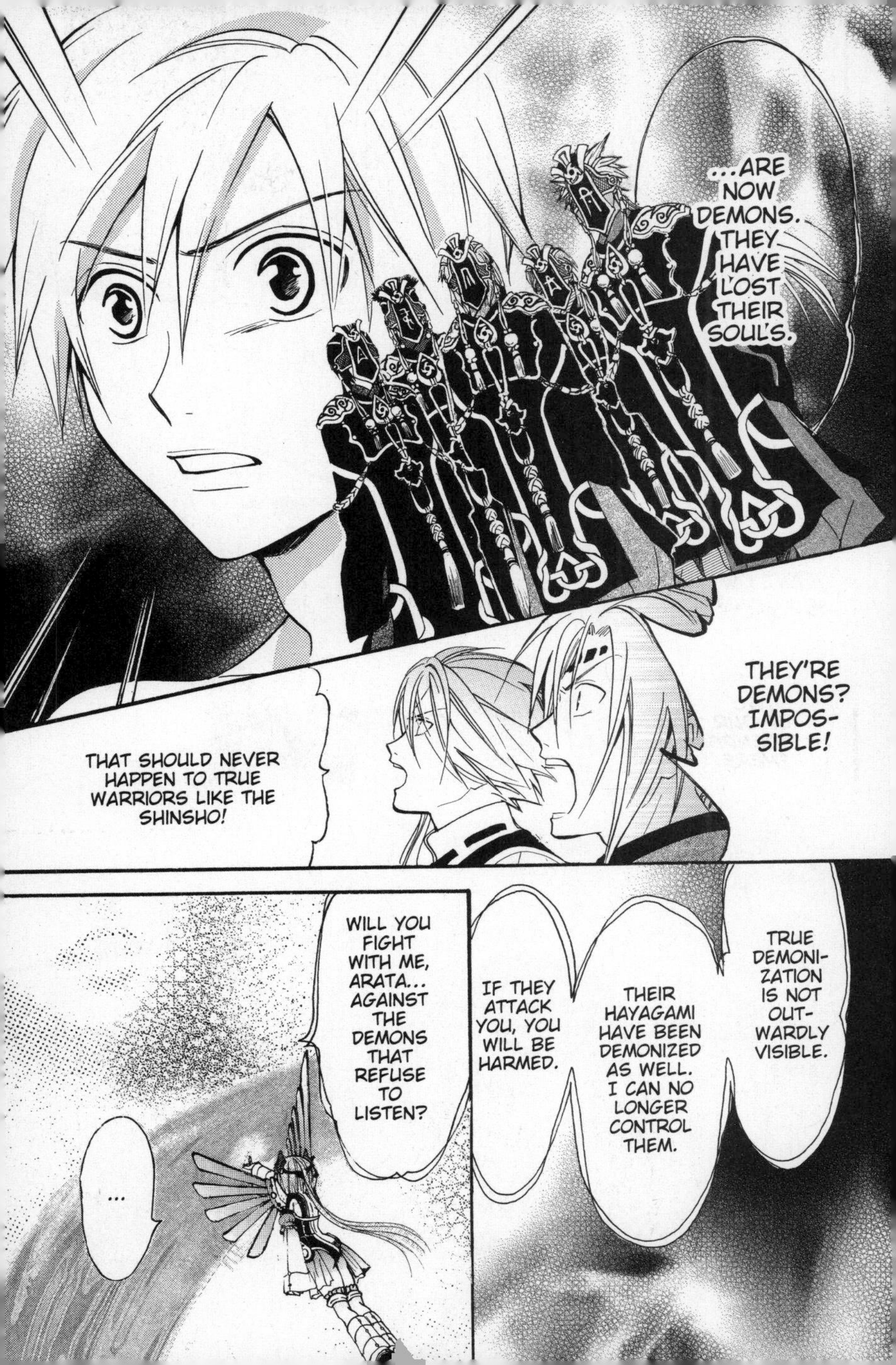
...ARE NOW DEMONS. THEY HAVE LOST THEIR SOULS.
THEY'RE DEMONS? IMPOSSIBLE!
THAT SHOULD NEVER HAPPEN TO TRUE WARRIORS LIKE THE SHINSHO!
TRUE DEMONIZATION IS NOT OUTWARDLY VISIBLE.
THEIR HAYAGAMI HAVE BEEN DEMONIZED AS WELL. I CAN NO LONGER CONTROL THEM.
IF THEY ATTACK YOU, YOU WILL BE HARMED.
WILL YOU FIGHT WITH ME, ARATA... AGAINST THE DEMONS THAT REFUSE TO LISTEN?
...

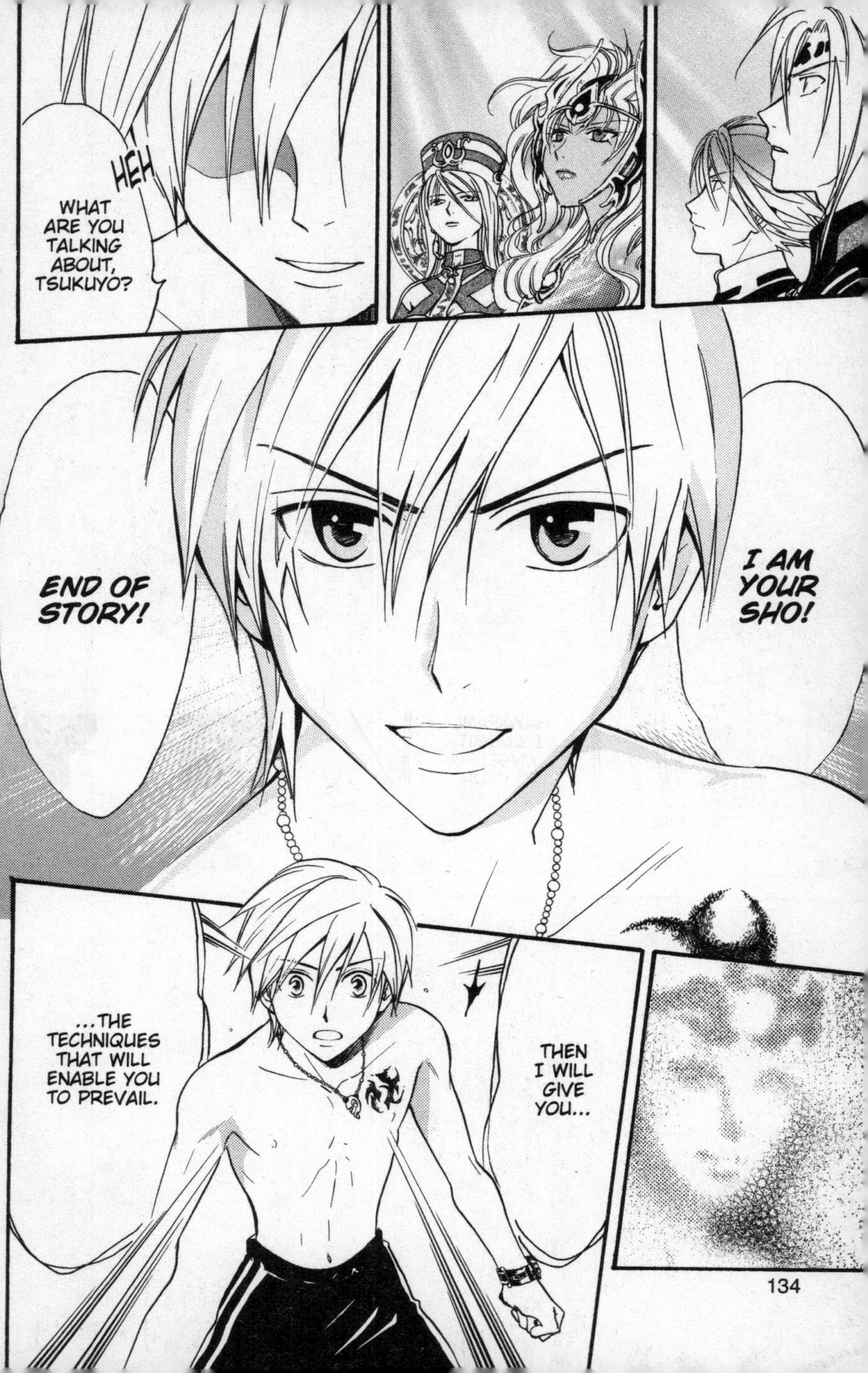
HEH
WHAT ARE YOU TALKING ABOUT, TSUKUYO?
I AM YOUR SHO!
END OF STORY!
THEN I WILL GIVE YOU...
...THE TECHNIQUES THAT WILL ENABLE YOU TO PREVAIL.

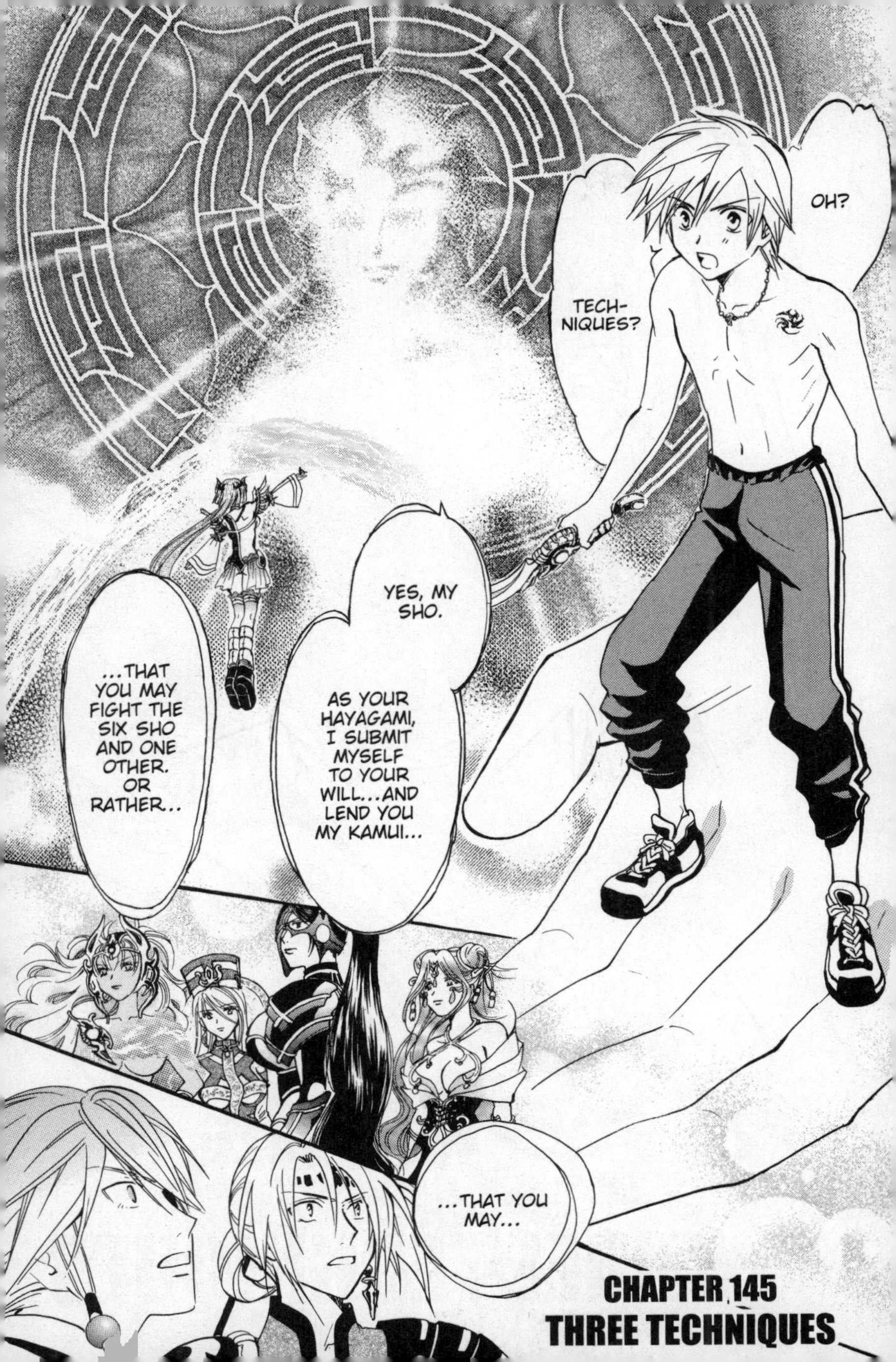
OH?
TECH-NIQUES?
YES, MY SHO.
AS YOUR HAYAGAMI, I SUBMIT MYSELF TO YOUR WILL...AND LEND YOU MY KAMUI...
...THAT YOU MAY FIGHT THE SIX SHO AND ONE OTHER. OR RATHER...
...THAT YOU MAY...
CHAPTER 145
THREE TECHNIQUES

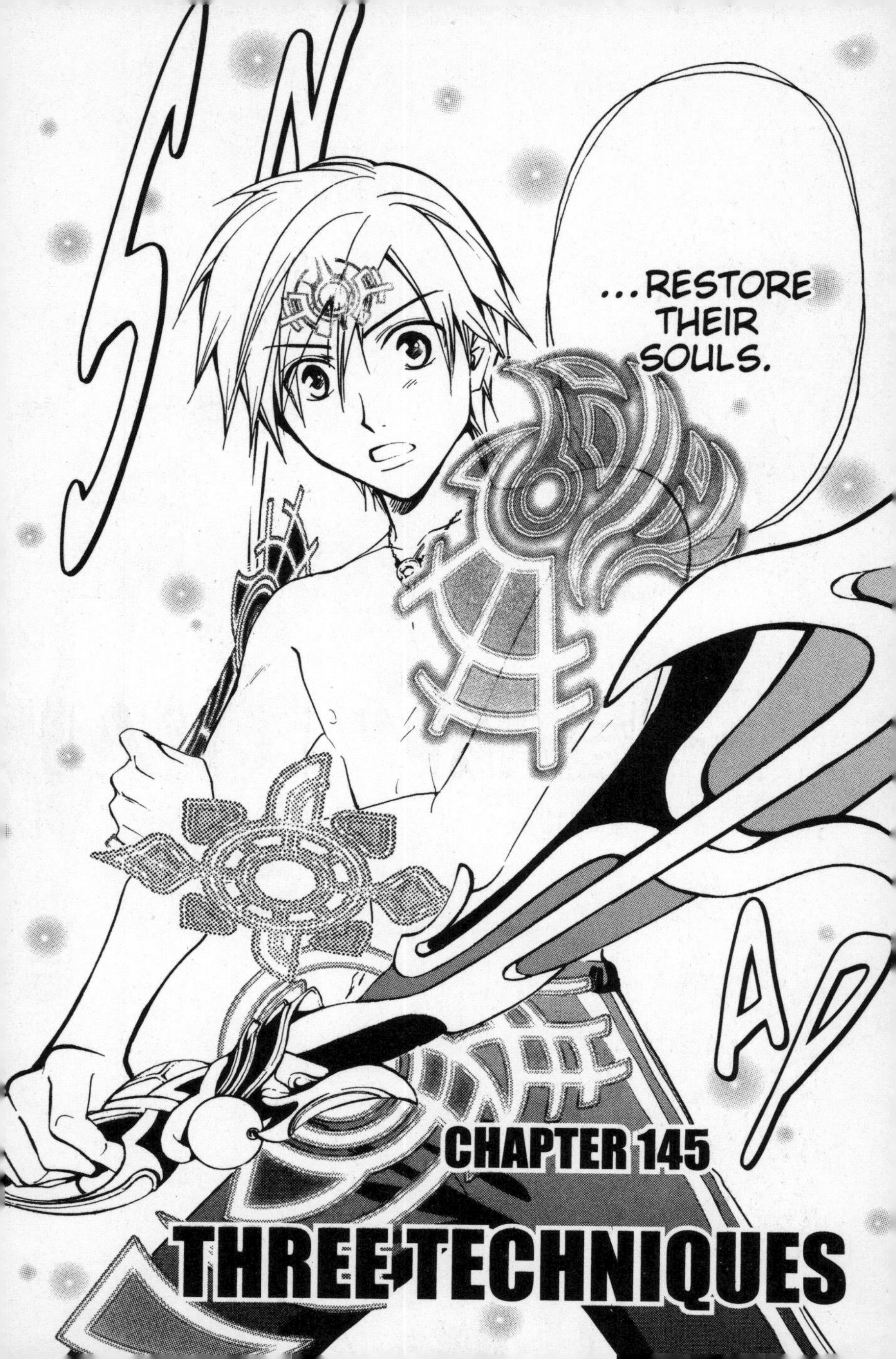
...RESTORE THEIR SOULS.

CHAPTER 145

THREE TECHNIQUES

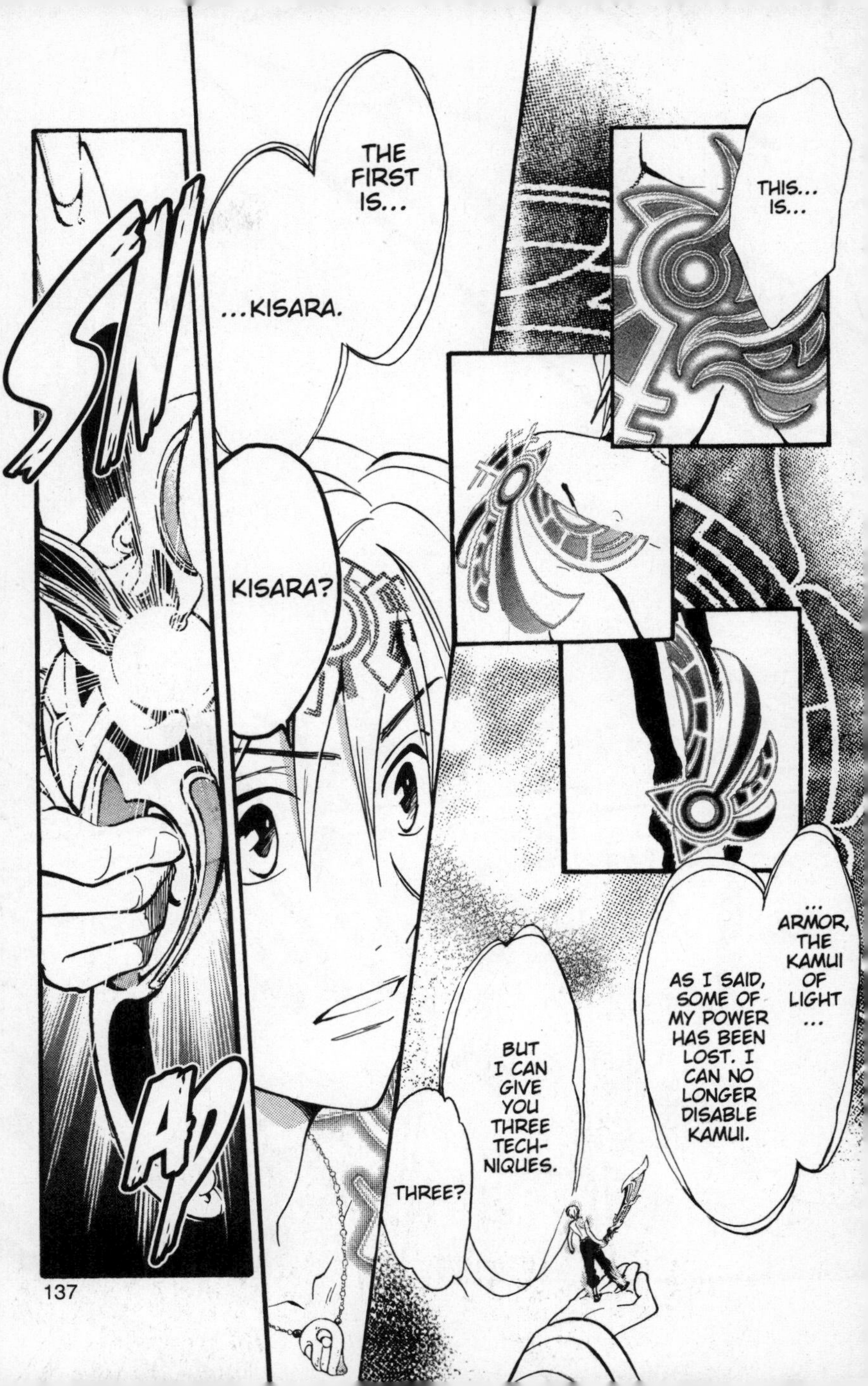
THIS... IS...
... ARMOR, THE KAMUI OF LIGHT ...
AS I SAID, SOME OF MY POWER HAS BEEN LOST. I CAN NO LONGER DISABLE KAMUI.
BUT I CAN GIVE YOU THREE TECH-NIQUES.
THREE?
THE FIRST IS...
...KISARA.
KISARA?

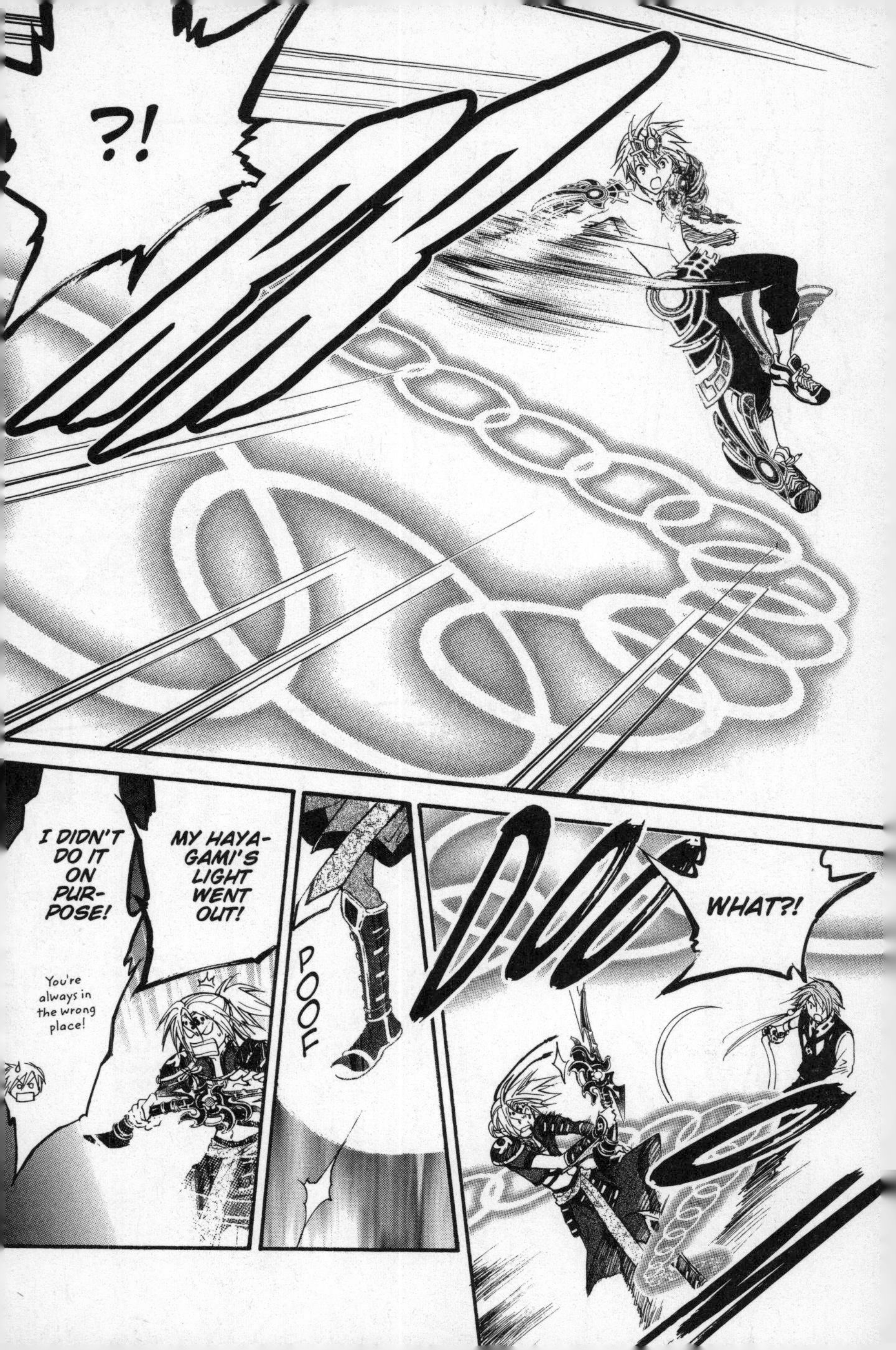
?!
WHAT?!
POOF
MY HAYA-GAMI'S LIGHT WENT OUT!
I DIDN'T DO IT ON PUR-POSE!
You're always in the wrong place!

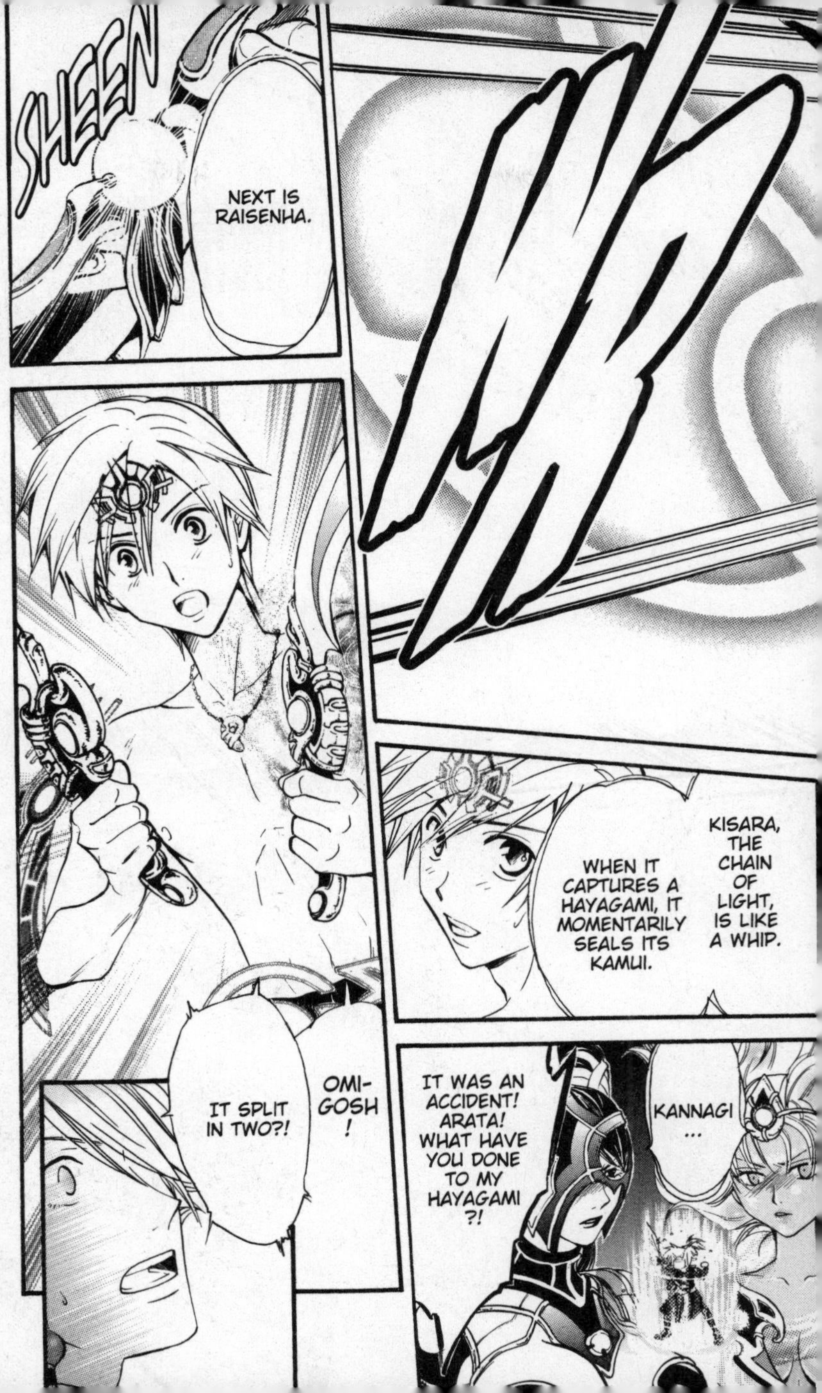
SHK
SHEEN
NEXT IS RAISENHA.
KISARA, THE CHAIN OF LIGHT, IS LIKE A WHIP.
WHEN IT CAPTURES A HAYAGAMI, IT MOMENTARILY SEALS ITS KAMUI.
KANNAGI...
IT WAS AN ACCIDENT! ARATA! WHAT HAVE YOU DONE TO MY HAYAGAMI?!
OMI-GOSH!
IT SPLIT IN TWO?!

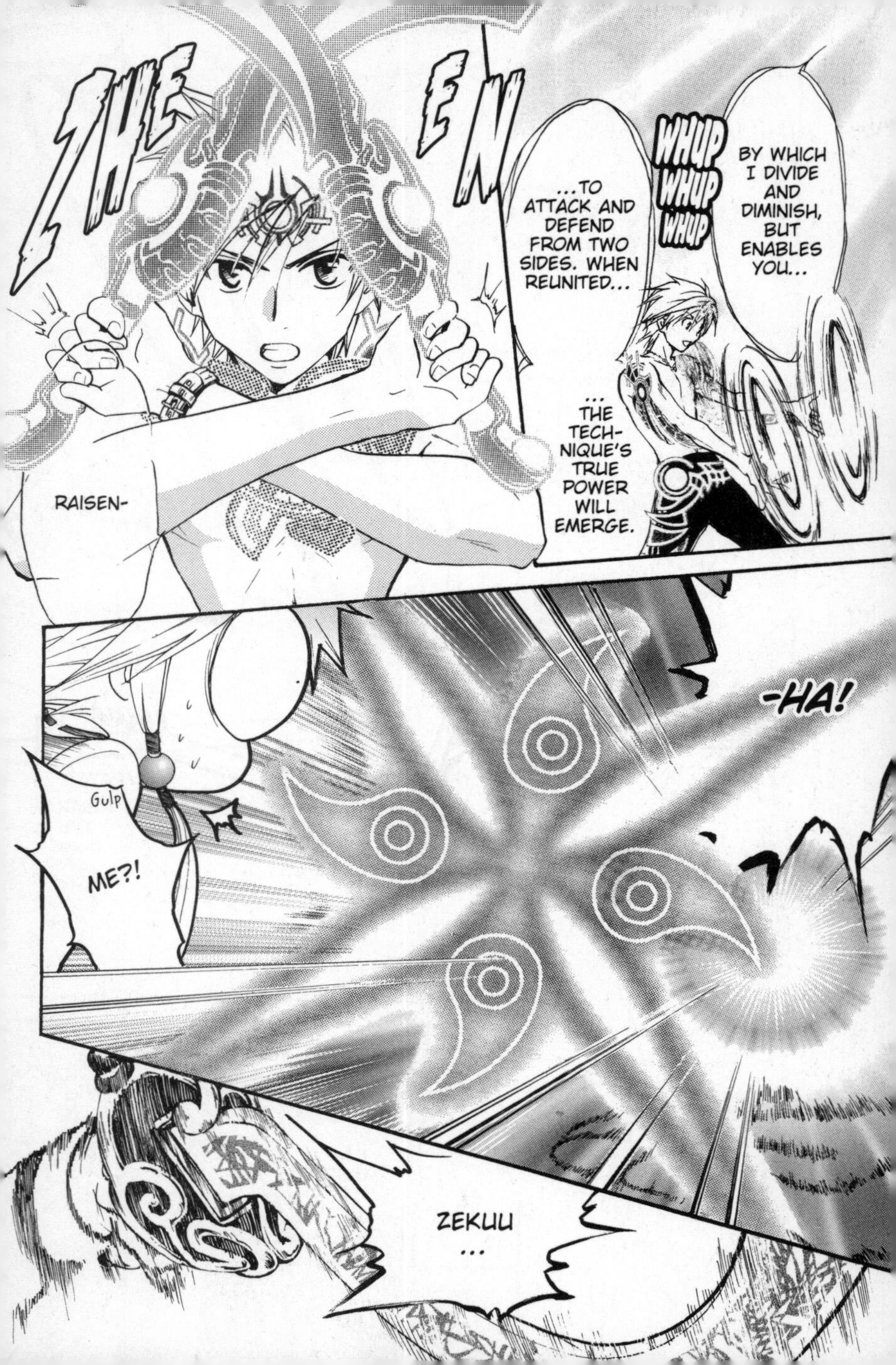
BY WHICH I DIVIDE AND DIMINISH, BUT ENABLES YOU...
WHUP WHUP WHUP
...TO ATTACK AND DEFEND FROM TWO SIDES. WHEN REUNITED...
...THE TECHNIQUE'S TRUE POWER WILL EMERGE.
ZHE
EN
RAISEN-
-HA!
Gulp
ME?!
ZEKUU ...

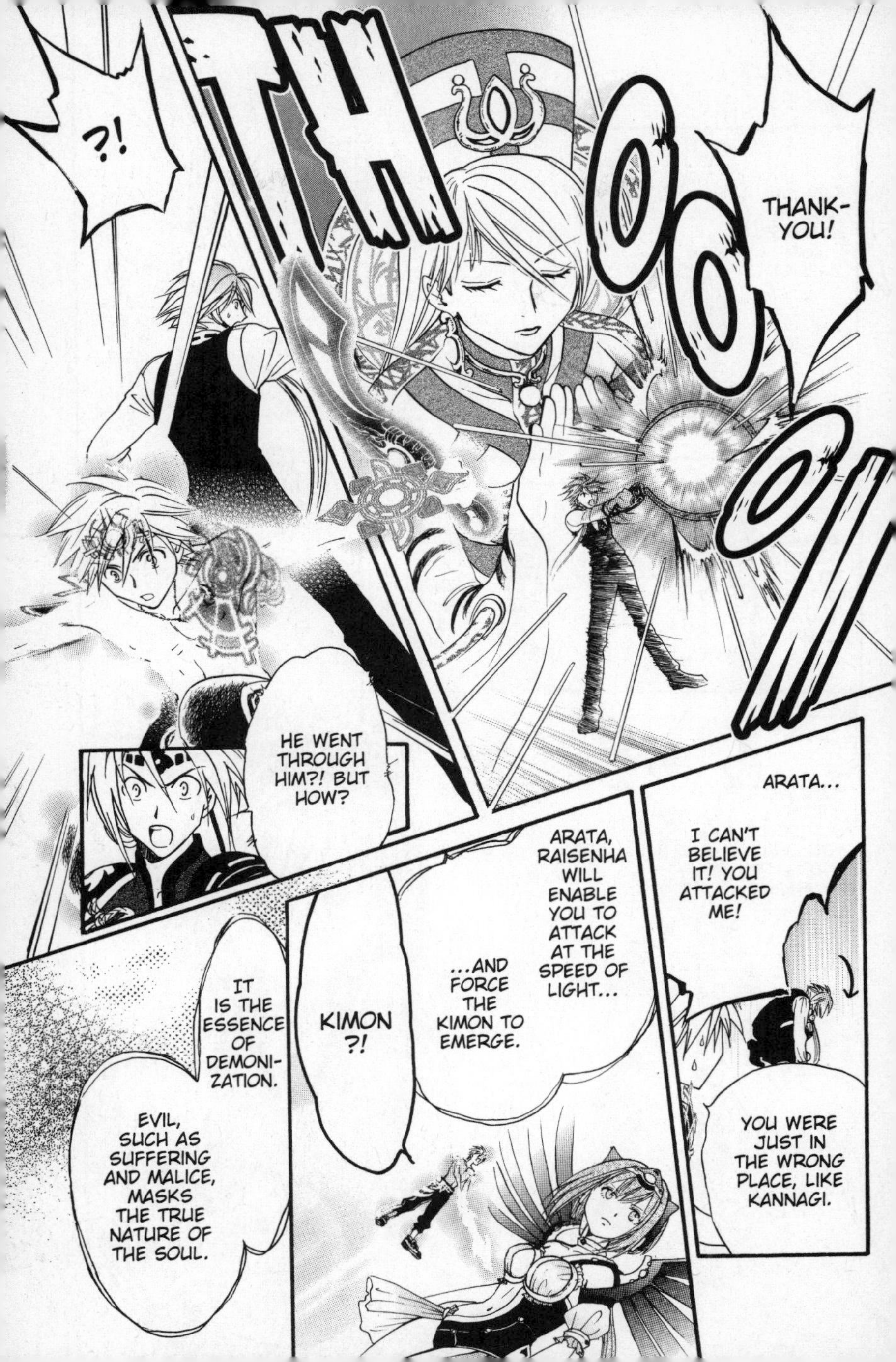
THANK-YOU!
THOOOO!
?!
HE WENT THROUGH HIM?! BUT HOW?
ARATA...
I CAN'T BELIEVE IT! YOU ATTACKED ME!
YOU WERE JUST IN THE WRONG PLACE, LIKE KANNAGI.
ARATA, RAISENHA WILL ENABLE YOU TO ATTACK AT THE SPEED OF LIGHT...
...AND FORCE THE KIMON TO EMERGE.
KIMON ?!
IT IS THE ESSENCE OF DEMONIZATION.
EVIL, SUCH AS SUFFERING AND MALICE, MASKS THE TRUE NATURE OF THE SOUL.

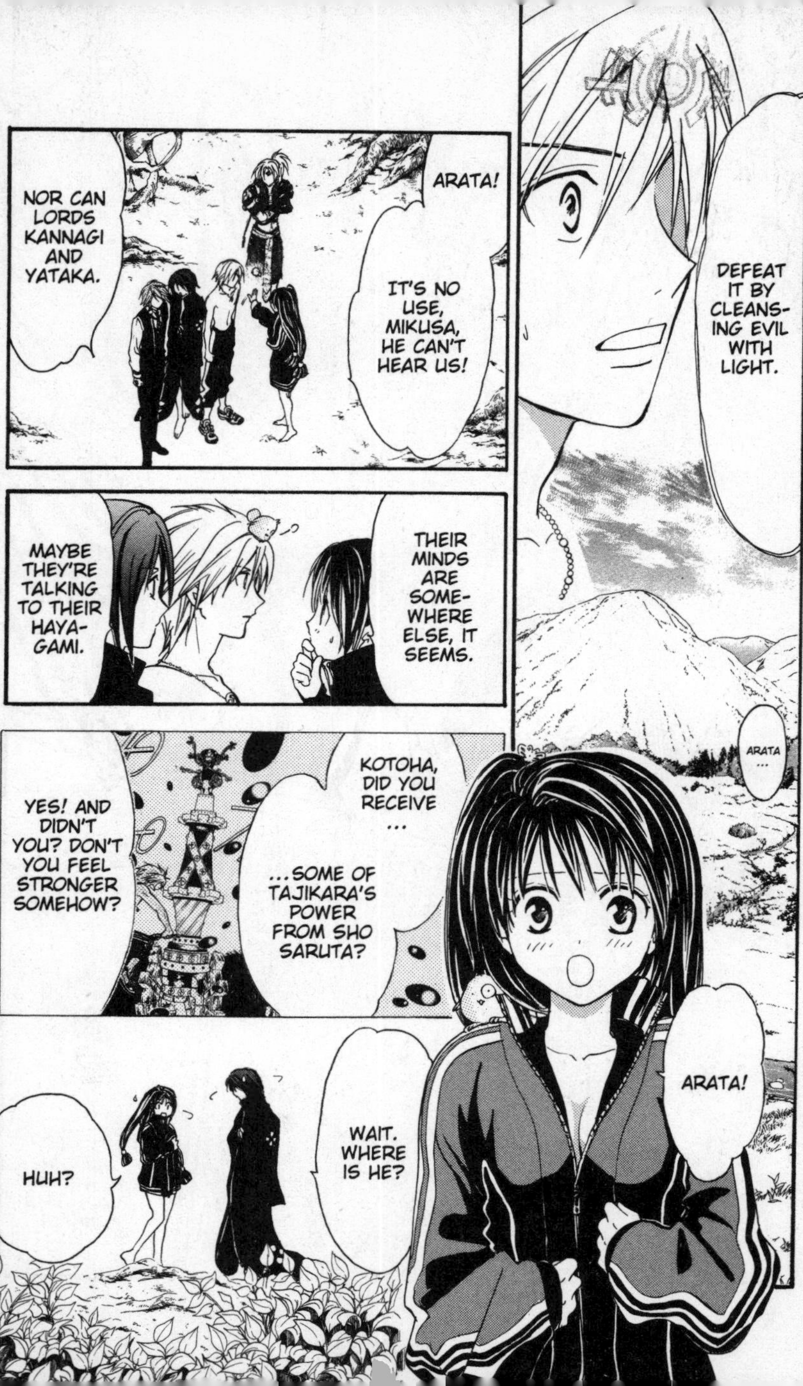
DEFEAT IT BY CLEANSING EVIL WITH LIGHT.
ARATA!
IT'S NO USE, MIKUSA, HE CAN'T HEAR US!
NOR CAN LORDS KANNAGI AND YATAKA.
THEIR MINDS ARE SOMEWHERE ELSE, IT SEEMS.
MAYBE THEY'RE TALKING TO THEIR HAYAGAMI.
KOTOHA, DID YOU RECEIVE...
...SOME OF TAJIKARA'S POWER FROM SHO SARUTA?
YES! AND DIDN'T YOU? DON'T YOU FEEL STRONGER SOMEHOW?
ARATA...
ARATA!
WAIT. WHERE IS HE?
HUH?

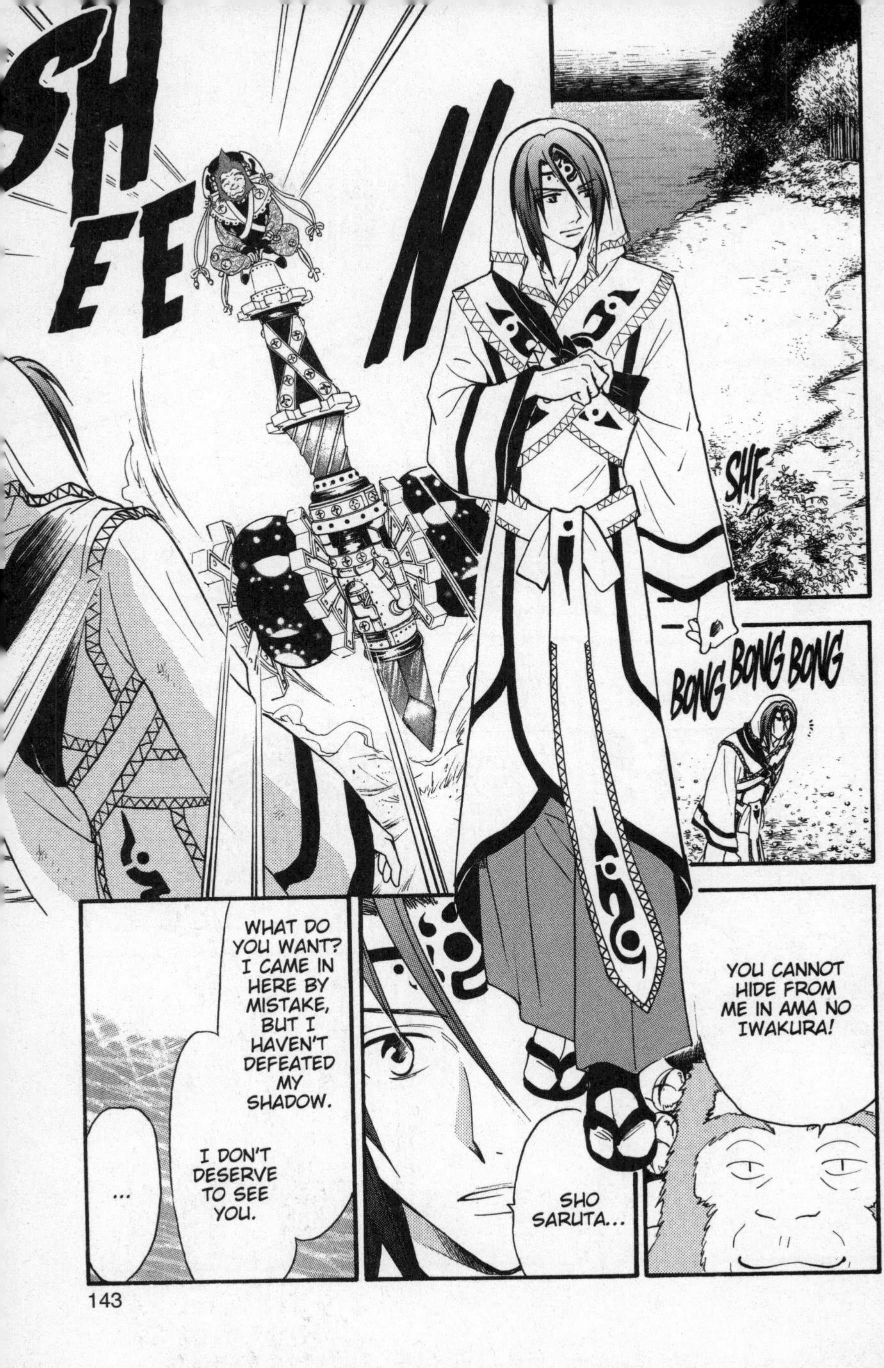
SHF
BONG BONG BONG
SHEEN
YOU CANNOT HIDE FROM ME IN AMA NO IWAKURA!
SHO SARUTA...
WHAT DO YOU WANT? I CAME IN HERE BY MISTAKE, BUT I HAVEN'T DEFEATED MY SHADOW.
I DON'T DESERVE TO SEE YOU.
...

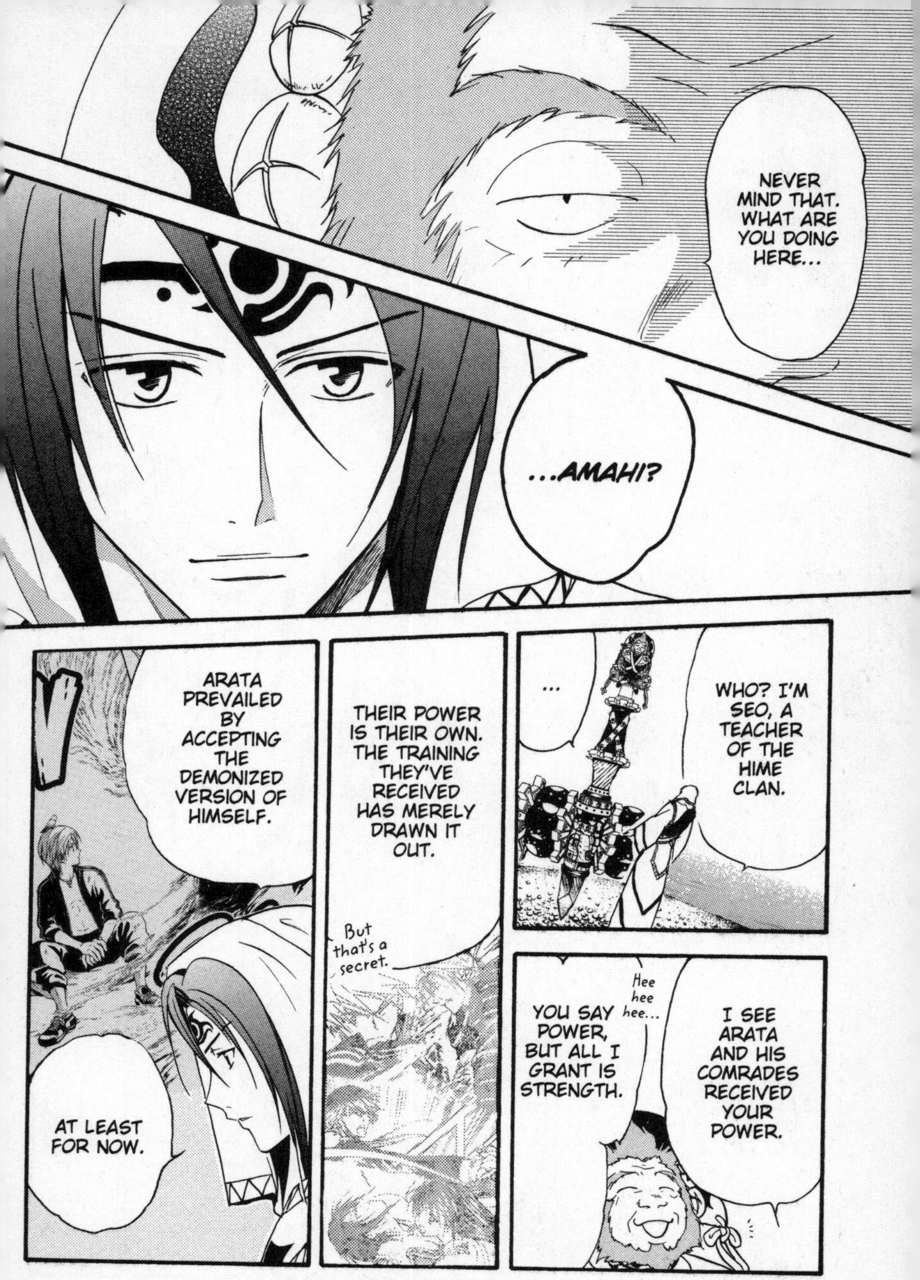
NEVER MIND THAT. WHAT ARE YOU DOING HERE...
...AMAHI?
WHO? I'M SEO, A TEACHER OF THE HIME CLAN.
...
I SEE ARATA AND HIS COMRADES RECEIVED YOUR POWER.
Hee hee hee...
YOU SAY POWER, BUT ALL I GRANT IS STRENGTH.
THEIR POWER IS THEIR OWN. THE TRAINING THEY'VE RECEIVED HAS MERELY DRAWN IT OUT.
But that's a secret.
ARATA PREVAILED BY ACCEPTING THE DEMONIZED VERSION OF HIMSELF.
AT LEAST FOR NOW.

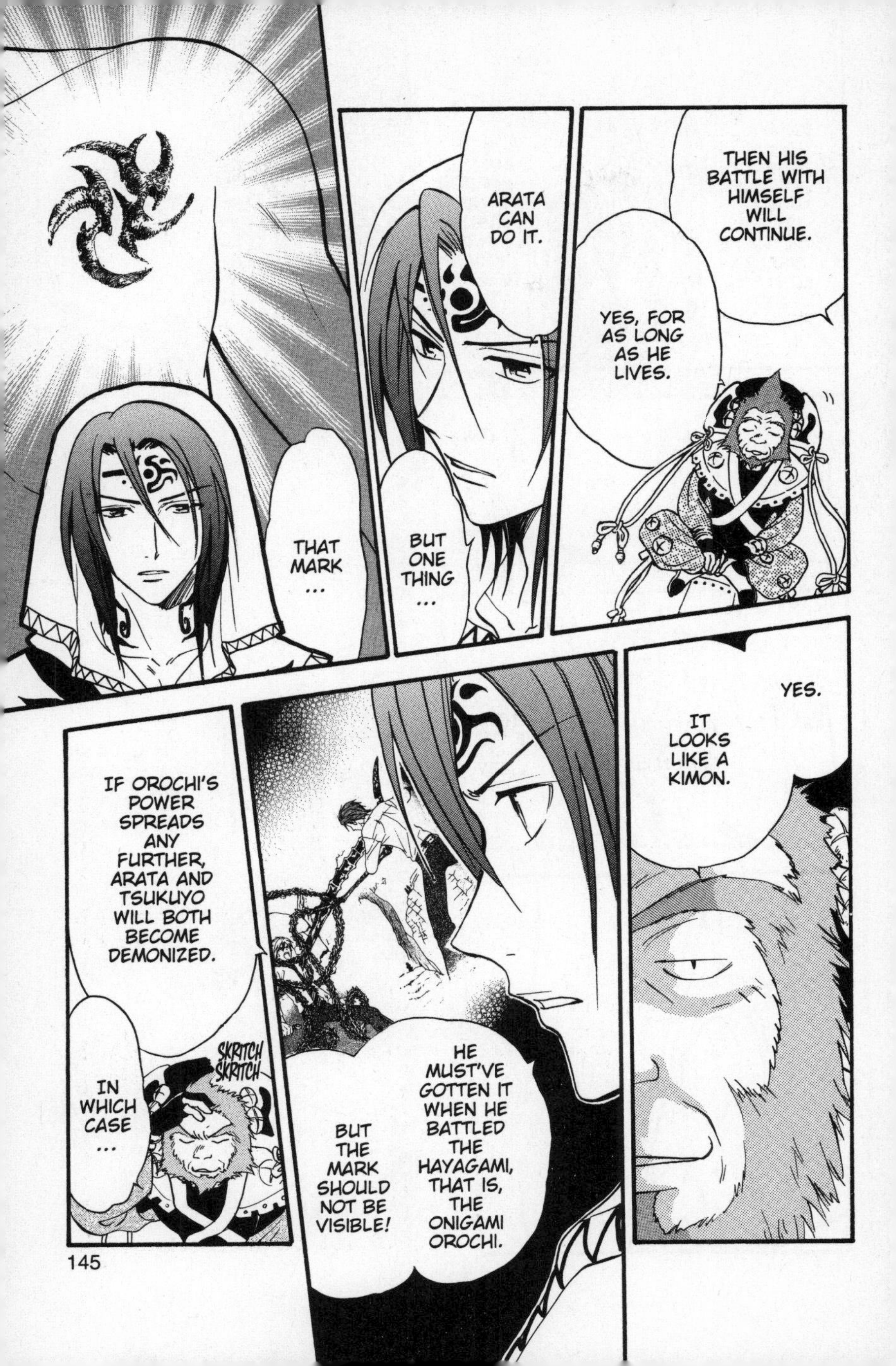
THEN HIS BATTLE WITH HIMSELF WILL CONTINUE.
YES, FOR AS LONG AS HE LIVES.
ARATA CAN DO IT.
BUT ONE THING...
THAT MARK...
YES.
IT LOOKS LIKE A KIMON.
HE MUST'VE GOTTEN IT WHEN HE BATTLED THE HAYAGAMI, THAT IS, THE ONIGAMI OROCHI.
BUT THE MARK SHOULD NOT BE VISIBLE!
IF OROCHI'S POWER SPREADS ANY FURTHER, ARATA AND TSUKUYO WILL BOTH BECOME DEMONIZED.
SKRITCH SKRITCH
IN WHICH CASE...

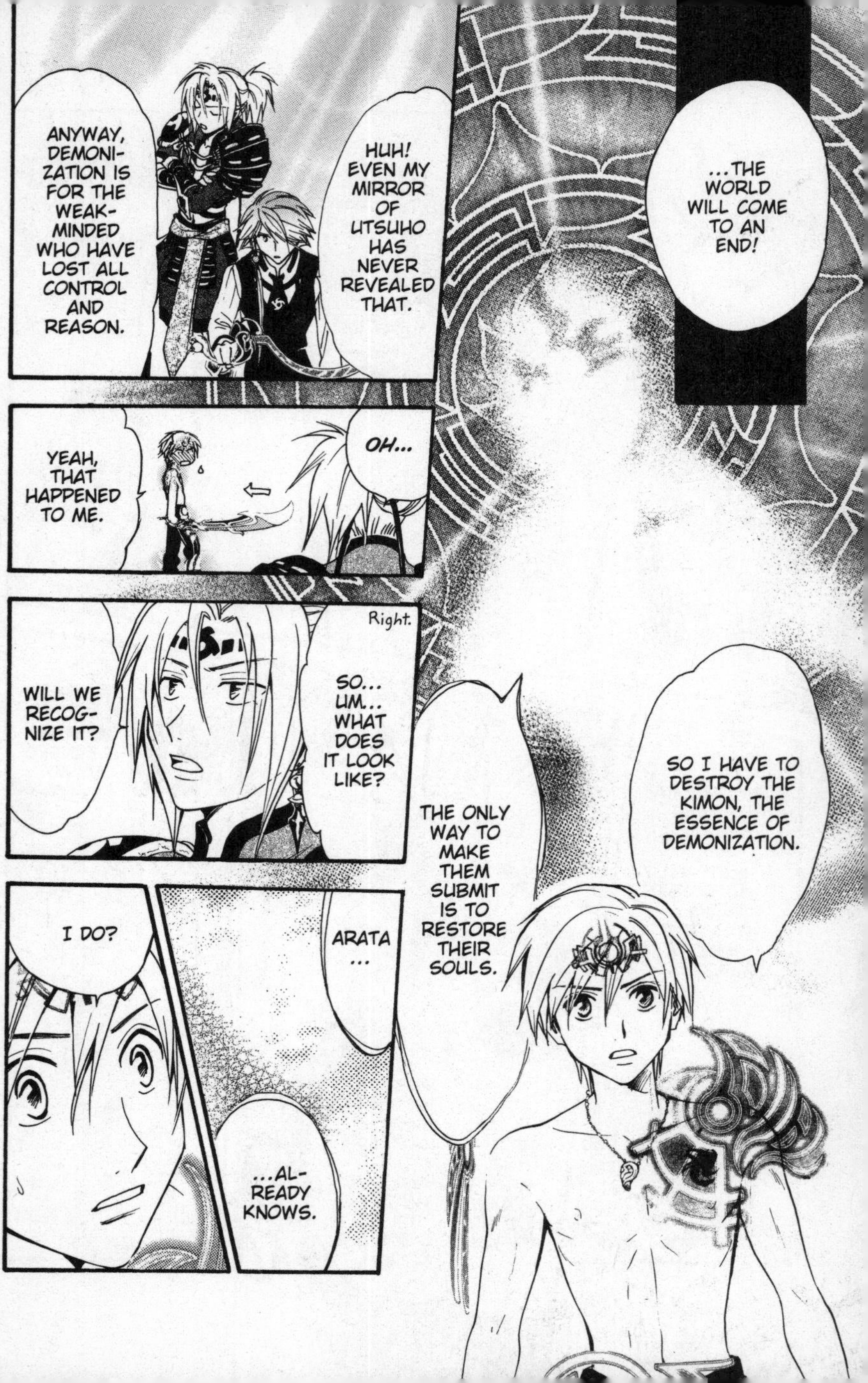
...THE WORLD WILL COME TO AN END!
SO I HAVE TO DESTROY THE KIMON, THE ESSENCE OF DEMONIZATION.
THE ONLY WAY TO MAKE THEM SUBMIT IS TO RESTORE THEIR SOULS.
HUH! EVEN MY MIRROR OF UTSUHO HAS NEVER REVEALED THAT.
ANYWAY, DEMONIZATION IS FOR THE WEAK-MINDED WHO HAVE LOST ALL CONTROL AND REASON.
OH...
YEAH, THAT HAPPENED TO ME.
Right.
SO... UM... WHAT DOES IT LOOK LIKE?
WILL WE RECOGNIZE IT?
ARATA ...
...AL-READY KNOWS.
I DO?

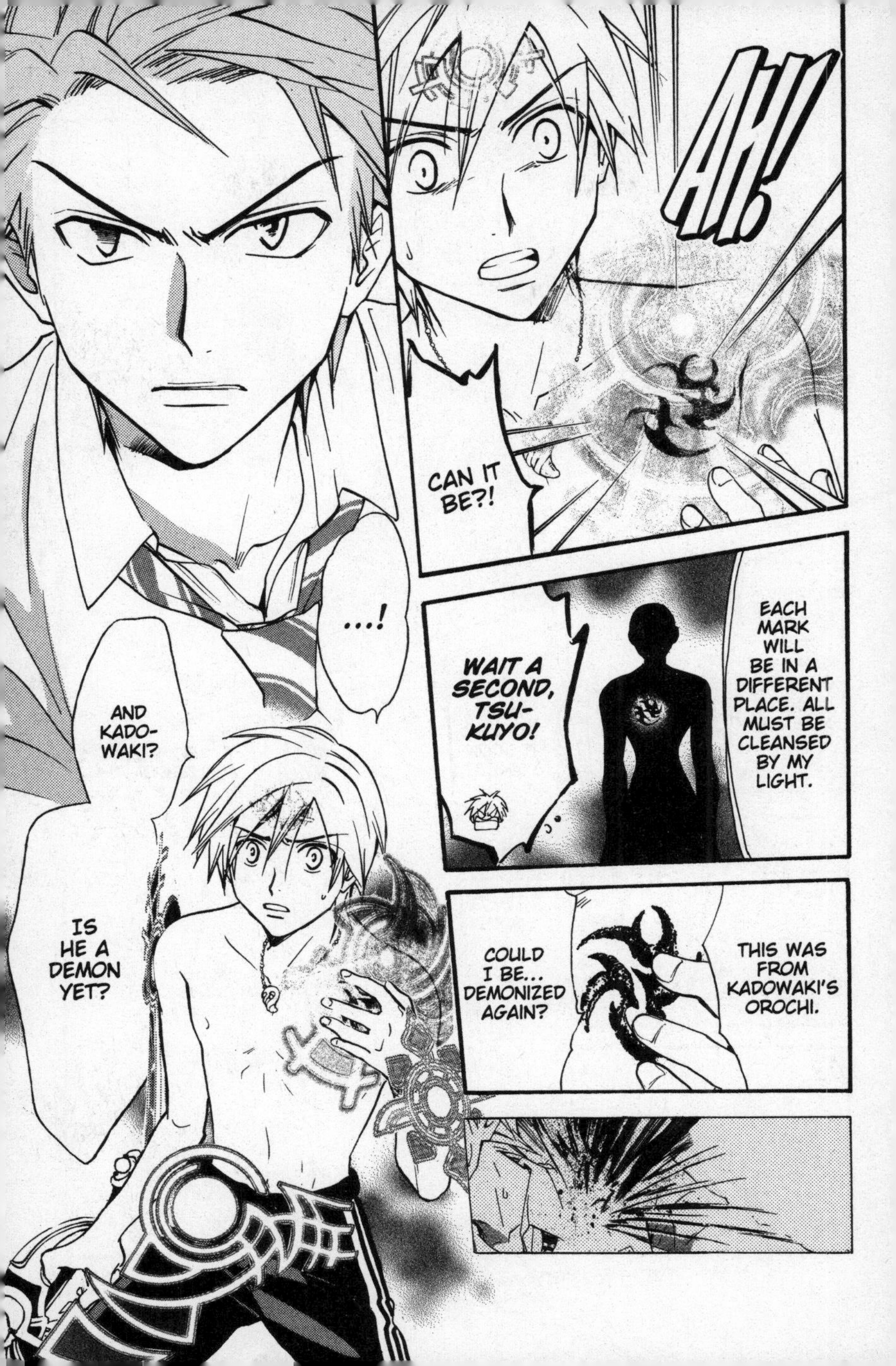
AH!
CAN IT BE?!
EACH MARK WILL BE IN A DIFFERENT PLACE. ALL MUST BE CLEANSED BY MY LIGHT.
WAIT A SECOND, TSUKUYO!
THIS WAS FROM KADOWAKI'S OROCHI.
COULD I BE... DEMONIZED AGAIN?
...!
AND KADOWAKI?
IS HE A DEMON YET?

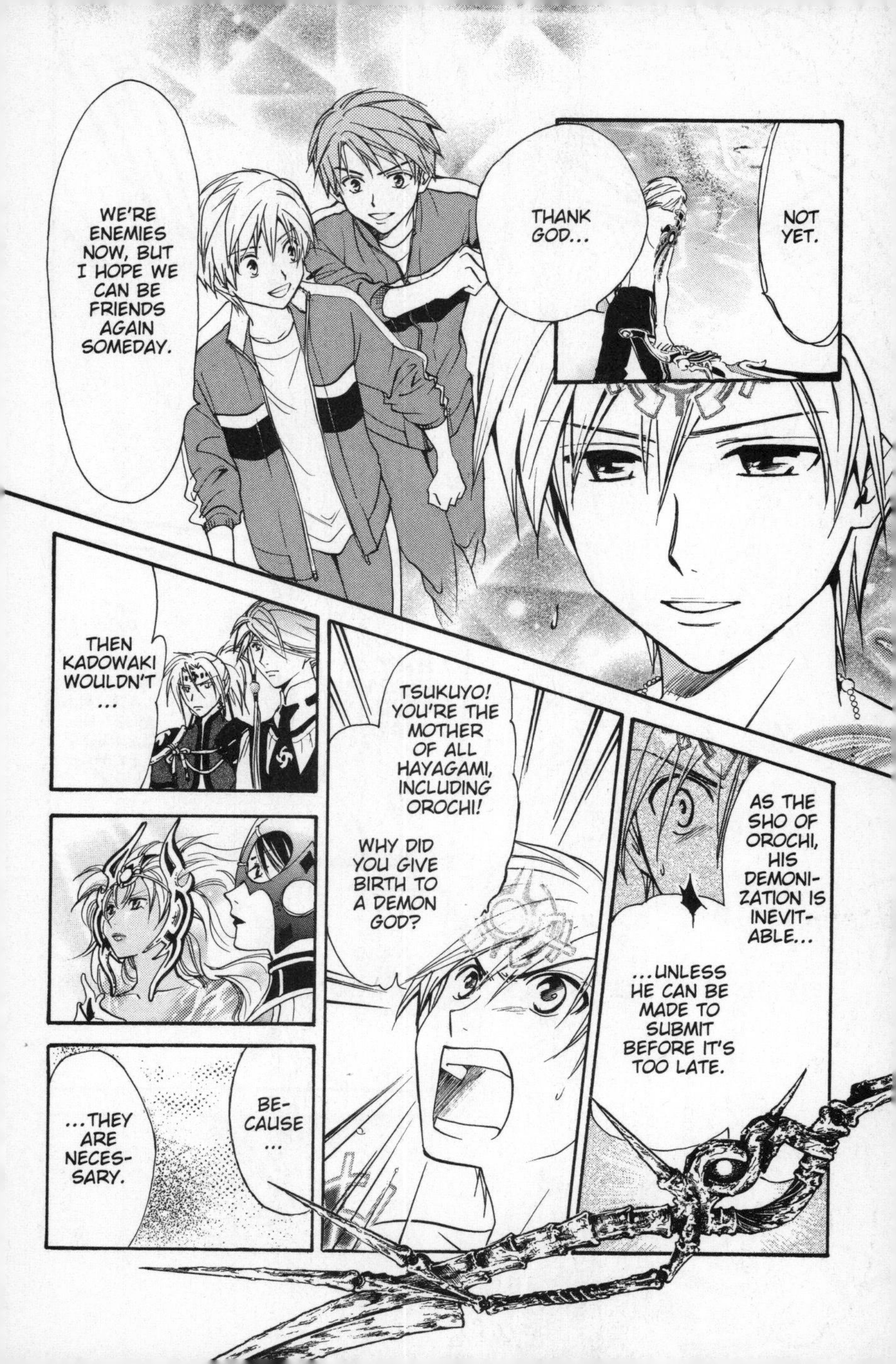
WE'RE ENEMIES NOW, BUT I HOPE WE CAN BE FRIENDS AGAIN SOMEDAY.
THANK GOD...
NOT YET.
AS THE SHO OF OROCHI, HIS DEMONI-ZATION IS INEVIT-ABLE...
...UNLESS HE CAN BE MADE TO SUBMIT BEFORE IT'S TOO LATE.
TSUKUYO! YOU'RE THE MOTHER OF ALL HAYAGAMI, INCLUDING OROCHI!
WHY DID YOU GIVE BIRTH TO A DEMON GOD?
THEN KADOWAKI WOULDN'T ...
BE-CAUSE ...
...THEY ARE NECES-SARY.

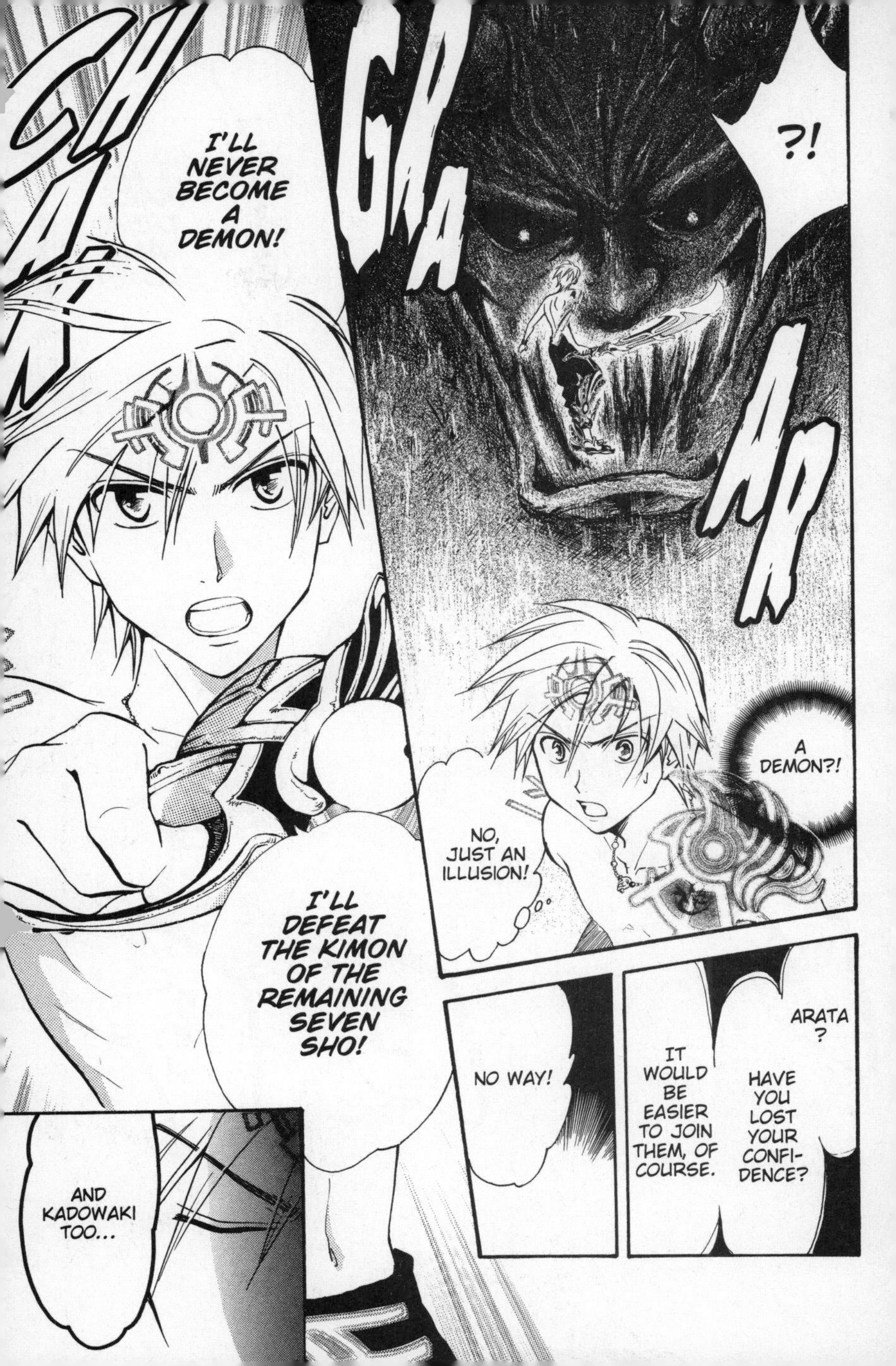
?!
A DEMON?!
NO, JUST AN ILLUSION!
ARATA?
HAVE YOU LOST YOUR CONFIDENCE?
IT WOULD BE EASIER TO JOIN THEM, OF COURSE.
NO WAY!
I'LL NEVER BECOME A DEMON!
I'LL DEFEAT THE KIMON OF THE REMAINING SEVEN SHO!
AND KADOWAKI TOO...

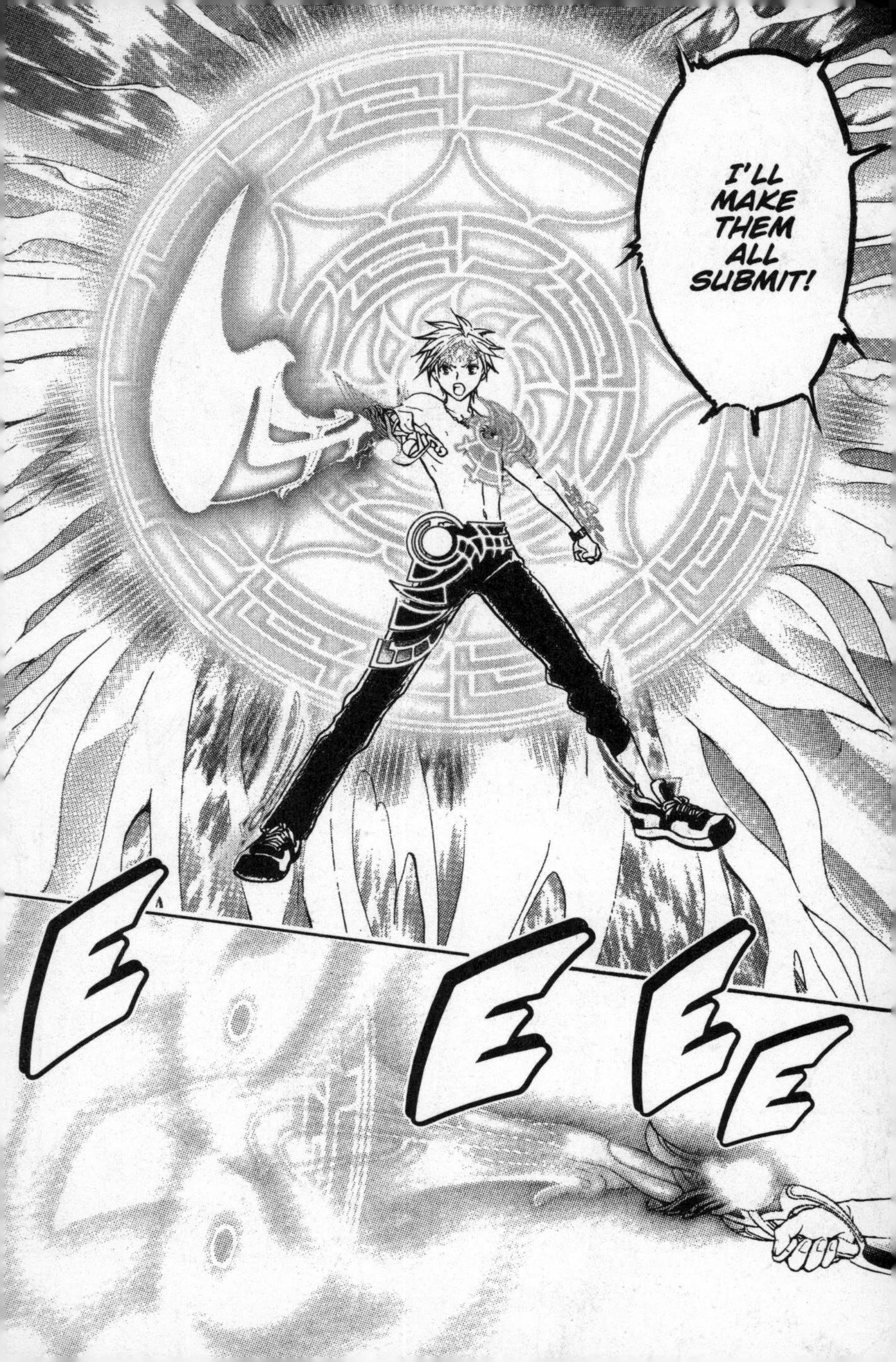
I'LL MAKE THEM ALL SUBMIT!
EEEE

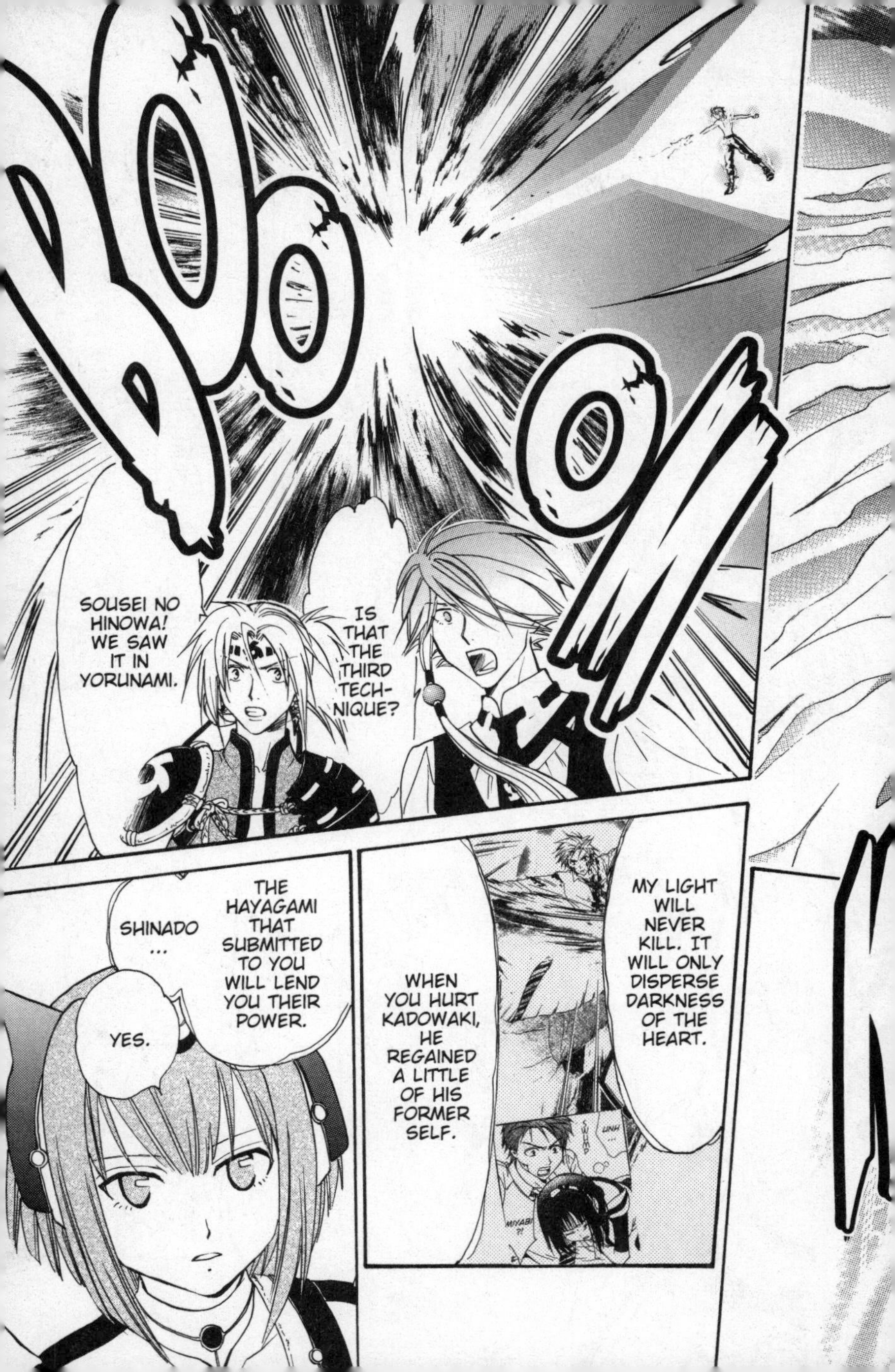
IS THAT THE THIRD TECH-NIQUE?
SOUSEI NO HINOWA! WE SAW IT IN YORUNAMI.
MY LIGHT WILL NEVER KILL. IT WILL ONLY DISPERSE DARKNESS OF THE HEART.
WHEN YOU HURT KADOWAKI, HE REGAINED A LITTLE OF HIS FORMER SELF.
UNH ...
MIYABI ?!
THE HAYAGAMI THAT SUBMITTED TO YOU WILL LEND YOU THEIR POWER.
SHINADO ...
YES.

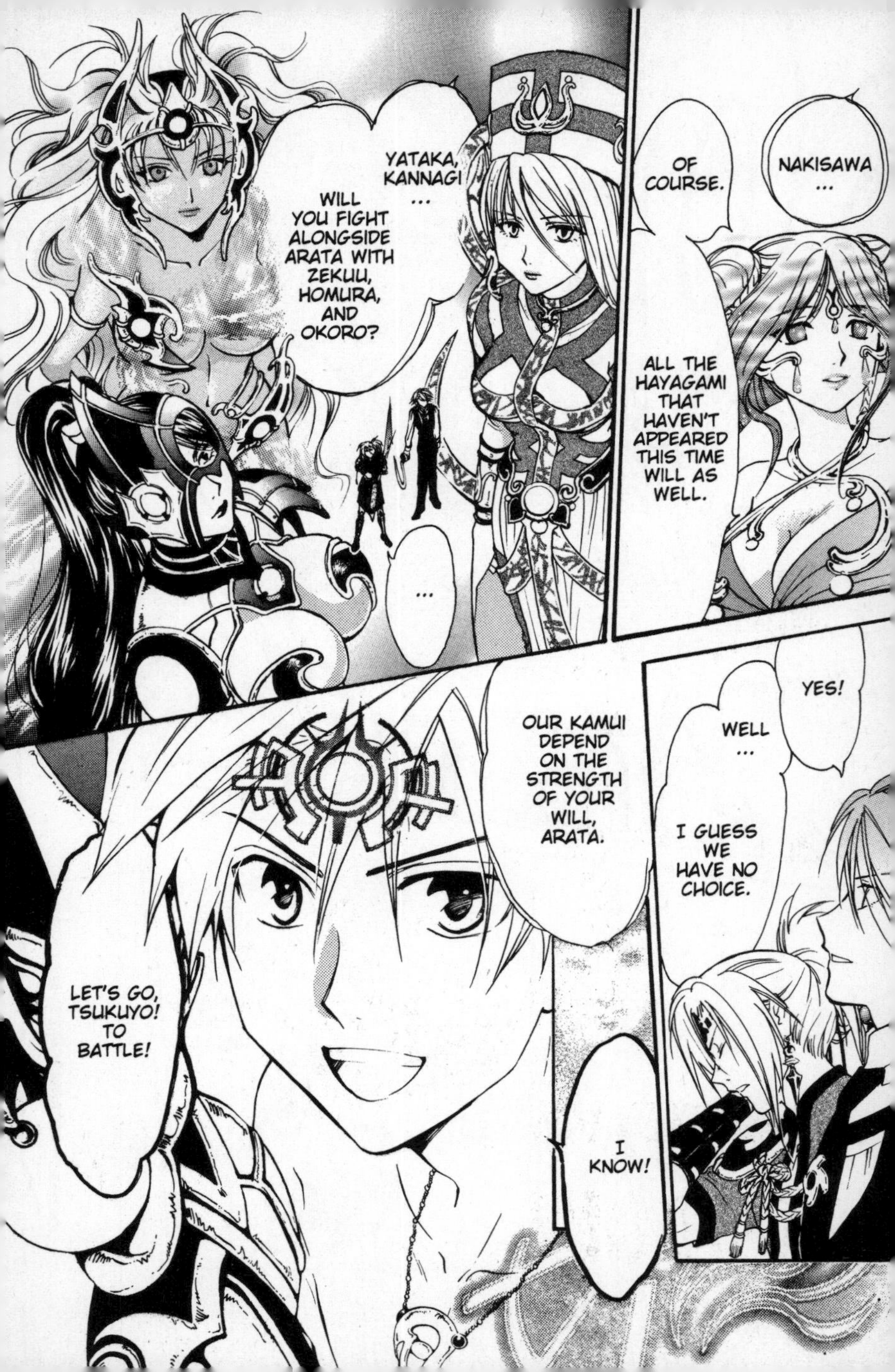
NAKISAWA ...
OF COURSE.
ALL THE HAYAGAMI THAT HAVEN'T APPEARED THIS TIME WILL AS WELL.
YATAKA, KANNAGI ...
WILL YOU FIGHT ALONGSIDE ARATA WITH ZEKUU, HOMURA, AND OKORO?
...
YES!
WELL ...
I GUESS WE HAVE NO CHOICE.
OUR KAMUI DEPEND ON THE STRENGTH OF YOUR WILL, ARATA.
I KNOW!
LET'S GO, TSUKUYO! TO BATTLE!

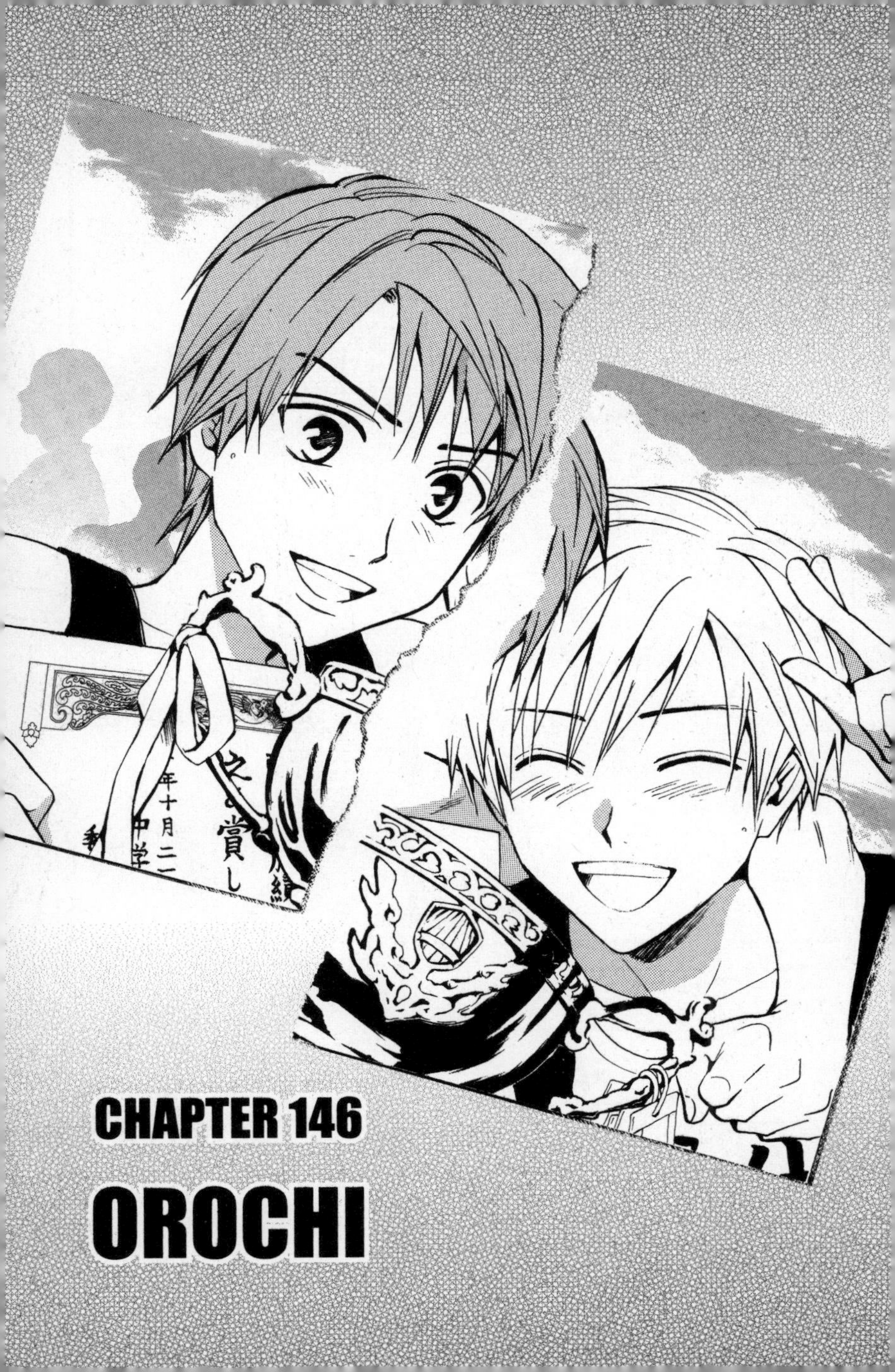

CHAPTER 146

OROCHI

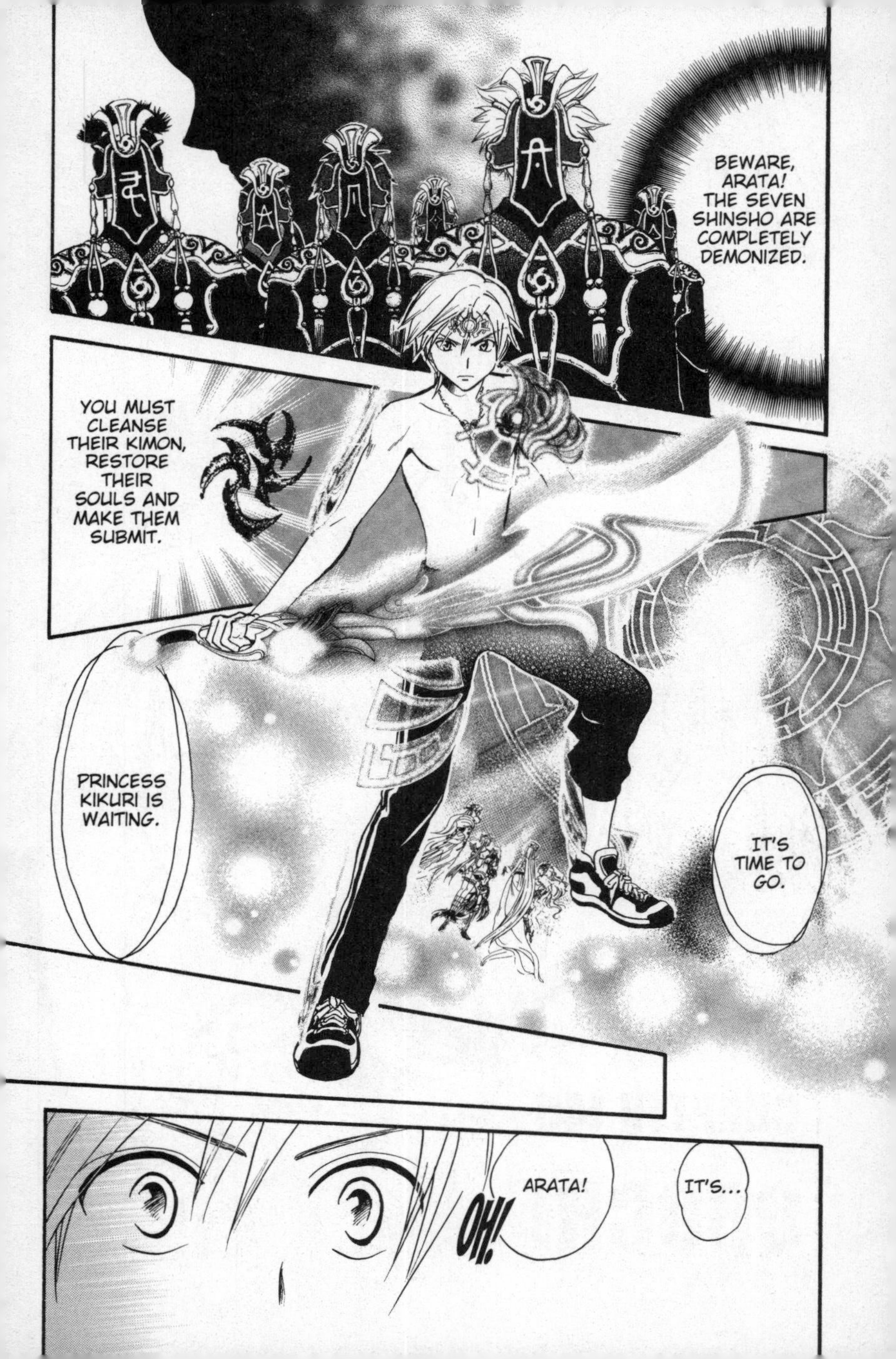
BEWARE, ARATA! THE SEVEN SHINSHO ARE COMPLETELY DEMONIZED.
YOU MUST CLEANSE THEIR KIMON, RESTORE THEIR SOULS AND MAKE THEM SUBMIT.
PRINCESS KIKURI IS WAITING.
IT'S TIME TO GO.
IT'S...
ARATA!
OH!

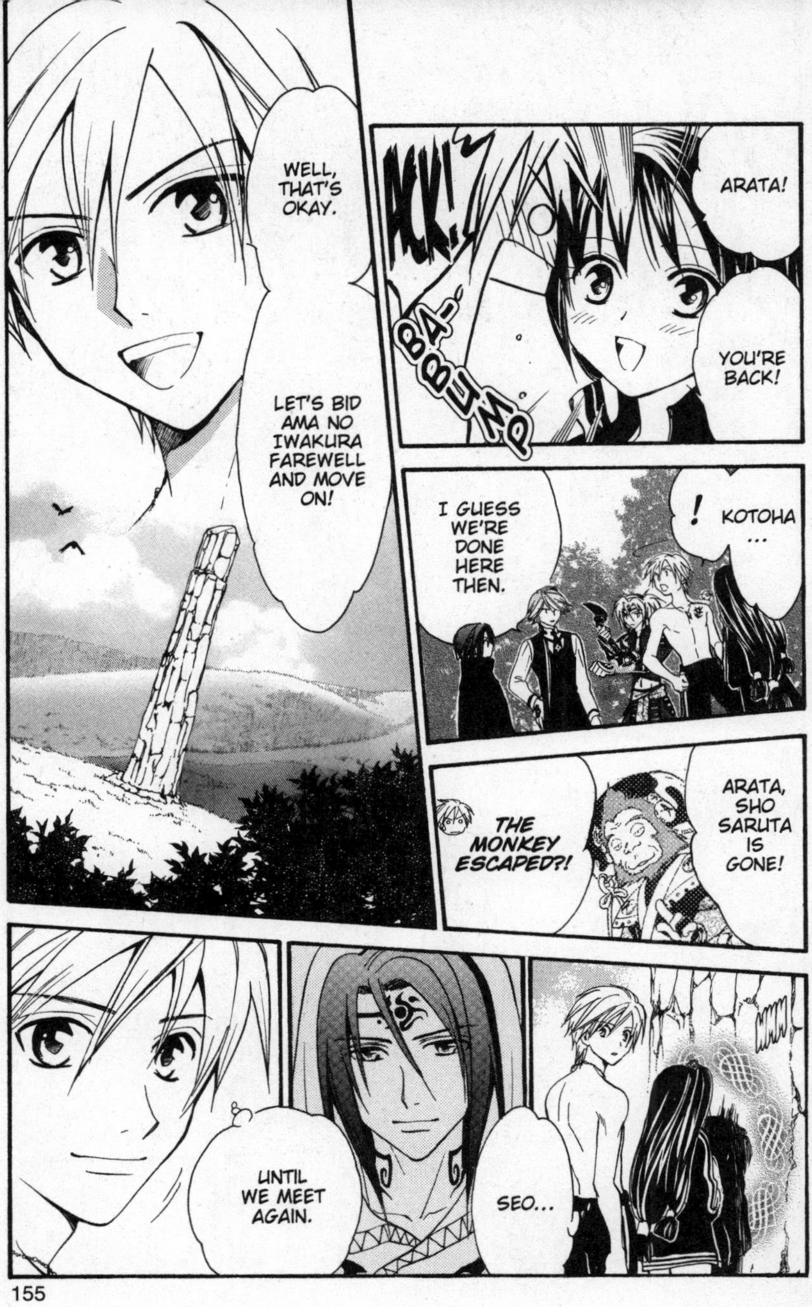

ARATA!
ACK!
YOU'RE BACK!
BA-BUMP
!
KOTOHA ...
I GUESS WE'RE DONE HERE THEN.
ARATA, SHO SARUTA IS GONE!
THE MONKEY ESCAPED?!
WELL, THAT'S OKAY.
LET'S BID AMA NO IWAKURA FAREWELL AND MOVE ON!
SEO...
UNTIL WE MEET AGAIN.

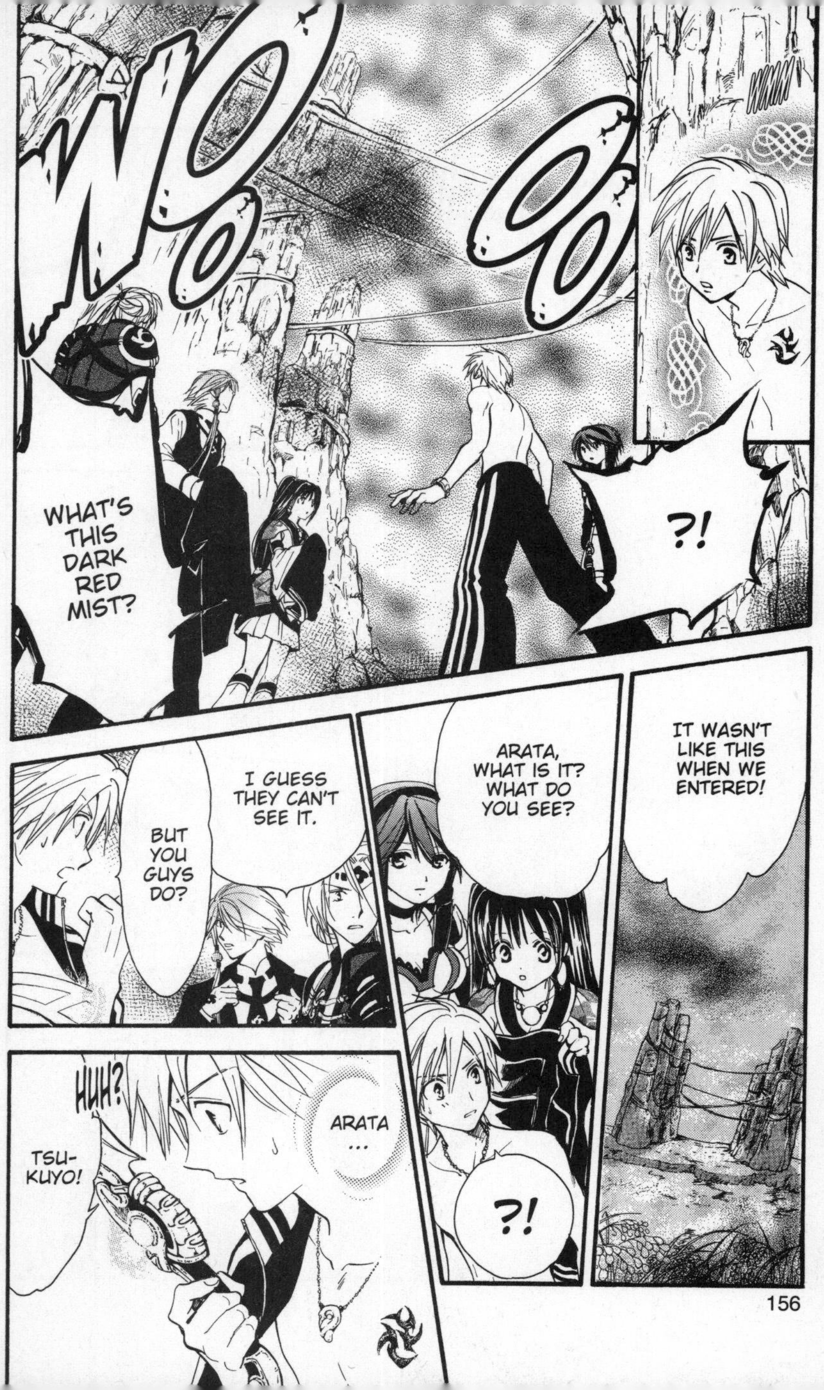
WOOOO
?!
WHAT'S THIS DARK RED MIST?
IT WASN'T LIKE THIS WHEN WE ENTERED!
ARATA, WHAT IS IT? WHAT DO YOU SEE?
?!
I GUESS THEY CAN'T SEE IT.
BUT YOU GUYS DO?
ARATA ...
HUH?
TSU-KUYO!

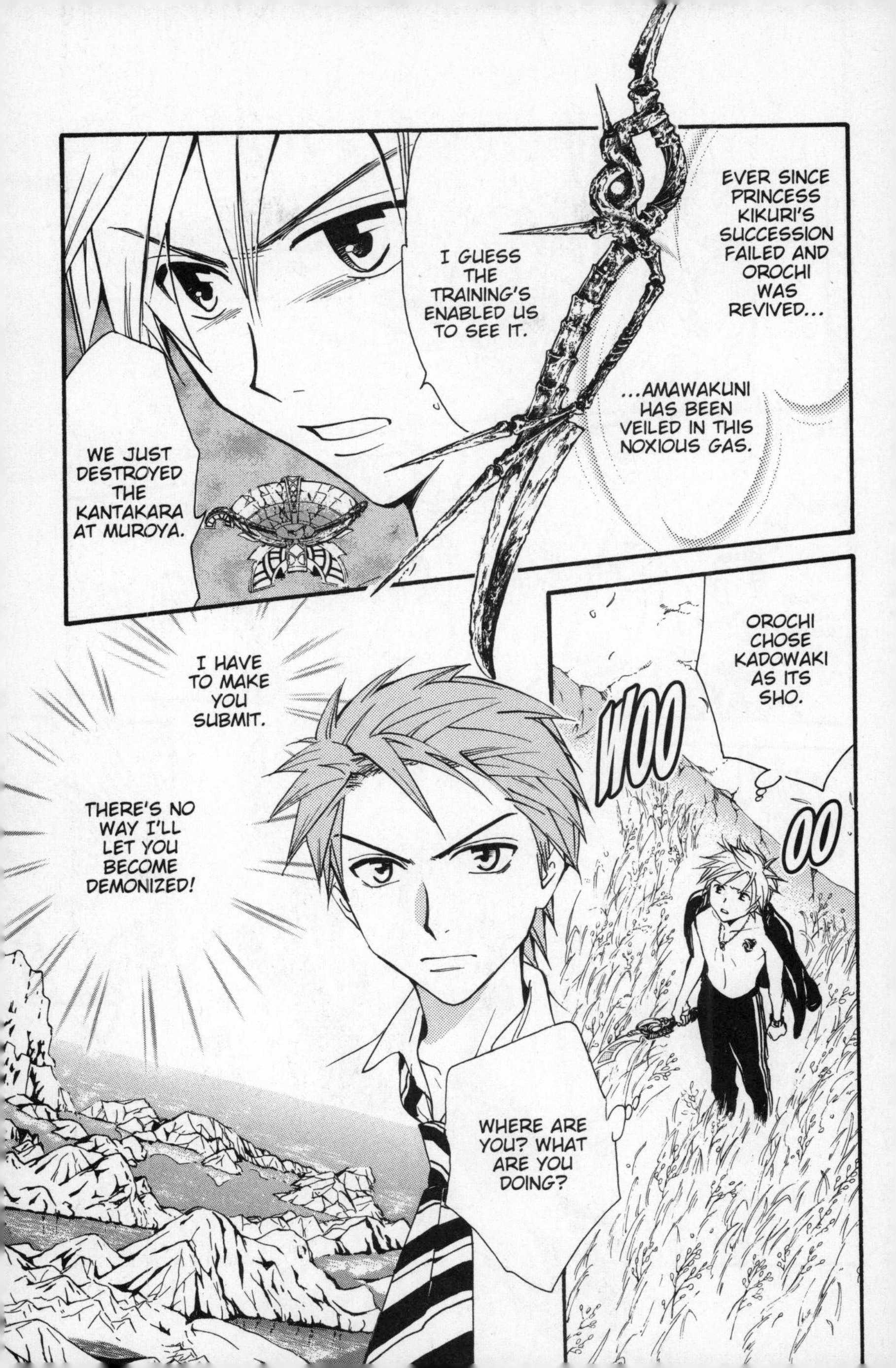
EVER SINCE PRINCESS KIKURI'S SUCCESSION FAILED AND OROCHI WAS REVIVED...
...AMAWAKUNI HAS BEEN VEILED IN THIS NOXIOUS GAS.
I GUESS THE TRAINING'S ENABLED US TO SEE IT.
WE JUST DESTROYED THE KANTAKARA AT MUROYA.
OROCHI CHOSE KADOWAKI AS ITS SHO.
WOO
OO
WHERE ARE YOU? WHAT ARE YOU DOING?
I HAVE TO MAKE YOU SUBMIT.
THERE'S NO WAY I'LL LET YOU BECOME DEMONIZED!

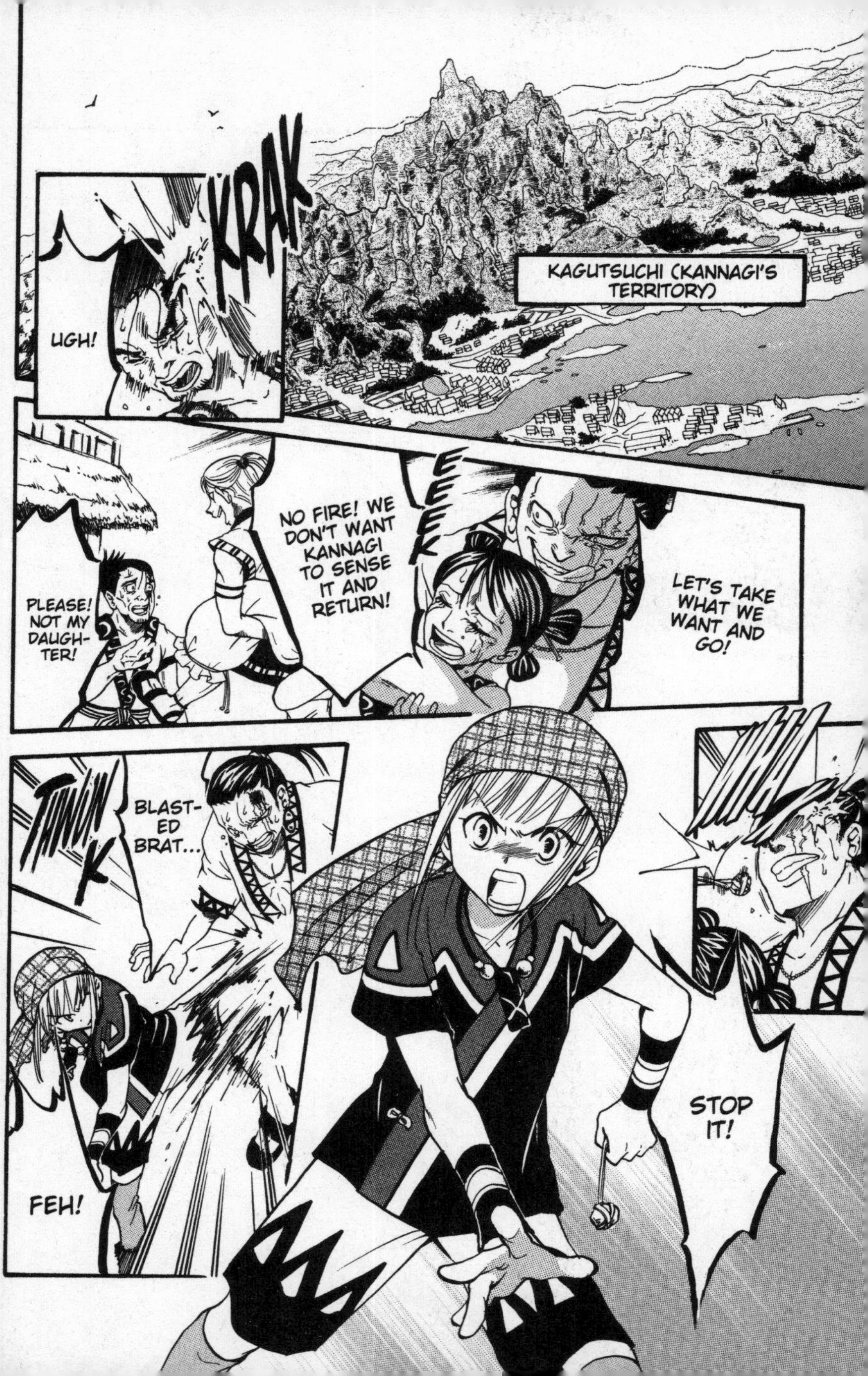
KAGUTSUCHI (KANNAGI'S TERRITORY)
KRAK
UGH!
LET'S TAKE WHAT WE WANT AND GO!
EEEEEK
NO FIRE! WE DON'T WANT KANNAGI TO SENSE IT AND RETURN!
PLEASE! NOT MY DAUGHTER!
STOP IT!
BLAST-ED BRAT...
TWUNK
FEH!

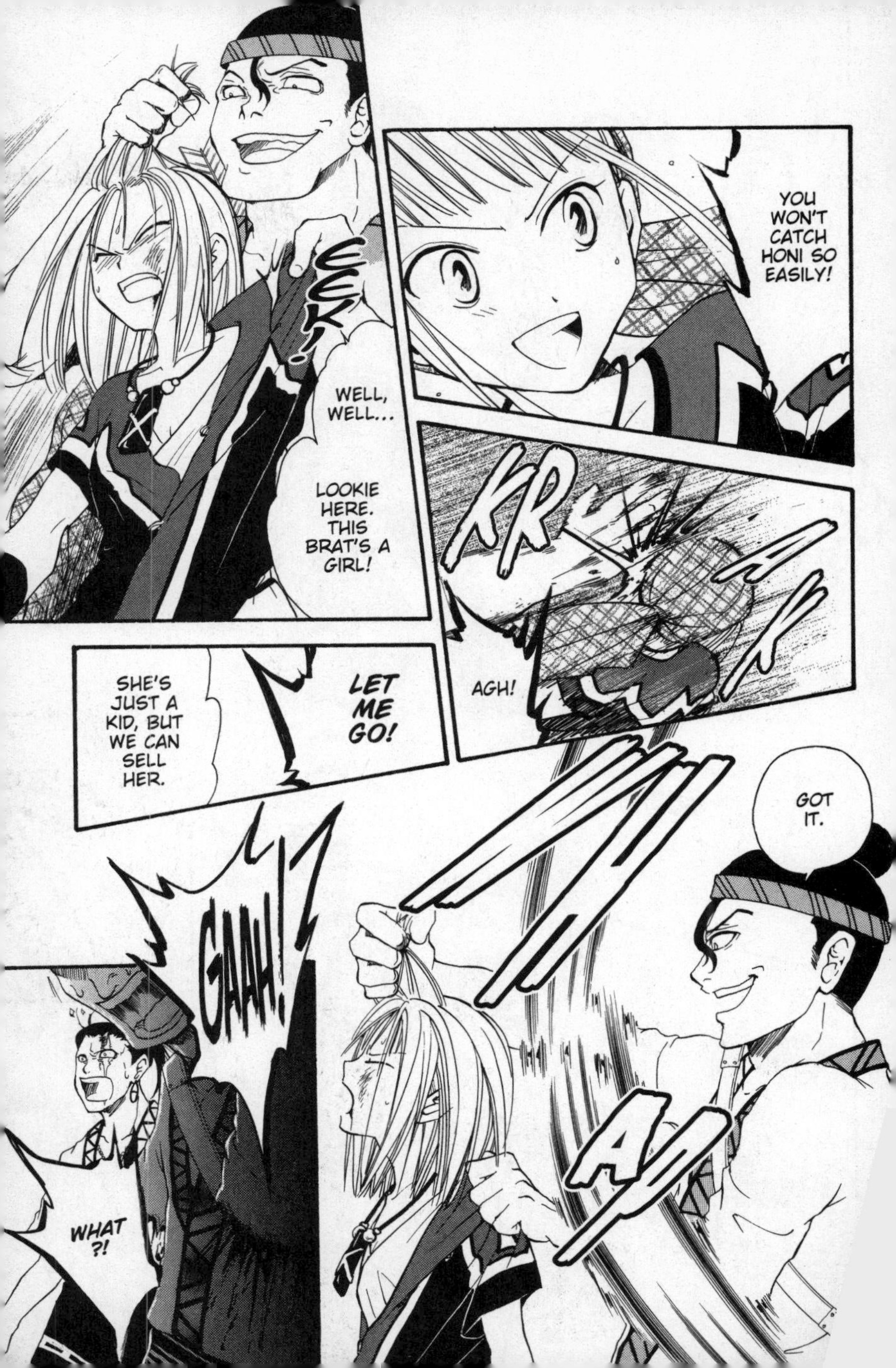
YOU WON'T CATCH HONI SO EASILY!
KRAAK
AGH!
EEK!
WELL, WELL...
LOOKIE HERE. THIS BRAT'S A GIRL!
LET ME GO!
SHE'S JUST A KID, BUT WE CAN SELL HER.
GOT IT.
AA
GAAH!
WHAT?!

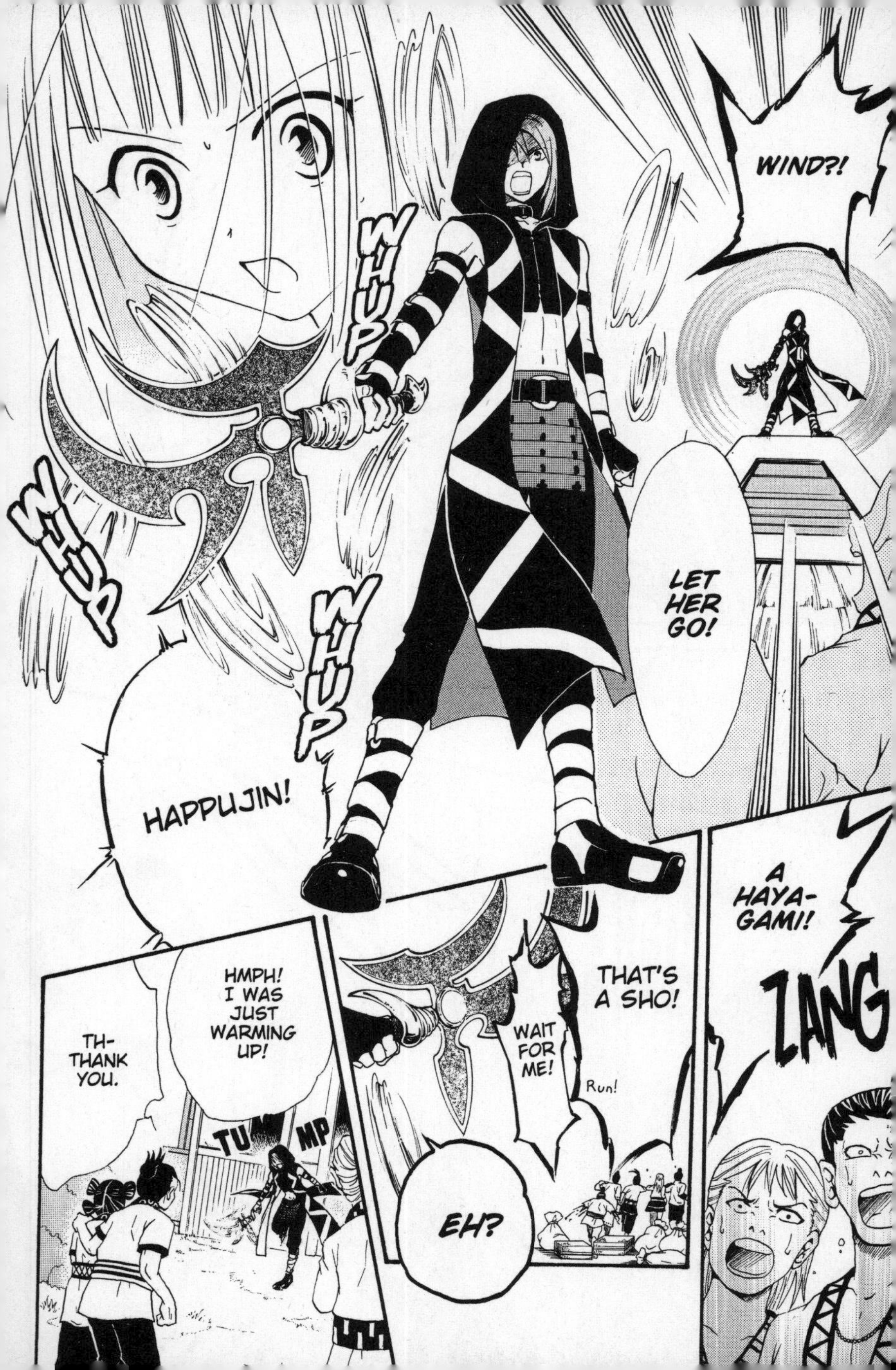
WIND?!
LET HER GO!
WHUP
WHUP
HAPPUJIN!
A HAYA-GAMI!
ZANG
THAT'S A SHO!
WAIT FOR ME!
Run!
EH?
HMPH! I WAS JUST WARMING UP!
TH-THANK YOU.
TUMP

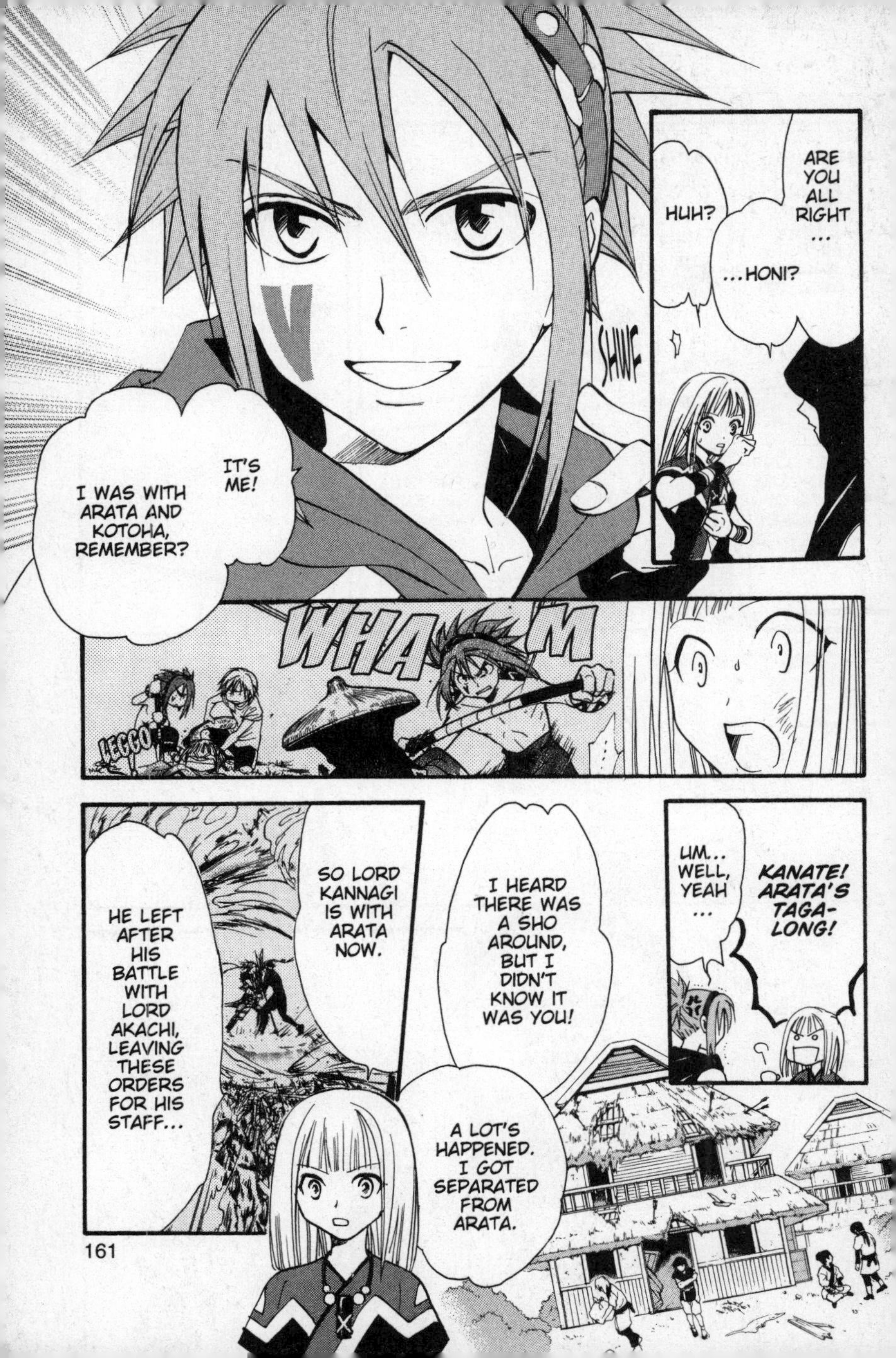

ARE YOU ALL RIGHT ...
HUH?
...HONI?
SHWF
IT'S ME!
I WAS WITH ARATA AND KOTOHA, REMEMBER?
WHAM
LEGGO
KANATE! ARATA'S TAGA-LONG!
UM... WELL, YEAH ...
I HEARD THERE WAS A SHO AROUND, BUT I DIDN'T KNOW IT WAS YOU!
A LOT'S HAPPENED. I GOT SEPARATED FROM ARATA.
SO LORD KANNAGI IS WITH ARATA NOW.
HE LEFT AFTER HIS BATTLE WITH LORD AKACHI, LEAVING THESE ORDERS FOR HIS STAFF...

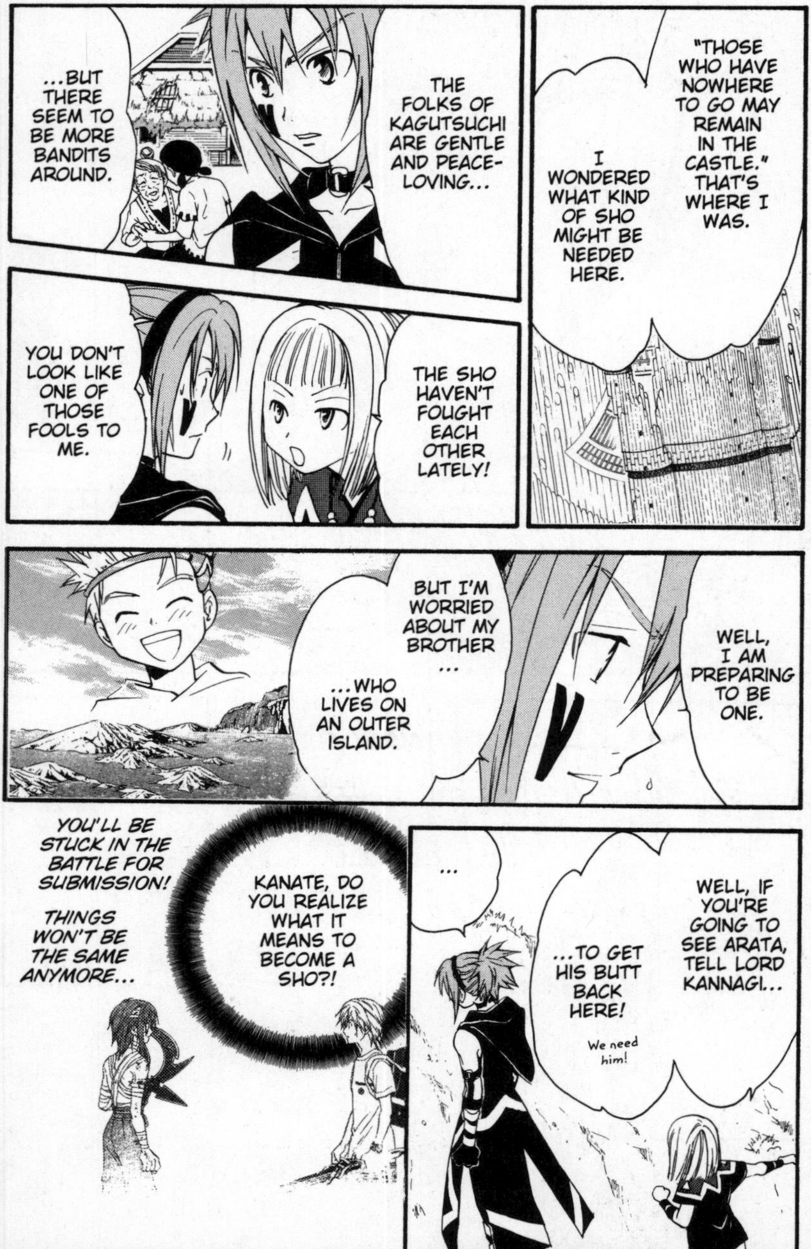
"THOSE WHO HAVE NOWHERE TO GO MAY REMAIN IN THE CASTLE." THAT'S WHERE I WAS.
I WONDERED WHAT KIND OF SHO MIGHT BE NEEDED HERE.
THE FOLKS OF KAGUTSUCHI ARE GENTLE AND PEACE-LOVING...
...BUT THERE SEEM TO BE MORE BANDITS AROUND.
THE SHO HAVEN'T FOUGHT EACH OTHER LATELY!
YOU DON'T LOOK LIKE ONE OF THOSE FOOLS TO ME.
WELL, I AM PREPARING TO BE ONE.
BUT I'M WORRIED ABOUT MY BROTHER ...
...WHO LIVES ON AN OUTER ISLAND.
WELL, IF YOU'RE GOING TO SEE ARATA, TELL LORD KANNAGI...
...TO GET HIS BUTT BACK HERE!
We need him!
...
KANATE, DO YOU REALIZE WHAT IT MEANS TO BECOME A SHO?!
YOU'LL BE STUCK IN THE BATTLE FOR SUBMISSION!
THINGS WON'T BE THE SAME ANYMORE...

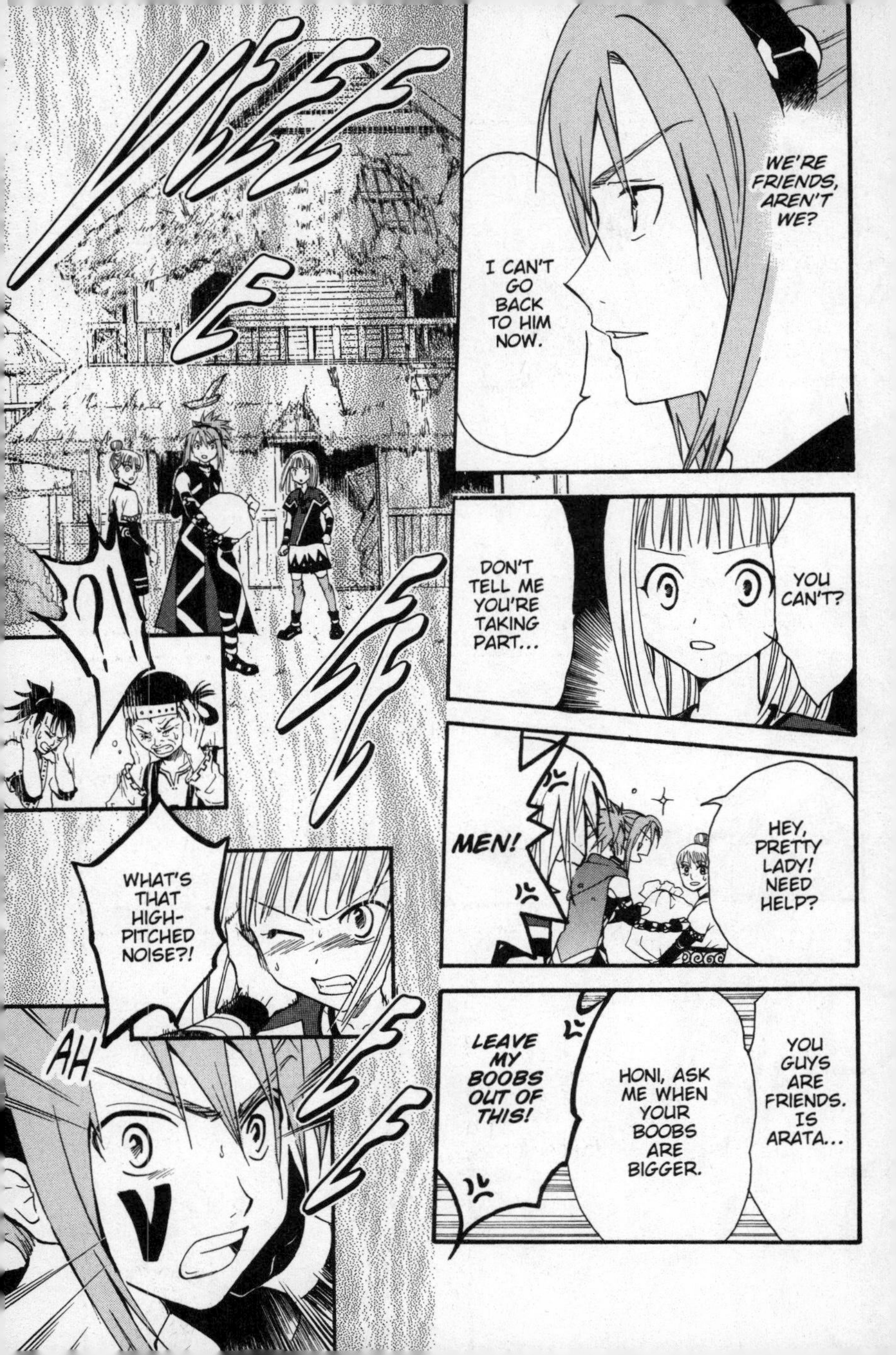
WE'RE FRIENDS, AREN'T WE?
I CAN'T GO BACK TO HIM NOW.
YOU CAN'T?
DON'T TELL ME YOU'RE TAKING PART...
HEY, PRETTY LADY! NEED HELP?
MEN!
YOU GUYS ARE FRIENDS. IS ARATA...
HONI, ASK ME WHEN YOUR BOOBS ARE BIGGER.
LEAVE MY BOOBS OUT OF THIS!
WEEEEEEEE
WHAT'S THAT HIGH-PITCHED NOISE?!
AH

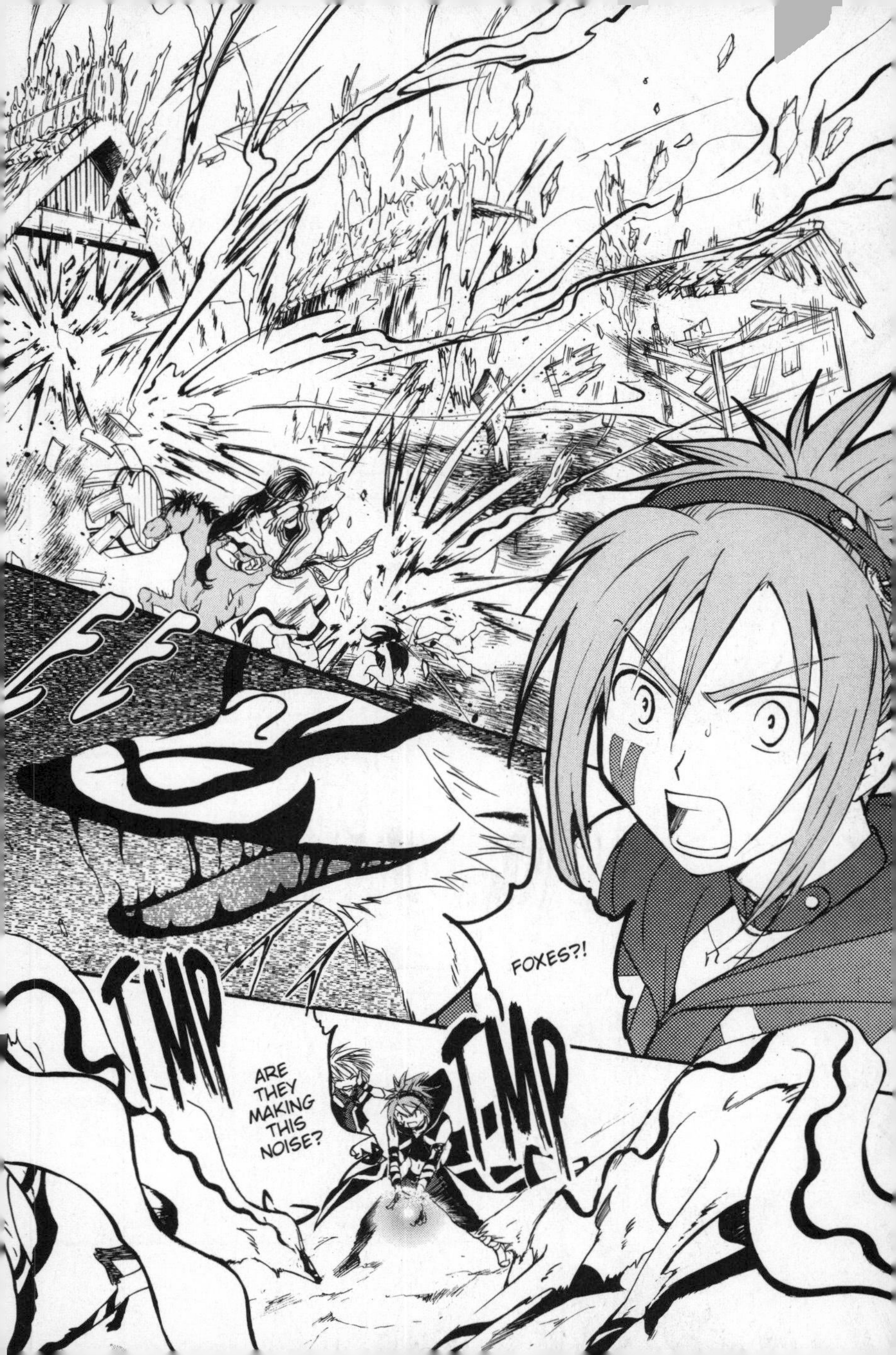
FOXES?!
T-MP
ARE THEY MAKING THIS NOISE?
TMP

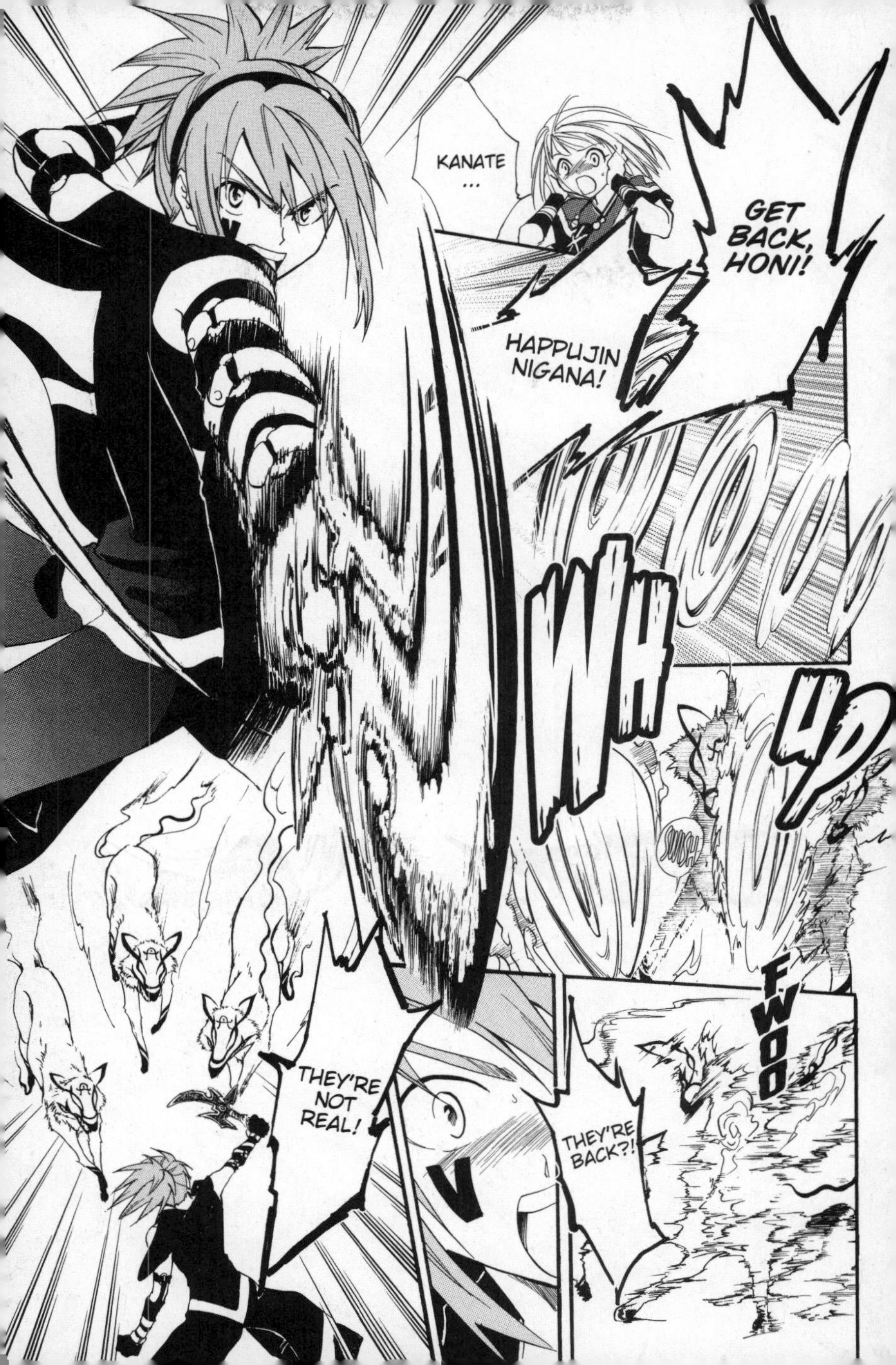
GET BACK, HONI!
KANATE ...
HAPPUJIN NIGANA!
WH
UP
SWISH
FWOO
THEY'RE BACK?!
THEY'RE NOT REAL!

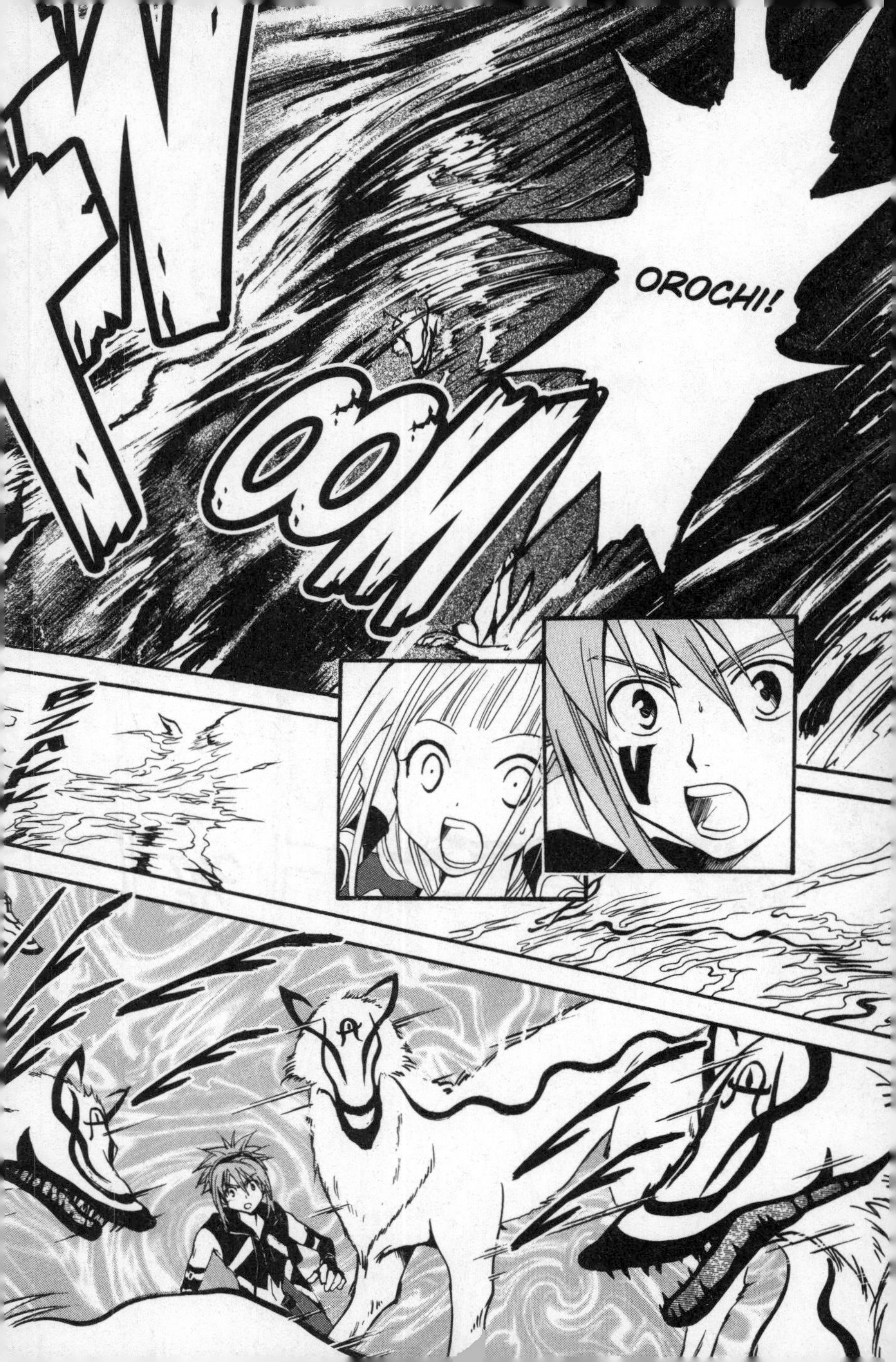
OROCHI!

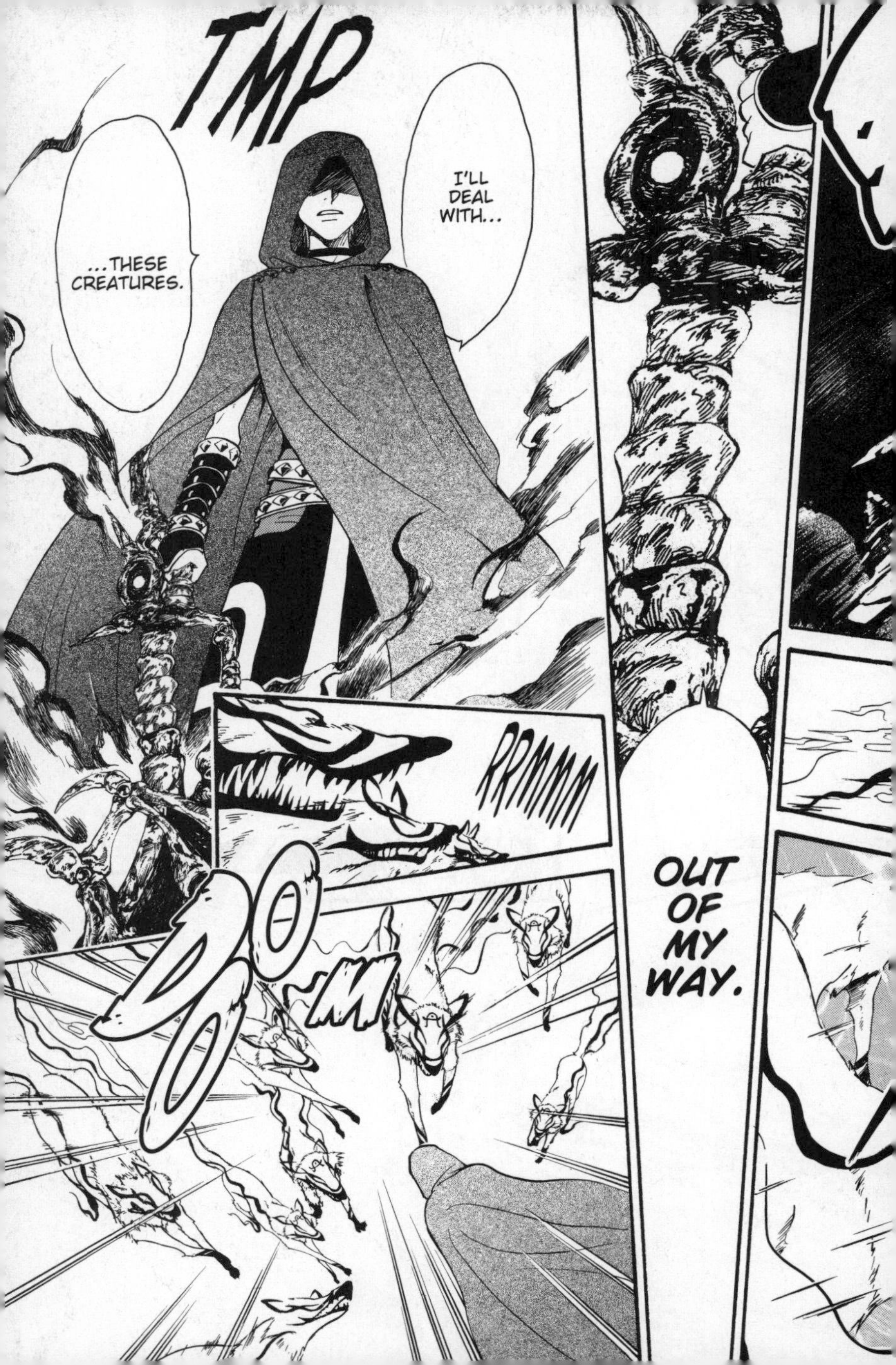
OUT OF MY WAY.
TMP
I'LL DEAL WITH...
...THESE CREATURES.
RRMMMM
DOOOM

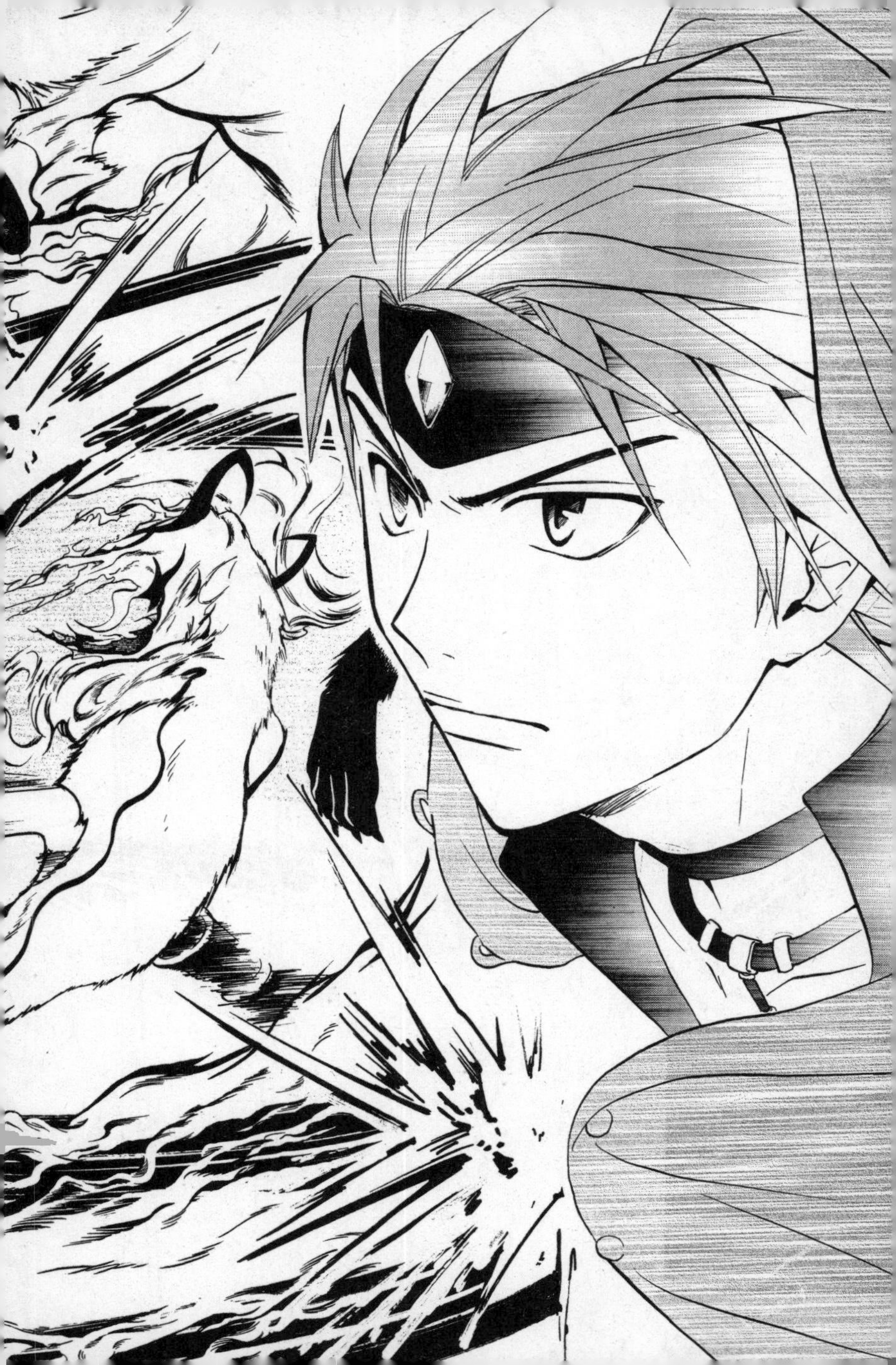

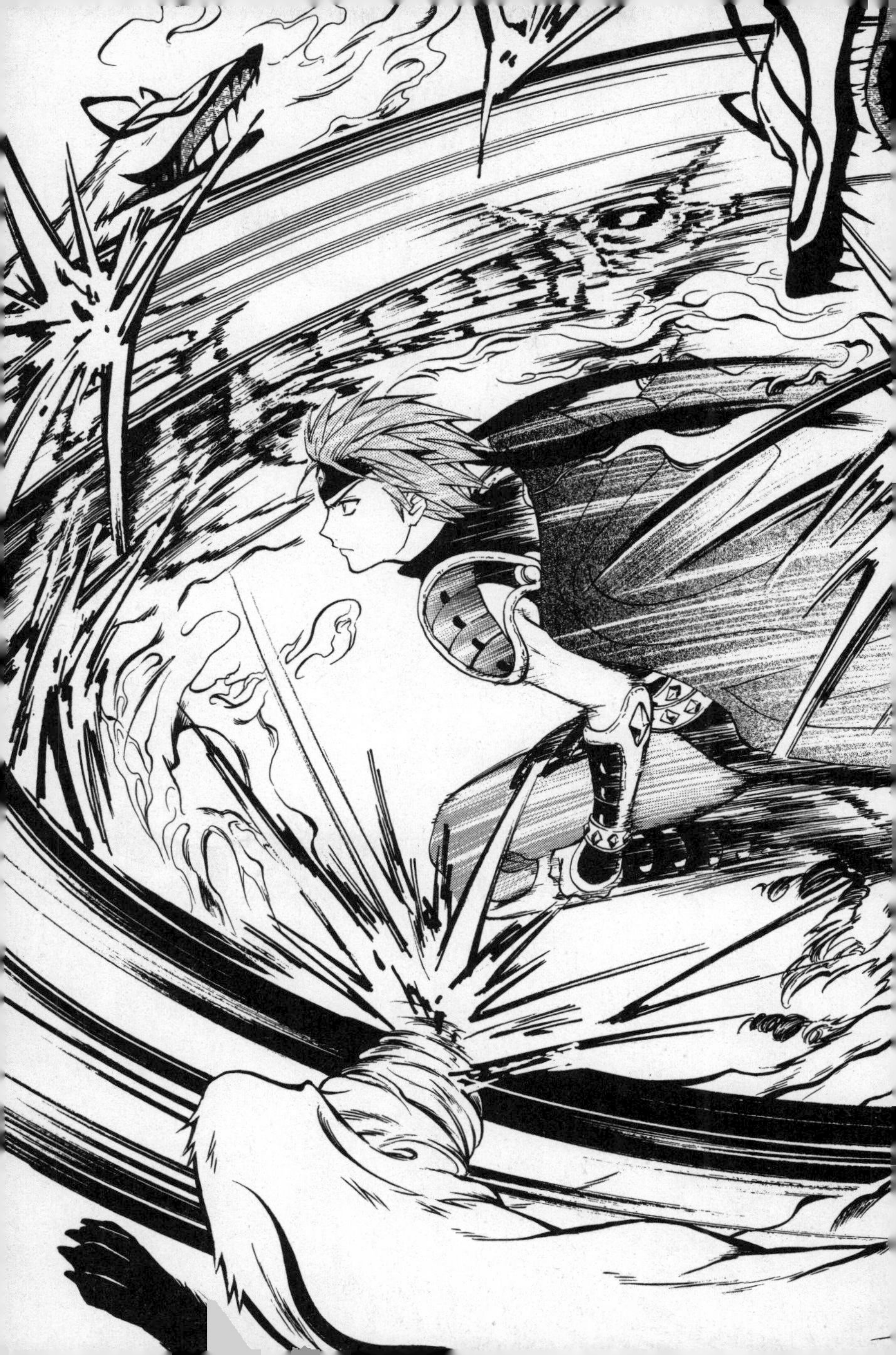

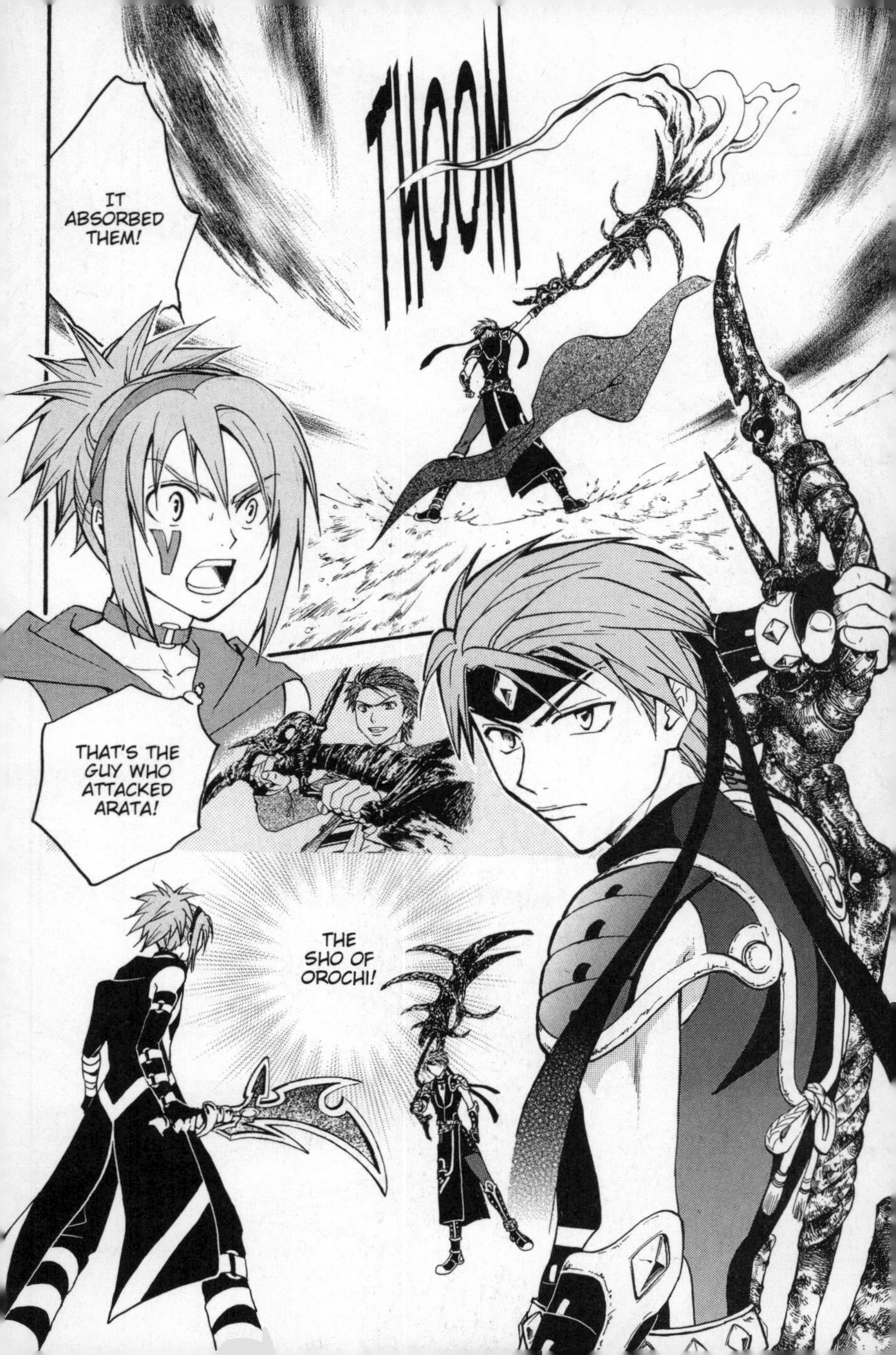
THOOM
IT ABSORBED THEM!
THAT'S THE GUY WHO ATTACKED ARATA!
THE SHO OF OROCHI!

CHAPTER 147
A TRUE FRIEND

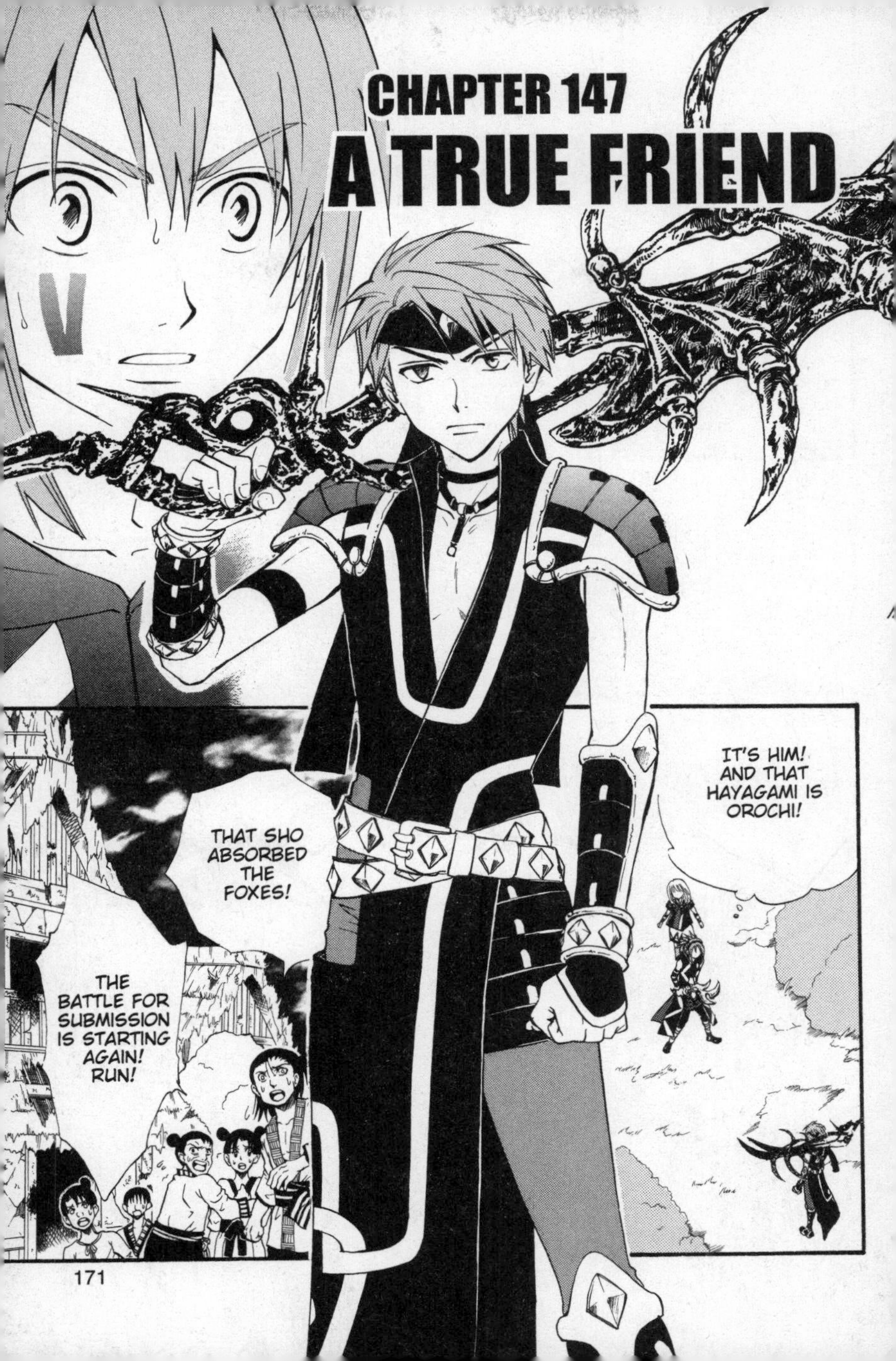
IT'S HIM! AND THAT HAYAGAMI IS OROCHI!
THAT SHO ABSORBED THE FOXES!
THE BATTLE FOR SUBMISSION IS STARTING AGAIN! RUN!

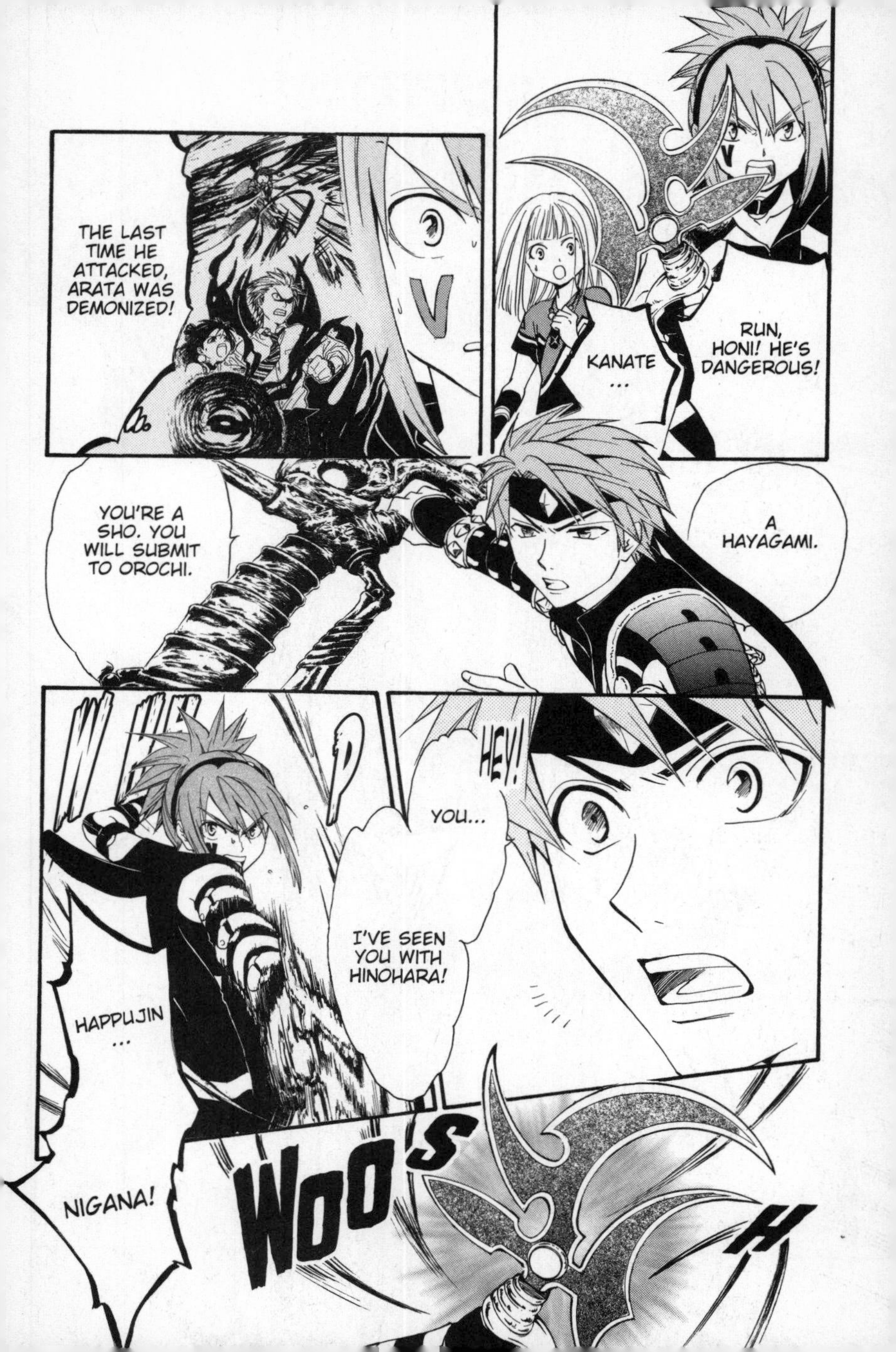
RUN, HONI! HE'S DANGEROUS!
KANATE ...
THE LAST TIME HE ATTACKED, ARATA WAS DEMONIZED!
A HAYAGAMI.
YOU'RE A SHO. YOU WILL SUBMIT TO OROCHI.
HEY!
YOU...
I'VE SEEN YOU WITH HINOHARA!
HAPPUJIN ...
NIGANA!
WOOSH

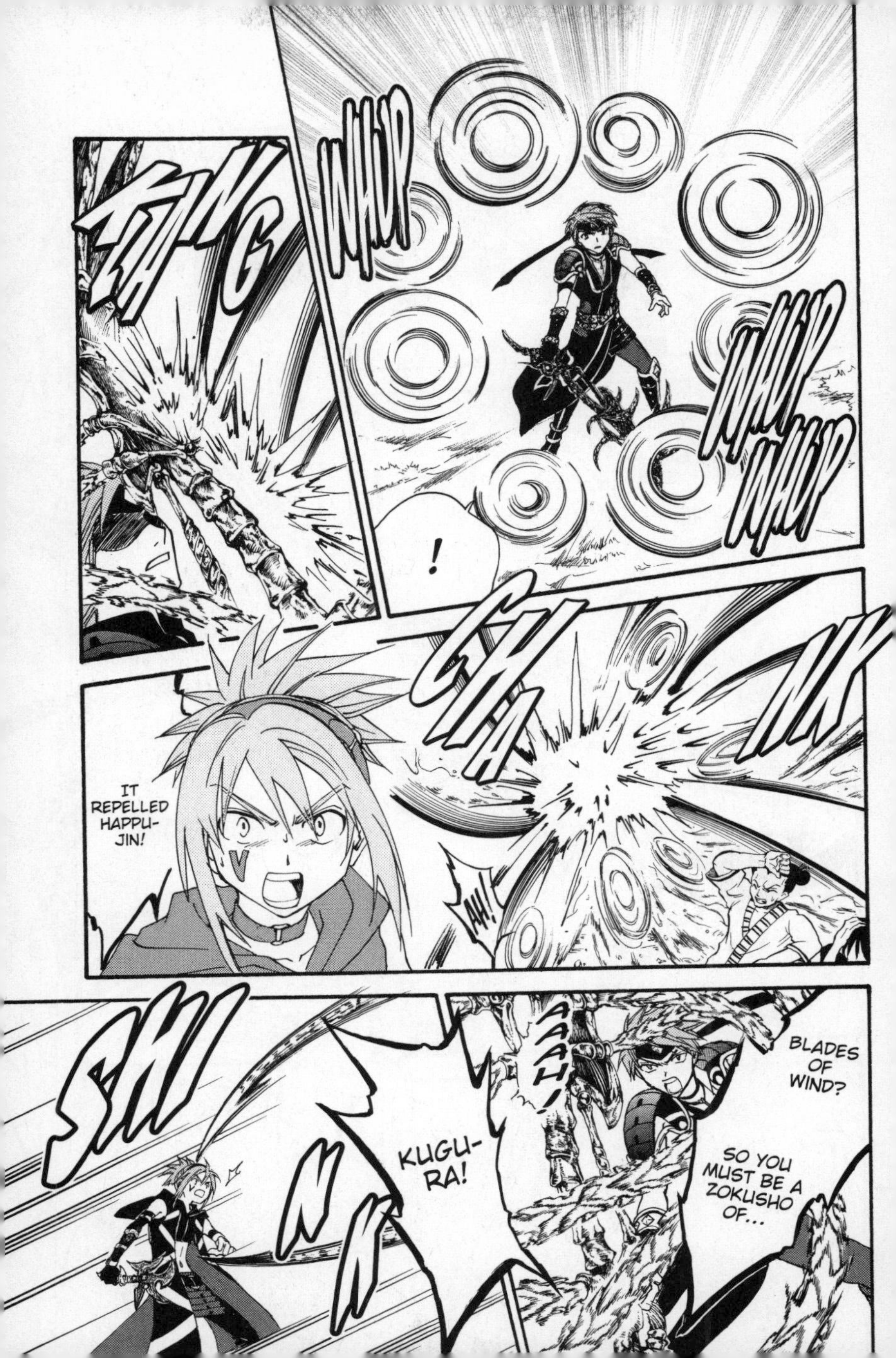
WHUP
WHUP
WHUP
!
ZHING
CHANK
AH!
IT REPELLED HAPPU-JIN!
BLADES OF WIND?
SO YOU MUST BE A ZOKUSHO OF...
AAAH!
KUGU-RA!
SHINNK

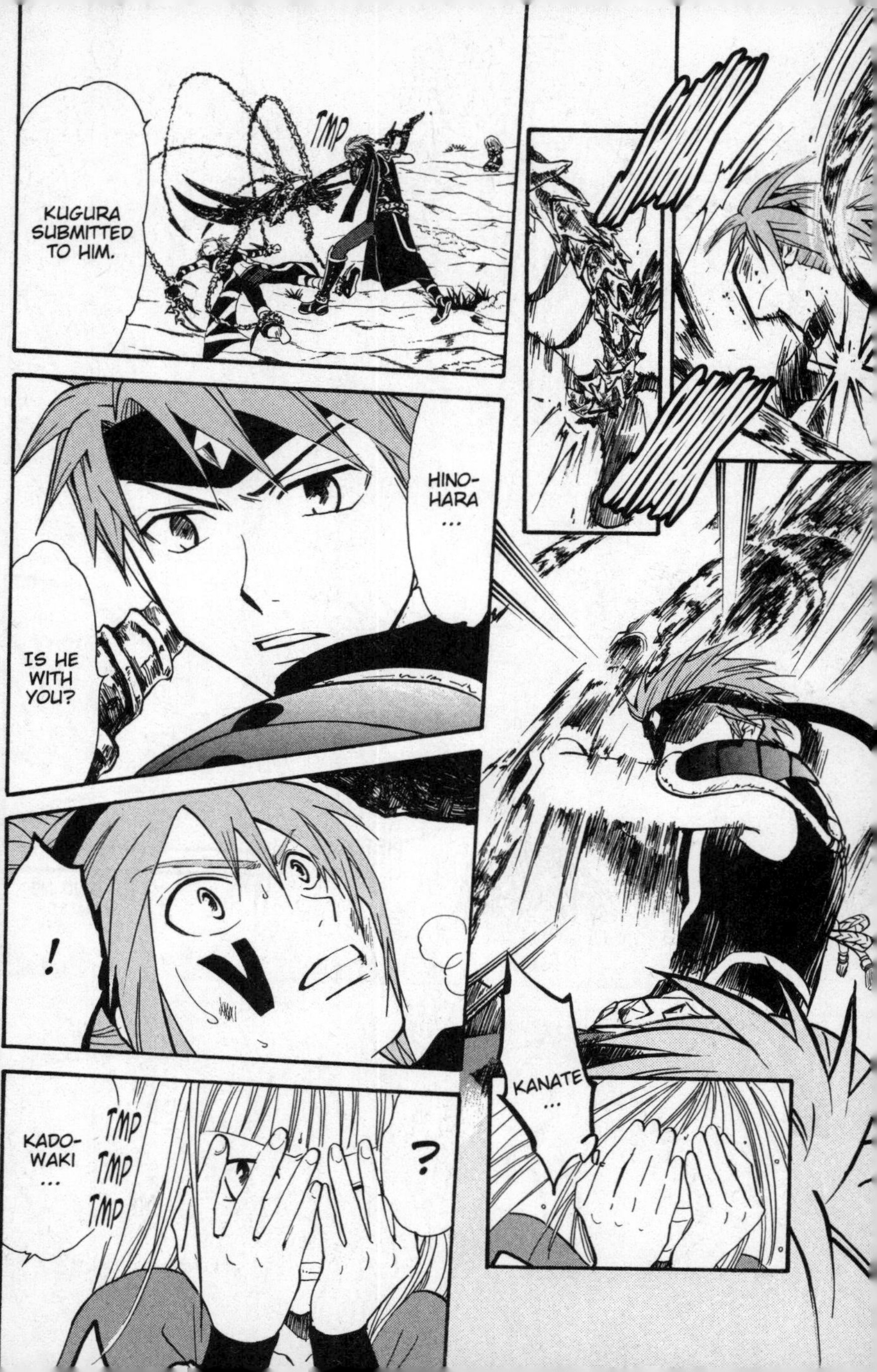
KANATE ...
TMP
KUGURA SUBMITTED TO HIM.
HINO-HARA ...
IS HE WITH YOU?
!
?
TMP TMP TMP
KADO-WAKI ...

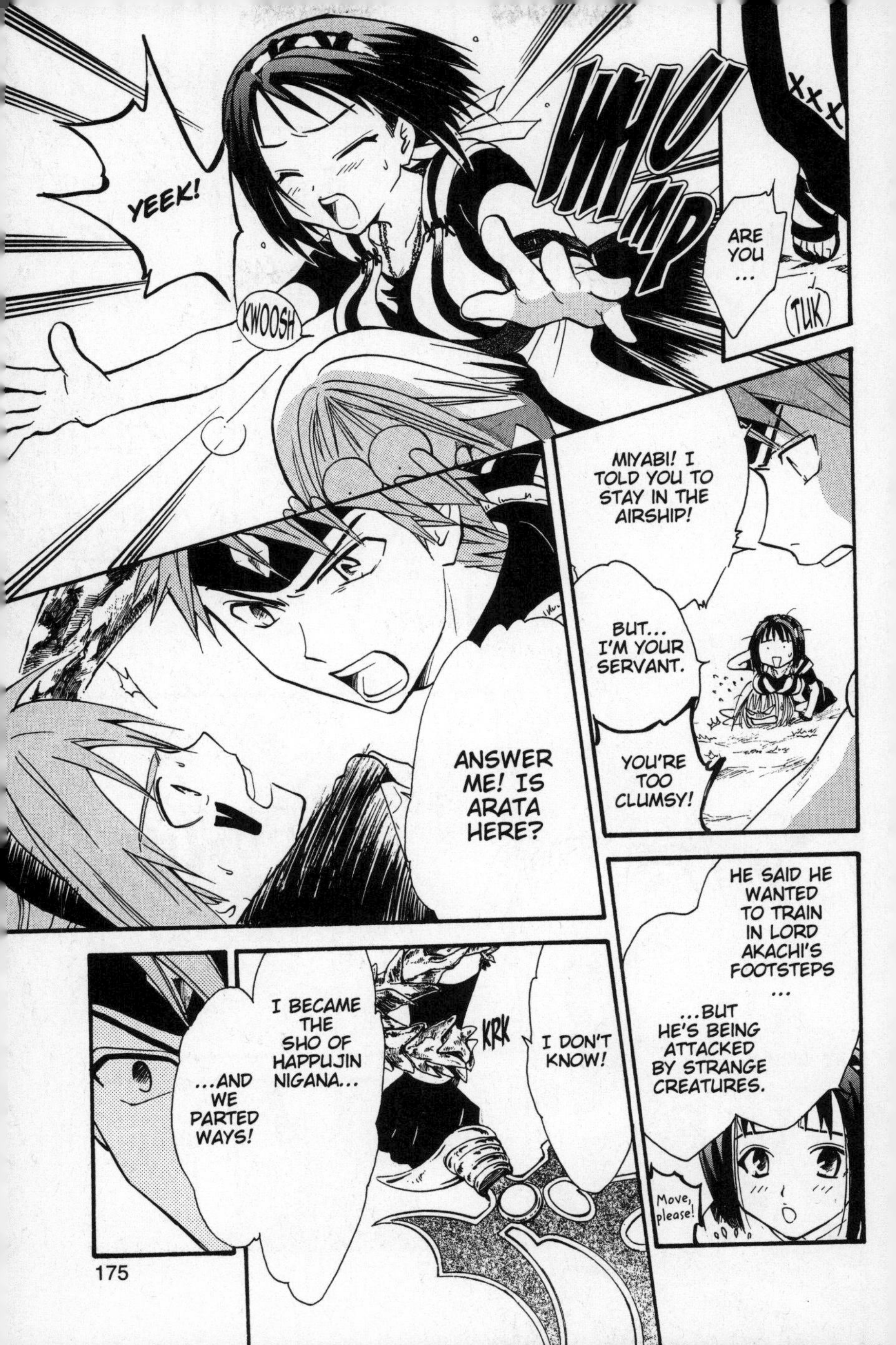

ARE YOU ...
TUK
WHUMP
YEEK!
KWOOSH
MIYABI! I TOLD YOU TO STAY IN THE AIRSHIP!
BUT... I'M YOUR SERVANT.
YOU'RE TOO CLUMSY!
ANSWER ME! IS ARATA HERE?
HE SAID HE WANTED TO TRAIN IN LORD AKACHI'S FOOTSTEPS ...
...BUT HE'S BEING ATTACKED BY STRANGE CREATURES.
Move, please!
I DON'T KNOW!
KRK
I BECAME THE SHO OF HAPPUJIN NIGANA...
...AND WE PARTED WAYS!

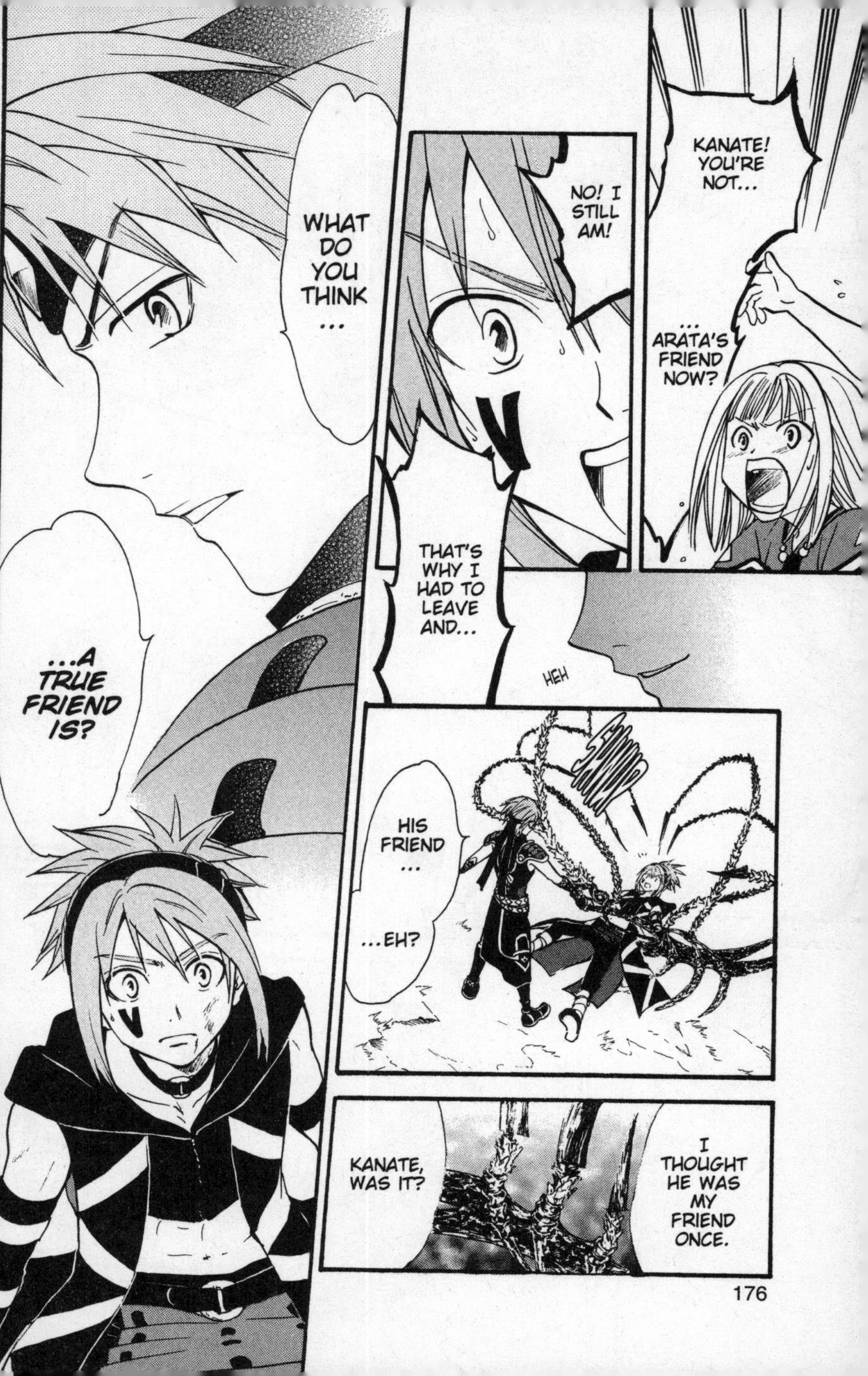
KANATE! YOU'RE NOT...
...ARATA'S FRIEND NOW?
NO! I STILL AM!
THAT'S WHY I HAD TO LEAVE AND...
HEH
HIS FRIEND...
...EH?
I THOUGHT HE WAS MY FRIEND ONCE.
KANATE, WAS IT?
WHAT DO YOU THINK...
...A TRUE FRIEND IS?

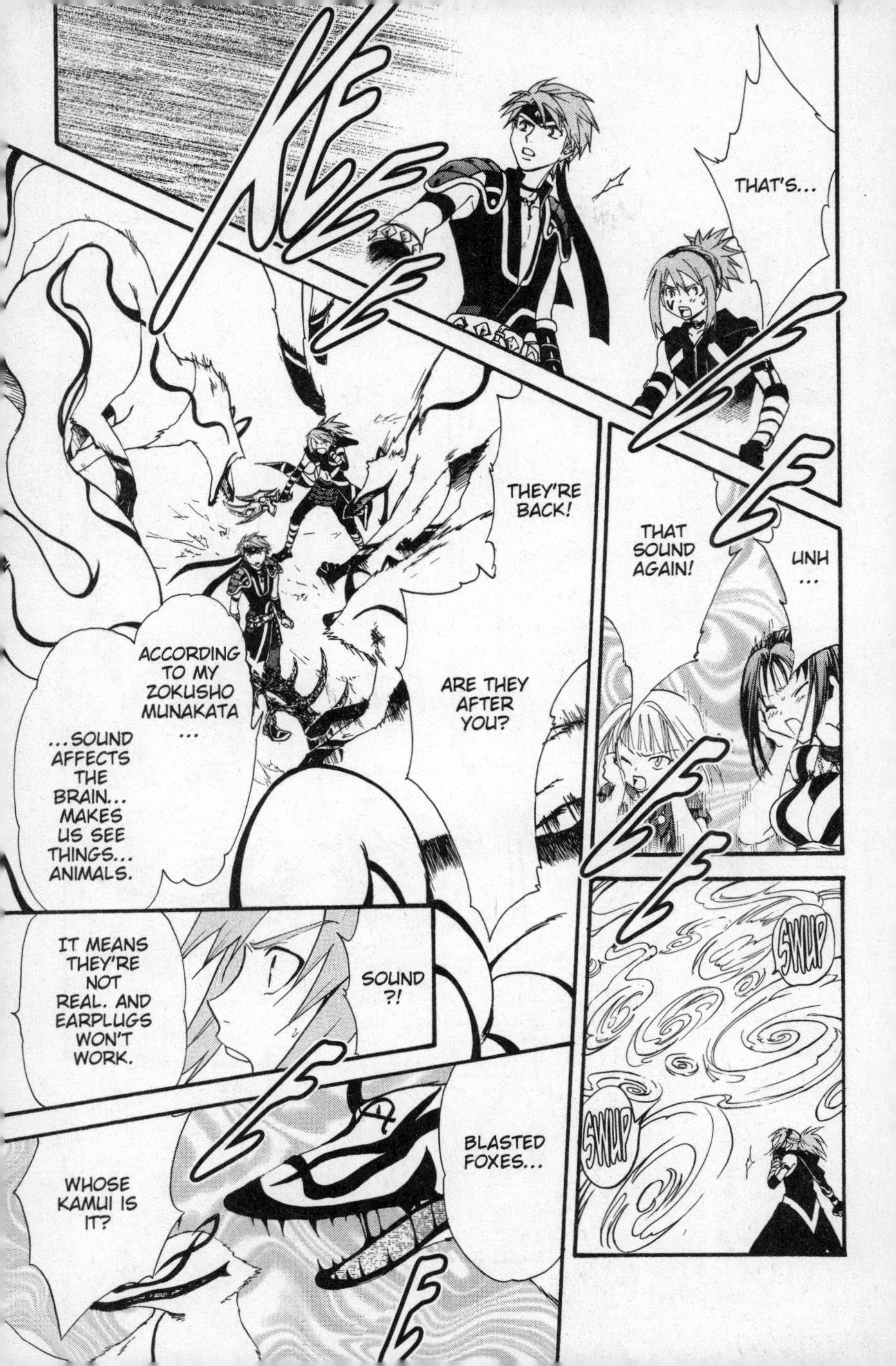
THAT'S...
UNH...
THAT SOUND AGAIN!
THEY'RE BACK!
ARE THEY AFTER YOU?
ACCORDING TO MY ZOKUSHO MUNAKATA...
...SOUND AFFECTS THE BRAIN... MAKES US SEE THINGS... ANIMALS.
SWUP
SWUP
SOUND?!
IT MEANS THEY'RE NOT REAL. AND EARPLUGS WON'T WORK.
BLASTED FOXES...
WHOSE KAMUI IS IT?

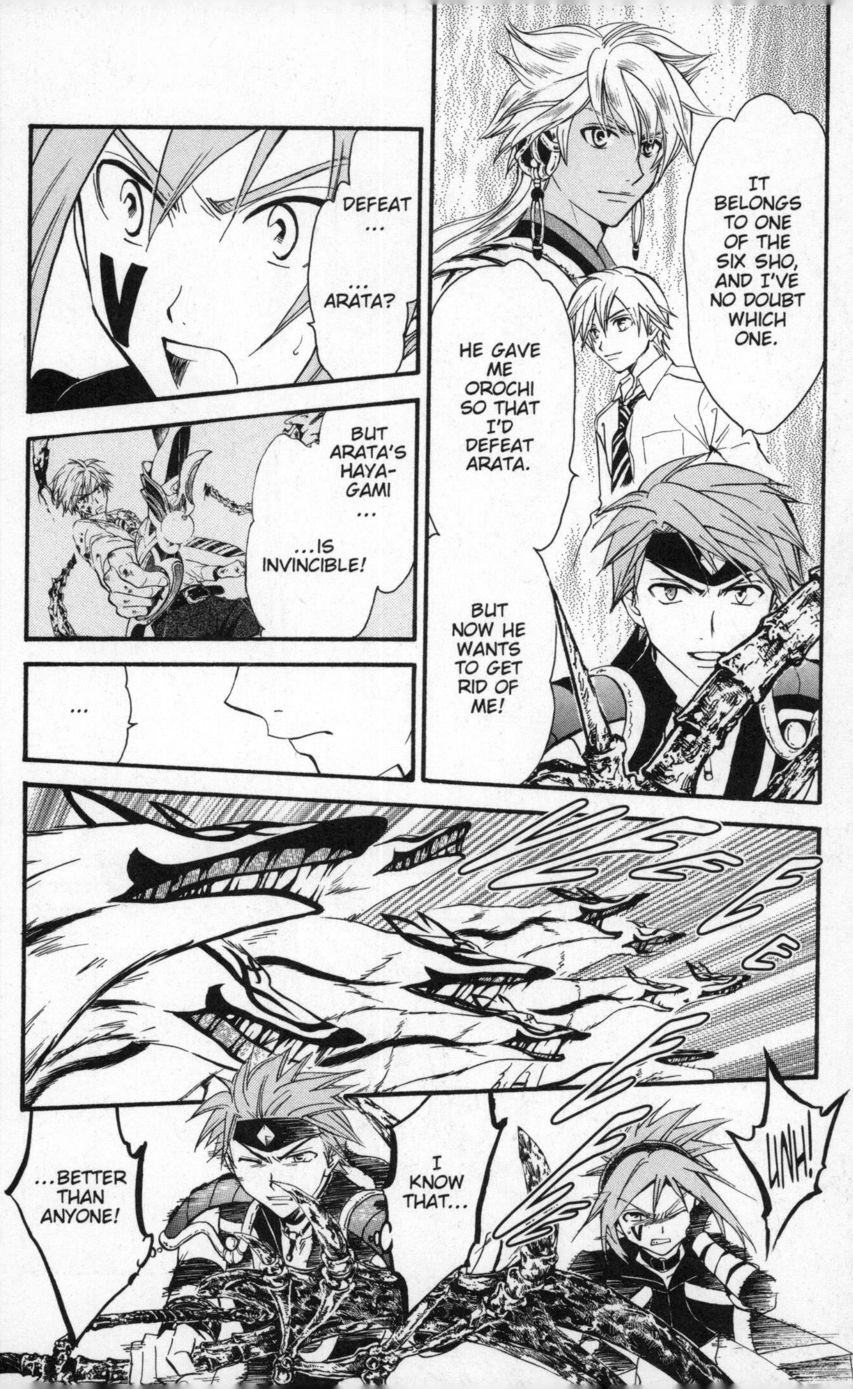
IT BELONGS TO ONE OF THE SIX SHO, AND I'VE NO DOUBT WHICH ONE.
HE GAVE ME OROCHI SO THAT I'D DEFEAT ARATA.
BUT NOW HE WANTS TO GET RID OF ME!
DEFEAT ...
... ARATA?
BUT ARATA'S HAYA-GAMI ...
...IS INVINCIBLE!
...
UNH!
I KNOW THAT...
...BETTER THAN ANYONE!

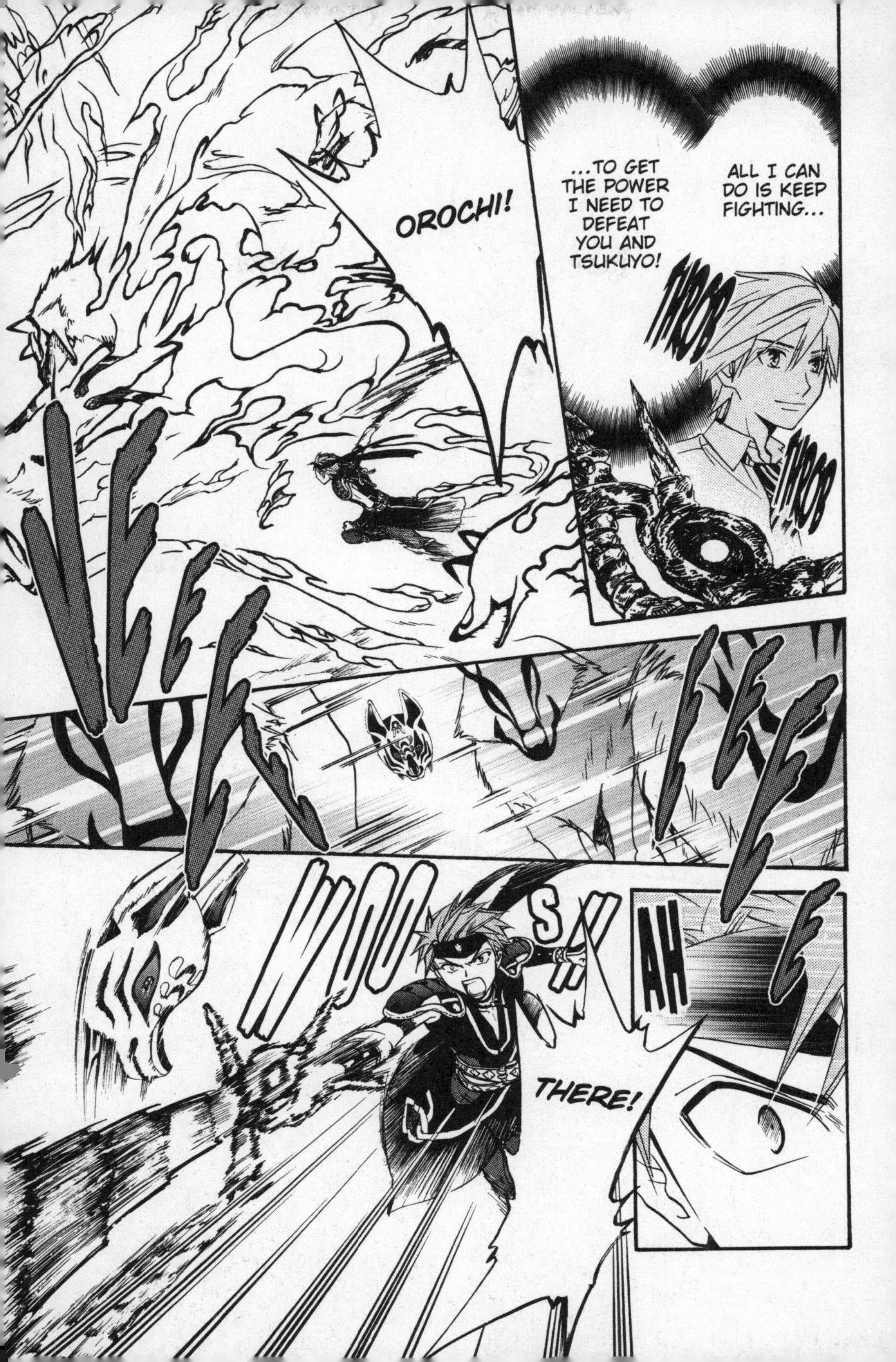
ALL I CAN DO IS KEEP FIGHTING...
...TO GET THE POWER I NEED TO DEFEAT YOU AND TSUKUYO!
THROB
THROB
OROCHI!
AH
WHOOSH
THERE!

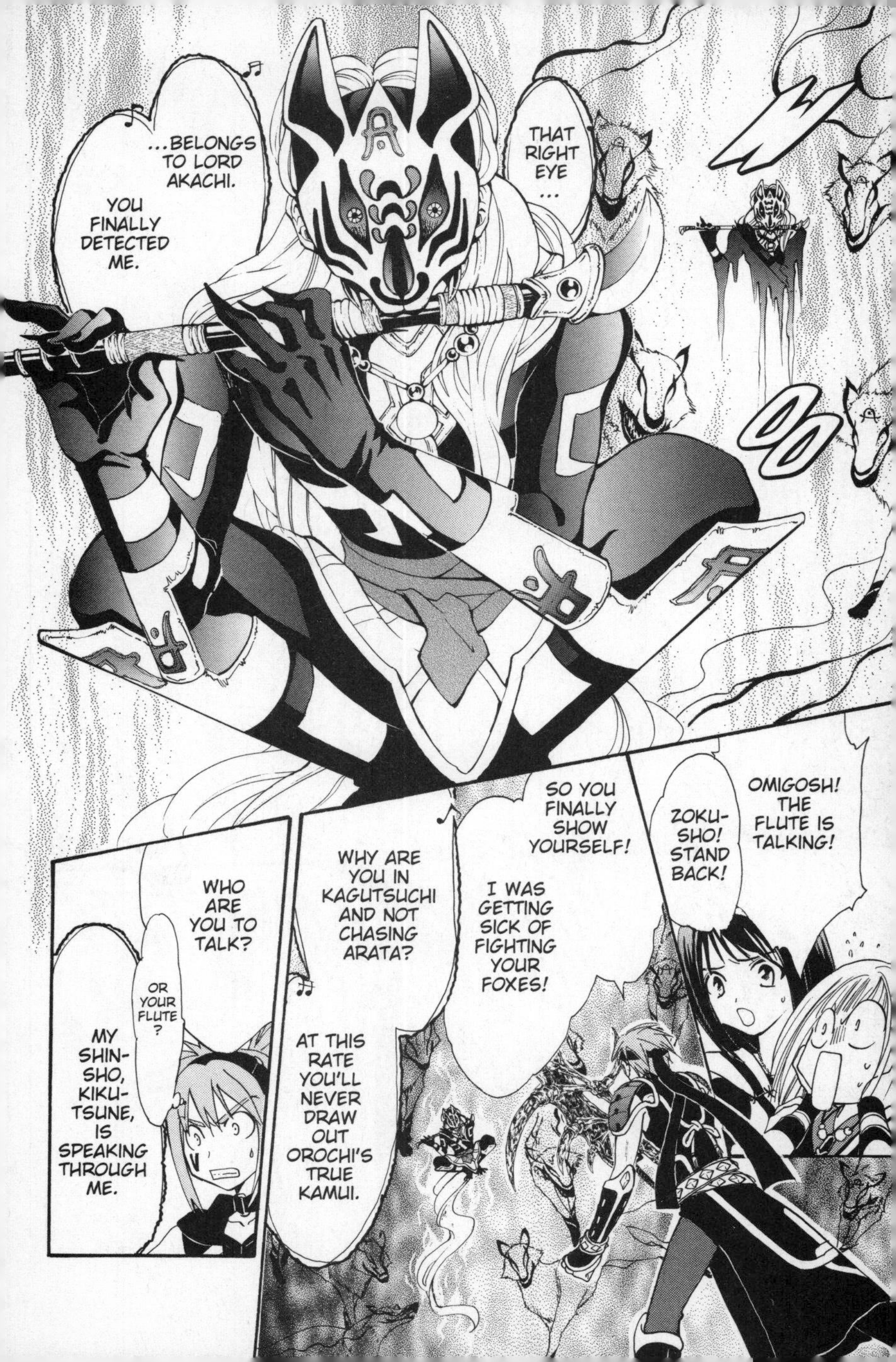
THAT RIGHT EYE...
...BELONGS TO LORD AKACHI.
YOU FINALLY DETECTED ME.
OMIGOSH! THE FLUTE IS TALKING!
ZOKU-SHO! STAND BACK!
SO YOU FINALLY SHOW YOURSELF!
I WAS GETTING SICK OF FIGHTING YOUR FOXES!
WHY ARE YOU IN KAGUTSUCHI AND NOT CHASING ARATA?
AT THIS RATE YOU'LL NEVER DRAW OUT OROCHI'S TRUE KAMUI.
WHO ARE YOU TO TALK?
OR YOUR FLUTE?
MY SHIN-SHO, KIKU-TSUNE, IS SPEAKING THROUGH ME.

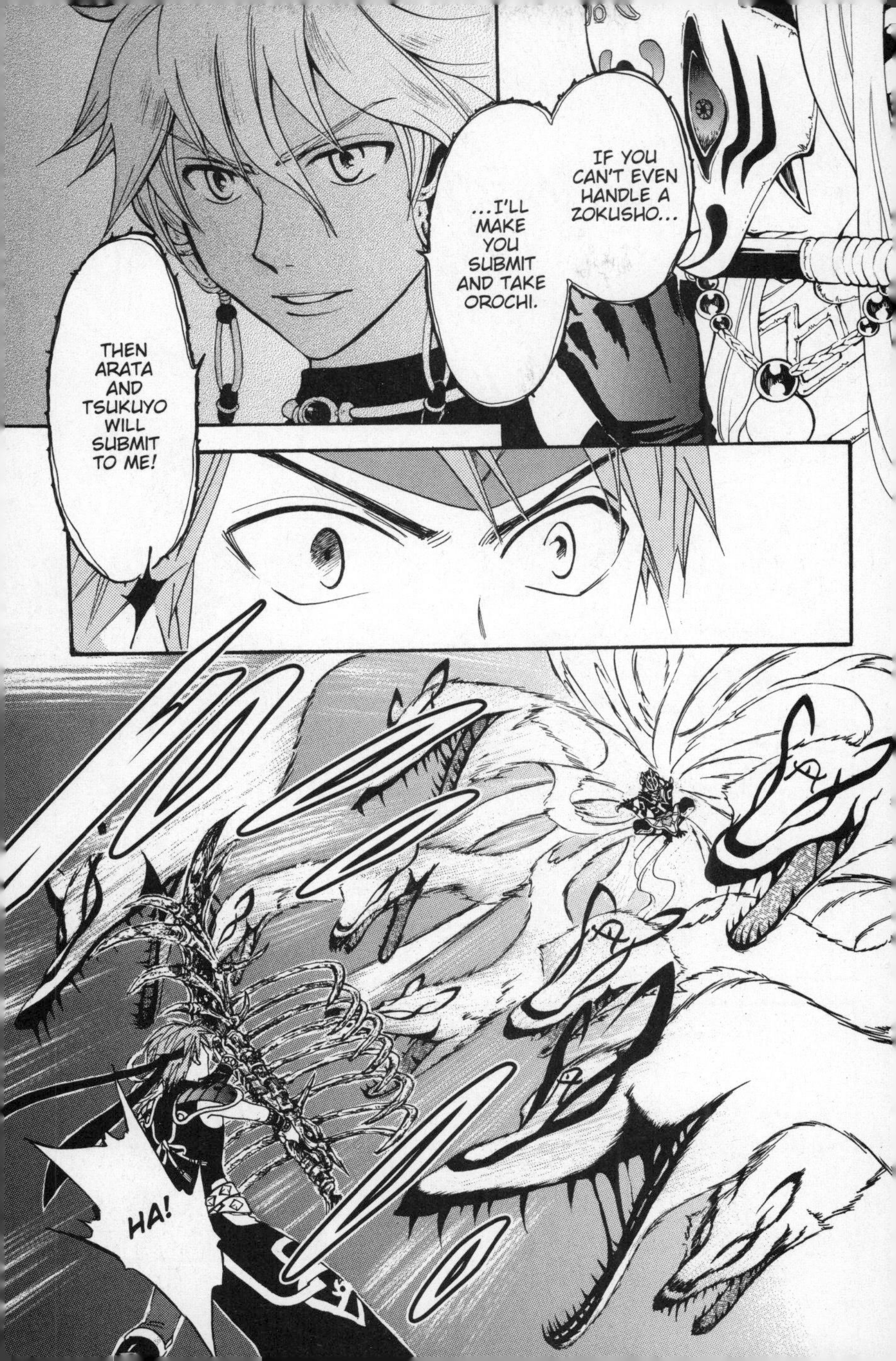
IF YOU CAN'T EVEN HANDLE A ZOKUSHO...
...I'LL MAKE YOU SUBMIT AND TAKE OROCHI.
THEN ARATA AND TSUKUYO WILL SUBMIT TO ME!
HA!

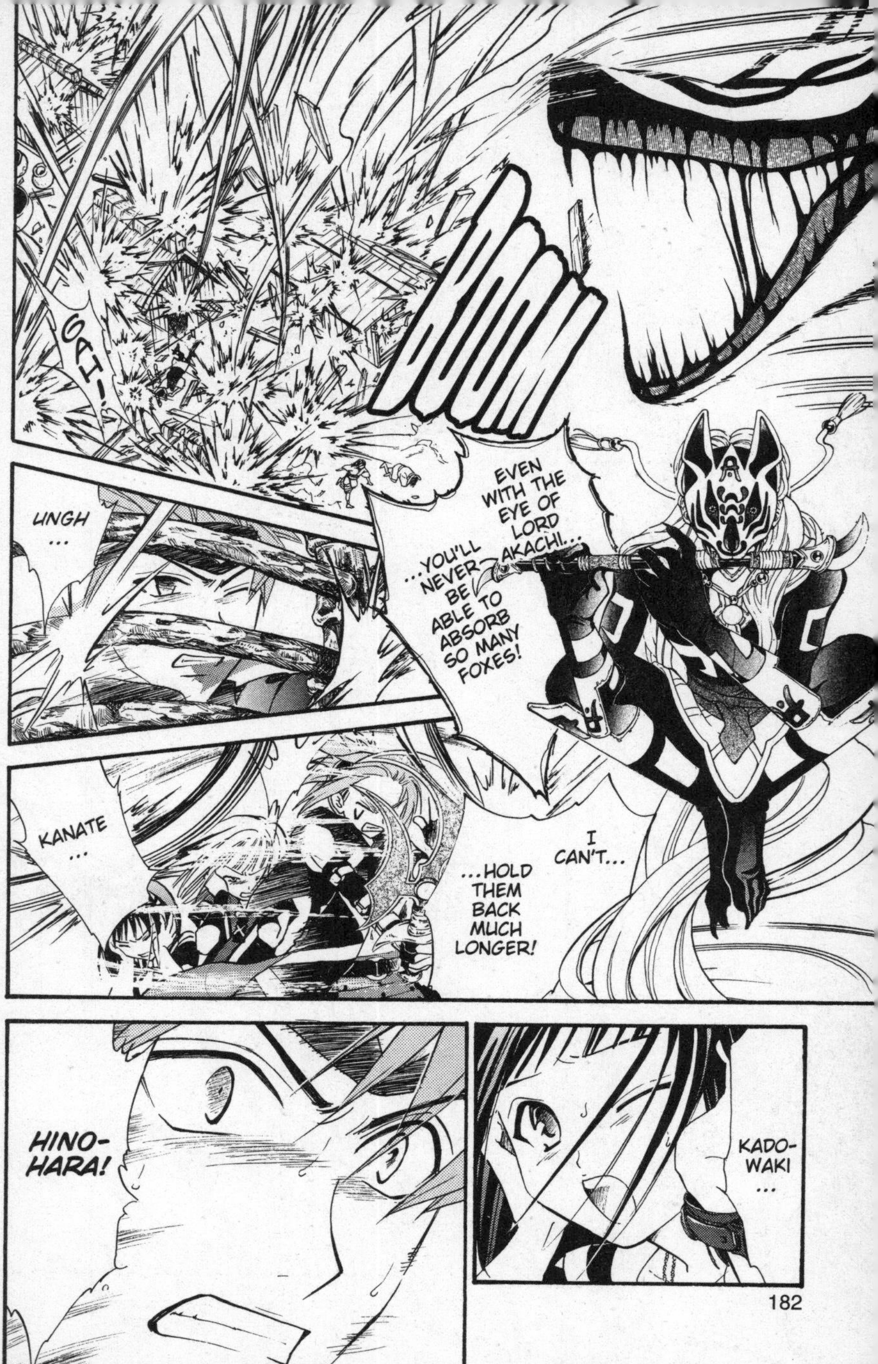
BOOM
GAH!!
EVEN WITH THE EYE OF LORD AKACHI...
...YOU'LL NEVER BE ABLE TO ABSORB SO MANY FOXES!
UNGH...
I CAN'T...
...HOLD THEM BACK MUCH LONGER!
KANATE...
KADO-WAKI...
HINO-HARA!

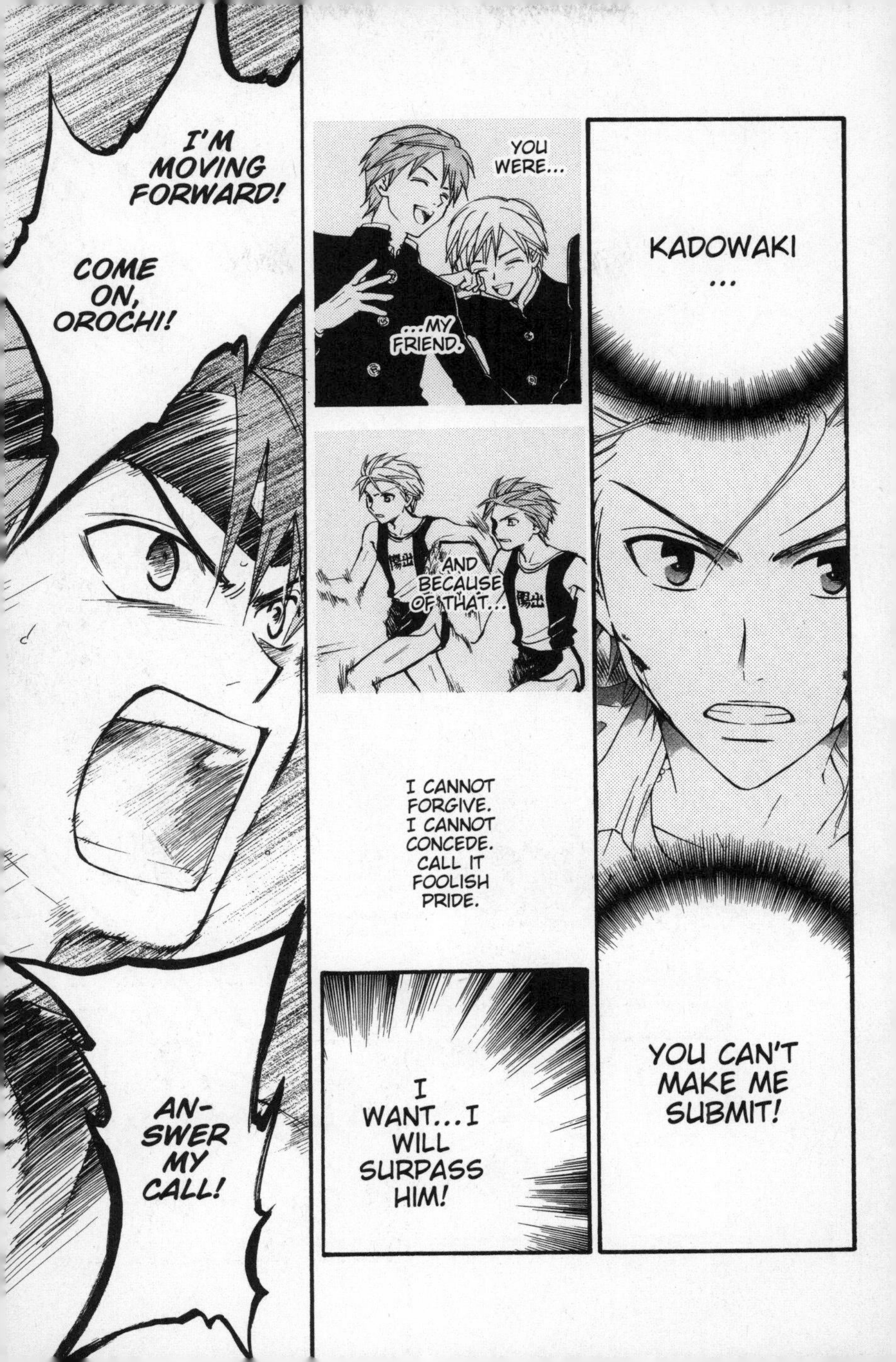
KADOWAKI ...
YOU CAN'T MAKE ME SUBMIT!
YOU WERE...
...MY FRIEND.
AND BECAUSE OF THAT...
I CANNOT FORGIVE. I CANNOT CONCEDE. CALL IT FOOLISH PRIDE.
I WANT...I WILL SURPASS HIM!
I'M MOVING FORWARD!
COME ON, OROCHI!
AN-SWER MY CALL!

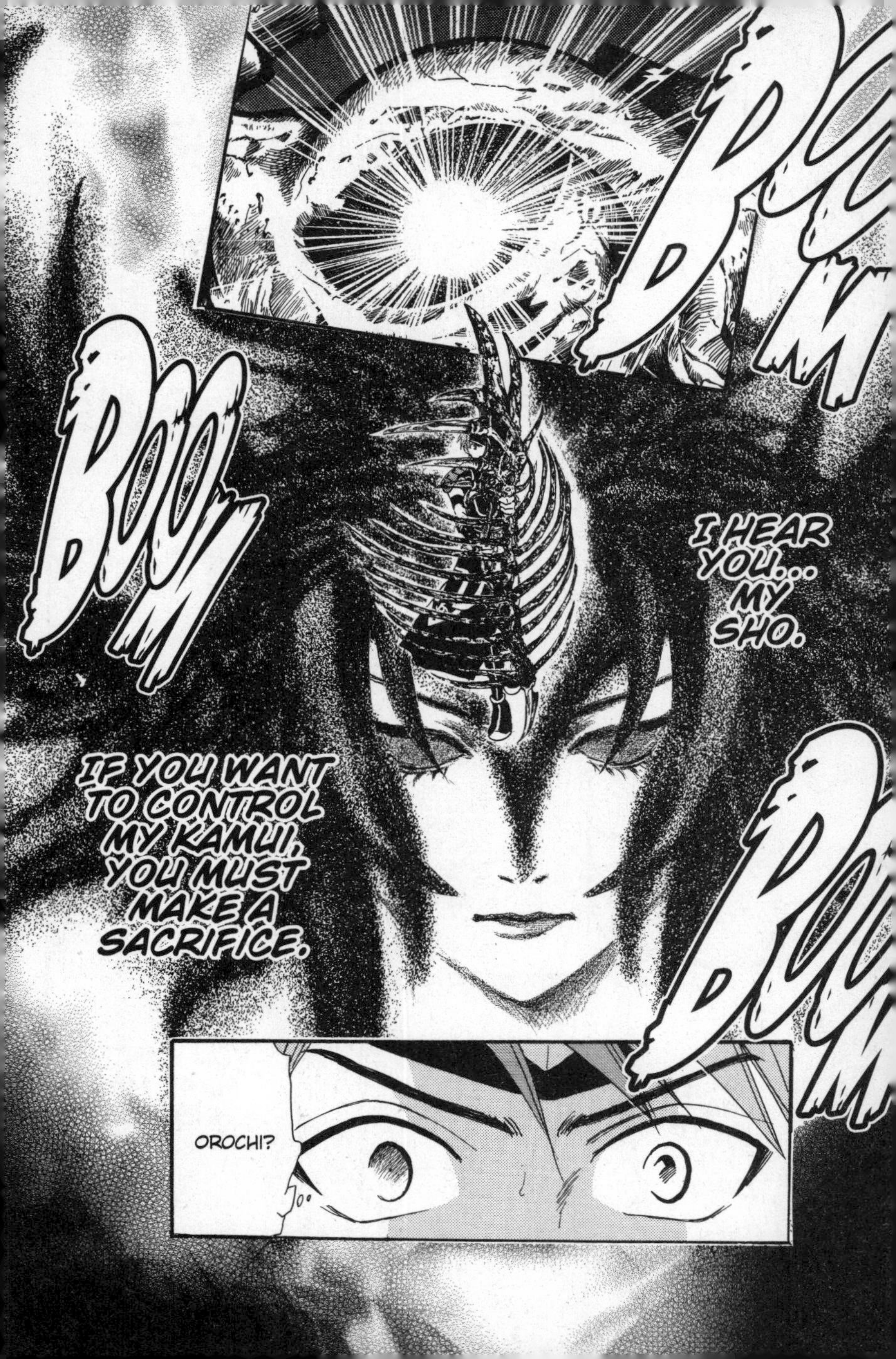
I HEAR YOU... MY SHO.
IF YOU WANT TO CONTROL MY KAMUI, YOU MUST MAKE A SACRIFICE.
OROCHI?

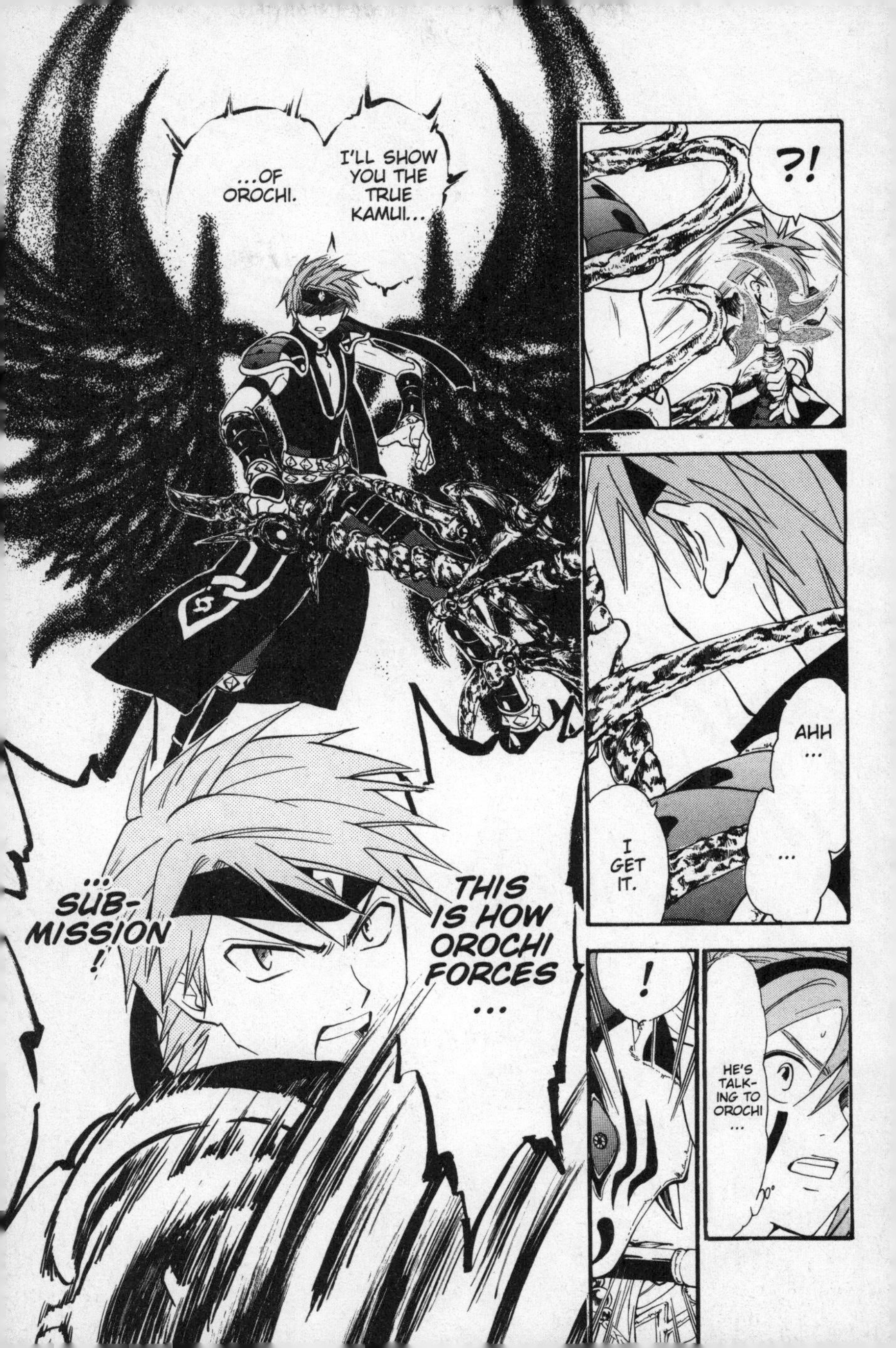
?!
AHH ...
...
I GET IT.
HE'S TALKING TO OROCHI ...
!
I'LL SHOW YOU THE TRUE KAMUI...
...OF OROCHI.
THIS IS HOW OROCHI FORCES ...
...SUBMISSION!

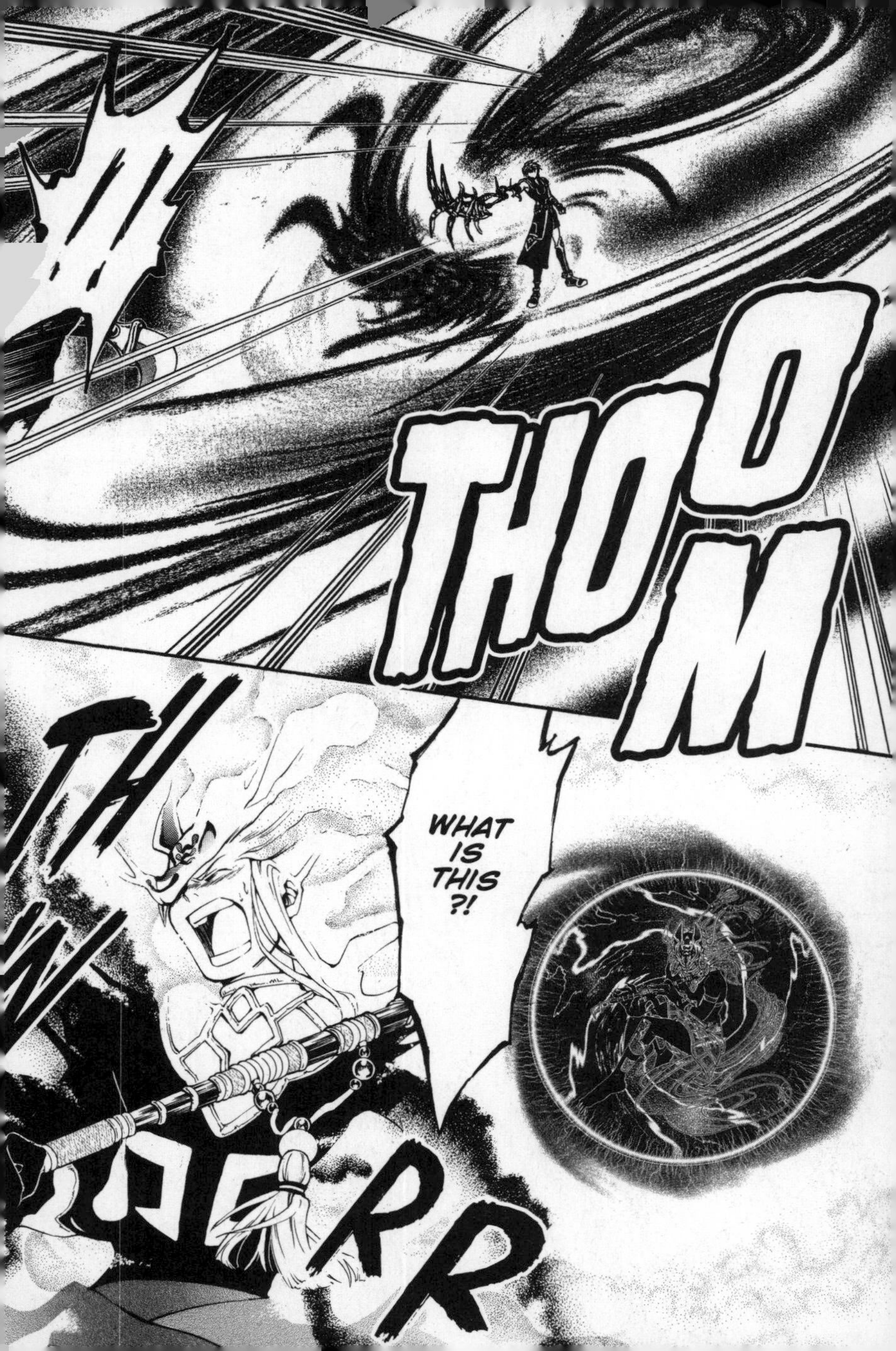
THOOM
WHAT IS THIS ?!
RR

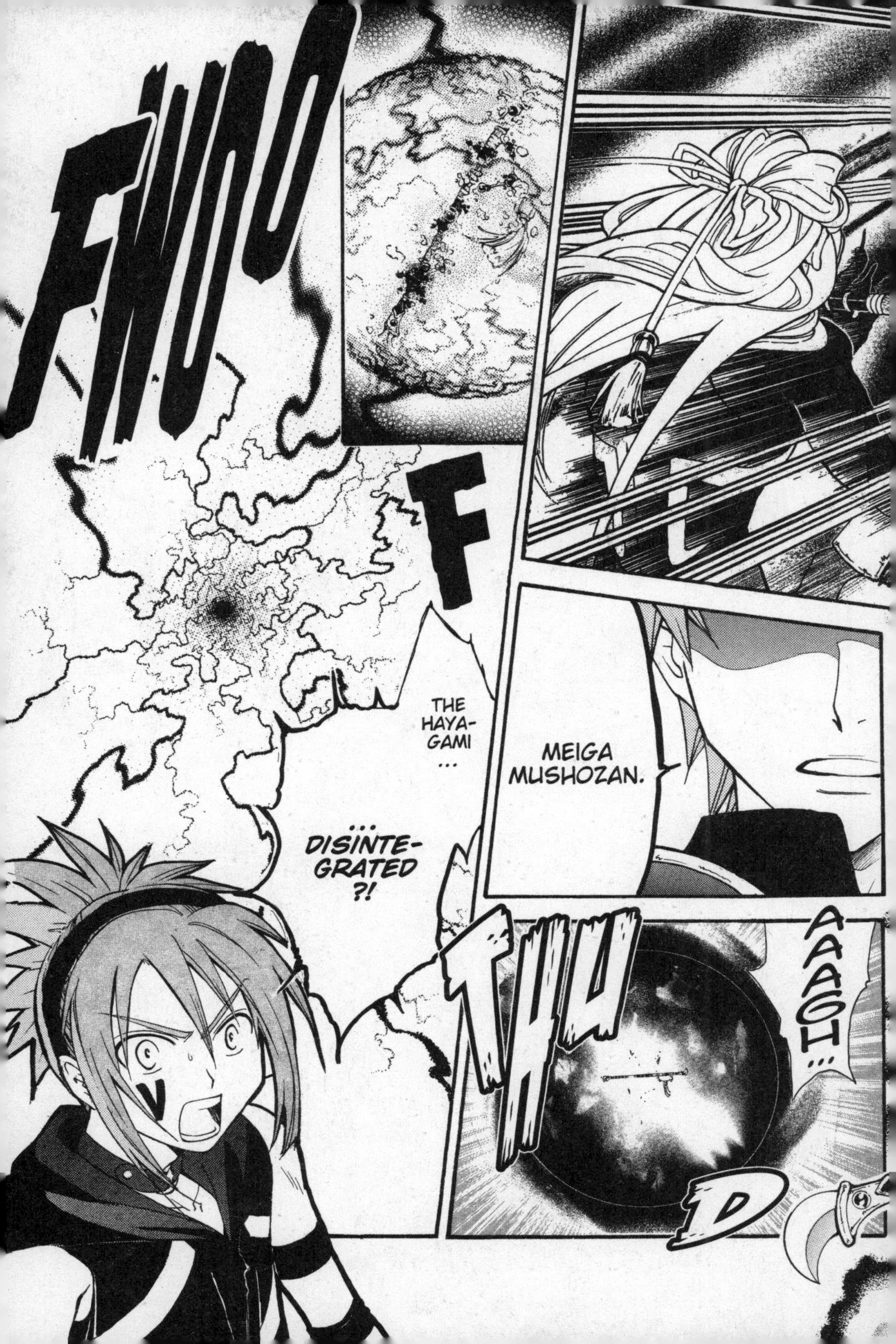
MEIGA MUSHOZAN.
AAAAGH...
THUD
FWOO
F
THE HAYA-GAMI...
...DISINTE-GRATED?!

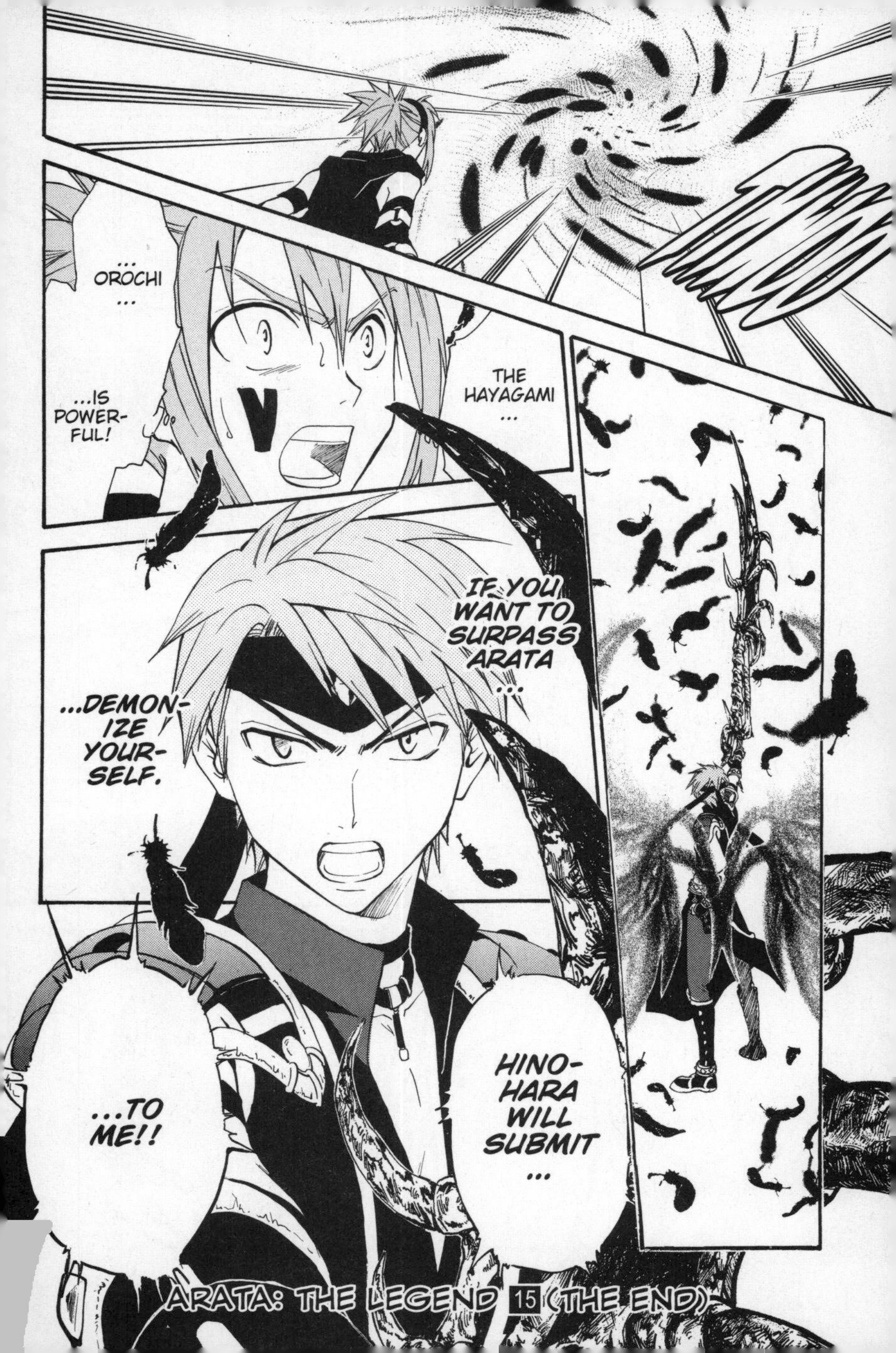
THE HAYAGAMI ...
... OROCHI ...
...IS POWER-FUL!
IF YOU WANT TO SURPASS ARATA ...
...DEMON-IZE YOUR-SELF.
HINO-HARA WILL SUBMIT ...
...TO ME!!
ARATA: THE LEGEND 15 (THE END)

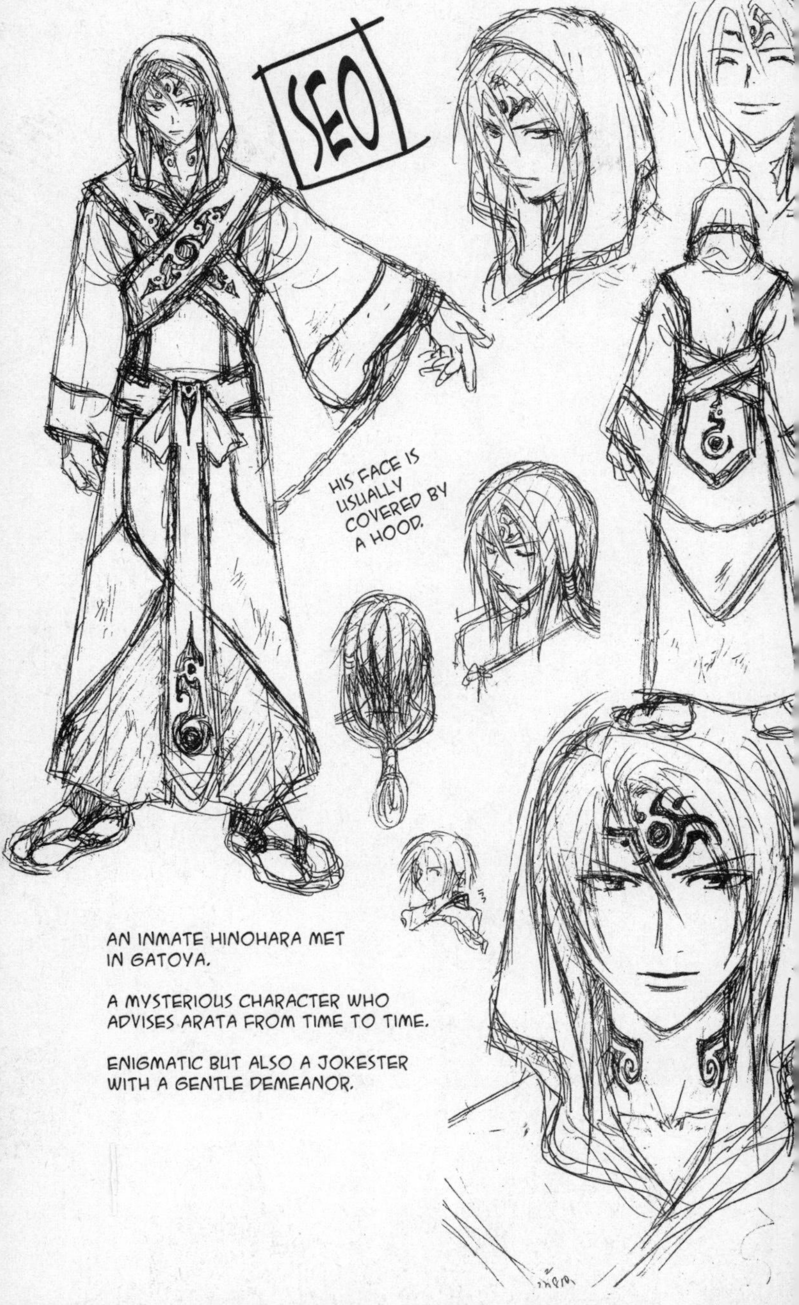
SEO
HIS FACE IS USUALLY COVERED BY A HOOD.

AN INMATE HINOHARA MET IN GATOYA.

A MYSTERIOUS CHARACTER WHO ADVISES ARATA FROM TIME TO TIME.

ENIGMATIC BUT ALSO A JOKESTER WITH A GENTLE DEMEANOR.

e color cover was all about girls this time, and although it was
n, it was a lot of work. Just as I was finishing up, I jabbed the
ticle of my thumb with the tip of my pen. Gyaaahhh!

ood gushed out, and it started to hurt. My right hand felt dull
d heavy and I couldn't work!

gh, did I lose too much blood? No, this is nothing! I gotta keep
pitching!!"

nsei! That's a line for a boy's magazine!"

the way, I can't pitch.

some reason, whenever Arata comes down with a fever, I do
. And if he sheds blood, I get injured and shed blood too. It's a
rd kind of synchronicity…

ta, don't you dare die!!

ny case, I look forward to a flood of entries for the autographed
d drawing.

–Yuu Watase

THOR BIO

March 5 in Osaka, Yuu Watase debuted in the *Shôjo Comic* manga anthology
89. She won the 43rd Shogakukan Manga Award with *Ceres: Celestial Legend*.
of her most famous works is *Fushigi Yûgi*, a series that has inspired the prequel
i Yûgi: Genbu Kaiden. In 2008, *Arata: The Legend* started serializing in

ARATA: THE LEGEND

Volume 15
Shonen Sunday Edition

Story and Art by YUU WATASE

ARATA KANGATARI Vol. 15
by Yuu WATASE
© 2009 Yuu WATASE
All rights reserved.
Original Japanese edition published by SHOGAKUKAN.
English translation rights in the United States of America, Canada, the United Kingdom and Ireland arranged with SHOGAKUKAN.

English Adaptation: Lance Caselman
Translation: JN Productions
Touch-up Art & Lettering: Rina Mapa
Design: Veronica Casson
Editor: Gary Leach

Printed in Canada

Published by VIZ Media, LLC
P.O. Box 77010
San Francisco, CA 94107

10 9 8 7 6 5 4 3 2 1
First printing, September 2013

PARENTAL ADVISORY
ARATA: THE LEGEND is rated T for Teen and is recommended for ages 13 and up. This volume contains fantasy violence.
ratings.viz.com

www.viz.com

WWW.SHONENSUNDAY.COM

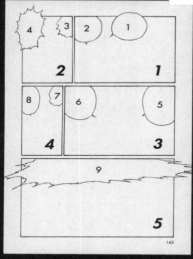

← Follow the action this way.

THIS IS THE LAST PAGE

Arata: The Legend has been printed in the original Japanese format in order to preserve the orientation of the original artwork.

Please turn it around and begin reading from right to left. Unlike English, Japanese is read right to left, so Japanese comics are read in reverse order from the way English comics are typically read. Have fun with it!